Verse by Verse Commentary on the Gospel of

LUKE

Enduring Word Commentary Series
By David Guzik

The grass withers, the flower fades,
but the word of our God stands forever.
Isaiah 40:8

Commentary on the Gospel of Luke
Copyright ©2019 by David Guzik
Printed in the United States of America
or in the United Kingdom
ISBN 987-1-939466-30-3

Enduring Word

5662 Calle Real #184
Goleta, CA 93117

Electronic Mail: ewm@enduringword.com
Internet Home Page: www.enduringword.com

Scripture references, unless noted, are from the New King James Version of the Bible, copyright ©1979, 1980, 1982, Thomas Nelson, Inc., Publisher.

Table of Contents

Luke 1—The Birth of John the Baptist

A. Introduction to the Gospel of Luke.

The first four verses are one sentence in the original Greek. They are written in refined, academic, classical style. But then, for the rest of the gospel, Luke didn't use the language of scholars but of the common man, the language of the village and the street. Through this, Luke said to us, "This account has all the proper academic and scholarly credentials. But it is written for the man on the street." Luke wrote so that people would understand Jesus, not so they would admire his brain and literary skill.

1. (1-2) Mention of the prior accounts of the life of Jesus.

Inasmuch as many have taken in hand to set in order a narrative of those things which have been fulfilled among us, just as those who from the beginning were eyewitnesses and ministers of the word delivered them to us,

a. **Many have taken in hand**: Luke wrote his gospel knowing that many had already written histories of the life of Jesus. This may be a reference to the works of Mark and Matthew (most scholars think John was written *after* Luke), and it may also refer to other biographies of Jesus not directly inspired by the Holy Spirit.

i. Some researchers claim that the writings about Jesus did not come about until two or perhaps three generations after His death on the cross. But the work of German papyrus expert Carsten Thiede (in December 1994) suggests that we actually possess copies of Matthew that date close to the very time of Jesus. Thiede's findings are based on a careful analysis of the handwriting script used on the recently discovered fragments.

b. **Those things which have been fulfilled among us**: The previously mentioned writings contain things already commonly *known* and **believed** among Christians of Luke's day. When Luke wrote, most Christians already knew all about the life of Jesus, both from the oral accounts passed on by the original disciples, and by the biographies that had already been written.

> i. With the word **us**, Luke put himself in the community of Christians who believed and received the accounts of Jesus' life. Luke was a companion of Paul (Acts 16:10-11; 2 Timothy 4:11; Philemon 1:24), and Paul called him the *beloved physician* (Colossians 4:14). Luke was a doctor and therefore a man of science and research, and this is reflected in his history of the life of Jesus.

> ii. By every indication, Luke was a Gentile. Colossians 4:10-11 and 4:14 show that he wasn't Jewish, because he was not included in the group *who are of the circumcision*. This makes Luke unique in that he is the only New Testament writer who was a Gentile.

> iii. God gave this lone Gentile writer a great privilege. Because he also wrote the book of Acts (which makes up the second volume of this Gospel), Luke wrote more of the New Testament than any other human writer did (assuming that Paul did *not* author the letter to the Hebrews).

c. **Just as those who from the beginning were eyewitnesses and ministers of the word delivered them to us**: Luke tells us that the prior accounts of the life of Jesus were based on the words of **eyewitnesses**.

> i. **Those who from the beginning** were undoubtedly the apostles, who were with Jesus from the very start. But **those who from the beginning** would also include people such as Mary herself, whom Luke probably interviewed in his research for this history of the life of Jesus.

> ii. Luke wrote to a first century world that was burnt out on "if it feels good, do it" living; yet it was offended by the crazy superstitions of most religions. The world then, as today, longs for what Christianity offers: *faith* founded on *fact*.

2. (3-4) Luke explains the reason for the writing of his account.

It seemed good to me also, having had perfect understanding of all things from the very first, to write to you an orderly account, most excellent Theophilus, that you may know the certainty of those things in which you were instructed.

a. **It seemed good to me also**: Luke was not one of those who was an *eyewitness* of events *from the beginning* of Jesus' ministry. Yet he put himself in the same line as others who wrote their accounts of Jesus' life from first-hand experience (such as Matthew and Mark), because his account was based on diligent research and a **perfect understanding** of events.

b. To write to you an orderly account: Having already read Matthew and Mark's account, Luke wanted to give a third account with an emphasis on comprehensiveness and order. Therefore, Luke is the most *comprehensive* gospel. He documents the story of Jesus all the way from the annunciation of John the Baptist to Jesus' ascension.

- Luke is the most *universal* gospel. In Luke, Gentiles are often put in a favorable light

- Luke's gospel is the one most interested in the roles of *women, children*, and *social outcasts*

- The gospel of Luke is the one most interested in *prayer*. He has seven different references to Jesus praying that are found in this gospel alone

- Luke's gospel is the one with the most emphasis on the *Holy Spirit* and on *joy*

- Luke's gospel is the one with the most emphasis on preaching the good news (the *gospel*). This term is used ten times in this gospel (and only once in any other gospel account), as well as fifteen additional times in Acts

c. Most excellent Theophilus: Luke addressed his gospel to a man named **Theophilus**, but it was also written with a wider audience in mind.

i. By his title (**most excellent**), we gather that Theophilus was probably a Roman government official. It is entirely likely that the books of Luke and Acts make up Paul's defense brief for his trial before Caesar, since Acts leaves Paul waiting for that trial.

ii. Whoever Theophilus was, he had already had some instruction in the faith (**in which you were instructed**).

B. The announcement of the birth of John the Baptist.

1. (5-7) The time and people beginning the history of the life of Jesus.

There was in the days of Herod, the king of Judea, a certain priest named Zacharias, of the division of Abijah. His wife *was* of the daughters of Aaron, and her name *was* Elizabeth. And they were both righteous before God, walking in all the commandments and ordinances of the Lord blameless. But they had no child, because Elizabeth was barren, and they were both well advanced in years.

a. **In the days of Herod**: *These events happened at a definite time.* This was the man known as *Herod the Great*, who was at the end of a long and terrible reign. Ethnically, he was not a descendant of Israel, but of Jacob's brother Esau—thereforean Edomite, or an Idumean. He was known for his spectacular building programs, but even more so for his paranoid cruelty, which drove him to execute many, including members of his own family.

b. **A certain priest named Zacharias…His wife…was Elizabeth**: *These events happened to definite people.* **Zacharias** and **Elizabeth** were righteous and obedient, yet also stigmatized by their barrenness (**but they had no child, because Elizabeth was barren**).

c. **Of the division of Abijah**: Priestly divisions (including the **division of Abijah**) were noted in 1 Chronicles 23-24.

2. (8-10) Zacharias' temple service.

So it was, that while he was serving as priest before God in the order of his division, according to the custom of the priesthood, his lot fell to burn incense when he went into the temple of the Lord. And the whole multitude of the people was praying outside at the hour of incense.

a. **According to the custom of the priesthood, his lot fell to burn incense**: Only priests from a particular lineage could serve in the temple. Over the years the number of priests multiplied, (there were said to be as many as 20,000 priests in the time of Jesus) so they used the **lot** to determine which priests would serve when. The **lot** to serve might fall to a priest only once in his life.

i. To a godly man like Zacharias, this was probably the biggest event of his life, a tremendous privilege, a once-in-a-lifetime opportunity. Surely he wondered what it would be like to enter the holy place, and if God had something special to speak to him in this special event of his life.

ii. It is also easy to imagine that Zacharias asked the other priests who had already performed this service what it was like; asking them if they had any unique spiritual experience when they ministered before the Lord. The whole event was filled with enormous anticipation.

b. **To burn incense**: According to the Law of Moses, incense was offered to God on the golden altar every morning and every evening (Exodus 30:7-8). By this time, there was an established ritual for the practice.

i. There were several lots cast to determine who did what at the morning sacrifice. The first lot determined who would cleanse the altar and prepare its fire; the second lot determined who would kill the morning sacrifice and sprinkle the altar, the golden candlestick, and the altar of incense. The third lot determined who would come and offer incense. This was the most privileged duty; those who received the first and second lots would repeat their duty at the evening sacrifice, but not with the third lot. To offer the incense would be a once-in-a-lifetime opportunity.

ii. Before dawn, hundreds of worshippers gathered at the temple. The morning sacrifice began when the incense priest walked toward the temple, through the outer courts, and struck a gong-like instrument known as the *Magrephah*. At this sound, the Levites assembled and got ready to lead the gathered people in songs of worship to God.

iii. The other two priests chosen by lot that morning walked up to the temple on each side of the priest chosen to offer the incense. All three entered the holy place together. One priest set burning coals on the golden altar; the other priest arranged the incense so it was ready to go. Then those two priests left the temple, and the incense priest was left all alone in the holy place.

iv. In front of him was the golden altar of incense; it was 18 inches square and 3 feet high. On that small table lay the burning coals, with little wisps of smoke rising up, ready for the incense. Behind the gold altar was a huge, thick curtain, and behind that curtain was the Holy of Holies, the Most Holy Place, where no man could enter, except the high priest, and that only on the Day of Atonement. As he faced the golden altar of incense, to his right would be the table of showbread, and to his left would be the golden lampstand, which provided the only light for the holy place.

c. **And the whole multitude of the people was praying outside at the hour of incense**: When the people outside saw the two men exit the temple, they knew that the time to offer the incense had come. Those hundreds of people bowed or kneeled before the Lord and spread their hands out in silent prayer. They knew that at that moment, the incense priest prayed in the holy place, in the very presence of God, for the entire nation.

i. There followed several minutes of dead silence in all the temple precincts—as Zacharias lingered in prayer in the holy place during this, the most solemn experience of his life.

ii. The connection between the burning of **incense** and prayer might seem strange to some, but in the Bible the burning of incense is a strong picture of prayer (Psalm 141:2; Revelation 5:8).

ii. Zacharias must have carefully thought about this prayer beforehand. He may have even brought a prayer list, though it is more likely he memorized it. He also knew how long to pray, because he had attended the morning sacrifice as a worshipper many times before, and he knew how long the incense priest stayed in the temple. He must have prayed for the needs of the nation of Israel, which was occupied and oppressed by the hated Romans. He must have prayed for God to send the Messiah. He probably would have thought it wrong to throw in his personal needs at such a holy moment.

3. (11-17) The angel's announcement to Zacharias.

Then an angel of the Lord appeared to him, standing on the right side of the altar of incense. And when Zacharias saw *him*, he was troubled, and fear fell upon him. But the angel said to him, "Do not be afraid, Zacharias, for your prayer is heard; and your wife Elizabeth will bear you a son, and you shall call his name John. And you will have joy and gladness, and many will rejoice at his birth. For he will be great in the sight of the Lord, and shall drink neither wine nor strong drink. He will also be filled with the Holy Spirit, even from his mother's womb. And he will turn many of the children of Israel to the Lord their God. He will also go before Him in the spirit and power of Elijah, 'to turn the hearts of the fathers to the children,' and the disobedient to the wisdom of the just, to make ready a people prepared for the Lord."

a. **Then an angel of the Lord appeared**: The angel simply stood **on the right side of the altar of incense**. Zacharias probably had his eyes tightly shut in passionate prayer, and when he opened them he saw this angel.

b. **When Zacharias saw him, he was troubled, and fear fell upon him**: The **angel** who appeared to Zacharias was not a romantic figure or a naked baby with wings. This angel was a glorious, fearful, and awesome creature. Like most angels in the Bible, the first thing this angel has to say to his human contact is **"Do not be afraid."**

i. Zacharias must have thought, "Does this happen to everyone who does this? The other priests didn't tell me anything about this."

c. **Your prayer is heard; and your wife Elizabeth will bear a son**: It is doubtful that Zacharias prayed for a son when he was at the golden altar of incense. First, it might have seemed like such a selfish need. Second, since he and Elizabeth *were both well advanced in years* (Luke 1:7), they had probably given up on this prayer a long time ago.

i. Sometimes we pray for something for a long, long time. We pray for the salvation of a spouse or a child. We pray for a calling or a ministry. We pray that God would bring that special person to us. But after years of heartfelt prayer, we give up out of discouragement. Zacharias and Elizabeth probably prayed years of passionate prayer for a son, but gave up a long time ago, and stopped believing God for so much anymore.

ii. When we are in that place, we sometimes begin—in the smallest of ways—to doubt the love and care of God for us. But God always loves, and His care never stops.

iii. Zacharias' reaction to the angel's promise was probably to think, "I don't know what you are talking about. I didn't pray for a son. We're old, you know. I gave up on that prayer a long time ago. I'm praying for the salvation of Israel. I'm praying that God will send the promised Messiah." Zacharias didn't know that God would answer both prayers at once, and use his miracle baby to be a part of sending the Messiah.

iv. Zacharias had no idea that God would answer the two greatest desires of his heart at once. He had probably completely given up on the idea of being a dad; it was a hope that was crushed over the years of disappointment. But God hadn't given up on it, even though Zacharias and Elizabeth had.

d. **You shall call his name John**: The boy was given a name before he was even conceived. This was a command from the Lord to name the boy **John**.

e. **He will be great in the sight of the Lord, and shall drink neither wine nor strong drink**: This is probably a reference to the vow of a Nazirite found in Numbers 6. Their son John would be specially consecrated to God all the days of his life, as Samson *should* have been.

i. Though John would be **great in the sight of the Lord**, by the grace of God, *he who is least in the kingdom of heaven is greater than he* (Matthew 11:11).

f. **He will also be filled with the Holy Spirit, even from his mother's womb**: Their son John would have a unique filling of the Holy Spirit, being **filled with the Holy Spirit** even while in the womb.

i. Calvin, on John being filled with the Holy Spirit from the womb: "Let us learn by this example that, from the earliest infancy to the latest old age, the operation of the Spirit in men is free."

g. **He will turn many of the children of Israel to the Lord their God**: John's great work would be to prepare the way of the Messiah by turning hearts to God before the Messiah came. The pattern for his ministry would be the great prophet Elijah—**in the spirit and power of Elijah**. Jesus later said this was fulfilled in John (Matthew 11:14 and 17:12).

h. **To turn the hearts of the fathers to the children**: This quotation from Malachi 4:5-6 is meaningful for more than its reference to Elijah. These were essentially the last words in the Old Testament, and now God's revelation is resuming where it had left off.

i. Elijah was a man who called Israel to a radical repentance (1 Kings 18:20-40).

4. (18-20) Zacharias' doubt and muteness.

And Zacharias said to the angel, "How shall I know this? For I am an old man, and my wife is well advanced in years." And the angel answered and said to him, "I am Gabriel, who stands in the presence of God, and was sent to speak to you and bring you these glad tidings. But behold, you will be mute and not able to speak until the day these things take place, because you did not believe my words which will be fulfilled in their own time."

> a. **How shall I know this? For I am an old man and my wife is well advanced in years**: Zacharias' attitude was, "Thanks for the promise, Angel. But knowing the condition of my wife and I, this is a big one. Can you give us a sign to prove it?"

>> i. It wasn't that Zacharias didn't *want* to believe this; he did. It is simply that he felt it must be too good to be true, and he had probably protected himself from disappointment by not setting his expectations too high. We may rob ourselves of a miracle by the same attitude.

>> ii. Zacharias looked at the circumstances first, and what God can do last; we are tempted to think this is logical, but if God is real, there is nothing logical about putting circumstances before God.

> b. **I am Gabriel who stands in the presence of God**: Gabriel reminds Zacharias of who *he is* and where he has come from. There is a big contrast between **I am an old man** and **I am Gabriel**. Which held more weight? Gabriel also "preaches the gospel" to Zacharias (**brings you glad tidings**).

>> i. It was nothing but good news to Zacharias that he would not only have a son, but that the son would have a significant role in God's plan of redemption. This is the good news that Gabriel brought to Zacharias.

>> ii. This gives a better idea of what it really means to preach the gospel—it is to bring good news to people who need it.

> c. **My words which will be fulfilled in their own time**: If there is no Zacharias, there is no John the Baptist. If there is no John the Baptist, there is no herald announcing the coming of the Messiah. If there is no herald announcing the coming of the Messiah, the prophecies in the Old Testament regarding the Messiah are unfulfilled. If any of the prophesies of the Old Testament regarding the first coming of the Messiah are unfulfilled, then Jesus did not fulfill all things. If Jesus did not fulfill all things, then He did not complete God's plan of redemption for you and I, and we must perish in our sins. This *was* good news.

d. **But behold, you will be mute and not able to speak**: Zacharias paid a price for his unbelief. His unbelief did not make God take his promise back; it just kept Zacharias from enjoying it.

i. When we do not believe God's promise for our lives, we do not necessarily destroy the promise, but we do destroy our ability to enjoy the promise. What made this such a severe punishment was that Zacharias had such great news to tell.

ii. Strangely, many Christians would not consider this a punishment—they don't mind keeping quiet about the good news of Jesus.

5. (21-23) Zacharias appears to the multitude.

And the people waited for Zacharias, and marveled that he lingered so long in the temple. But when he came out, he could not speak to them; and they perceived that he had seen a vision in the temple, for he beckoned to them and remained speechless. And so it was, as soon as the days of his service were completed, that he departed to his own house.

a. **And the people waited for Zacharias, and marveled that he lingered so long**: The custom was for the priest to come from the temple as soon as he finished praying to assure the people he had not been struck dead by God. Zacharias' delay had started to make the crowd nervous.

i. After the incense priest finished his work, he came out of the holy place through the great doors of the temple, and met the other two priests right outside the doors. Then the incense priest raised his hands and blessed the people with the blessing from Numbers 6:24-26. The hundreds of gathered worshippers knew what to do; they responded by saying, "Blessed be the Lord God, the God of Israel, from everlasting to everlasting."

ii. After all this, the Levites got the worship singers and musicians started. They began with a blast from special silver trumpets; then a priest struck the cymbals, and the choir of Levites began to sing the Psalm of the day. The choir was made up of not less than twelve voices, which mingled young and old for a full range of sound and probably some great harmonies.

b. **But when he came out, he could not speak to them**: When Zacharias came out, he was supposed to stand on the temple steps, overlooking the crowd, and pronounce the priestly blessing on the people (Numbers 6:24-26), and the other priests would repeat it after him. But Zacharias couldn't speak.

i. Doing the best he could through hand motions, he told the story of what happened to him in the temple. It's hard to know if everyone believed him.

6. (24-25) Elizabeth's conception and joy.

Now after those days his wife Elizabeth conceived; and she hid herself five months, saying, "Thus the Lord has dealt with me, in the days when He looked on *me*, to take away my reproach among people."

a. **His wife Elizabeth conceived**: Zacharias had normal relations with his wife; he partnered with God to fulfill the promise. He did not count on this child coming from a miraculous conception.

b. **She hid herself five months**: Elizabeth did not go away to hide her pregnancy; she was gone for the first five months, the time when she would be *least* noticed as pregnant. She went away to spend time with the Lord, and to meditate on the destiny of the child within her.

C. The announcement of the birth of Jesus.

1. (26-27) Gabriel is sent to Mary in **Nazareth**.

Now in the sixth month the angel Gabriel was sent by God to a city of Galilee named Nazareth, to a virgin betrothed to a man whose name was Joseph, of the house of David. The virgin's name *was* Mary.

a. **In the sixth month the angel Gabriel**: Gabriel's work was not finished with the announcement to Zacharias in the temple. In the **sixth month** of Elizabeth's pregnancy, he came to a village in Galilee.

b. **A city of Galilee named Nazareth**: Chronologically, this is the first mention of **Nazareth** in the Old or New Testament. Nazareth is perhaps remarkable for its unremarkable nature; it was unmentioned in the Old Testament, in the Apocrypha, and in the writings of Josephus.

i. Though **Nazareth** is in the general region of Galilee, it is 15 miles away from the Sea of Galilee. It is six miles from the closest major road. **Nazareth** had no good water supply, only one fairly weak well in the center of the village.

ii. Jesus would forever be identified with this place, being repeatedly called *Jesus of Nazareth* (Mark 1:24, John 18:7, John 19:19, Acts 2:22). His followers were also called "Nazarenes" (Acts 24:5).

c. **To a virgin betrothed**: Mary was **betrothed** to Joseph. There were three stages to a Jewish wedding in that day.

- *Engagement* (a formal agreement made by the fathers)
- *Betrothal* (the ceremony where mutual promises were made)
- *Marriage* (approximately one year later, when the bridegroom came for his bride at an unexpected time)

i. When a couple was **betrothed**, they were under the obligations of faithfulness, and a divorce was required to break the betrothal. This was not a casual promise.

d. **The virgin's name was Mary**: Mary is clearly said to be a **virgin**. There is no ambiguity about the idea here—Mary had never had sexual relations with any man.

i. The conception of John the Baptist, the forerunner, was miraculous; we should expect an even more remarkable conception of the Messiah.

ii. "The name 'Mary' is the Greek form of the Hebrew name *Miriam*, the sister of Moses. It means 'exalted one,' a fitting description of the soon-to-be mother of the Messiah." (Pate)

2. (28-29) Gabriel greets Mary.

And having come in, the angel said to her, "Rejoice, highly favored *one*, the Lord *is* with you; blessed *are* you among women!" But when she saw *him*, she was troubled at his saying, and considered what manner of greeting this was.

a. **The angel said to her**: Gabriel said three things to Mary. Each of these were certainly true of Mary, who had a unique privilege among any person to ever live.

- She was **highly favored**
- That the **Lord is with** her
- She was **blessed**

  i. However, all these things are true of the believer in Jesus. We are highly favored as Mary was (Ephesians 1:6), the Lord is with us (Matthew 28:20), and we are blessed (Ephesians 1:3).

  ii. The Roman Catholic prayer that begins "Hail Mary, full of grace" is accurate. Mary *was* full of grace, and so is the believer; but Mary's grace was a *received* grace, not grace to give to others.

b. **But when she saw him, she was troubled at his saying**: The fact that Mary was **troubled at his saying** shows her humility. Mary was surprised to hear such extravagant words said of her.

3. (30-33) Gabriel announces the birth of the Messiah, born to Mary.

Then the angel said to her, "Do not be afraid, Mary, for you have found favor with God. And behold, you will conceive in your womb and bring forth a Son, and shall call His name JESUS. He will be great, and will be called the Son of the Highest; and the Lord God will give Him the

throne of His father David. And He will reign over the house of Jacob forever, and of His kingdom there will be no end."

a. **You have found favor with God...you will conceive in your womb and bring forth a Son**: The focus was not on Mary, but on **a Son**, to be named JESUS (a common name). This **Son** was unmistakably identified as the Messiah predicted by the Old Testament.

i. **He will be great**: No one has influenced history more than Jesus Christ. "Is it not proven that he is great? Conquerors are great, and he is the greatest of them. Deliverers are great, and he is the greatest of them. Liberators are great, and he is the greatest of them. Saviours are great, and he is the greatest of them." (Spurgeon)

- Jesus is great in the perfection of His nature
- Jesus is great in the grandeur of His offices
- Jesus is great in the splendor of his achievements
- Jesus is great in the numbers of those He rescues
- Jesus is great in the estimation of His people

ii. **He will be called the Son of the Highest**: Jesus would be the son of Mary, but not *only* her son; He would also be, and be known as, the Son of God.

iii. **The throne of His father David**: He will be the Messiah prophesied to David (2 Samuel 7:12-16), who has the rightful authority to rule over Israel, **and of His kingdom there will be no end.**

b. **You will conceive in your womb and bring forth a Son**: Mary knew exactly what Gabriel was talking about because she was a woman of the word of God. When Gabriel said this, Mary knew he quoted from Isaiah 7:14: *the virgin shall conceive and bear a Son.*

4. (34-37) Mary's question and Gabriel's response.

Then Mary said to the angel, "How can this be, since I do not know a man?" And the angel answered and said to her, *"The* Holy Spirit will come upon you, and the power of the Highest will overshadow you; therefore, also, that Holy One who is to be born will be called the Son of God. Now indeed, Elizabeth your relative has also conceived a son in her old age; and this is now the sixth month for her who was called barren. For with God nothing will be impossible."

a. **How can this be, since I do not know a man?** Mary's question was logical. She asked the same question Zacharias asked (Luke 1:18), but his question was asked in skeptical unbelief, and her question was asked in wonder-filled faith.

b. **The power of the Highest will overshadow you**: Gabriel answered that **the power of the Highest**, in the Person of the **Holy Spirit**, would **overshadow** Mary.

> i. The word **overshadow** means "to cover with a cloud," as in the cloud of Shekinah glory (Exodus 16:10, 19:9, 24:16, 34:5, 40:34) or the cloud of transfiguration (Matthew 17:5, Mark 9:7, Luke 9:34).

> ii. This cloud was a visible manifestation of the glory and presence of God; this means that the same power of God that was with Moses and others in the Old Testament was now going to do a unique work in the life of Mary.

> iii. "This delicate expression rules out crude ideas of a 'mating' of the Holy Spirit with Mary." (Morris)

> iv. "Technically speaking, however, the angel predicted a virginal *conception*, rather than a virginal birth. As far as anyone can tell, the actual birth of Jesus was normal; not so his conception." (Pate)

c. **That Holy One who is to be born**: Because this will be the manner of His conception, He would be the **Holy One** (different from all others), and He **will be called the Son of God**.

> i. This doesn't have the same impact on us today because of our unfamiliarity with the idea of being a **Son of God**. But Mary (and all other Jewish people from her culture) knew what this meant: this child would be equal to God (John 5:18).

> ii. Jesus did not *become* the Son of God; He was **called the Son of God**, recognizing His nature from all eternity.

d. **Now indeed, Elizabeth your relative has also conceived a son in her old age**: With such an amazing promise, Gabriel also brought evidence, explaining that Elizabeth was pregnant. If God could do that, He could do what He promised for Mary.

> i. "Though believers are satisfied with the bare word of God, yet they do not disregard any of his works which they find to be conducive to strengthen their faith." (Calvin)

e. **With God nothing shall be impossible**: The point is clear. More literally, one could translate this *for no word of God shall be powerless*. God will absolutely perform what He has said.

> i. The words, 'for nothing' (literally, 'no word') 'will be impossible for God,' recall the divine promise of a son addressed to Sarah (Genesis 18:14 [Septuagint]) and, in so doing, provide another confirming example of God's ability to carry out His promise to Mary." (Pate)

5. (38) Mary's response of faith.

Then Mary said, "Behold the maidservant of the Lord! Let it be to me according to your word." And the angel departed from her.

a. **Behold, the maidservant of the Lord!** Mary first responded by agreeing with what Gabriel said about her. She *was* **the maidservant of the Lord**, and it was not her position to debate with her Master, but to accept what He said.

> i. "It was inevitable that clouds would gather around her character, which would sorely perplex the good man to whom she was betrothed. But as soon as she realized that this lot was ordained for her by God, she humbly acquiesced, with these model words of patient faith." (Meyer)

b. **Let it be to me according to your word**: Mary then responded with an affirmation of faith. "**Let it be to me according to Your word**" is the proper response of every believer to every promise of God.

> i. This all took more trust in the Lord than we might think. Mary agreed to receive a pregnancy that would be seen as suspicious, and this in a culture that had a potential death penalty for adultery. Mary identified herself with sinners so that the purpose of God would be fulfilled.

> ii. Spiritually speaking, there are similarities between God's work in Mary and His work in every believer.

> - Jesus lives within the believer spiritually, as He did in Mary physically
> - Jesus lives within us spiritually by His word, as He did in Mary physically
> - Jesus is made visible to the world through us, as He was through Mary physically

> iii. "Truly did our Lord speak when he said to his disciples, 'These are my mother, and sister, and brother.' We bear as close a relationship to Christ as did the Virgin mother, and we in some sense take the same position spiritually which she took up corporeally [bodily] in reference to him." (Spurgeon)

c. **And the angel departed from her**: We don't know the exact moment Jesus was conceived in the womb of Mary. It may have been when Gabriel spoke to her, or soon after. Whenever it was, the cloud of God's glory *overshadowed* Mary (Luke 1:35), and Jesus was miraculously conceived in Mary's womb. Jesus' birth from this conception is what we call the *Virgin Birth*.

i. When we approach the event we call Virgin Birth, we have to agree with Paul's analysis: *great is the mystery of godliness* (1 Timothy 3:16). But the message of the Scriptures is clear regarding the Virgin Birth. There can be no question about the Virgin Birth, only questions on the authority of Scripture.

ii. The Virgin Birth is unique. Many mythologies have legends about a god who had sexual relations with a woman and produced offspring, but the idea of a _virgin_ birth is unique to Christianity.

D. Mary's song.

1. (39-41) Mary's visit to Elizabeth.

Now Mary arose in those days and went into the hill country with haste, to a city of Judah, and entered the house of Zacharias and greeted Elizabeth. And it happened, when Elizabeth heard the greeting of Mary, that the babe leaped in her womb; and Elizabeth was filled with the Holy Spirit.

a. **Mary arose in those days and went into the hill country with haste**: Mary heard from Gabriel that her relative Elizabeth was pregnant (Luke 1:36); so she went the considerable distance (somewhere between 80 and 100 miles or 130 to 160 kilometers) from the region of Galilee to the **hill country** of Judea for a visit.

i. Mary probably understood that not many people could understand her experience with Gabriel and miraculous conception. If anyone could understand, it might be Elizabeth.

b. **The babe leaped in her womb**: When Elizabeth saw Mary, her unborn child—John the Baptist—**leaped**, because he was filled with **joy**. Though John wasn't born yet, he had a spiritual awareness and could respond to the Spirit of God.

i. "Such comfort there is in the presence of Christ (though but in the womb) as it made John to spring. What then shall it be in heaven, think we?" (Trapp)

2. (42-45) Elizabeth's blessing to Mary.

Then she spoke out with a loud voice and said, "Blessed *are* you among women, and blessed *is* the fruit of your womb! But why *is* this *granted* to me, that the mother of my Lord should come to me? For indeed, as soon as the voice of your greeting sounded in my ears, the babe leaped in my womb for joy. Blessed *is* she who believed, for there will be a fulfillment of those things which were told her from the Lord."

a. **Blessed are you among women, and blessed is the fruit of your womb!** John the Baptist had not yet been born, and Zacharias was still mute, yet Elizabeth *believed* the word of the Lord given to her husband Zacharias when he was in the temple. In the temple, Gabriel told him that their promised son would *make ready a people prepared for the Lord* (Luke 1:17).

> i. Elizabeth believed that, and also believed that the baby in Mary's womb was the **Lord**, who Elizabeth's son would prepare the way for (**the mother of my Lord**). This faith was in Elizabeth, because she **was filled with the Holy Spirit**.

b. **Blessed is she who believed, for there will be a fulfillment of those things**: Elizabeth recognized that Mary's faith played an active role in receiving the promise. God's promises should never make us passive; they should prompt us to seize them by faith. Elizabeth wanted to encourage Mary's faith so she declared "**there will be a fulfillment of those things which were told her from the Lord.**"

3. (46-56) Mary's song of praise to the Lord.

And Mary said: "My soul magnifies the Lord, and my spirit has rejoiced in God my Savior. For He has regarded the lowly state of His maidservant; for behold, henceforth all generations will call me blessed. For He who is mighty has done great things for me, and holy *is* His name. And His mercy *is* on those who fear Him from generation to generation. He has shown strength with His arm; He has scattered *the* proud in the imagination of their hearts. He has put down the mighty from *their* thrones, and exalted *the* lowly. He has filled *the* hungry with good things, and *the* rich He has sent away empty. He has helped His servant Israel, in remembrance of *His* mercy, as He spoke to our fathers, to Abraham and to his seed forever." And Mary remained with her about three months, and returned to her house.

a. **My soul magnifies the Lord**: This song (often called *the Magnificat*, after the Latin translation of the first few words) resembles Hannah's song in 1 Samuel 2:1-10, but it also has at least 12 other allusions to the Old Testament. This means that Mary was a woman who studied and knew God's Word. The Scriptures were on her heart, and came out through her song.

> i. "It appears by the whole frame of this holy song, that the blessed Virgin was well versed in the Scripture, which she here makes so much use of in sundry passages…She had by her much reading made her bosom *Bibliothecam Christi*, Christ's library, as a Father saith; and may seem to have been exercised in the good word of God from her infancy." (Trapp)

ii. Mary was greatly gifted, highly privileged. She did exactly what such greatly blessed people should do: *Mary magnified the Lord.* This remedies pride and self-congratulation, and is something every blessed believer should do.

b. **My spirit has rejoiced in God my Savior**: This means Mary needed a **Savior**, and she *knew* that she needed a **Savior**.

i. "Mary answered the Roman Catholic dogma of the immaculate conception, which holds that from the moment of her conception Mary was by God's grace 'kept free from all taint of Original Sin.' Only sinners need a Savior." (Liefeld)

ii. "Mary was a member of the sinning race…but the honour conferred on her was of the highest, and our thoughts of her, our language concerning her, should at least not lack the dignity and respect manifested in the word of Gabriel. Hers was the crown and glory of all Motherhood, and we should ever think and speak of her reverently." (Morgan)

c. **He who is mighty has done great things for me**: This song mainly celebrates God's goodness, faithfulness and power. Mary's song shows the futility of trusting in self, of trusting in political power, or of trusting in riches. Mary's trust was in God, and it was rewarded.

i. Trapp on **has done great things for me**: "No small things can fall from so great a hand. He gives like himself."

ii. Mary rejoiced and gloried in God, though the child was not yet born. "Brothers, there are some of you who cannot even sing over a mercy when it is born, but here is a woman who sings over an unborn mercy." (Spurgeon)

iii. "To Mary was granted the blessedness of being the mother of the Son of God…Yet that very blessedness was to be a sword to pierce her heart. It meant that some day she would see her son hanging on a cross." (Barclay)

E. John the Baptist's birth.

1. (57-66) The birth and naming of John the Baptist.

Now Elizabeth's full time came for her to be delivered, and she brought forth a son. When her neighbors and relatives heard how the Lord had shown great mercy to her, they rejoiced with her. So it was, on the eighth day, that they came to circumcise the child; and they would have called him by the name of his father, Zacharias. His mother answered and said, "No; he shall be called John." But they said to her, "There is no one among your relatives who is called by this name." So

they made signs to his father; what he would have him called. And he asked for a writing tablet, and wrote, saying, "His name is John." So they all marveled. Immediately his mouth was opened and his tongue *loosed,* and he spoke, praising God. Then fear came on all who dwelt around them; and all these sayings were discussed throughout all the hill country of Judea. And all those who heard *them* kept *them* in their hearts, saying, "What kind of child will this be?" And the hand of the Lord was with him.

a. **She brought forth a son**: The promise was fulfilled just as God said it would be. God always keeps His promises.

b. **They rejoiced with her**: This fulfilled Gabriel's promise recorded at Luke 1:14 (*many will rejoice at his birth*).

i. William Barclay relates the custom of the time: "When the time of the birth was near at hand, friends and local musicians gathered near the house. When the birth was announced and it was a boy, the musicians broke into song, and there was universal congratulation and rejoicing. If it was a girl, the musicians went silently and regretfully away."

c. **They would have called him by the name of his father, Zacharias**: Both Zacharias and Elizabeth knew the name of the child had to be John, according to the command from the angel (Luke 1:13).

d. **They made signs to his father**: They treated Zacharias as if he were deaf, not mute. This must have been constantly annoying to Zacharias.

e. **His name is John**: Now, Zacharias responded in total faith. It wasn't, "I think his name should be John." For Zacharias, this was recognition of a fact, not a suggestion.

i. Even though he had failed before, God gave Zacharias a *second chance* at faith. He gives the same to us today.

ii. "This was a return from the point of unbelief, and the exercise of will in the appointed way." (Morgan)

f. **Immediately his mouth was opened**: Just as Gabriel said, Zacharias could speak again. **He spoke, praising God**. It was fitting that Zacharias' first words were praise to God. His chastisement for disobedience had not made him bitter. Instead, it made him want to trust God all the more, at every opportunity.

2. (67-80) Zacharias' prophecy.

Now his father Zacharias was filled with the Holy Spirit, and prophesied, saying: "Blessed *is* the Lord God of Israel, for He has visited and redeemed His people, and has raised up a horn of salvation for us in the house of His servant David, as He spoke by the mouth of His holy prophets, who *have been* since the world began, that we should be saved from our enemies and from the hand of all who hate us, to perform the mercy *promised* to our fathers and to remember His holy covenant, the oath which He swore to our father Abraham: To grant us that we, being delivered from the hand of our enemies, might serve Him without fear, in holiness and righteousness before Him all the days of our life. And you, child, will be called the prophet of the Highest; for you will go before the face of the Lord to prepare His ways, to give knowledge of salvation to His people by the remission of their sins, through the tender mercy of our God, with which the Dayspring from on high has visited us; to give light to those who sit in darkness and the shadow of death, to guide our feet into the way of peace." So the child grew and became strong in spirit, and was in the deserts till the day of his manifestation to Israel.

a. **Zacharias was filled with the Holy Spirit, and prophesied**: The prophetic voice of the Lord had been silent for 400 years. Now, God spoke through Gabriel (Luke 1:13, 1:28), through Elizabeth (Luke 1:41-42), through Mary (Luke 1:46-55), and now through Zacharias. When God spoke again, it was all connected to the theme of Jesus and His work.

i. Zacharias could truly say, "**Blessed is the Lord God of Israel, for He has visited and redeemed His people.**" It was as if God was present for Israel (**has visited**) in a way not experienced for a long time.

ii. Zacharias' song has been called the *Benedictus*, from its first words in the Latin translation.

b. **Has raised up a horn of salvation for us in the house of His servant David**: We know this was truly Spirit-inspired prophecy because the first focus of his prophecy is the unborn Jesus, not Zacharias' new son John.

- Jesus is **the horn of salvation for us** (Luke 1:69)
- Jesus is the One who saves us from our enemies (Luke 1:71)
- Jesus is the One **to perform the mercy promised to our fathers** (Luke 1:72)
- Jesus is the One **to remember the covenant** (Luke 1:72)
- Jesus makes us able to **serve Him without fear** (Luke 1:74)

i. "It was a song of salvation, and has within it truth deeper than most likely the singer then understood." (Morgan)

ii. Zacharias didn't even *know* Jesus yet, but he praised Him, he loved Him, and he was passionate about Jesus. We know so much more about Jesus than Zacharias did, so what can excuse the coldness of our hearts?

iii. i. Trapp on **by the mouth of His holy prophets**: "There were so many prophets, yet they all had one mouth, so sweet is their harmony."

c. **And you, child, will be called the prophet of the Highest**: After the initial focus on Jesus, the Holy Spirit then led Zacharias to speak of his new-born son and his place in God's great plan.

- John was a true prophet, **the prophet of the Highest** (Luke 1:76)
- John had the unique calling to **go before the face of the Lord to prepare His ways** (Luke 1:76)
- John would teach, and **give knowledge of salvation** to God's people (Luke 1:77)
- John would show people **the remission of their sins** (Luke 1:77)
- John would **give light to those who sit in darkness** (Luke 1:79)
- John would **guide** God's people **into the way of peace** (Luke 1:79)

d. **The child grew and became strong in spirit**: The promise of God came to fruition in John's life. John was **in the desert till the day of his manifestation** because that is where God trains many of His prophets.

Luke 2—Jesus' Birth and Boyhood

A. The world Jesus was born into.

1. (1) A decree from Rome reaches the whole Mediterranean world.

And it came to pass in those days *that* a decree went out from Caesar Augustus that all the world should be registered.

a. **It came to pass in those days**: Luke clearly tells us that he recorded *actual history* and *real events*. This is not "once upon a time." These are not fanciful stories of Zeus and Apollo on Mount Olympus. This is *real*.

b. **A decree went out from Caesar Augustus**: The story of Jesus' birth began during the reign of one of the most remarkable men of ancient history.

i. He was born with the name Octavian, named after his father. His grandmother was the sister of Julius Caesar, and being a talented young man, Octavian came to the attention of his great uncle. Julius Caesar eventually adopted Octavian as his son, and he was made his official heir in 45 B.C. Within a year Caesar was murdered, and Octavian joined with two others—Mark Antony and Lepidus—in splitting the domination of Rome three ways. For decades, the whole Mediterranean world was filled with wars and violence. Now, under the Triumvirate, it became far worse. There were years of bloody, brutal fighting for power and money in Rome and the provinces.

ii. Octavian and Antony soon pushed Lepidus out of the picture. Even though his sister married Antony, for thirteen years Octavian and Antony existed together as rivals, until 31 B.C. For a year, their huge armies assembled and positioned themselves. Antony, with the help of Cleopatra, brought 500 warships; 100,000 foot soldiers; and 12,000 cavalry. Octavian answered with 400 warships, 80,000 infantry and 12,000 horsemen. Octavian had the better strategy and the more mobile ships, and he defeated the combined forces of Antony and Queen Cleopatra of Egypt at the battle of Actium. Now Octavian was the sole ruler of the Roman world, and took the title **Caesar Augustus**.

c. **That all the world**: For decades, the **world** Augustus lived in and Jesus would be born into, the world of the Mediterranean basin, was wrecked by war, destruction, brutality, and immorality.

i. "The lusty peninsula was worn out with twenty years of civil war. Its farms had been neglected, its towns had been sacked or besieged, much of its wealth had been stolen or destroyed. Administration and protection had broken down; robbers made every street unsafe at night; highwaymen roamed the roads, kidnapped travelers, and sold them into slavery. Trade diminished, investment stood still, interest rates soared, property values fell. Morals, which had been loosened by riches and luxury, had not been improved by destitution and chaos, for few conditions are more demoralizing than poverty that comes after wealth. Rome was full of men who had lost their economic footing and then their moral stability: soldiers who had tasted adventure and had learned to kill; citizens who had seen their savings consumed in the taxes and inflation of war and waited vacuously for some returning tide to lift them back to affluence; women dizzy with freedom, multiplying divorces, abortions, and adulteries." (Durant)

d. **A decree went out from Caesar Augustus**: It seemed that the authority of this man changed the chaos of that time in a dramatic way. He brought three things that turned the tide miraculously. First, he brought peace because he had defeated all his rivals. Second, he brought political and administrative skill, perhaps even brilliance. Third, he brought vast sums of money from Egypt to pay the soldiers and to help the Roman economy.

i. "Jesus was born in the reign of Augustus. After a long period of wars which had racked the Mediterranean and its shores, political unity had been achieved and the Roman Empire had become roughly coterminous with the Mediterranean Basin. Here and there it was soon to spread beyond it. Augustus was the first Emperor. Building on the foundations laid by his uncle, Julius Caesar, he brought peace and under the guise of the chief citizen of a restored republic ruled the realm that for several generations Rome had been building. The internal peace and order that Augustus achieved endured, with occasional interruptions, for about two centuries. Never before had all the shores of the Mediterranean been under one rule and never had they enjoyed such prosperity. The *pax Romana* made for the spread of ideas and religions over the area where it prevailed." (Latourette)

ii. But as great a man as **Caesar Augustus** was, he was only a man. And the man who brought the answers also took a dear price. He demanded absolute power over the Roman Empire. For hundreds and hundreds of years, Rome prided itself on being a *republic*—a nation governed by laws, not by any man, and no man was above the law. The Roman Senate and the army and various political leaders lived together in a sometimes-difficult arrangement. Octavius would change all that. In 27 B.C. he arranged for the Roman Senate to give him the title *Augustus*, which means, "exalted" and "sacred." From then on, Rome wasn't a *republic* governed by laws; it was an *empire* governed by an *emperor*. The first Emperor of Rome was this same **Caesar Augustus**.

iii. Durant on the title **Augustus**: "Hitherto the word had been applied only to holy objects and places, and to certain creative or augmenting divinities; applied to Octavian it clothed him with a halo of sanctity, and the protection of religion and the gods."

iv. One of his early titles was *imperator*, the commander in chief of all the armed forces of the state. But he came to make the title mean *emperor*.

v. This says something important about the world Jesus was born into. It was a world hungry for a savior, and a world that was living in the reign of a *political* savior—**Caesar Augustus**—but that wasn't enough.

vi. "In the century before Christ was born the evidences of disintegration were so palpable in wars, in the passing of the old order, and in moral corruption, that the thoughtful feared early collapse. From this disaster the Mediterranean Basin was saved by Julius Caesar and Augustus Caesar…[but] we must note that the principiate devised by Augustus did not cure but only temporarily halted the course of the disease from which Graeco-Roman culture was suffering." (Latourette)

vii. "Augustus and his successors had not solved the basic problems of the Mediterranean world. They had obscured them. For what appeared to be a failure in government they had substituted more government, and government was not the answer." (Latourette)

2. (2) The governor of the Roman administrative region near Galilee.

This census first took place while Quirinius was governing Syria.

a. **This census**: The registration and **census** described wasn't for simple record keeping or statistics. It was to efficiently and effectively tax everyone in the Roman Empire.

i. According to Leon Morris, Justin Martyr, who wrote in the middle of the second century, said that in his own day (more than a hundred years after the time of Jesus) the record of the **census** Luke mentioned could be seen in Roman archives.

b. **First took place**: The idea in the original language is that this was "the first enrollment." Using a census for taxation was common in ancient Rome, so Luke called this one "the first enrollment" to distinguish it from the well-known enrollment in A.D. 6 that he later mentioned in Acts 5:37.

c. **While Quirinius was governing Syria**: This is another historical anchor, securing Luke's account with the reign of known, verifiable historical people.

3. (3) The world responds to the command of Caesar Augustus.

So all went to be registered, everyone to his own city.

a. **So all went to be registered**: It is an impressive thought; one man, in the ivory palaces of Rome, gave a command—and the whole world responded. It may well be that up to that point there had never been a man with power over more lives than Caesar Augustus.

i. Overall, Caesar Augustus was a good ruler. He expanded the territory of the Roman Empire and he did much for his people. The greatest sorrows of his life came from his home, because he had an out-of-control daughter, no son, and all of his nephews, grandsons, and his favorite stepson died young. But like most every man of such ambition and authority, he thought a lot of himself. It is easy to imagine how invincible he felt when he made a *decree… that all the world should be registered* for taxation. It's pretty heady to think, "I make the command and the whole Roman world has to obey it."

ii. But Augustus wasn't really powerful at all. In John 19:10-11, Jesus confronted another Roman who believed he was powerful. *Then Pilate said to Him, "Are You not speaking to me? Do You not know that I have power to crucify You, and power to release You?" Jesus answered, "You could have no power at all against Me unless it had been given you from above."* The same principle applied towards Caesar Augustus; whatever power he had was power given from God.

iii. As he sat in his palace and made his decree, he thought it was the supreme exercise of his will, the ultimate flexing of his muscle. But he was just a tool in God's hand. God had promised that the Messiah would be born in Bethlehem (Micah 5:2), and that promise would be fulfilled. So how does one get a young couple from Nazareth down to Bethlehem when they might not be inclined to travel? Simple. Just work through the *political* "savior of the world," and use him as a pawn in your plan.

iv. We also see that Augustus, for all his accomplishments, couldn't really be the answer. God allowed Caesar Augustus to rise to unheard of human power for many reasons; in some ways, he was like a Roman John the Baptist preparing the way for Jesus. At the end of the story, what is important is Jesus. Who does the world know more today—Jesus or Caesar Augustus? Who has a more lasting legacy?

b. **Everyone to his own city**: There is no record in secular history that Augustus decreed this census and commanded it be performed in this manner, but it was consistent with what we do know of him from history. Augustus was known to be very sensitive to the nationalistic feelings of his subjects, and so he commanded them to return to their cities of family origin for the census.

i. Barclay and others cite a government edict from a Roman census commanded in Egypt in the same era, that each person had to go to their own city for the census enrollment.

ii. In this way, Augustus softened the blow for many. They had to travel, they had to pay taxes—but they would also gather together with family, and see relatives that they perhaps had not seen for a long time.

B. The birth of Jesus.

1. (4-7) Joseph and Mary come to Bethlehem; Jesus is born.

Joseph also went up from Galilee, out of the city of Nazareth, into Judea, to the city of David, which is called Bethlehem, because he was of the house and lineage of David, to be registered with Mary, his betrothed wife, who was with child. So it was, that while they were there, the days were completed for her to be delivered. And she brought forth her firstborn Son, and wrapped Him in swaddling cloths, and laid Him in a manger, because there was no room for them in the inn.

a. **Joseph also went up from Galilee**: The trip from Nazareth to Bethlehem (just outside of Jerusalem) is about 80 miles. This was not a short distance in those days. It was a significant undertaking, costing time and money.

b. **With Mary, his betrothed wife, who was with child**: We often think that Mary was close to delivery when they made this journey, but this may not have been the case at all. Joseph may have been anxious to get her out of Nazareth to avoid the pressure of scandal. Luke tells us that it was while they were in Bethlehem, **that while they were there, the days were completed for her to be delivered**.

i. According to the Roman law, Mary didn't have to go with Joseph for the tax census; but it made sense for her to go with Joseph, especially because she was in the latter stages of a controversial pregnancy, surely the subject of much gossip in Nazareth.

ii. "It is possible that he used the emperor's order as a means of removing Mary from possible gossip and emotional stress in her own village. He had already accepted her as his wife (Matthew 1:24), but apparently continued in betrothal (Luke 2:5), pledged to be married, till after the birth." (Liefeld)

c. **And she brought forth her firstborn Son**: One of the striking things about Luke's narrative is how simple it is in contrast to how great the events are. In our modern age, small events are often inflated with over-description and presented as more important than they actually are. Yet under the inspiration of the Holy Spirit, Luke presented this most amazing event in an understated manner.

d. **She brought forth**: This phrase is filled with wonder. We are not told that anyone assisted Mary in the birth, though someone may have. One way or another, this young woman was completely separated from all her family and supporting friends, who lived back in Nazareth.

i. "The narrative runs as if Mary did these things herself, whence the patristic inference of a painless birth." (Bruce) "That Mary wrapped the child herself points to a lonely birth." (Morris)

ii. When did this happen? The date of December 25 is improbable but not impossible; this date was first popularized in the church the fourth century.

iii. In A.D. 150, Justin Martyr said that the place Jesus was born was a cave in Bethlehem. Later (330), under Constantine the Great, a church was built over the cave, which many believe is still the most probable place where Jesus was born.

e. **Her firstborn son**: This invites the logical conclusion that Mary had other children as well, despite the Roman Catholic dogma of the perpetual virginity of Mary.

f. **Wrapped Him in swaddling cloths**: These are snugly wrapped strips of cloth. More remarkable than the **swaddling cloths** is the fact that He was laid in a **manger**—a feeding trough for animals.

i. Trapp points out that the word translated *swaddling cloths* comes from the ancient Greek word meaning "to tear," meaning they were torn strips of cloth wrapped around Jesus.

g. **There was no room for them in the inn**: This happened in a public place, with other travelers and residents. "Men were trafficking, and little children playing, and women gossiping beside the well—and lo! The kingdom of heaven was among them." (Morrison)

> i. "That there was no room in the inn was symbolic of what was to happen to Jesus. The only place where there was room for him was on a cross." (Barclay)

2. (8) Shepherds watch over their flocks.

Now there were in the same country shepherds living out in the fields, keeping watch over their flock by night.

> a. **Now there were in the same country shepherds**: Bethlehem's shepherds were known to care for the temple flock. These men may have also protected and cared for the lambs used in temple sacrifice.

> b. **Living out in the fields**: Many have said that a late December date is impossible, because shepherds would not have been out at night at that time of year. Nevertheless, warm winters are not unknown in Judea, which has a climate remarkably similar to Southern California.

3. (9-14) The angelic announcement.

And behold, an angel of the Lord stood before them, and the glory of the Lord shone around them, and they were greatly afraid. Then the angel said to them, "Do not be afraid, for behold, I bring you good tidings of great joy which will be to all people. For there is born to you this day in the city of David a Savior, who is Christ the Lord. And this *will be* the sign to you: You will find a Babe wrapped in swaddling cloths, lying in a manger." And suddenly there was with the angel a multitude of the heavenly host praising God and saying: "Glory to God in the highest, And on earth peace, goodwill toward men!"

> a. **An angel of the Lord stood before them**: Interrupting this quiet, dark night was the shining presence of an angel and **the glory of the Lord**. This first angel brought **good tidings** (literally it means that they preached the gospel) to these shepherds, who were regarded as social outcasts.

> > i. "As a class shepherds had a bad reputation…More regrettable was their habit of confusing 'mine' with 'thine' as they moved about the country. They were considered unreliable and were not allowed to give testimony in the law courts." (Morris)

> > ii. "The first preacher of the gospel was an angel. God hath now taken this honour from the angels, and put it upon the ministers, who in Scripture are called angels, Revelation 2:1." (Trapp)

> b. **For there is born to you this day in the city of David a Savior**: They announced the birth of a **Savior**, which was (and is) exactly the need of

mankind. We don't need another advisor, a reformer, or a committee, but a **Savior**.

c. **Suddenly there was with the angel a multitude of the heavenly host praising God**: After the single angel's announcement, a whole group of angels appeared. This was a **heavenly host** (a band of soldiers) that proclaimed peace. What the world needed then and needs now **peace**.

> i. Even the pagans of the first century world sensed this need for peace and a savior. Epictetus, a first century pagan writer, expressed this: "While the emperor may give peace from war on land and sea, he is unable to give peace from passion, grief, and envy; he cannot give peace of heart, for which man yearns for more than even outward peace."

> ii. The contrast between the angelic glory and the humble Jesus must have seemed extreme. God loves to put His glory in unlikely packages so His glory is more clearly displayed (2 Corinthians 4:7).

> iii. "Let God have all the glory, so we may have the peace." (Trapp)

4. (15-16) The shepherds come and see the child Jesus.

So it was, when the angels had gone away from them into heaven, that the shepherds said to one another, "Let us now go to Bethlehem and see this thing that has come to pass, which the Lord has made known to us." And they came with haste and found Mary and Joseph, and the Babe lying in a manger.

a. **Let us now go**: This shows a genuine urgency. They didn't hesitate at all.

b. **And see this thing that has come to pass**: The angel told them to look for *a Babe wrapped in swaddling cloths, lying in a manger* (Luke 2:12). It wasn't an unusual *sign* to see a baby *wrapped in swaddling cloths*, but it was strange to see a baby *lying in a manger*—a feeding trough. If the angel had not told them to look for such a specific sign, they would never have believed it.

c. **And found Mary and Joseph, and the Babe lying in a manger**: This was a strange sight, and the specific sign they were told to look for. They no longer heard or saw angels, but they had the abiding encounter with Jesus. Angels may go, but Jesus remains.

> i. "This was a revolting sight, and was sufficient of itself to produce an aversion to Christ. For what could be more improbable than to believe that he was the King of the whole people, who was deemed unworthy to be ranked with the lowest of the multitude?" (Calvin)

ii. "It is a lovely thought that the shepherds who looked after the Temple lambs were the first to see the Lamb of God who takes away the sin of the world." (Barclay)

5. (17-20) The shepherds spread the news of Jesus' birth.

Now when they had seen *Him*, they made widely known the saying which was told them concerning this Child. And all those who heard *it* marveled at those things which were told them by the shepherds. But Mary kept all these things and pondered *them* in her heart. Then the shepherds returned, glorifying and praising God for all the things that they had heard and seen, as it was told them.

a. **They made widely known the saying which was told them concerning this Child**: The combination of the angelic announcement and the sign of a child in a feeding trough inspired the shepherds to tell as many as they could of what they heard and experienced.

b. **All those who heard it marveled at those things which were told them by the shepherds**: The shepherds' good news amazed all who heard it. Even if they didn't really understand it, they recognized that something significant had happened.

i. "God, to show that he respected not persons, revealed this grand mystery to the shepherds and the wise men; the one poor, the other rich; the one learned, the other unlearned; the one Jews, the other Gentiles; the one near, the other far off." (Trapp)

c. **Mary kept all these things and pondered them in her heart**: Mary's reaction was different than either the shepherds or those who heard them. She calmly took it all in and meditated over it **in her heart**, seeking to understand the deep meaning of it all.

i. "The wonder of the many was a transient emotion (aorist), this recollecting and brooding of Mary was an abiding habit (imperfect)." (Bruce)

ii. Mary had good reason to meditate. What brought her to Bethlehem? She came there because of a Roman emperor's great decree and perhaps gossiping tongues in Nazareth. God works through all kinds of people and all kinds of events to accomplish His plan.

d. **The shepherds returned, glorifying and praising God for all the things they had heard and seen, as it was told them**: The shepherds had such happiness and praise to God because *the word was fulfilled just as it was told them*.

i. "Their zeal in *glorifying and praising God* is an implied reproof of our indolence, or rather of our ingratitude. If the cradle of Christ had such an effect upon them, as to make them rise from the stable and the manger to heaven, how much more powerful ought the death and resurrection of Christ to be in raising us to God?" (Calvin)

C. Jesus' presentation in the temple.

1. (21-24) The circumcision and presentation of Jesus.

And when eight days were completed for the circumcision of the Child, His name was called Jesus, the name given by the angel before He was conceived in the womb. Now when the days of her purification according to the law of Moses were completed, they brought Him to Jerusalem to present *Him* to the Lord (as it is written in the law of the Lord, "Every male who opens the womb shall be called holy to the Lord"), and to offer a sacrifice according to what is said in the law of the Lord, "A pair of turtledoves or two young pigeons."

a. **And when eight days were completed**: This was done so Jesus might fulfill every aspect of the law (as commanded in Leviticus 12:2-3). It also shows that Joseph and Mary were truly devout, obedient parents. They obeyed God's command in Leviticus 12, so Jesus obeyed it also.

b. **Circumcision...the days of her purification**: The circumcision and purification ceremonies were necessary as a reminder that we are all born in sin (Psalm 51:5). Jesus *could* have been excused because He was not born in sin. Yet we see Him even as a baby, identifying with sinners, as He also later did at His baptism and on the cross.

i. The correct reading of Luke 2:22 is, "Now when the days of *their* purification...were completed." Jesus was identified with sinners even as a baby.

ii. "Let us now speak first of the purification. Luke makes it apply both to Mary and to Christ: for the pronoun *of them*, can have no reference whatever to Joseph." (Calvin)

iii. "For He who knew no sin, and who never was to know sin, was already in His circumcision made sin for us. He was not so much as eight days in this world till he began to be numbered with the transgressors. Mary's firstborn son was a lamb without blemish and without spot, but before He was a week old, He began to bear the sins of many...And as He began in the temple that day, so He continued every day to lead a life of pain, and shame, and bloodshedding, for us, for our children, till He finished on the cross the sin-atoning work His Father had given Him to do. And ever after that first day of His wounding of our transgressions, that Holy Thing bore in His body the marks of our redemption." (Whyte)

c. **A pair of turtledoves or two young pigeons**: Leviticus 12 commands that at the birth of a son, a *lamb* be offered as part of the purification and dedication ceremony. Yet it allowed for two birds to be offered if the family could not afford to present a lamb.

> i. "The offering of the two pigeons instead of the lamb and the pigeon was technically called *The Offering of the Poor*…we see that it was into an ordinary home that Jesus was born." (Barclay)

> ii. This suggests that this all happened before the wise men came from the east (Matthew 2:1-12). Mary and Joseph would not have returned to Jerusalem after being warned by the angel (Matthew 2:13), and they would not have offered only two birds after receiving the rich gifts from the wise men (Matthew 2:11).

2. (25-32) A promise fulfilled to Simeon.

And behold, there was a man in Jerusalem whose name was Simeon, and this man was just and devout, waiting for the Consolation of Israel, and the Holy Spirit was upon him. And it had been revealed to him by the Holy Spirit that he would not see death before he had seen the Lord's Christ. So he came by the Spirit into the temple. And when the parents brought in the Child Jesus, to do for Him according to the custom of the law, he took Him up in his arms and blessed God and said: "Lord, now You are letting Your servant depart in peace, according to Your word; for my eyes have seen Your salvation which You have prepared before the face of all peoples, a light to *bring* revelation to the Gentiles, and the glory of Your people Israel."

a. **Waiting for the Consolation of Israel**: Simeon may have known that there were rumors regarding the coming of the Messiah. The news of John the Baptist's birth and its meaning was widely publicized (Luke 1:65), and the shepherds who heard the angelic announcement may have kept temple flocks, and they may have reported what happened among the people of the temple.

b. **So he came by the Spirit into the temple**: Yet it was not rumors, but the **Spirit** who led him into the temple on that day. Simeon was a man who knew how to be led by the Holy Spirit, both in hearing God's promise to him and being prompted to go to the temple at the right time.

c. **He took Him up in his arms**: Simeon's prophecy was filled with love for his Savior; and he hardly knew Jesus. We who know so much more about Him should love Him even more.

d. **According to Your word**: Simeon now had the peace of seeing God's promise fulfilled in his life.

e. **You are letting Your servant depart in peace, according to Your word; for my eyes have seen Your salvation**: It was as if Simeon were commanded by God to keep a lonely watch through the night until he saw the sun come up. This now was, for him, God's sunrise, and because Jesus had come, Simeon could be relieved of his watch.

f. **A light to bring revelation to the Gentiles**: The amazing thing about Simeon's prophecy is that it shows that this **light** is for the Gentiles, also. The salvation of Jesus began with Israel, but was always to be extended beyond Israel.

i. John Trapp quoted a poet's expression of Simeon's heart:

"I fear no sin, I dread no death;
I have lived long enough, I have my life;
I have longed enough, I have my love;
I have seen long enough, I have my light;
I have served enough, I have my saint;
I have sorrowed enough, I have my joy;
Sweet babe, let this psalm serve as a lullaby to thee, and for a funeral for me. Oh, sleep in my arms, and let me sleep in thy peace."

3. (33-35) A promise and a warning from Simeon.

And Joseph and His mother marveled at those things which were spoken of Him. Then Simeon blessed them, and said to Mary His mother, "Behold, this *Child* is destined for the fall and rising of many in Israel, and for a sign which will be spoken against (yes, a sword will pierce through your own soul also), that the thoughts of many hearts may be revealed."

a. **Joseph and His mother marveled**: We can imagine their combination of joy and surprise to see how God has touched the hearts of *others* with an understanding of their Son. No matter how well you know Jesus, there is something special about seeing someone else come to know Him.

b. **For the fall and rising of many**: This would be shown in the way that Peter repented, but Judas despaired; in that one thief blasphemed, the other believed. Jesus is like a magnet that is attractive to some, but others are repelled from Him.

c. **And a sign which will be spoken against**: **Sign** is literally "a target that people shoot at." Jesus would be the target of great evil.

d. **A sword will pierce through your own soul also**: It was important for Mary to know that mothering the Messiah would not be all sweetness and light. It was both a great privilege and a great burden.

i. Possibly no other human agonized as much over Jesus' rejection and suffering as His mother did. This was not only because of the natural love of a mother, but also because His rejection was her rejection. Wonderfully, His vindication was hers also.

4. (36-38) Anna's testimony to the Redeemer.

Now there was one, Anna, a prophetess, the daughter of Phanuel, of the tribe of Asher. She was of a great age, and had lived with a husband seven years from her virginity; and this woman *was* a widow of about eighty-four years, who did not depart from the temple, but served *God* with fastings and prayers night and day. And coming in that instant she gave thanks to the Lord, and spoke of Him to all those who looked for redemption in Jerusalem.

a. **Anna, a prophetess**: We don't know in what capacity Anna was a **prophetess**. Perhaps it was in the way that she brought forth this specific word about Jesus.

b. **Who did not depart from the temple, but served God with fastings and prayers night and day**: This godly woman served God with total devotion. Anna's close walk with God was shown by her *love* for Jesus, and her desire to *tell others* about Jesus (**spoke of Him to all those who looked for redemption**).

i. Anna was a remarkable woman. As a widow, she knew pain and loss, but had not become bitter. As an elderly woman, she had not lost hope. Perhaps it was because she was a woman of *worship* and a woman of *prayer*.

5. (39-40) The return to Nazareth.

So when they had performed all things according to the law of the Lord, they returned to Galilee, to their *own* city, Nazareth. And the Child grew and became strong in spirit, filled with wisdom; and the grace of God was upon Him.

a. **When they had performed all things according to the law of the Lord**: Luke emphasizes that Jesus was perfectly obedient to God, even as a child.

b. **The child grew and became strong in spirit, filled with wisdom**: Jesus **grew** and developed as other children; yet His *spiritual* development is here first noted. We might say that Jesus was aware of His identity and His calling as appropriate to His age development. At age 5 He did not have the understanding of a 30 year-old; but had the greatest capacity for understanding appropriate for a 5 year-old.

i. The development of Jesus gives inspiration for believing parents today. They also pray for children to become **strong in spirit** and to be **filled with wisdom**, and they guide their children in those paths.

c. **The grace of God was upon Him**: The goodness and favor of God was evident in His life, even as a child. The legends of bizarre miracles connected to the childhood of Jesus are nothing more than superstitious tales; but **the grace of God was upon Him**.

i. We know little of Jesus' life from the time He was one month old to the time when He was twelve, except for the general statement in Luke 2:40. We may be curious about the details of His childhood, but there isn't anything we *need* to know except what we are told by the Holy Spirit in the Word.

ii. To satisfy this curiosity, men wrote their own so-called Infancy Gospels. They contain spectacular and silly miracles like Jesus talking from the manger; healing a man made into a mule by a spell; bringing clay birds to life with a clap of His hands; healing people with a sprinkling with his old bath water, and so forth. Yet, "Where the Scripture hath no tongue, we must have no ears." (Trapp)

D. Jesus in His Father's house.

1. (41-45) Jesus is lost on a Passover pilgrimage.

His parents went to Jerusalem every year at the Feast of the Passover. And when He was twelve years old, they went up to Jerusalem according to the custom of the feast. When they had finished the days, as they returned, the Boy Jesus lingered behind in Jerusalem. And Joseph and His mother did not know *it;* but supposing Him to have been in the company, they went a day's journey, and sought Him among *their* relatives and acquaintances. So when they did not find Him, they returned to Jerusalem, seeking Him.

a. **His parents went to Jerusalem every year at the Feast of the Passover**: Attendance at the major feasts was commanded in Exodus 23:17 and Deuteronomy 16:16. It was customary for the faithful of Galilee to make these pilgrimages at feast time in large groups.

i. It would not be difficult to lose track of a young boy with such a large group of travelers—we shouldn't accuse Joseph and Mary of child neglect. But Mary must have felt badly enough, losing the Messiah.

b. **They returned to Jerusalem, seeking Him**: As we would expect from diligent and godly parents, they took the effort to find their son Jesus.

2. (46-50) They find Jesus teaching and learning in the temple.

Now so it was *that* after three days they found Him in the temple, sitting in the midst of the teachers, both listening to them and asking them questions. And all who heard Him were astonished at His under-

standing and answers. So when they saw Him, they were amazed; and His mother said to Him, "Son, why have You done this to us? Look, Your father and I have sought You anxiously." And He said to them, "Why did you seek Me? Did you not know that I must be about My Father's business?" But they did not understand the statement which He spoke to them.

a. **Sitting in the midst of the teachers, both listening to them and asking them questions**: For **three days**, a 12-year-old Jesus discussed God's Word and astonished His listeners with **His understanding and answers**.

> i. "For the Passover season it was the custom for the Sanhedrin to meet in public in the Temple court to discuss, in the presence of all who would listen, religious and theological questions." (Barclay)

> ii. When we realize the impressive intellectual insight and analysis of Jewish Rabbis, this *is* impressive. This is something like a middle-school child discussing physics with a rocket scientist. Jesus did have a unique advantage, having a special relationship with the writer of God's Word.

b. **I must be about My Father's business**: In that day, there was nothing more natural than a son taking up his father's business. Jesus did follow in Joseph's footsteps as a carpenter, but His words here show that He was at least *beginning* to understand His unique relationship to His Father.

> i. It is impossible to say when, in the context of the self-imposed limitations of His humanity, Jesus realized who He was and what He was sent to do, but it was early—this is probably not when it began, but when it was in full flower.

c. **I must be about My Father's business**: These first recorded words of Jesus are significant. The *surprise* implied by these words of Jesus means that He knew that Mary and Joseph *did know* of His special relationship with God His Father. It means that it must have been an item of discussion and perhaps instruction in the upbringing of Jesus in their home.

d. **They did not understand the statement which He spoke to them**: Jesus' statement told them something about His identity as a unique Son of God the Father, though **they did not understand** it. In Judaism of that day, a boy began to learn his father's trade at about 12 years of age. Jesus fulfilled this by instructing the teachers in the temple.

3. (51-52) The growth and development of Jesus.

Then He went down with them and came to Nazareth, and was subject to them, but His mother kept all these things in her heart. And Jesus increased in wisdom and stature, and in favor with God and men.

a. **Then He went down with them and came to Nazareth**: Growing up in Nazareth, Jesus would mature in boyhood and then in His young adulthood. He would fulfill the responsibilities expected of an eldest son; and then at some time Joseph disappeared from the scene, and Jesus became the "man of the family." He worked His trade, supported His family, loved His God, and proved Himself utterly faithful in a thousand small things before He formally entered His appointed ministry.

i. "A Christian does not always do extraordinary things. He does ordinary things in extraordinary ways." (Morrison)

b. **And was subject to them**: The knowledge of who He was did not make Jesus proud or haughty; Jesus **was subject to** His parents. Jesus went from vision to duty, even as He later did from the Mount of Transfiguration.

c. **His mother kept all these things in her heart**: Luke probably heard of all this (and of the events about John's and Jesus' births) in personal interviews with Mary as he compiled his Gospel.

d. **Jesus increased in wisdom**: The development described first in Luke 2:40 continued.

e. **Jesus increased in...stature**: Not only did He become bigger physically, He also became a bigger *person.*

f. **Jesus increased in...favor with God and men**: He grew in a close, personal relationship with His heavenly Father, and He also grew in His human friendships and relationships.

i. The word translated **favor** is the same word translated *grace* in the rest of the New Testament, but this was not *saving grace* in the pattern of grace extended to sinners. " 'The good pleasure of God was upon Him,' that would be the best way to render the text." (Whyte)

ii. Jesus was not born a superman. He developed as He grew. "He passed through a natural but perfect spiritual and physical development. At every stage, He was perfect for that stage." (Geldenhuys)

Luke 3—The Work of John the Baptist

A. The mission of John the Baptist.

1. (1-2a) The time is described in reference to the contemporary political and religious leaders.

Now in the fifteenth year of the reign of Tiberius Caesar, Pontius Pilate being governor of Judea, Herod being tetrarch of Galilee, his brother Philip tetrarch of Iturea and the region of Trachonitis, and Lysanias tetrarch of Abilene, while Annas and Caiaphas were high priests...

a. **In the fifteenth year of the reign of Tiberius Caesar**: Biblical chronology can be a complicated matter. From secular historical records we know with certainty the *general* time this was, but it is difficult to be certain *exactly* when this was. The best reckonings set it anywhere from A.D. 27 to 29.

b. **Tiberius Caesar…Pontius Pilate…Herod…Philip…Lysanias**: Luke listed the *political* leaders of the region Jesus lived and served in. Like any good historian, Luke gave a real, historical framework. This is not a fairy tale beginning with "once upon a time."

i. Luke gave more than a chronological measure; he also told us something of the tenor of the times.

- **Tiberius** was an emperor known for his cruelty and severity
- **Pontius Pilate** was also renowned for his brutal massacres of the Jewish people in Judea, and his insensitivity towards the Jews
- The rulers from the family of Herod the Great (**Herod**, **Philip**, and **Lysanias**) were known for their corruption and cruelty

ii. With all this, Luke reminds both his original readers and us today of the corruption and moral degradation of the Roman Empire, especially in the distant provinces like Judea.

iii. The historical reality of these rulers is beyond dispute. Archaeologists have discovered specific, undeniable evidence that these people lived and ruled in these places and at these times.

iv. When Herod the Great died, he divided his kingdom among his three sons **Herod**, **Philip**, and **Lysanias**. "The title tetrarch literally means *governor of a fourth part*…later the word widened its meaning and came to mean the governor of any part." (Barclay)

c. **Caiaphas…Annas**: Luke also listed the *religious* leaders of Judea in the period of Jesus' ministry. **Caiaphas** was actually the High Priest, but his father-in-law **Annas** (the patriarch of the family) was the real influence among the priestly class.

i. The mention of these two corrupt high priests reminds us that the Jewish leaders were more interested in power politics than in serving God.

ii. In November 1990, scholars discovered what some believe to be the family tomb of **Caiaphas**. On an ancient burial box (an *ossuary*) from the era is an inscription reading *Joseph, Son of Caiaphas*. Remains of a 60-year-old male were discovered in the box.

2. (2b-3) The ministry of John the Baptist.

The word of God came to John the son of Zacharias in the wilderness. And he went into all the region around the Jordan, preaching a baptism of repentance for the remission of sins...

a. **The word of God came to John the son of Zacharias in the wilderness**: John lived in the desert since his youth (Luke 1:80). Now, prompted by **the word of God**, John began to fulfill his ultimate calling—to be a forerunner of the Messiah.

i. Luke carefully set the work of John in historical context because, "To Luke the emergence of John the Baptist was one of the hinges on which history turned." (Barclay)

b. **Preaching a baptism of repentance for the remission of sins**: The idea behind **remission** is not only forgiveness, but also liberty and deliverance (as in *to preach deliverance…to set at liberty* in Luke 4:18). **Repentance** could bring true liberty in the Messiah for those who received it.

i. John's message was a call to **repentance**. Some people think that repentance is mostly about *feelings*, especially feeling sorry for your sin. It is wonderful to feel sorry about your sin, but **repent** isn't a "feelings" word. It is an *action* word. John told his listeners to make a change of the mind, not merely to feel sorry for what they had done. Repentance speaks of a change of direction, not a sorrow in the heart.

c. **Baptism of repentance**: There was nothing strange in the ceremony of **baptism** (a ceremonial immersion) itself. The strange thing was that *Jews* submitted to baptism. This was a common ritual for Gentiles who wanted to become Jews. For a Jew to submit to baptism was to say something like, "I'm as bad as a heathen Gentile." This was a true mark of humble repentance, a radical rededication to the Lord.

> i. "Baptism by water, whether understood by the Qumran community as applicable to itself or as preached by Jewish missionaries to Gentile converts symbolized spiritual cleansing from sin, the result of forgiveness." (Pate)

> ii. This is different than our *baptism into Christ* (Romans 6:3-4) where our immersion in water identifies us with Jesus' death and resurrection. This **baptism of repentance** John presented identified a person with his or her need to get right with God and be cleansed.

3. (4-6) John's ministry as a fulfillment of prophecy.

As it is written in the book of the words of Isaiah the prophet, saying: "The voice of one crying in the wilderness: 'Prepare the way of the LORD; make His paths straight. Every valley shall be filled and every mountain and hill brought low; the crooked places shall be made straight and the rough ways smooth; and all flesh shall see the salvation of God.'"

a. **As it is written in the book of the words of Isaiah the prophet**: Luke connected John the Baptist with the one prophesied by Isaiah (Isaiah 40:3-5). John himself was aware of this from his early days, because his father was aware of it from before John's birth (Luke 1:76-77).

b. **Prepare the way of the LORD**: John's great message was that things *can* be set right. The Messiah is here to do things that are too big for man: filling valleys, leveling mountains, setting crooked roads straight and rough roads smooth.

> i. The Jews at that time thought that the problem was mainly "*them*," that is, the Romans who politically oppressed them. John made them see that when you got right down to it, the problem was really with *me*, not *them*. *I* have to get right with God.

c. **All flesh shall see the salvation of God**: The way of the Messiah must be made ready. He came to *all mankind*. (NIV)

> i. "Simply stated, the theme of John's preaching was that the messianic age was at hand." (Pate)

B. The message of John the Baptist.

1. (7-9) John's message to the multitudes.

Then he said to the multitudes that came out to be baptized by him, "Brood of vipers! Who warned you to flee from the wrath to come? Therefore bear fruits worthy of repentance, and do not begin to say to yourselves, 'We have Abraham as *our* father.' For I say to you that God is able to raise up children to Abraham from these stones. And even now the ax is laid to the root of the trees. Therefore every tree which does not bear good fruit is cut down and thrown into the fire."

a. **Brood of vipers! Who warned you to flee from the wrath to come?** Addressing your audience as a *family of snakes* is not a customary way to begin a sermon. Asking them, "*Why are you here anyway?*" isn't a smooth introduction. But John wasn't interested in preaching a soft message or in tickling ears.

i. Simply said, John was weird. Any man who preached like this, lived in the desert, wore funny clothes and lived on grasshoppers and wild honey was just plain *strange*. Jesus didn't have a polished advance man with a thousand-dollar suit and a two-hundred-dollar haircut. God often uses weird people.

b. **Do not begin to say to yourselves, 'We have Abraham as our father':** John cautioned against trusting in Abraham's merits as sufficient for salvation. It was widely taught that Abraham's merits were plenty for any Jew's salvation, and that it was *impossible* for any descendant of Abraham, Isaac and Jacob to go to hell.

c. **Bear fruits worthy of repentance**: John was not unreasonable in demanding **good fruit**. True repentance will always have fruit—and the basic fruit of the Christian life is *love* (Galatians 5:22 and 1 Corinthians 13:1-3).

2. (10-14) John's message to specific individuals.

So the people asked him, saying, "What shall we do then?" He answered and said to them, "He who has two tunics, let him give to him who has none; and he who has food, let him do likewise." Then tax collectors also came to be baptized, and said to him, "Teacher, what shall we do?" And he said to them, "Collect no more than what is appointed for you." Likewise the soldiers asked him, saying, "And what shall we do?" So he said to them, "Do not intimidate anyone or accuse falsely, and be content with your wages."

a. **What shall we do then?** John's instructions were quite ordinary. He demanded that people share, that they be fair with each other, and that they not be mean and cruel; that they be happy with what they get. These are things we teach our smallest children.

i. Integrity in the *ordinary* things is still a mark of true repentance. We sometimes think God requires us to do great or impossible things to demonstrate repentance. Often He instead looks for integrity in the ordinary things.

ii. *He has shown you, O man, what is good; and what does the* LORD *require of you but to do justly, to love mercy, and to walk humbly with your God?* (Micah 6:8)

b. **Collect no more than what is appointed for you…Do not intimidate anyone or accuse falsely, and be content with your wages**: John did not see tax collecting or soldiering as inherently evil. He did not command them to quit their professions, but to conduct themselves honestly in them.

i. The Romans taxed by auctioning the rights to collect taxes to the highest bidder. Because the tax collector could only cover his costs and make a profit by getting as much as he could, these men were hated intensely.

ii. "These were the toll-takers, custom-gatherers for the Romans, and most of them greedy gripers. Publicans they were called, because they took up *publica*, the goods of the empire." (Trapp)

3. (15-18) John points forward to a greater One and a greater baptism.

Now as the people were in expectation, and all reasoned in their hearts about John, whether he was the Christ *or* not, John answered, saying to all, "I indeed baptize you with water; but One mightier than I is coming, whose sandal strap I am not worthy to loose. He will baptize you with the Holy Spirit and fire. His winnowing fan *is* in His hand, and He will thoroughly clean out His threshing floor, and gather the wheat into His barn; but the chaff He will burn with unquenchable fire." And with many other exhortations he preached to the people.

a. **All reasoned in their hearts about John, whether he was the Christ or not**: John made such an impact that people logically wondered if he was the Messiah. Instead of cultivating his own popularity, he gave it all to Jesus. John pointed to **One mightier than I**.

b. **Whose sandal strap I am not worthy to loose**: The rabbis of Jesus' day taught that a teacher might require just about anything of his followers *except* to have them take off his sandals. That was considered too humiliating to demand. Yet John said that he was not even worthy to do *this* for Jesus.

i. John had many reasons to be proud, yet he was humble. He had a miraculous birth, a prophesied destiny, he was called to personally fulfill great prophetic promises, a powerful preacher, and a man with a great following.

ii. "What was the reason, think you, of John's always retaining his proper position? Was it not because he had a high idea of his Master, and a deep reverence for him? Ah, brethren, because of our little estimate of Christ, it is often unsafe for the Lord to trust us in any but the very lowest positions." (Spurgeon)

iii. John was both *strict* and *humble*. That is an all-too-rare combination.

c. **He will baptize you with the Holy Spirit and fire**: John said that the Messiah was coming with a different baptism. The Holy Spirit's outpouring was promised as part of the New Covenant. We are promised an *immersion*, an *overflowing* of the Holy Spirit in our lives. This was often experienced as people were prayed for with hands laid on them (Acts 6:6, 8:17, 9:17, 13:3-4, and 19:6).

d. **His winnowing fan is in His hand, and He will thoroughly clean out His threshing floor**: The Messiah would also bring a baptism of fire, fire that would both *purify* and *destroy* what is lacking, like fire burns up the worthless chaff. God's power is always a transforming power, a purifying power.

i. The Messiah will also be the one to divide the true from the false, to separate the wheat from the chaff; **the winnowing fan is in His hand**. Judas is set apart from Peter; one thief blasphemes, another believes.

4. (19-20) The boldness of John's message is illustrated.

But Herod the tetrarch, being rebuked by him concerning Herodias, his brother Philip's wife, and for all the evils which Herod had done, also added this, above all, that he shut John up in prison.

a. **Herod the tetrarch, being rebuked by him concerning Herodias**: The relationship between Herod and Herodias was both complicated and sinful. He was her uncle, and he seduced her from his half-brother. In marrying Herodias, Herod at once married a woman both his niece and his sister-in-law.

i. "In light of passages like Leviticus 18:16 and 20:21, which specifically forbid a man having sexual relations with his brother's wife, Herod's actions called for condemnation." (Pate)

b. **He shut John up in prison**: Because John made such a bold stand for the truth, Herod, who was steeped in immorality, punished him.

i. "Josephus says that the reason for the arrest was that Herod 'feared lest the great influence John had over the people might put it in his power and inclination to raise a rebellion; for they seemed ready to do anything he should advise.'" (Barclay)

C. John baptizes Jesus.

1. (21a) Jesus is baptized along with the others.

When all the people were baptized, it came to pass that Jesus also was baptized...

a. **When all the people were baptized**: There was a remarkable response to the work of John the Baptist, and many came to repent and receive baptism. One day, in the midst of the crowd, Jesus came to also be baptized.

b. **Jesus also was baptized**: Jesus did not receive baptism because He was a sinner that needed to repent and be cleansed from His sins. He did it to completely identify Himself with sinful man. This was the same heart that would lead to His ultimate identification with sinful man on the cross.

2. (21b-22) The Divine witness to Jesus' standing as the Son of God.

And while He prayed, the heaven was opened. And the Holy Spirit descended in bodily form like a dove upon Him, and a voice came from heaven which said, "You are My beloved Son; in You I am well pleased."

a. **And while He prayed**: We notice Luke's repeated emphasis on prayer. Other gospel writers describe this occasion, but only Luke points out that it happened **while He prayed**.

b. **The Holy Spirit...and a voice came from heaven**: The three Persons of the Trinity were all manifested at once. The Holy Spirit came **in bodily form like a dove**, the **voice** of God the Father was heard, and the **beloved Son** was baptized.

i. There was some visible, tangible evidence that the Holy Spirit had come upon Jesus. A similar thing happened with the apostles when something like tongues of fire appeared over their heads on Pentecost.

ii. "What this scene was in the life of the Lord, Pentecost was for the Church. Then she was anointed for her divine mission among men; the unction of the Holy One rested upon her, to be continued and renewed as the centuries slowly passed." (Meyer)

c. **You are My beloved Son; in You I am well pleased**: The **voice** from heaven left no doubt. This wasn't just another sinner being baptized; this was the sinless, Eternal Son of God, pleasing the Father by His identification with sinful man.

- **You are My beloved Son** is an echo of Psalm 2:7, a glorious Messianic Psalm.

- **In You I am well pleased** is an echo of Isaiah 42:7, marking Jesus as the suffering Servant spoken of in that broader passage.

d. **In You I am well pleased**: Jesus began His earthly ministry with the blessing of the Father and the enabling power of the Holy Spirit. In Jesus, we can have the same things.

i. In Jesus, we can hear the Father say to us, *This is My beloved son, in you I am well pleased.*

ii. In Jesus, the Holy Spirit can come upon us for empowering and blessing.

D. The genealogy of Jesus.

1. (23a) The age of Jesus when He began His ministry.

Now Jesus Himself began *His ministry at* about thirty years of age...

a. **Thirty years of age**: This seems to have been the age of full maturity in the Jewish mind. Priests could begin their service only at 30 (Numbers 4:2-3).

2. (23b-38) Luke's genealogy of Jesus.

Being (as was supposed) *the son* of Joseph, *the son* of Heli, *the son* of Matthat, *the son* of Levi, *the son* of Melchi, *the son* of Janna, *the son* of Joseph, *the son* of Mattathiah, *the son* of Amos, *the son* of Nahum, *the son* of Esli, *the son* of Naggai, *the son* of Maath, *the son* of Mattathiah, *the son* of Semei, *the son* of Joseph, *the son* of Judah, *the son* of Joannas, *the son* of Rhesa, *the son* of Zerubbabel, *the son* of Shealtiel, *the son* of Neri, *the son* of Melchi, *the son* of Addi, *the son* of Cosam, *the son* of Elmodam, *the son* of Er, *the son* of Jose, *the son* of Eliezer, *the son* of Jorim, *the son* of Matthat, *the son* of Levi, *the son* of Simeon, *the son* of Judah, *the son* of Joseph, *the son* of Jonan, *the son* of Eliakim, *the son* of Melea, *the son* of Menan, *the son* of Mattathah, *the son* of Nathan, *the son* of David, *the son* of Jesse, *the son* of Obed, *the son* of Boaz, *the son* of Salmon, *the son* of Nahshon, *the son* of Amminadab, *the son* of Ram, *the son* of Hezron, *the son* of Perez, *the son* of Judah, *the son* of Jacob, *the son* of Isaac, *the son* of Abraham, *the son* of Terah, *the son* of Nahor, *the son* of Serug, *the son* of Reu, *the son* of Peleg, *the son* of Eber, *the son* of Shelah, *the son* of Cainan, *the son* of Arphaxad, *the son* of Shem, *the son* of Noah, *the son* of Lamech, *the son* of Methuselah, *the son* of Enoch, *the son* of Jared, *the son* of Mahalalel, *the son* of Cainan, *the son* of Enos, *the son* of Seth, *the son* of Adam, *the son* of God.

a. **Being (as was supposed) the son of Joseph**: According to ancient custom, genealogies were almost always traced through the father, not the mother. This was a problem in the unique situation of a virgin birth.

> i. Luke differs in the account of Matthew from David onward, but they both end their genealogies with Joseph. The best explanation for this seems to be that Luke followed Mary's line (Jesus' *actual* lineage) while Matthew followed Joseph's line (His *legal* lineage by adoption). This was Luke's point in his important phrase "**being (as was supposed) the son of Joseph**."

> ii. Luke began with **Joseph** because he followed proper form and included no women in his genealogy

b. **The son of…the son of**: The fact that Luke could give Jesus' genealogical history was not unusual. Josephus traced his own genealogy from "the public records" (*Autobiography*, paragraph 1). It was also well known that the famous Rabbi Hillel could prove his descent from King David with reference from the public registers.

c. **The son of Adam, the son of God**: Luke traced his genealogy all the way back to Adam to show that Jesus belonged to all mankind, not only to the Jewish people.

> i. A genealogy may not seem like much, but it exactly established Jesus' credentials as a member of the human race. A Bible translator to a distant tribe saved the genealogies for last, because he thought them the least important part of the gospels. But when he finally finished them last of all, the tribesmen were astounded—they told the translator, "You mean to tell us that this Jesus was a *real* person, with *real* ancestors? We had no idea."

Luke 4—Jesus' Temptation, First Galilean Ministry

A. The temptation of Jesus.

1. (1-2a) Jesus is led by the Spirit into the wilderness.

Then Jesus, being filled with the Holy Spirit, returned from the Jordan and was led by the Spirit into the wilderness, being tempted for forty days by the devil.

a. **Being filled with the Holy Spirit**: In Luke 3:21-22 we read of how the Holy Spirit came upon Jesus in an unusual way at His baptism. We should not infer that He was *not* filled with the Holy Spirit before, only that He was now **filled with the Holy Spirit** in an unusual and public way.

i. We can say—certainly for the most part, and perhaps entirely—that Jesus lived His life and performed His ministry *as a Spirit-filled man*, choosing *not* to rely on the resources of His divine nature, but willingly limiting Himself to what could be done by the guidance of God the Father and the empowering of God the Holy Spirit.

b. **Was led by the Spirit into the wilderness, being tempted**: After identifying with sinners in baptism (Luke 3:21-22), He then identified with them in temptation. *For we do not have a High Priest who cannot sympathize with our weaknesses, but was in all points tempted as we are, yet without sin.* (Hebrews 4:15)

i. We sometimes think that Jesus' temptations were not real because they were not exactly like ours. There was never a sinful pull or a sinful memory inside of Jesus, like in us. But in many ways, Jesus' temptations were more real and more severe. For us, oftentimes the pressure of temptation only relents when we give in—and Jesus never did. He had to withstand a much greater pressure of temptation than you or I ever will.

ii. The word or idea of *temptation* is used in three different senses in the Bible.

- Satan, working through our own lusts, tempts us to perform evil acts—a solicitation or enticement to evil (1 Corinthians 7:5 and James 1:13-14)

- We may tempt God in the sense of wrongly putting Him to the test (Acts 5:9 and 1 Corinthians 10:9)

- God may test us, but never with a solicitation or enticement to evil (Hebrews 11:17)

iii. "This is the most sacred of stories, for it can have come from no other source than his own lips. At some time he must have had himself told his disciples about this most intimate experience of his soul." (Barclay)

c. **Filled with the Holy Spirit...led by the Spirit into the wilderness**: Walking in the Spirit, Jesus was still led **into the wilderness** where He was **tempted**. The Holy Spirit leads us into seasons of wilderness as well as seasons of green pastures.

i. There are parallels with the way that Jesus was tested and the way that Adam was tested; but Adam faced his temptation in the most favorable circumstances imaginable, and Jesus faced His temptations in bad and severe circumstances.

d. **Being tempted for forty days**: Jesus was tempted for the entire **forty days**. What follows are highlights of that season of temptation.

2. (2b-4) The first temptation: transform stone into bread for personal needs.

And in those days He ate nothing, and afterward, when they had ended, He was hungry. And the devil said to Him, "If You are the Son of God, command this stone to become bread." But Jesus answered him, saying, "It is written, 'Man shall not live by bread alone, but by every word of God.'"

a. **He ate nothing...He was hungry**: To tempt a man who has fasted for forty days with food seems almost unfair; yet the Father allowed it because He knew Jesus could endure it. God will never allow us to be tempted beyond our ability to resist (1 Corinthians 10:13).

i. The fact that Luke, the physician, noted that **afterward...He was hungry** is important. After such a long fast, renewed hunger often points to a critical need for food. Jesus was beginning to starve to death.

ii. Jesus was hungry, but full of the Spirit. We are sometimes just the opposite—full stomachs and empty spirits.

b. **And the devil said to Him**: The Bible clearly teaches the existence and activity of an evil being of great power and cunning, who sets himself against God and God's people. This one is sometimes called **the devil**, sometimes Satan (Luke 4:8), and many other names or titles.

c. **If You are the Son of God**: This could be more accurately translated *since You are the Son of God*. Satan didn't suggest doubt about Jesus' identity;. instead, he challenged Jesus to *display* His identity.

> i. The temptation was basically this: "Since You're the Messiah, why are You so deprived? Do a little something for Yourself." The same temptation comes to us: "If you're a child of God, why are things so tough? Do a little something for yourself."

d. **Command this stone to become bread**: Satan enticed Jesus to use the power of God for selfish purposes. The temptation to eat something inappropriate worked well with the first sinless man (Genesis 3:6), so the devil thought to try it on the second sinless man.

> i. "This wilderness was not a wilderness of sand. It was covered by little bits of limestone exactly like loaves." (Barclay)
>
> ii. By this, we also see how temptation often works. Often, this is the pattern of temptation:
>
> - Satan appealed to a *legitimate* desire within Jesus (the desire to eat and survive)
> - Satan suggested that Jesus fulfill this legitimate desire in an *illegitimate* way

e. **But Jesus answered him, saying, "It is written, 'Man shall not live by bread alone, but by every word of God.'"** Jesus countered Satan's suggestion with Scripture (Deuteronomy 8:3). What Satan said made sense— "Why starve yourself to death?" But what **is written** makes even more sense. Jesus reminded Satan of Biblical truth, that **every word of God** is more important than the very bread we eat.

> i. Jesus used *Scripture* to battle Satan's temptation, not some elaborate spiritual power inaccessible to us. Jesus fought this battle as a Spirit-filled, Word-of-God-filled man. He drew on no divine resources that are unavailable to us.
>
> ii. We effectively resist temptation in the same way Jesus did: filled with the Holy Spirit, we answer Satan's seductive lies by shining the light of God's truth upon them. If we are ignorant of God's truth, we are poorly armed in the fight against temptation.

3. (5-8) The second temptation: all the kingdoms of this world in exchange for a moment of worship.

Then the devil, taking Him up on a high mountain, showed Him all the kingdoms of the world in a moment of time. And the devil said to Him,

"All this authority I will give You, and their glory; for *this* has been delivered to me, and I give it to whomever I wish. Therefore, if You will worship before me, all will be Yours." And Jesus answered and said to him, "Get behind Me, Satan! For it is written, 'You shall worship the Lord your God, and Him only you shall serve.'"

a. **Taking Him up on a high mountain, showed Him all the kingdoms of the world in a moment of time**: It seems best to understand this as a mental or spiritual vision. The experience and the temptation were real, but there doesn't seem to be a mountain high enough to literally see **all the kingdoms of the world in a moment of time**.

b. **All the kingdoms of the world…All this authority I will give to You, and their glory**: The devil knew Jesus had come to win **the kingdoms of the world**. This was an invitation to win back the world without going to the cross. Satan would simply **give** it to Jesus, if Jesus would **worship before** the devil.

i. **For this has been delivered to me, and I give it to whomever I wish**: Satan claimed that authority over the earth's kingdoms was **delivered** to him, and Jesus never challenged the statement. We might say that Adam and all of his collective descendants **delivered** to Satan when God gave man dominion over the earth, and Adam and his descendants forfeited it to Satan (Genesis 1).

ii. Satan is *the ruler of this world* (John 12:31) and *the prince of the power of the air* (Ephesians 2:2) by the popular election of mankind since the days of Adam.

iii. Since Satan possesses the glory of the kingdoms of this world, and can **give it to whomever I wish**, it should not surprise us to see the ungodly in positions of power and prestige.

c. **If You will worship before me, all will be Yours**: The Father's plan for Jesus was for Him to suffer first, then enter His glory (Luke 24:25-26). Satan offered Jesus a way out of the suffering.

i. One day, it will be said that *The kingdoms of this world have become the kingdoms of our Lord and of His Christ, and He shall reign forever and ever* (Revelation 11:15). Satan offered this to Jesus now, before the agony of the cross.

ii. If Jesus accepted this, our salvation would be impossible. He might have gained some sort of authority to rule, delegated from Satan, but He could not redeem individual sinners through His sacrifice.

d. **And Jesus answered and said to him, "Get behind Me, Satan!"** Satan brought a powerful temptation to Jesus, and Jesus *resisted* the influence of Satan, first by saying, **"Get behind Me, Satan!"** In this, Jesus fulfilled the exhortation later expressed in James 4:7: *Resist the devil and he will flee from you.*

e. **For it is written, "You shall worship the** Lord **your God, and Him only you shall serve."** For the second time, Jesus countered Satan's deception with Biblical truth, quoting from Deuteronomy 6:13. There might have seemed to be an advantage in Jesus avoiding the cross, but Jesus affirmed to Himself and reminded Satan that the command to **worship the Lord your God** and serve **Him only** is far above any supposed advantage in bowing to Satan.

i. Again, Jesus answered Satan with the same resource available to every believer: the Word of God used by a Spirit-filled believer. In resisting these temptations as a man, Jesus proved that Adam did not *have* to sin; there was not something faulty in his makeup. Jesus faced worse than what Adam did and Jesus never sinned.

4. (9-13) The third temptation: testing God through signs and wonders.

Then he brought Him to Jerusalem, set Him on the pinnacle of the temple, and said to Him, "If You are the Son of God, throw Yourself down from here. For it is written: 'He shall give His angels charge over you, to keep you,' and, 'In their hands they shall bear you up, lest you dash your foot against a stone.'" And Jesus answered and said to him, "It has been said, 'You shall not tempt the Lord **your God.'" Now when the devil had ended every temptation, he departed from Him until an opportune time.**

a. **Set Him on the pinnacle of the temple**: Satan took Jesus to a prominent, high place. From this wall surrounding the temple mount, it was hundreds of feet to the rocky valley floor below. If Jesus followed Satan's request to **throw Yourself down from here**, it would be a spectacular event.

i. According to Geldenhuys, the ancient Jewish writing *Pesiqta Rabbati* (162a) records a traditional belief that the Messiah would show Himself to Israel standing on the roof of the temple. If Jesus did what Satan suggested, it would fulfill the Messianic expectation of His day.

b. **Throw Yourself down from here**: Satan could not himself throw Jesus off the pinnacle of the temple. He could do no more than suggest, so he had to ask Jesus to throw *Himself* down.

c. **For it is written: "He shall give His angels charge over you, to keep you"**: This time, the devil knew and quoted Scripture in his temptation (Psalm 91:11-12). "Go ahead, Jesus; if You do this, then the Bible promises angels will help You, and it will be spectacular self-promotion."

i. When Satan says, **"For it is written,"** it reminds us that Satan is a Bible expert and knows how to twist Bible passages out of their context. Sadly, many people will accept anyone who quotes a Bible verse as if they taught God's truth, but the mere use of Bible words does not necessarily convey the will of God.

ii. Some suggest that Satan is such a Bible expert because he has spent centuries looking for loopholes.

d. **And Jesus answered and said to him, "It has been said, 'You shall not tempt the LORD your God.'"** Jesus answered Satan's misuse of Scripture with the proper use of the Bible, quoting from Deuteronomy 6:16. As Jesus rejected Satan's twisting of Scripture, He rightly divided the word of truth, understanding it in its context.

i. Jesus understood from His knowledge of the *whole counsel of God* (Acts 20:27) that Satan twisted this passage from Psalm 91. Jesus knew how to rightly divide the word of truth (2 Timothy 2:15).

ii. Jesus understood that Satan enticed Him to take a step of "faith" that would actually test (**tempt**) God in an ungodly way. "The temptation may have been to perform a spectacular, but pointless miracle in order to compel wonder and belief of a kind." (Morris)

e. **Now when the devil had ended every temptation, he departed from Him until an opportune time**: When Satan saw that he couldn't get anywhere, he left for a while. The devil will always seek to come back at an **opportune time**, so we should never give him the opportunity.

i. "Evil had nothing more to suggest. The thoroughness of the temptation was the completeness of the victory." (Morgan)

ii. Satan is not stupid; he will not continually put his limited resources into an ineffective battle. If you want Satan to leave you alone for a while, you must continually resist him. Many are *so attacked* because they resist *so little*.

iii. Jesus resisted these temptations because He walked in the Word and in the Spirit; these two are the resources for Christian living. Too much Word and not enough Spirit and you *puff up* (in the sense of pride). Too much Spirit and not enough Word and you *blow up*. With the Word and the Spirit together, you *grow up*.

B. Jesus is rejected at Nazareth.

1. (14-15) The early Galilean ministry.

Then Jesus returned in the power of the Spirit to Galilee, and news of Him went out through all the surrounding region. And He taught in their synagogues, being glorified by all.

a. **Jesus returned in the power of the Spirit**: Jesus came through His time of testing stronger than ever. Though He was already filled with the Spirit (Luke 4:1), He continued to walk **in the power of the Spirit** after experiencing victory over temptation.

> i. "He who, through the grace of God, resists and overcomes temptation, is always *bettered* by it. This is one of the wonders of God's grace, that those very things which are designed for our utter ruin he makes the instruments of our greatest good. Thus Satan is ever duped by his own proceeding, and caught in his own craft." (Clarke)

b. **To Galilee...the surrounding region**: The **region** of **Galilee** was a fertile, progressive, highly-populated region. According to figures from the Jewish historian Josephus, there were some 3 million people populating Galilee, an area smaller than the state of Connecticut. Even allowing for some exaggeration from Josephus, it indicates a highly-populated area.

> i. Josephus—who was at one time a governor of Galilee—wrote that there were 240 villages and cities in Galilee (*Life* 235), each with a population of at least 15,000 people.

c. **He taught in their synagogues**: Jesus' focus in ministry was teaching, and at this early point in His ministry, He had no organized opposition (**being glorified by all**).

2. (16-17) Jesus comes to His own synagogue in Nazareth.

So He came to Nazareth, where He had been brought up. And as His custom was, He went into the synagogue on the Sabbath day, and stood up to read. And He was handed the book of the prophet Isaiah. And when He had opened the book, He found the place where it was written:

a. **He came to Nazareth, where He had been brought up**: Since this was early in the ministry of Jesus, it was not long from the time when He lived and worked in **Nazareth**. The people of that village knew Him, and He had probably done work as a carpenter or builder for many of them.

> i. Shortly before this, Jesus moved from Nazareth to Capernaum on the shores of the Sea of Galilee (Matthew 4:12-13).

b. **And as His custom was, He went into the synagogue on the Sabbath day**: Jesus made it **His custom** to get together with God's people for worship and the Word of God. If anyone didn't need to go to church (so to speak), it was Jesus—yet, it was **His custom** to do so.

c. **And stood up to read**: The usual order of service in a synagogue began with an opening prayer and praise; then a reading from the Law; then a reading from the prophets and then a sermon, perhaps from a learned visitor. On this occasion Jesus was the learned visitor. Since this synagogue was in **Nazareth**, Jesus would have attended it often before, and now He would **read** and teach in His hometown synagogue.

3. (18-19) Jesus reads from Isaiah 61:1-2.

"The Spirit of the LORD *is* upon Me, because He has anointed Me to preach the gospel to *the* poor; He has sent Me to heal the brokenhearted, to proclaim liberty to *the* captives and recovery of sight to *the* blind, to set at liberty those who are oppressed; to proclaim the acceptable year of the LORD."

a. **The Spirit of the LORD is upon Me**: The one speaking in this Isaiah passage is the Anointed One; the Messiah, the Christ.

> i. **Anointed Me**: The word *anoint* means, *to rub or sprinkle on; apply an unguent, ointment, or oily liquid to*. Persons in the Old Testament were often literally anointed with oil. For example, priests were anointed for their special service to the LORD (Exodus 28:41). Literal oil was applied, but as a sign of the Holy Spirit upon their life and service. The oil on the head was only the outward representation of the real, spiritual work going on inside them.

b. **He has anointed Me to…**: In this prophecy, the Messiah announced that He came to heal the fivefold damage that sin brings. Sin does great damage, so there must be a great work of redemption.

- **To preach the gospel to the poor**: Sin impoverishes, and the Messiah brings good news to the **poor**
- **To heal the brokenhearted**: Sin breaks hearts, and the Messiah has good news for **brokenhearted**
- **To proclaim liberty to the captives**: Sin makes people captive and enslaves them, and the Messiah comes to set them free
- **Recovery of sight to the blind**: Sin blinds us, and the Messiah comes to heal our spiritual and moral blindness
- **To set at liberty those who are oppressed**: Sin oppresses its victims, and the Messiah comes to bring **liberty** to the **oppressed**

  > i. Thankfully, Jesus didn't come to only *preach* deliverance or even to only *bring* deliverance. Jesus came to *be* deliverance for us. "Christ was the great enemy of bonds. He was the lover and the light of liberty." (Morrison)

c. **To proclaim the acceptable year of the LORD**: This seems to describe the Old Testament concept of the year of Jubilee (Leviticus 25:9-15 and following). In the year of Jubilee slaves were set free, debts cancelled, and things set to a new start.

i. "Jesus came to preach the Lord's acceptable year, a reference to the year of Jubilee. It is just possible that the reason Jesus returned to His hometown was because it was Jubilee year." (Pate)

ii. Where Jesus *stopped* reading from Isaiah helps show us the nature of prophecy and its relation to time. The Isaiah passage goes on to describe what Jesus would do at His *second* coming (*and the day of vengeance of our God*, Isaiah 61:2). This is a 2,000-year-old comma between the two phrases.

4. (20-22) Jesus teaches on Isaiah 61:1-2.

Then He closed the book, and gave *it* back to the attendant and sat down. And the eyes of all who were in the synagogue were fixed on Him. And He began to say to them, "Today this Scripture is fulfilled in your hearing." So all bore witness to Him, and marveled at the gracious words which proceeded out of His mouth. And they said, "Is this not Joseph's son?"

a. **And sat down**: As Jesus sat, He prepared to teach instead of returning to His seat among the congregation. Everyone wondered how He would explain what He had just read.

b. **Today this Scripture is fulfilled in your hearing**: With these words, Jesus answered two questions.

- "Whom did Isaiah write of?" Jesus answered, "Isaiah wrote of Me."
- "When will this come to pass?" Jesus answered, "Isaiah wrote of now."

c. **Marveled at the gracious words which proceeded out of His mouth**: This seems to mean that Jesus *continued* to speak on the theme just mentioned, and He did it with words that were literally *full of grace*. They sensed the goodness and grace of God in the announcement that the ministry of the Messiah was now present.

d. **Is this not Joseph's son?** The following response of Jesus shows that this was not an impartial comment. After their initial amazement, they then began to resent that someone so familiar (**Joseph's son**) could speak with such grace and claim to be the fulfillment of such remarkable prophecies.

5. (23-27) Jesus answers their objections.

He said to them, "You will surely say this proverb to Me, 'Physician, heal yourself! Whatever we have heard done in Capernaum, do also here in Your country.'" Then He said, "Assuredly, I say to you, no prophet is accepted in his own country. But I tell you truly, many widows were in Israel in the days of Elijah, when the heaven was shut up three years and six months, and there was a great famine throughout

all the land; but to none of them was Elijah sent except to Zarephath, *in the region* **of Sidon, to a woman** *who was* **a widow. And many lepers were in Israel in the time of Elisha the prophet, and none of them was cleansed except Naaman the Syrian."**

a. **Whatever we have heard done in Capernaum, do also here in Your country**: Luke doesn't directly tell us that the people said this; perhaps they did and Jesus quoted their words back to them, or it is just as likely that Jesus understood and explained their objection. They wanted Jesus to *prove* His claims with miraculous signs.

> i. Apparently, Jesus had already done miracles in **Capernaum**, not recorded in Luke (but in places like John 1-4). The people of Nazareth wanted to see the same kind of thing, demanding the miraculous as a show or a sign.

> ii. "They no doubt argued, 'He is a Nazareth man, and of course he is in duty bound to help Nazareth. They considered themselves as being in a sort his proprietors, who could command his powers at their own discretion." (Spurgeon)

b. **No prophet is accepted in his own country**: Jesus understood that it is easy to doubt the power and work of God among those most familiar to us. It was easier for those in Nazareth to doubt or reject Jesus because He seemed so *normal* and *familiar* to them.

> i. "I learn, from this incident in our Lord's life, that it, is not the preacher's business to seek to please his congregation. If he labors for that end, he will in all probability not attain it; but, if he should succeed in gaining it, what a miserable success it would be!" (Spurgeon)

c. **To none of them was Elijah sent except to Zarephath, in the region of Sidon…none of them was cleansed except Naaman the Syrian**: Jesus' audience wanted special favors because He was in His hometown. Jesus pointed out that this doesn't matter to God, using God's work among the Gentiles in the days of Elijah and Elisha as examples.

> i. Jesus made at least two points. First, the fact that they did not receive Jesus had nothing to do with Jesus, but everything to do with them. He was truly from God, but they would not receive Him. Their rejection said more about them than it did about Jesus.

> ii. Second, it showed that God's miraculous power operates in unexpected and sovereign ways. People that we often consider undeserving and perhaps strange are many times recipients of God's miraculous power.

> iii. Spurgeon points out that it was true that Naaman's healing was an example of sovereign grace and election at work; but it could also

be turned around to say, "Every foreign, heathen leper who came to Elisha and did what he said to do in seeking the Lord was healed and received a blessing." This was also true, and can be set alongside the first aspect.

iv. Naaman was healed by sovereign grace, but note how it happened. First, he heard a word that he could be healed. He then responded to that word in faith that connected with action (the act of travelling to Israel). Next, Naaman obeyed the word of the prophet to wash in the Jordan seven times, and he obeyed with humility, surrendering his pride to the word of God through the prophet.

6. (28-30) Jesus walks away from a murderous mob.

So all those in the synagogue, when they heard these things, were filled with wrath, and rose up and thrust Him out of the city; and they led Him to the brow of the hill on which their city was built, that they might throw Him down over the cliff. Then passing through the midst of them, He went His way.

a. **When they heard these things, were filled with wrath, and rose up and thrust Him out of the city**: This was quite a response to a sermon. They were angry to be told that there was something wrong with them, that their request for a miracle was denied, and that Jesus implied that God also loved the Gentiles.

i. Jesus didn't primarily seek to please His audience, and He didn't use their approval as the measure of His success.

b. **That they might throw Him down over the cliff**: Pushing someone off a small cliff was often the first step in the process of stoning. Once the victim fell down, they were pelted with rocks until dead.

i. Luke set the tone for the whole story of Jesus' life here in Luke 4. Jesus came, sinless and doing nothing but good for all—and they wanted to kill Him.

c. **Passing through the midst of them**: They wanted a miracle, and Jesus did an unexpected one right in front of them, escaping miraculously.

i. In this situation, Jesus could have backed off the cliff and been rescued by angels—as Satan suggested in the third temptation. Instead, Jesus chose a more normal miracle, if there is such a thing. "Like a second Samson; his own arm saved him. This might have convinced his adversaries, but that they were mad with malice." (Trapp)

C. Further ministry in Galilee.

1. (31-37) Jesus rebukes an unclean spirit in the Capernaum synagogue.

Then He went down to Capernaum, a city of Galilee, and was teaching them on the Sabbaths. And they were astonished at His teaching, for His word was with authority. Now in the synagogue there was a man who had a spirit of an unclean demon. And he cried out with a loud voice, saying, "Let *us* alone! What have we to do with You, Jesus of Nazareth? Did You come to destroy us? I know who You are; the Holy One of God!" But Jesus rebuked him, saying, "Be quiet, and come out of him!" And when the demon had thrown him in *their* midst, it came out of him and did not hurt him. Then they were all amazed and spoke among themselves, saying, "What a word this *is!* For with authority and power He commands the unclean spirits, and they come out." And the report about Him went out into every place in the surrounding region.

a. **And was teaching them on the Sabbaths...they were astonished at His teaching, for His word was with authority**: Jesus pursued His primary calling as a teacher, taking advantage of the courtesy of the synagogue. We are not told what Jesus taught, but we are told of the effect the teaching had on His audience. **They were astonished**. They had never heard anyone teach quite like this before.

i. The **authority** of Jesus was not only evident as He taught, but also in His life. This would be demonstrated in the encounter with the demon-possessed man.

b. **There was a man who had a spirit of an unclean demon**: The terms unclean *spirit*, *evil spirit*, and **demon** all seem to be the same, referring to evil powers of darkness who are the enemies of God and man. These powers are organized (Ephesians 6:12) and led by Satan himself.

c. **What have we to do with You, Jesus of Nazareth?** It is ironic that the demons knew who Jesus was, but the chosen people—those from His own city—did not appreciate who Jesus was.

i. **Did You come to destroy us?** This question "reflects the belief that the advent of the kingdom of God would spell the demise of demonic control over the world." (Pate)

d. **I know who You are; the Holy One of God!** The demon himself testified that Jesus was holy and pure. The demons admitted that their wilderness temptations failed to corrupt Jesus.

e. **But Jesus rebuked him, saying, "Be quiet, and come out of him!"** The manner of Jesus' dealings with the demon in this passage is a clear demonstration of His power and authority over the spirit realm. People were amazed at the authority of His word in both teaching and in spiritual living.

i. "This may have distinguished Jesus from the 'ordinary' exorcist's fanfare of incantations, charms, and superstitions." (Pate)

2. (38-39) Peter's mother-in-law is healed of a fever.

Now He arose from the synagogue and entered Simon's house. But Simon's wife's mother was sick with a high fever, and they made request of Him concerning her. So He stood over her and rebuked the fever, and it left her. And immediately she arose and served them.

a. **Entered Simon's house**: Jesus did a rather public miracle in the synagogue. Now He would display His power in a private setting. Jesus was not a mere performer for the crowds.

b. **Simon's wife's mother**: Simon will later be identified as Peter, the leader among the disciples of Jesus. This shows that Simon Peter was married. Clement of Alexandria, an early Christian writer, said that Peter's wife helped him in ministry by meeting the needs of other women.

c. **He stood over her and rebuked the fever**: In this situation, Jesus saw the fever itself as something to be rebuked. Perhaps He perceived that there was some spiritual dynamic behind this seemingly natural illness.

i. Barclay on the phrase, **sick with a high fever**, "every word is a medical word…the medical Greek for someone definitely laid up with an illness…Luke knew just how to describe this illness."

d. **And it left her…immediately she arose and served them**: This was not only the healing of a disease, but also the immediate granting of strength. One doesn't normally go from a high fever to serving others.

i. "He who healed her of the fever did not need her to minister to him; he who had power to heal diseases had certainly power to subsist without human ministry. If Christ could raise her up he must be omnipotent and divine, what need then had he of a womanly service?" (Spurgeon)

3. (40-41) Jesus heals many who are sick and demon possessed.

When the sun was setting, all those who had any that were sick with various diseases brought them to Him; and He laid His hands on every one of them and healed them. And demons also came out of many, crying out and saying, "You are the Christ, the Son of God!" And He, rebuking *them*, did not allow them to speak, for they knew that He was the Christ.

a. **When the sun was setting**: This marked the start of a new day, the day after the Sabbath (Luke 4:31). Freed from the Sabbath restrictions on travel and activity, the people come to Him freely to be healed.

b. **He laid His hands on every one of them and healed them**: Jesus worked hard to serve the needs of others, and put their needs before His.

c. **Did not allow them to speak**: Jesus restrained the demons from speaking about Him because He did not want their testimony to be relied upon.

i. Because the Biblical accounts of the ministry of Jesus are compressed, stressing the important and exceptional events, it is easy to think that Jesus encountered demon-possessed people more than He actually did. In fact, Scripture records fewer than ten specific individuals delivered from demon possession in Jesus' ministry, plus two general occasions where it describes people being delivered. This doesn't seem abnormally high over a period of three years, among a dense, pre-Christian population.

4. (42-44) Jesus continues His preaching ministry in Galilee.

Now when it was day, He departed and went into a deserted place. And the crowd sought Him and came to Him, and tried to keep Him from leaving them; but He said to them, "I must preach the kingdom of God to the other cities also, because for this purpose I have been sent." And He was preaching in the synagogues of Galilee.

a. **Went into a deserted place**: Jesus knew the value of solitude with God the Father. He spent most of His time ministering among the people, but needed such times in **a deserted place**.

i. The great work that Jesus did in His ministry did not draw on the resource of His divine nature, but on His constant communion with God the Father and His empowering by God the Holy Spirit. The time in **a deserted place** was essential for that.

b. **I must preach the kingdom of God to the other cities also**: He taught about the **kingdom of God**, in the sense of announcing the presence of the King and correcting misconceptions about the kingdom.

c. **For this purpose I have been sent**: Jesus saw His main ministry, at this point, to be **preaching the kingdom**. Miracles were a part of that work, but not His main focus.

d. **And He was preaching in the synagogues of Galilee**: This was the clear emphasis of Jesus' work before the great work of atonement on the cross—he was a teacher and a preacher, both in the open air and in houses of worship. His work of miracles and healings was impressive, but it was never His emphasis.

Luke 5—Disciples Are Called

A. The call of four fishermen.

1. (1-3) Jesus teaches from a boat.

So it was, as the multitude pressed about Him to hear the word of God, that He stood by the Lake of Gennesaret, and saw two boats standing by the lake; but the fishermen had gone from them and were washing *their* nets. Then He got into one of the boats, which was Simon's, and asked him to put out a little from the land. And He sat down and taught the multitudes from the boat.

a. **The multitude pressed around Him to hear the word of God**: The large crowd showed the increasing popularity of Jesus as a teacher. The crowd was so big that Jesus **got into one of the boats** and **taught the multitudes from the boat**.

i. "Note the many strange pulpits in which Christ preached." (Morrison)

b. **The Lake of Gennesaret**: This was another name for the Sea of Galilee, as it is more familiarly known. It was also sometimes called the Sea of Tiberias.

c. **One of the boats, which was Simon's**: Simon must have felt privileged that Jesus wanted to teach from his boat. We can also be sure that Simon listened to this teaching all the more attentively.

2. (4-5) Peter receives as Jesus directs his service.

When He had stopped speaking, He said to Simon, "Launch out into the deep and let down your nets for a catch." But Simon answered and said to Him, "Master, we have toiled all night and caught nothing; nevertheless at Your word I will let down the net."

a. **He said to Simon, "Launch out into the deep and let down your nets"**: After Jesus had finished teaching, He wanted to do something good for Simon, who had lent Him the use of the boat. Peter could not give something to Jesus without Jesus giving even more back to him.

i. As far as we can tell, *Jesus was in the boat with them, as He directed this*. His presence gave confidence. "It is a blessed thing to see Christ sitting in the boat while you cast out the net. If you catch a glimpse of his approving smile as he watches you, you will work right heartily." (Spurgeon)

b. **Master, we have toiled all night**: The particular ancient Greek word Luke used for **Master** (*epistata*) is unique to Luke's Gospel. The word has the ideas "commander," "leader," or perhaps even "boss." With this title, Peter showed he was willing to take orders from Jesus.

c. **We have toiled all night and caught nothing; nevertheless at Your word I will let down the net**: Peter could have come up with any number of possible excuses.

- "I worked all night and I'm tired"
- "I know a lot more about fishing than a carpenter does"
- "The best fishing is at night, not in the daytime"
- "All these crowds and loud teaching have scared the fish away"
- "We already washed our nets"
- "Jesus may know religion but He doesn't know fishing"

d. **At Your word I will let down the net**: This was Peter's great statement of faith, and trust in Jesus' word. God's people throughout all ages have lived and gone forth with this confidence in the word of Jesus.

- **At Your word**, there was light
- **At Your word**, the sun, moon, stars, and planets were created
- **At Your word**, life came to this earth
- **At Your word**, creation is held together and sustained
- **At Your word**, empires rise and fall; history unfolds Your great plan

3. (6-7) The miraculous catch of fish.

And when they had done this, they caught a great number of fish, and their net was breaking. So they signaled to *their* partners in the other boat to come and help them. And they came and filled both the boats, so that they began to sink.

a. **They caught a great number of fish**: Peter *didn't* make such excuses, and His faith in Jesus was well rewarded. Peter understood that he probably knew more about fishing than a carpenter did and that he had worked all night without any results. The only reason why Peter did what

Jesus asked was because *he believed in Jesus*, not because the circumstances seemed right.

i. When Jesus *directs* our work, it makes all the difference. We can work—even work hard—for a long time with no results. But when Jesus directs our work, we see results; and we always miss something great when we make excuses instead of allowing Jesus to direct our work.

ii. "Here the dumb fishes do clearly preach Christ to be the Son of God." (Trapp)

b. **So they signaled to their partners in the other boat to come and help them**: Peter had to work with others to get the job done. This is reminiscent of what God did in a man named James McGready on the frontiers of Kentucky starting in the 1790s. In Kentucky he pastored three small churches that met in roughly-built shacks. He said that the winter of 1799, for the most part, was weeping and mourning with the people of God and that it was like living in Sodom and Gomorrah on the rough, lawless, and often godless frontier. McGready started the concerts of prayer, but he also got his congregations praying for him and for his ministry of the word of God—for a half an hour before they went to bed on Saturday night and for a half an hour when they woke up on Sunday morning. In 1800 came an extraordinary outpouring of the Holy Spirit, and so many people began to come to Christ that McGready called out: "Any preacher of any kind who loves the Lord Jesus come and help me."

i. "Some will rather leave souls to perish than admit of *partners* in the sacred work. It is an intolerable pride to think nothing done well but what we do ourselves; and a diabolic envy to be afraid lest others should be more successful than we are." (Clarke)

4. (8-11) Peter's reaction and the call of four disciples.

When Simon Peter saw *it*, he fell down at Jesus' knees, saying, "Depart from me, for I am a sinful man, O Lord!" For he and all who were with him were astonished at the catch of fish which they had taken; and so also *were* James and John, the sons of Zebedee, who were partners with Simon. And Jesus said to Simon, "Do not be afraid. From now on you will catch men." So when they had brought their boats to land, they forsook all and followed Him.

a. **He fell down at Jesus' knees**: Jesus had already miraculously healed Peter's mother-in-law (Luke 4:38-39). Yet there was something about *this* miracle of the blessed catch that made Peter worship Jesus and surrender himself to Him.

b. **Depart from me, for I am a sinful man, O Lord!** When Peter saw the great power of Jesus—displayed in Jesus' knowledge in an area where He should have no knowledge—it made Peter realize his own spiritual bankruptcy compared to Jesus.

i. Because Peter was such an experienced fisherman, and because he knew how unfavorable the conditions were, he knew all the more what a great miracle this was.

ii. Peter had hardly met Jesus, yet he already knew much about Jesus; and because of that, he understood some things about himself.

- Peter knew that Jesus was **Lord**
- Peter knew he was a **man**
- Peter knew he was a **sinful man**
- Peter let this make him a humble man

iii. We might say that Peter's prayer was good, but there is even a better prayer to pray: "*Come nearer to me,* for I am a sinful man, O Lord!"

c. **Do not be afraid**: In the grammar of the ancient Greek, this is literally *stop being fearful*; it calms an existing fear. Peter was afraid of Jesus in the sense of holding Him in such great awe, but Jesus told Him to put away that fear. God wants to relate to us on the principle of love, not the principle of a cowering fear.

d. **From now on you will catch men**: When Jesus told Simon that he would **catch men**, He told Simon that he would do what Jesus Himself did. There was never a greater fisher of men than Jesus Himself, but He wanted others to do the work He did. Jesus started with these three, then twelve, then hundreds, then thousands, and millions up on through the centuries.

i. Clarke says that the word **catch** signifies to catch something *alive*. That is true evangelism; it isn't to bring dead people into a building, but to bring real life.

e. **They forsook all and followed Him**: This seems to mean that they left the miraculous catch of fish behind, because it was not as important as what it showed them about Jesus. It showed them that Jesus was much more than any carpenter, and this caused them to follow Him.

f. **They forsook all and followed Him**: They **followed Him** in the way that students followed their teaching rabbi in those days. In some aspects Jesus offered them a traditional education at the feet of a rabbi; in other aspects this was very different from a normal rabbinical education.

i. They started out relatively untrained and uneducated, but Jesus taught them. Their education and training came more upon an *apprenticeship* model than a *classroom* model.

ii. "The word 'follow' is a technical term in Luke for discipleship (9:23, 49, 57, 59, 61; especially 18:22, 28). As such, it is similar in nature to his term in Acts for following Christ, the 'way' (Acts 9:2, 19:9, 23; 22:4; 24:14, 22)." (Pate)

B. Jesus heals a leper.

1. (12) The leper begs Jesus for help.

And it happened when He was in a certain city, that behold, a man who was full of leprosy saw Jesus; and he fell on *his* face and implored Him, saying, "Lord, if You are willing, You can make me clean."

a. **A man who was full of leprosy saw Jesus**: In the ancient world, leprosy was a terrible, destructive disease—and still is in some parts of the world. Being **full of leprosy**, this man had no hope of improvement, so he came to Jesus with a great sense of need and desperation.

i. "In Palestine there were two kinds of leprosy. There was one which was rather like a very bad skin disease, and it was the less serious of the two. There was the one in which the disease, starting from a small spot, ate away the flesh until the wretched sufferer was left with only the stump of a hand or a leg. It was literally a living death." (Barclay)

ii. According to Jewish law and customs, one had to keep 6 feet (2 meters) from a leper. If the wind blew toward a person from a leper, they had to keep 150 feet (45 meters) away. The only thing *more* defiling than contact with a leper was contact with a dead body.

iii. For these reasons, leprosy was considered a picture of sin and its effects. It is a contagious, debilitating disease that corrupts its victim and makes him essentially dead while alive. Therefore society and religious people scorned lepers. Rabbis especially despised them, and saw lepers as those under the special judgment of God, deserving no pity or mercy.

iv. Nevertheless, the leper came to Jesus by himself and despite many discouragements.

- He knew how terrible his problem was
- He knew most everyone thought his condition was hopeless
- He had no one who would or could take him to Jesus
- He had no previous example of Jesus healing a leper to give him hope

- He had no promise that Jesus would heal him

- He had no invitation from Jesus or the disciples

- He must have felt ashamed and alone in the crowd

b. **Lord, if You are willing**: The leper had no doubt about the *ability* of Jesus to heal; his only question was if Jesus was **willing** to heal. This was significant, because leprosy was so hopeless in the ancient world that healing a leper was compared to raising the dead; yet this leper knew that all Jesus needed was to be **willing**.

c. **Lord, if You are willing, You can make me clean**: This leper wanted more than healing. He wants *cleansing*, not only from the leprosy, but also from all its debilitating effects on his life and soul.

i. Barclay quotes Dr. A. B. MacDonald, who was in charge of a leper colony in Itu: "The leper is sick in mind as well as body. For some reason there is an attitude to leprosy different from the attitude to any other disfiguring disease. It is associated with shame and horror, and carries, in some mysterious way, a sense of guilt…shunned and despised, frequently do lepers consider taking their own lives and some do."

2. (13) Jesus touches the leper and he is cleansed.

Then He put out *His* hand and touched him, saying, "I am willing; be cleansed." Immediately the leprosy left him.

a. **He put out His hand and touched him**: Jesus did not have to touch the leper in order to heal him. He could have healed him with a word or even a thought. Yet He healed the leper with a *touch* to show compassion to this man thought to be untouchable, and to show that the touch of the Messiah makes men clean instead of receiving their impurity.

i. "On the one hand, He knew that the ceremonial restrictions were abolished in Himself: on the other, He desired to teach that sin cannot defile the divine holiness of the Saviour." (Meyer)

b. **I am willing**: By both His words and His touch, Jesus showed that He was in fact **willing**. He showed the leper more than His power to heal; He also showed His willing and compassionate heart to heal. It is common for people to doubt the *love* of God more than His *power*.

c. **Immediately the leprosy left him**: The former leper's life was changed forever. He was not only healed, but as he had requested, he was also **cleansed**.

3. (14) Jesus commands the healed man to give testimony of his healing to the priests only.

And He charged him to tell no one, "But go and show yourself to the priest, and make an offering for your cleansing, as a testimony to them, just as Moses commanded."

a. **He charged him to tell no one**: Jesus often commanded people to be quiet about a healing or some miraculous work that He had done for them. He did this because He wanted to calm the excitement of the crowds until the proper time for His formal revelation to Israel, which was an exact date as prophesied in Daniel 9.

i. In addition, Jesus' miracles were not primarily calculated to make Him famous or a celebrity (though they certainly did give testimony to His ministry). More so, Jesus healed to meet the needs of specific individuals and to demonstrate the evident power of the Messiah in the setting of love and care for the personal needs of humble people.

b. **Go and show yourself to the priest**: Jesus commanded the man to give **a testimony** to the priests, and what a testimony it was! The Mosaic Law commanded certain sacrifices upon the healing of a leper, and when the man reported it to the priests, they had to perform ceremonies (Leviticus 14) that were rarely (if ever) practiced.

i. "This gift was *two living, clean birds, some cedar wood, with scarlet and hyssop*, Leviticus 14:4, which were to be brought *for* his cleansing; and, *when* clean, *two he lambs, one ewe lamb, three tenth deals of flour, and one log of oil*, Leviticus 14:10; but if the person was *poor*, then he was to bring *one lamb, one tenth deal of flour, one log of oil and two turtle doves, or young pigeons*, Leviticus 14:21, 22." (Clarke)

ii. Going to the priest also helped to bring the former leper back into society. Jesus wanted the healing of the man's disease to have as much benefit as possible.

4. (15-16) Jesus' increasing fame as a healer.

However, the report went around concerning Him all the more; and great multitudes came together to hear, and to be healed by Him of their infirmities. So He Himself *often* withdrew into the wilderness and prayed.

a. **The report went around concerning Him all the more**: The news of the remarkable healing of the leper became widely known. Luke doesn't specifically tell us that the leper himself was responsible for this, but Mark does tell us (Mark 1:44-45). He told many despite the command of Jesus to *tell no one*.

i. It is strange that the one Jesus commanded to tell no one told everyone, and we who are commanded to tell everyone often tell no one.

b. **Great multitudes came together to hear, and to be healed by Him of their infirmities**: Jesus had a great following as a healer, but He never seemed to promote or encourage it. The crowds came to **hear**, and he also **healed** them.

> i. The Messiah's ministry as a healer was prophesied: *Then the eyes of the blind shall be opened, and the ears of the deaf shall be unstopped. Then the lame shall leap like a deer, and the tongue of the dumb sing. For waters shall burst forth in the wilderness, and streams in the desert.* (Isaiah 35:5-6)

> ii. The presence of so much sickness and disease among Israel was evidence of their disobedience to the Sinai Covenant and of their low spiritual state. God promised that such curses would come upon them if they were disobedient to His covenant (Deuteronomy 28).

c. **So He Himself often withdrew into the wilderness and prayed**: In this season of increasing popularity and publicity, Jesus made a special point to withdraw into the wilderness for prayer. The demands of life pushed Jesus *to* prayer, not *from* it.

> i. "The love in the eyes of God compensated him for the hate in the eyes of men." (Barclay)

> ii. "He made it a frequent custom to withdraw from the multitudes for a time, and pray, teaching hereby ministers of the Gospel that they are to receive *fresh* supplies of *light* and *power* from God by prayers, that they may be the more successful in their work; and that they ought to seek frequent opportunities of being in private with *God* and their *books*." (Clarke)

C. Jesus' power to forgive and heal.

1. (17-19) Jesus' teaching is interrupted.

Now it happened on a certain day, as He was teaching, that there were Pharisees and teachers of the law sitting by, who had come out of every town of Galilee, Judea, and Jerusalem. And the power of the Lord was *present* to heal them. Then behold, men brought on a bed a man who was paralyzed, whom they sought to bring in and lay before Him. And when they could not find how they might bring him in, because of the crowd, they went up on the housetop and let him down with *his* bed through the tiling into the midst before Jesus.

a. **As He was teaching, that there were Pharisees and teachers of the law sitting by**: In Capernaum (Mark 2:1) Jesus continued His teaching work and in His audience were religious and spiritual leaders (**Pharisees** and **teachers of the law**). Some of them had come from considerable distances (**Judea, and Jerusalem**).

i. The **Pharisees** were devoted and zealous, but for many of them religion was focused on an exact outward obedience to the law, and they believed that God only loved those that did as they did.

ii. **Pharisees** means *separated ones*. They separated themselves from everything they thought was unholy, and they thought everyone was separated from the love of God, except themselves.

iii. These men were **sitting by** with critical eyes and hearts, ready to twist and pounce upon some word of Jesus. Yet at least they were *there*. "We are glad to have these people 'sitting by' rather than not coming at all. Being in the way, the Lord may meet with them. If you go where shots are flying you may be wounded one of these days. Better to come and hear the gospel from a low motive than not to come at all." (Spurgeon)

b. **And the power of the Lord was present to heal them**: One might have seen that whenever Jesus was present, the **power of the Lord was present to heal**. Yet even in the ministry of Jesus, there seemed to be times of a greater demonstration and reception of God's healing work.

i. There were times when Jesus did not do many miraculous works because of the general unbelief of His audience (Matthew 13:58).

ii. We note that the **power of the Lord was present to heal them** after Jesus *withdrew into the wilderness and prayed* (Luke 5:16).

c. **They went up on the housetop and let him down with his bed through the tiling into the midst before Jesus**: Because of the crowded room, the friends of the paralyzed man had to lower him down through the roof—certainly, an unusual interruption to a sermon.

i. **Through the tiling**: The roof was usually accessible by means of an outside stairway and was made of thatch, dirt or tile set over beams. It could be taken apart, and the friends of the paralyzed man could lower their friend down to Jesus.

ii. This proved the determination and faith of friends of the paralytic. They counted on Jesus healing their friend, because it would be harder to bring him back up through the roof than lowering him down.

iii. Spurgeon spoke of the quality of men who would bring a friend to Jesus in such a way: "They need be strong, for the burden is heavy; they need be resolute, for the work will try their faith; they need be prayerful, for otherwise they labor in vain; they must be believing, or they will be utterly useless."

2. (20-22) Jesus declares the paralyzed man's sins forgiven.

When He saw their faith, He said to him, "Man, your sins are forgiven you." And the scribes and the Pharisees began to reason, saying, "Who is this who speaks blasphemies? Who can forgive sins but God alone?" But when Jesus perceived their thoughts, He answered and said to them, "Why are you reasoning in your hearts?

a. **When He saw their faith**: Jesus looked up at the four men struggling with crude ropes tied to each corner of the stretcher with a paralytic on it. He looked at them and **saw their faith**.

i. Their faith could be *seen*. Their bold, determined action to bring their friend to Jesus proved they had real faith. There is something lacking in faith if it can never be *seen*.

ii. In this account, the emphasis is on the faith of the *friends of the paralyzed man*. We need to have faith for more than our own needs, but also have faith that Jesus can and will meet the needs of others whom we bring to Him.

b. **Man, your sins are forgiven you**: We can imagine how the friends on the roof felt. They went to a lot of trouble to see their friend healed of his paralysis, and now the teacher seemed to only be concerned with his spiritual problems.

i. Jesus knew what the man's *real* need was, and what his *greatest* need was. What good was it if the man had two whole legs, and walked right into hell with them?

ii. Jesus did not mean that the paralyzed man was especially sinful, or that his paralysis was directly caused by sin. Instead, He addressed the man's greatest need, and the common root of all pain and suffering—man's sinful condition.

c. **Who can forgive sins but God alone?** The religious leaders used the right kind of logic. They correctly believed that only God could forgive sins, and they were even correct for examining this new teacher. Their error was in refusing to see who Jesus actually was: God the Son, who has the authority to forgive sins.

i. "Again and again during the life of Christ the same dilemma was to re-appear. If he were not divine, then he was indeed a blasphemer; there could be no third way out." (Cole)

ii. This reminds us that only God can solve our sin problem. We can't even forgive ourselves, because we don't have the power and authority to forgive ourselves. We must be persuaded that God has truly and rightly forgiven us in light of what Jesus did at the cross.

3. (23-26) Jesus demonstrates the power and authority of God alone.

"Which is easier, to say, 'Your sins are forgiven you,' or to say, 'Rise up and walk'? But that you may know that the Son of Man has power on earth to forgive sins"; He said to the man who was paralyzed, "I say to you, arise, take up your bed, and go to your house." Immediately he rose up before them, took up what he had been lying on, and departed to his own house, glorifying God. And they were all amazed, and they glorified God and were filled with fear, saying, "We have seen strange things today!"

a. **Which is easier, to say**: For men, both real forgiveness and the power to heal are impossible; but for God, both are easy. It is a logical assumption that if Jesus had the power to heal the man's disease, He also had the authority to forgive his sins.

i. In a way, it was "harder" to heal the man than to forgive his sins, because forgiveness is invisible—no one could verify at that moment the man was forgiven before God. Yet it could be instantly verified whether or not the man could walk. Jesus was willing to put Himself to the test in a way where the results would be immediate.

b. **But that you may know that the Son of Man**: Jesus often referred to Himself as **the Son of Man**. The idea was not of the "perfect man" or the "ideal man" or even the "common man." Instead, it was a reference to Daniel 7:13-14, where the coming King of Glory, coming to judge the world, has the title *Son of Man*.

i. Jesus used this title often, because in His day it was a Messianic title free from political and nationalistic sentiment. Jesus could have more commonly referred to Himself as "King" or "Christ" but those titles, in the ears of His audience, sounded like "the One Who Will Defeat the Romans."

ii. Robertson on **Son of Man**: "Christ's favourite designation of himself, a claim to be the Messiah in terms that could not easily be attacked."

c. **Immediately he arose**: Imagine the tension in this scene. The scribes were tense, because Jesus challenged them, and said He would demonstrate He was the Son of God. The paralyzed man was tense, because he wondered if Jesus really would heal him. The crowd was tense, because they sensed the tension of everyone else. The owner of the house was tense, because he wonders how much it would cost to repair his roof. And the four friends were tense, because they were tired by now. The only one *not* tense was Jesus, because He had perfect peace when He said, "**arise, take up your bed, and go to your house**." At those words, **immediately he arose**. Jesus' *power* to heal and *authority* to forgive sins was **immediately** vindicated.

i. Imagine if Jesus *had failed*. His ministry would be shattered. The crowd would slowly make their way out of the house. The scribes would smile and say, "He can't heal *or* forgive." The four men would struggle to pull up the paralyzed man, who looked more dejected and embarrassed than ever. The homeowner would look at his roof and think it was all for nothing.

ii. But Jesus did not fail and could not fail. There is wonderful healing power in the word of Jesus, in the promises of Jesus, for those who *come to Him in faith*. This man came to Jesus in faith, even if it was on the borrowed faith of his friends.

d. **They were all amazed, and they glorified God and were filled with fear**: Jesus carried the day, and the people were **amazed** to see the power of God in action.

D. The call of Levi (Matthew).

1. (27-28) A tax collector is called to follow Jesus.

After these things He went out and saw a tax collector named Levi, sitting at the tax office. And He said to him, "Follow Me." So he left all, rose up, and followed Him.

a. **After these things**: To this point in Luke's account, Jesus dealt with a paralytic, a leper, and a demoniac. Now He was ready for **a tax collector**.

b. **A tax collector named Levi...sitting at the tax office**: Levi (also known as Matthew in Matthew 9:9) was a tax collector. In that day, tax collectors were despised as traitors and extortioners.

i. The Jewish people rightly considered them *traitors*, because they worked for the Roman government, and had the force of Roman soldiers behind them to make people pay taxes. They were the most visible Jewish traitors with Rome.

ii. The Jewish people rightly considered them *extortioners*, because they could keep whatever they over-collected. A tax collector bid against others for the tax-collecting contract. The Romans awarded the contract to the highest bidder. He then collected taxes, paid the Romans what he promised, and kept the remainder. Therefore, there was great motivation for tax collectors to overcharge and cheat any way they could. It was pure profit for them.

iii. "When a Jew entered the customs service he was regarded as an outcast from society: he was disqualified as a judge or a witness in a court session, was excommunicated from the synagogue, and in the eyes of the community his disgrace extended to his family." (Lane)

iv. "A Roman writer tells us that he once saw a monument to an honest tax collector. An honest specimen of this renegade profession was so rare that he received a monument." (Barclay)

c. **And He said to him, "Follow Me"**: Understanding how almost everyone hated tax collectors, it is remarkable to see how Jesus loved and called Levi. It was a well-placed love; Levi responded to Jesus' invitation by leaving his tax collecting business and following Jesus.

i. In one way, this was more of a sacrifice than some of the other disciples made. Peter, James, and John could more easily go back to their fishing business, but it would be hard for Levi to go back to tax collecting. "Tax collector jobs were greatly sought after as a sure way to get rich quickly." (Wessel)

ii. There is archaeological evidence that fish taken from the Sea of Galilee were taxed. So Jesus took as His disciple the taxman that took money from Peter, James, and John and the other fishermen among the disciples.

d. **He left all**: "This must have meant a considerable sacrifice, for tax collectors were normally wealthy. Matthew must have been the richest of the apostles." (Morris)

2. (29-32) Jesus is accused of associating with sinners.

Then Levi gave Him a great feast in his own house. And there were a great number of tax collectors and others who sat down with them. And their scribes and the Pharisees complained against His disciples, saying, "Why do You eat and drink with tax collectors and sinners?" Jesus answered and said to them, "Those who are well have no need of a physician, but those who are sick. I have not come to call *the* righteous, but sinners, to repentance."

a. **Then Levi gave Him a great feast in his own house**: Levi (Matthew) gave up much to follow Jesus, but he wasn't sad. He was happy enough to give a party for Jesus.

i. One reason Matthew gave the party was to have his friends meet Jesus. A saved man doesn't want to go to heaven alone.

b. **And their scribes and the Pharisees complained against His disciples**: Their complaint was that they had friendly relationships with notorious sinners, eating at the same table, attending the same **feast**.

i. The accusation came indirectly against Jesus, through His **disciples**. People often attack Jesus in the same way today, through His disciples.

ii. "Nothing puzzled the religionists of the Lord's time more than His eating and drinking on terms of familiarity with publicans and sin-

ners. Here He revealed the reason for doing so. He was among men as
the great Physician." (Morgan)

c. **Those who are well have no need of a physician**: Jesus' answer was
both simple and profound. Jesus is the **physician** of the soul, and it makes
sense for Him to be with those who are sick with sin.

i. Of course, His critics were sick with sin also, but they refused to
see themselves that way. They thought *other* people were sick with sin,
not themselves.

ii. There are many possible reasons why a sick person might refuse the
services of a doctor.

- Perhaps you don't know that you are sick
- Perhaps you know you are sick, but you think you will get better
  on your own—you don't know that you *need* to go to the doctor
- Perhaps you know you are sick, and know you need a doctor,
  but *do not know* there is a doctor to help you
- Perhaps you know you are sick, and know you need a doctor,
  and know there is a doctor, but do not know the doctor *can*
  help you
- Perhaps you know you are sick, and know you need a doctor,
  and know there is a doctor, and know the doctor can help you,
  but do not know the doctor *wants* to help you
- Perhaps you know you are sick, and know you need a doctor,
  and know there is a doctor, and know the doctor can help you,
  and know the doctor wants to help you, but you know what the
  doctor will tell you to do and *you just don't want to do it*

iii. Jesus is the perfect doctor to heal us of our sin.

- He is always available
- He always makes a perfect diagnosis
- He provides a complete cure
- Jesus even pays the bill

3. (33-39) Jesus declares that under Him, things are different.

**Then they said to Him, "Why do the disciples of John fast often and
make prayers, and likewise those of the Pharisees, but Yours eat and
drink?" And He said to them, "Can you make the friends of the bridegroom fast while the bridegroom is with them? But the days will come
when the bridegroom will be taken away from them; then they will fast
in those days." Then He spoke a parable to them: "No one puts a piece
from a new garment on an old one; otherwise the new makes a tear,**

and also the piece that was *taken* out of the new does not match the old. And no one puts new wine into old wineskins; or else the new wine will burst the wineskins and be spilled, and the wineskins will be ruined. But new wine must be put into new wineskins, and both are preserved. And no one, having drunk old *wine,* immediately desires new; for he says, 'The old is better.'"

a. **Can you make the friends of the bridegroom fast while the bridegroom is with them?** Jesus answered their question with an allusion to the wedding practices of His day. A wedding feast was the most vivid picture of joy and happiness in that culture. During the weeklong wedding feast, it was understood that joy was more important than conformity to religious rituals. If any ceremonial observance would detract from the joy of a wedding feast, it was not required. Jesus said that His followers should have this kind of happiness.

i. Basically, they thought *Jesus was too happy.* When was the last time you were accused of being too cheerful or too happy?

ii. According to Pate, there was a popular rabbinic text called the *Scroll of Fasting,* and in it was a custom that said that fasting was forbidden on certain specified days devoted to joyous celebration of Israel's blessings from God. Jesus appealed to this kind of thinking.

b. **But the days will come**: There would come a day when fasting was appropriate for Jesus' followers; but at the present time, when Jesus was among them, it was not that day.

i. There is a slight dark note in the words, "**the days will come when the bridegroom will be taken away from them**." It was as if Jesus said, "They are going to take Me away; I threaten their system." It is one of the first slight hints of His coming rejection.

c. **But new wine must be put into new wineskins, and both are preserved**: Jesus' point is clear. You can't fit His new life into the old forms. This explains why Jesus did not begin a reform movement within Judaism, working with the rabbinical schools and such. Jesus says, "I haven't come to patch up your old practices. I come with a whole new set of clothes."

i. Jesus formed a new institution—the church—that brought Jew and Gentile together into a completely new body (Ephesians 2:16).

ii. Jesus reminds us that what is old and stagnant often cannot be renewed or reformed. God will often look for new vessels to contain new work, until those vessels eventually make themselves unusable. This reminds us that the religious establishment of any age is not necessarily pleasing to Jesus. Sometimes it is in direct opposition to His work, or at least resisting His work.

iii. **No one puts a piece from a new garment on an old one**: "Patching up an old garment with a piece of a new garment not only disfigures the new garment, but also causes the old garment to become more ragged than ever, for the new piece has still to shrink and will then pull the old threadbare garment to pieces. Just as fatal will it be to adapt the principles of Jesus to the old systems." (Geldenhuys)

d. **And no one, having drunk old wine, immediately desires new; for he says, "The old is better"**: Just because people are more comfortable with the old, some assume that it is better. Our modern age is more taken with the shiny and new rather than what is old; yet we shouldn't accept or reject anything simply because it is old or new.

i. Jesus came to introduce something new, not to patch up something old. This is what salvation is all about. In doing this, Jesus doesn't destroy the old (the law), but He fulfills it, just as an acorn is fulfilled when it grows into an oak tree. There is a sense in which the acorn is gone, but its purpose is fulfilled in greatness.

Luke 6—The Sermon on the Plain

A. Jesus and Sabbath controversy.

1. (1-2) The source of the controversy: the disciples are accused of "harvesting" on the Sabbath.

Now it happened on the second Sabbath after the first that He went through the grainfields. And His disciples plucked the heads of grain and ate *them,* **rubbing** *them* **in** *their* **hands. And some of the Pharisees said to them, "Why are you doing what is not lawful to do on the Sabbath?"**

a. **Now it happened on the second Sabbath**: If the unnamed *first* Sabbath was the one mentioned in Luke 4:31, Luke gave this time marker to show how *busy* Jesus had been in the two weeks (**second Sabbath**) since the Sabbath mentioned in Luke 4:31.

i. Clarke, along with others, believe this phrase refers to the first Sabbath *after* the Passover. There are some textual complications here as well, and the idea may simply be "on the Sabbath."

b. **His disciples plucked the heads of grain and ate them, rubbing them in their hands**: There was nothing wrong with what they did. Their gleaning was not considered stealing, according to the provision for the poor of the land given in Deuteronomy 23:25.

c. **Why are you doing what is not lawful to do on the Sabbath?** The problem was with *the day* on which they did it. The rabbis made an elaborate list of "do" and "don't" items relevant to the Sabbath and this violated one of the items on this list.

i. When the disciples did what they did, in the eyes of the religious leaders they were guilty of *reaping, threshing, winnowing,* and *preparing* food. There were therefore four violations of the Sabbath in one mouthful.

ii. This approach to the Sabbath continues in modern times among Orthodox Jews. In early 1992, tenants let three apartments in an Orthodox neighborhood in Israel burn to the ground while they asked a rabbi whether a telephone call to the fire department on the Sabbath would violate Jewish law. Observant Jews are forbidden to use the phone on the Sabbath, because doing so would break an electrical current, which is considered a form of work. In the half-hour it took the rabbi to decide "yes," the fire spread to two neighboring apartments.

iii. At this time, many rabbis filled Judaism with elaborate rituals related to the Sabbath and observance of other laws. Ancient rabbis taught that on the Sabbath one was forbidden to tie a knot—except a woman could tie a knot in her girdle. So if a bucket of water had to be raised from a well, one could not tie a rope to the bucket, but a woman could tie her girdle to the bucket and then to the rope.

2. (3-5) Jesus responds to the accusation with two important principles.

But Jesus answering them said, "Have you not even read this, what David did when he was hungry, he and those who were with him: how he went into the house of God, took and ate the showbread, and also gave some to those with him, which is not lawful for any but the priests to eat?" And He said to them, "The Son of Man is also Lord of the Sabbath."

a. **Have you not even read this**: This was a not-so-subtle rebuke to the religious leaders (the *Pharisees* of Luke 6:2) who were confident in their knowledge of the Scriptures. In effect, Jesus questioned whether or not they ever read or understood their Bibles; He implied that they were ignorant of the essential point of the following Old Testament event.

i. "It is possible to read scripture meticulously, to know the Bible inside our from cover to cover, to be able to quote it verbatim and to pass any examination on it—and yet completely miss its real meaning." (Barclay)

b. **What David did when he was hungry**: The reference to David's use of the holy bread (**showbread**, or *Bread of the Presence*) in 1 Samuel 21:1-6 showed the first principle: *human need is more important than religious ritual*.

i. This is exactly what many people, steeped in tradition, simply cannot accept.

- They don't believe that what God really wants is mercy before sacrifice (Hosea 6:6)

- They don't believe that love to others is more important than religious rituals (Isaiah 58:1-9)

- They don't believe that *the sacrifices of God are a broken spirit, a broken and a contrite heart; these, O God, You will not despise* (Psalm 51:17)

ii. "Any application of the Sabbath Law which operates to the detriment of man is out of harmony with God's purpose." (Morgan)

iii. The incident with David was a valid defense, because:

- It was a case of eating
- It probably happened on the Sabbath (1 Samuel 21:6)
- It concerned not only David, but also his followers

c. **The Son of Man is also Lord of the Sabbath**: The second principle was even more dramatic. Jesus said that He is the **Lord of the Sabbath**, and if the Lord of the Sabbath was not offended by His disciples' actions, then these religious leaders should not have been offended.

i. This was a direct claim to Deity. Jesus said that He had the authority to know if His disciples broke the Sabbath law, because He is the **Lord of the Sabbath**.

3. (6-8) The Lord of the Sabbath heals on the Sabbath.

Now it happened on another Sabbath, also, that He entered the synagogue and taught. And a man was there whose right hand was withered. So the scribes and Pharisees watched Him closely, whether He would heal on the Sabbath, that they might find an accusation against Him. But He knew their thoughts, and said to the man who had the withered hand, "Arise and stand here." And he arose and stood.

a. **He entered the synagogue**: Luke showed the rising resistance to Jesus and His followers. Yet, Jesus still attended synagogue services and did not forsake the gathering together of God's people—even when we might think He had reason to.

b. **The scribes and Pharisees watched Him closely, whether He would heal on the Sabbath**: By their very actions, the Pharisees admitted that Jesus had the power of God to work miracles, yet they sought to trap Him. It was as if a man could fly, and the authorities arrested him for not landing at airports.

i. The religious leaders **watched** Jesus **closely**, but with no heart of love for Him. We can watch Jesus, but our hearts can still be far from Him.

ii. "It may even be that they purposely set Jesus up by bringing the man into the synagogue." (Pate) Perhaps they had a greater expectation that Jesus would do such a miracle than the followers of Jesus had.

4. (9-11) The Lord of the Sabbath heals on the Sabbath.

Then Jesus said to them, "I will ask you one thing: Is it lawful on the Sabbath to do good or to do evil, to save life or to destroy?" And when He had looked around at them all, He said to the man, "Stretch out your hand." And he did so, and his hand was restored as whole as the other. But they were filled with rage, and discussed with one another what they might do to Jesus.

a. **Is it lawful on the Sabbath to do good or to do evil, to save life or to destroy?** In His question to the religious leaders, Jesus emphasized the truth about the Sabbath. There is never a *wrong* day to do something truly *good*.

i. In the legalistic approach taken by the religious leaders of Jesus' day (which went *beyond* the commands of the Bible itself), they clearly neglected acts of compassion and love to the needy. "Surely, there is no desecration of divine ordinances so powerful as that which clogs the stream of compassion." (Morgan)

ii. The modern Christian has the challenge of displaying love and compassion to all, *and* faithfully upholding God's clearly-stated moral standard on matters of social controversy.

b. **Stretch out your hand**: When Jesus commanded the man "**stretch out your hand**," He commanded the man to do something impossible in his current condition. But Jesus gave both the command and the ability to fulfill it, and the man put forth the effort and was healed.

c. **They were filled with rage**: The reaction of the religious leaders was shocking, but true. When Jesus did this miracle on the Sabbath, He met the needs of simple people and broke the petty religious traditions of the establishment. Obviously their **rage** and plotting of murder (**discussed with one another what they might do to Jesus**) were far great violations of the Sabbath than the healing of the man's withered hand.

i. Jesus often rebuked the religious leaders of his day for this kind of heart. He said of them, *laying aside the commandment of God, you hold the tradition of men…all too well you reject the commandment of God, that you may keep your tradition…making the word of God of no effect through your tradition* (Mark 7:8-9, 7:13).

iii. Jesus wasn't trying to reform the Sabbath. He tried to show that in their understanding of the Sabbath, they missed the whole point. A legalist wants to debate the *rules*; but the point wasn't *which* rules were the correct rules; the point was *the basic way to approach God.* We emphasize that it is based not on what we do for Him, but it is based on what He has done for us in Jesus Christ.

B. The choosing of the twelve apostles.

1. (12-13) Jesus chooses the twelve.

Now it came to pass in those days that He went out to the mountain to pray, and continued all night in prayer to God. And when it was day, He called His disciples to *Himself*; and from them He chose twelve whom He also named apostles:

a. **Now it came to pass in those days that He went out to the mountain to pray**: Jesus was at a critical point in His ministry:

- He offended the traditions of the religious leadership, and they began to plot His death

- The political leadership also began to plot His destruction (according to Mark 3:6)

- Great crowds followed Him, but they were not interested in spiritual things, and could be quickly turned against Jesus

  i. In response to these pressures and changing situations, Jesus *secluded Himself for this time of special prayer*. We suppose that Jesus prayed constantly, but for this particular need **He went out to the mountain to pray**. "Jesus, therefore, to prevent interruption, to give himself the opportunity of pouring out his whole soul, and to avoid ostentation, sought the mountain." (Spurgeon)

  ii. Then, being alone out on **the mountain**, Jesus **continued all night** in prayer and before choosing twelve among the disciples who would become His **apostles**.

b. **And continued all night in prayer to God**: Jesus was about to choose His disciples. In one sense, there was nothing in Jesus' three years of ministry before the cross more important than this. These were the men who would carry on what He had done, and without them the work of Jesus would never extend to the whole world. No wonder Jesus gave this critical choice an entire night of prayer.

  i. Jesus was God; yet He did not simply use His infinite knowledge to pick the apostles. Instead, He prayed all night. Like every other struggle Jesus faced, He faced this one as a man; a man who needed to seek the will of His Father and rely on the power of the Holy Spirit just as we do.

  ii. **All night**: "One night alone in prayer might make us new men, changed from poverty of soul to spiritual wealth, from trembling to triumphing." (Spurgeon)

c. He called His disciples to Himself: The disciples (and also the apostles for that matter) belonged to Jesus. Disciples never belong to any man; they only belong to Jesus. They are **His disciples.**

> i. "A disciple was a learner, a student, but in the first century a student did not simply study a subject; he followed a teacher. There is an element of personal attachment in 'disciple' that is lacking in 'student.'" (Morris)

d. From them He chose twelve: Jesus chose **twelve** apostles because this was the foundation of the new chosen people, and as Israel had twelve tribes, Jesus would also have twelve apostles.

e. Whom He also named apostles: From among the group of His followers (the larger group of disciples), He picked twelve to be **apostles.**

> i. The idea behind the ancient Greek word for *apostle* is "ambassador." "The Greek word is *apostolos*, which means 'sent one'." (Pate) It describes someone who represents another, and has a message from their sender. In this broader sense, Jesus was also an apostle according to Hebrews 3:1: *consider the Apostle and High Priest of our confession, Christ Jesus.*

2. (14-16) The twelve listed.

Simon, whom He also named Peter, and Andrew his brother; James and John; Philip and Bartholomew; Matthew and Thomas; James the *son* of Alphaeus, and Simon called the Zealot; Judas *the son* of James, and Judas Iscariot who also became a traitor.

a. Peter...Andrew...James and John...: We really do not know much about most of these men. **Peter, James, John,** and **Judas** we know something about. Yet of the other eight, we pretty much only know their names. Their fame is reserved for heaven, where their names are on the twelve foundations of God's heavenly city (Revelation 21:14).

b. There are many interesting connections with this group. There are brothers (**James and John, Peter** and **Andrew**); business associates (**Peter, James,** and **John** were all fishermen); opposing political viewpoints (**Matthew** the Roman-friendly tax collector, and **Simon**, the Roman-hating **Zealot**); and one who would betray Jesus (**Judas Iscariot who also became a traitor**).

> i. "Judas's surname of Iscariot probably indicates that he was a man from Kerioth: he thus seems to have been the only Judean among the twelve." (Geldenhuys)

ii. It seems that the names of the twelve disciples are usually arranged in pairs. "Since Jesus sent His Apostles out two by two, this was a logical way to list them." (Wiersbe)

- Peter and Andrew

- James and John

- Philip and Bartholomew (also called Nathanael in John 1:45)

- Matthew (Levi) and Thomas (his name means "twin")

- James, son of Alphaeus and Simon the Zealot

- Judas, the son of James (also called Thaddaeus in Mark 3:18) and Judas Iscariot

c. **Judas Iscariot who also became a traitor**: Jesus chose Judas, knowing how he would turn out and become **a traitor**. Jesus later told His disciples that He chose them, and He knew one of them was a devil (John 6:70).

i. *Jesus also had many others to choose from.* He chose these twelve from among many others.

ii. *Jesus wasn't looking for an edgy person to make scandal or controversy.* We read of no other scandal surrounding Judas during Jesus' ministry. The other disciples seemed to do worse things during their three years with Jesus.

iii. Jesus chose Judas knowing him and what he would do, but also knowing that God would allow and even use the great evil Judas did for great good, despite the intention of Judas.

iv. A man once asked a theologian, "Why did Jesus choose Judas Iscariot to be his disciple?" The teacher replied, "I don't know, but I have an even harder question: Why did Jesus choose me?"

3. (17-19) Jesus ministers healing and deliverance to a multitude.

And He came down with them and stood on a level place with a crowd of His disciples and a great multitude of people from all Judea and Jerusalem, and from the seacoast of Tyre and Sidon, who came to hear Him and be healed of their diseases, as well as those who were tormented with unclean spirits. And they were healed. And the whole multitude sought to touch Him, for power went out from Him and healed *them* all.

a. **He came down with them**: Jesus came down **with them** (His disciples) to serve and bless this crowd. Jesus not only taught them *about* serving others; He wanted them to help Him. Here, they seemed to work as a team.

i. Jesus could have done it all by Himself. But it was important that He work together as a team with these twelve, both for their sake and for the sake of the work.

b. **And stood on a level place**: The work described in these few verses and the teaching recorded till the end of the chapter took place **on a level place**. For some, this is a helpful distinction marking the following teaching from the teaching *on a mountain* described in Matthew 5-7.

i. However, some have observed that the area around the Sea of Galilee, including the traditional Mount of Beatitudes where the Sermon on the Mount is said to be delivered, is like a mountain when looking from the Sea of Galilee, but like a level place when one stands on or above it.

c. **A great multitude of people from all Judea and Jerusalem, and from the seacoast of Tyre and Sidon**: People came from great distances to be healed and delivered from demonic spirits by Jesus, even from Gentile cities such as **Tyre and Sidon**.

d. **And the whole multitude sought to touch Him**: This was a dramatic scene with hundreds or thousands crowding in upon Jesus to **touch Him**, hoping to receive something miraculous from Him. In *that* scene and context, Jesus *taught them*. We might say that He interrupted the healing service, and had a Bible study.

e. **Power went out from Him and healed them all**: Jesus not only *had* the power of God in Him; it was also true that **power went out from Him** as He **healed them all**.

i. When the woman with an issue of blood touched the hem of Jesus' garment and was healed, it says of Jesus: *immediately knowing in Himself that power had gone out of Him* (Mark 5:30). As Jesus served the needs of others, both in His preaching/teaching work and in miraculous deeds, *something went out of Him*. It cost Him something to be used of God and to serve others.

4. (20a) Jesus prepares to teach His disciples and the multitude.

Then He lifted up His eyes toward His disciples, and said:

a. **He lifted up His eyes toward His disciples**: Jesus here began a section of recorded teaching often called *the Sermon on the Plain*, because it was done *on a level place* (Luke 6:17) and to distinguish it from the *Sermon on the Mount* recorded in Matthew 5-7.

i. The recorded teaching in Matthew 5-7 is similar in many ways to this passage in Luke, but there are also differences. Mainly, the Luke account is much shorter. Many wonder if these are two separate occasions of teaching, or the same occasion.

ii. Scholarly opinion is divided on this issue. But we should remember that Jesus was an itinerant preacher, whose main emphasis was the Kingdom of God (see Luke 4:43).

iii. Itinerant preachers often repeat themselves to different crowds, especially when teaching upon the same topic. This is probably the same *sermon* as Matthew 5-7, but possibly at a different time and a different place.

b. **Toward His disciples**: In Luke's gospel, it is no accident that this great message of Jesus comes immediately *after* Jesus chose the twelve (Luke 6:12-16) and *before* He sent those disciples to preach throughout the towns of Galilee (Luke 9:1-6). It was part of their teaching to hear and understand this message, because it helped explain clearly what it meant to be a follower of Jesus the Messiah.

i. "It may be surmised that the sermon served a twofold function: to encourage faithfulness among Jesus' disciples and to challenge non-disciples to follow Him." (Pate)

ii. It is clear that the Sermon on the Plain (and the Sermon on the Mount) had a significant impact on the early church. The early Christians made constant reference to it and their lives shined with the glory of radical disciples.

c. **And said**: *What* Jesus said in the Sermon on the Plain (and in the Sermon on the Mount) has long been recognized as the sum of Jesus'—or anyone's—ethical teaching. In the Sermon on the Plain, Jesus told His followers and would-be-followers how to live.

i. It has been said if you took all the good advice for how to live ever uttered by any philosopher or psychiatrist or counselor, took out the foolishness and boiled it all down to the real essentials, you would be left with a poor imitation of this great message by Jesus.

ii. The Sermon on the Mount is sometimes thought of as Jesus' "Declaration of the Kingdom." The American Revolutionaries had their *Declaration of Independence*. Karl Marx had his *Communist Manifesto*. With this message, Jesus explained the agenda and plan of His Kingdom.

iii. It presents a radically different agenda from what the nation of Israel expected from the Messiah. It does not present the political or material blessings of the Messiah's reign. Instead, it expresses the spiritual implications of the rule of Jesus in our lives. This great message tells us how will we live when Jesus is our Lord.

iv. It is important to understand that the Sermon on the Mount does not deal with salvation as such, but it lays out for the disciple and the potential disciple how regarding Jesus as King translates into ethics and daily living.

v. "This may be an instance of the Jewish method of preaching. The Jews called preaching *Charaz*, which means *stringing beads*. The Rabbis held that the preacher must never linger more than a few moments on any topic but, in order to maintain interest, must move quickly from one topic to another." (Barclay)

C. The surprising plan of God's kingdom.

1. (20b) Blessings to the poor.

"Blessed *are you* poor, for yours is the kingdom of God."

a. **Blessed**: Jesus promised blessing to His disciples, promising that the **poor in spirit** are **blessed**. The idea behind the ancient Greek word for **blessed** is "*happy*," but in the truest, godly sense of the word, not in our modern sense of merely being comfortable or entertained at the moment.

i. This same word for *blessed*—which in some sense means "happy"— is applied to God in 1 Timothy 1:11: *according to the glorious gospel of the blessed God*. "*Makarios* then describes that joy which has its secret within itself, that joy which is serene and untouchable, and self-contained, that joy which is completely independent of all the chances and changes of life." (Barclay)

ii. In Matthew 25:34, Jesus said that on the Day of Judgment He would say to His people, *Come, you blessed of My Father, inherit the kingdom prepared for you from the foundation of the world*. On that day, He will judge between the blessed and the cursed—He both knows and explains what are the requirements for the blessed one. We can also say that no one was ever blessed more than Jesus; He knows what goes into a blessed life.

iii. "Note, also, with delight, that *the blessing is in every case in the present tense*, a happiness to be now enjoyed and delighted in. It is not 'Blessed *shall* be,' but 'Blessed *are*.'" (Spurgeon)

b. **Blessed are you poor**: In the ancient Greek vocabulary there are several words that can be used to describe poverty. Jesus used the word that indicates a severe poverty; the idea is someone who must *beg* for whatever they have or will get.

i. Immediately, this statement strikes us with its strangeness. **Blessed** by being **poor**? That makes no sense at all. Yet the power and wisdom in this truth lies in the fact that the **poor** man *must look to others for* *what he needs*. He has no illusions about his ability to provide for himself.

ii. Though there is much practical wisdom in the teaching of Jesus, He was a spiritual man and taught on spiritual themes. The poverty Jesus had most in mind is *poverty of spirit*, and that was exactly how He phrased it in the sermon recorded in Matthew 5.

iii. The **poor** in spirit recognize that they have no spiritual assets. They know they are spiritually bankrupt. Poverty of spirit cannot be artificially induced by self-hatred. It comes as the Holy Spirit works in our heart and we respond to Him.

iv. *Everyone* can start here; it isn't first blessed are the pure or the holy or the spiritual or the wonderful. Everyone can be **poor** in spirit. "Not what I have, but what I have not, is the first point of contact, between my soul and God." (Spurgeon)

c. **For yours is the kingdom of God**: Yet those who are **poor** in spirit, so poor they must beg, are rewarded: they receive **the kingdom of God**. Therefore poverty of spirit is an absolute prerequisite for receiving the kingdom, because as long as we keep illusions about our own spiritual resources, we will never receive from God what we absolutely need.

i. This blessing to the poor is placed first for a reason, because it puts the following commands into perspective. They cannot be fulfilled in our own strength, but only by a beggar's reliance on God's power.

2. (21a) Blessings to the hungry.

"Blessed *are you* who hunger now, for you shall be filled."

a. **Blessed are you who hunger now**: The hungry person *seeks*. They look for food, and hope to satisfy their appetite. Their hunger drives them and gives them a single focus. Jesus described the blessedness of those who focus on Him and His righteousness like a hungry man focuses on food.

- This passion is *real*, just like hunger is real
- This passion is *natural*, like hunger is natural in a healthy person
- This passion is *intense*, just like hunger is
- This passion can be *painful*, just like real hunger can cause pain
- This passion is a *driving force*, just like hunger can drive a man
- This passion is a *sign of health*, just like hunger shows health

i. It is good to remember that Jesus said this in a day and to a culture that really knew what it was to be hungry and thirsty. Modern man— at least in the western world—is often distant from the basic needs of hunger and thirst. We find it difficult to hunger and thirst after Jesus and His righteousness.

ii. Matthew recorded Jesus giving a similar message, and recorded Jesus with these words: *Blessed are those who hunger and thirst for righteousness* (Matthew 5:6). Since Jesus spoke of more than physical hunger, even His sermon in Luke implies this kind of longing. Hunger for righteousness may express itself in several ways:

- A man longs to have a righteous nature
- A man wants to be sanctified, to be made more holy
- A man longs to continue in God's righteousness
- A man longs to see righteousness promoted in the world

b. **For you shall be filled**: Jesus promised to *fill* this hungry one; to fill them with as much as they could eat. This is a strange filling that both satisfies us and keeps us longing for more.

3. (21b) Blessings to those who weep.

"Blessed *are you* who weep now, for you shall laugh."

a. **Blessed are you who weep now**: The weeping is for the low and needy condition of both the individual and society, but with the awareness that they are low and needy because of *sin*. **You who weep** actually **weep** over sin and its effects.

i. This mourning is the *godly sorrow* that *produces repentance to salvation* that Paul described in 2 Corinthians 7:10. Those who **weep** can know something special of God; the fellowship of His sufferings (Philippians 3:10), a closeness to the Man of Sorrows who was acquainted with grief (Isaiah 53:3).

ii. "I do not believe in that faith which has not a tear in its eye when it looks to Jesus. Dry-eyed faith seems to me to be bastard faith, not born of the Spirit of God." (Spurgeon)

b. **For you shall laugh**: The one who does grieve over their spiritual condition can genuinely **laugh** when God makes things right. *Weeping may endure for a night, but joy comes in the morning.* (Psalm 30:5).

c. **Now**: In each of these three paradoxical statements—describing a person's spiritual condition in terms of poverty, hunger, and weeping—Jesus used the hopeful word **now**.

- You are poor **now**; you will one day receive the kingdom
- You are hungry **now**; you will one day be filled
- You weep **now**; you will one day laugh

i. Some are taken with the idea that Jesus was more a community organizer or revolutionary than a true preacher and teacher, and that Jesus meant for these statements of blessing to subvert the social order and give power to the oppressed.

ii. Jesus was in fact extremely concerned to give power to the oppressed, but set His focus against the greatest oppression of all—the tyranny of sin and separation from God in and over a man. While not ignoring the need of those poor, hungry, and weeping in the physical sense, Jesus focused on the spiritual revolution that would change them, and eventually society.

iii. In fact, what Jesus said here is *against* the spirit of the social revolutionary because He gave people *hope* in their present poverty, hunger, and weeping. The revolutionary wants to take away all present hope, and demands that people take immediate action (often violent, sometimes murderous) to supposedly change things. The bitter fruit of this thinking can be numbered in the hundreds of millions dead by the murderers of Communist ideology. Jesus shows a better way, a way of true hope.

4. (22-23) Blessings to the hated.

"Blessed are you when men hate you, and when they exclude you, and revile *you,* and cast out your name as evil, for the Son of Man's sake. Rejoice in that day and leap for joy! For indeed your reward *is* great in heaven, for in like manner their fathers did to the prophets."

a. **Blessed are you when men hate you**: We think of the people who see themselves as spiritually poor and hungry; who with weeping seek God. It seems impossible that these people would be hated, but they are.

b. **Exclude you…revile you…cast out your name as evil**: This speaks of the extent of hatred that would be brought against the followers of Jesus; and even worse would come upon them. Jesus said that for this, His followers (**for the Son of Man's sake**) would be **blessed**.

i. It did not take long for these words of Jesus to become true of His followers. Early Christians heard many enemies **exclude** them, **revile** them, and regard their **name as evil**. Christians were accused of:

- Cannibalism, because of gross and deliberate misrepresentation of the practice of the Lord's Supper

- Immorality, because of gross deliberate misrepresentation of weekly "Love Feast" and their private meetings

- Revolutionary fanaticism, because they believed that Jesus would return and there would be an apocalyptic end to history

- Splitting families, because when one marriage partner or parent became a Christian there was often change and division in the family
- Treason, because they would not honor the Roman gods and participate in emperor worship

c. **Rejoice in that day and leap for joy**: It is a paradox to be so happy when so hated, yet these persecuted ones can because their **reward is great in heaven**, and because the persecuted are in good company: the **prophets** before them were also persecuted.

> i. Trapp named some men who did in fact **rejoice** and **leap for joy** when persecuted. George Roper came to the stake leaping for joy, and hugged the stake he was burned at like a friend. Dr. Taylor leapt and danced a little as he came to his execution, saying when asked how he was, "Well, God be praised, good Master Sheriff, never better; for now I am almost home…I am even at my Father's house." Lawrence Saunders, who with a smiling face embraced the stake of his execution and kissed it saying, "Welcome the cross of Christ, welcome everlasting life."

5. (24-26) Strange woes.

**"But woe to you who are rich, for you have received your consolation.
Woe to you who are full, for you shall hunger.
Woe to you who laugh now, for you shall mourn and weep.
Woe to you when all men speak well of you, for so did their fathers to the false prophets."**

a. **Woe**: This was an expression of regret and compassion, not a threat. The woes Jesus spoke seem just as paradoxical as His blessings. We normally see no **woe** in being **rich** or **full** or in laughing or in being spoken **well of**.

b. **But woe to you who are rich…Woe to you who are full**: Riches, no sense of need, and continual excitement and good times are a genuine obstacle to the kingdom. We normally won't come to Jesus the way we should until we know we are poor, hungry, and needing comfort.

> i. In each of these paradoxical sayings, Jesus contrasted the current expectations of the kingdom with the spiritual reality of His Kingdom. Jesus told us that God does unexpected things. Jesus mocked the world's values. He exalted what the world despises and rejected what the world admires. Jesus turned upside-down (rather, right-side-up) their perception of the Kingdom of God.

D. God's agenda is a plan of love.

1. (27-28) Love your enemies.

"But I say to you who hear: Love your enemies, do good to those who hate you, bless those who curse you, and pray for those who spitefully use you."

a. **Love your enemies**: This is a shockingly simple command to understand, but a difficult one to obey. Jesus told us exactly how to actually love our enemies: **do good**, **bless**, and **pray for those who spitefully use you**.

i. Jesus recognized that *we will have enemies*. This plan of God's Kingdom takes into account real-world problems. Though we *will* have enemies, yet we are to respond to them in love, trusting that God will protect our cause and destroy our enemies in the best way possible, by transforming them into our friends.

b. **Do good...bless...pray for those who spitefully use you**: The love Jesus told us to have for our enemies was not a warm, fuzzy feeling deep in the heart. If we wait for that, we may never love them. The love for our enemies is a love that *does* something for them, quite apart from how we might feel about them.

i. **Bless those who curse you** means that we must speak well of those who speak ill of us.

ii. "We cannot love our enemies as we love our nearest and dearest. To do so would be unnatural, impossible, and even wrong. But we can see to it that, no matter what a man does to us, even if he insults, ill-treats and injures us, we will seek nothing but his highest good." (Barclay)

2. (29-30) Be willing to suffer wrong.

To him who strikes you on the *one* cheek, offer the other also. And from him who takes away your cloak, do not withhold *your* tunic either. Give to everyone who asks of you. And from him who takes away your goods do not ask *them* back."

a. **To him who strikes you on the one cheek, offer the other also**: Continuing His astonishing teaching, Jesus said we must accept certain evils committed against us.

i. When a person insults us (**strikes you on the one cheek**), we want to give them back what they gave to us, plus more. Jesus said we should patiently bear such insults and offences, and not resist an evil person who insults us this way. Instead, we trust God to defend us. France points out that ancient Jewish writings state that striking someone with the back of the hand—a severe insult—was punishable by a very heavy fine, according to Mishnah *BK* 8:6.

ii. It is wrong to think Jesus meant evil should never be resisted. Jesus demonstrated with His life that evil should and must be resisted, such as when He turned the tables over in the temple.

iii. "Jesus is here saying that the true Christian has learned to resent no insult and to seek retaliation for no slight" (Barclay). When we think how Jesus Himself was insulted and spoken against (as a glutton, a drunkard, and an illegitimate child, a blasphemer, a madman, and so forth), we see how He lived this principle Himself.

iv. It is wrong to think that Jesus meant a physical attack cannot be resisted or defended against. When Jesus spoke of a slap **on the one cheek**, it was culturally understood as a deep insult, not a physical attack. Jesus did not mean that if someone hits us across the right side of our head with a weapon, we should allow them to then hit the left side. 2 Corinthians 11:20 probably had in mind this kind of insult slap.

v. It is also wrong to think Jesus meant that there is no place for punishment or retribution in society. Jesus here spoke to personal relationships, and not to the proper functions of government in restraining evil (Romans 13:1-4). I must turn my cheek when I am personally insulted, but the government has a responsibility to restrain the evil man from physical assault.

b. **And from him who takes away your cloak, do not withhold your tunic either. Give to everyone who asks of you**: With this, Jesus told us how to deal with people who mistreat, coerce, and manipulate us. We should take command of the situation by sacrificial giving and love.

i. Under the Law of Moses, the outer cloak was something that could not be taken from someone (Exodus 22:26; Deuteronomy 24:13).

ii. "Jesus' disciples, if sued for their tunics (an inner garment like our suit but worn next to the skin), far from seeking satisfaction, will gladly part with what they may legally keep." (Carson)

iii. "The old said, Insist on your own right, and loving your neighbor, hate your enemy, and so secure your safety. The new says, Suffer wrong, and lavish your love on all." (Morgan)

c. **From him who takes away your goods do not ask them back**: We can only practice this kind of sacrificial love when we know that God will take care of us. We know that if we give away our tunic, God has plenty more of them to give us.

i. The only limit to this kind of sacrifice is the limit that love itself will impose. It isn't loving to give into someone's manipulation without our transforming it into a free act of love. It isn't always loving to give or to not resist.

ii. We might say that Paul repeated this idea of Jesus: *Do not be overcome by evil, but overcome evil with good.* (Romans 12:21)

3. (31) The Golden Rule.

"And just as you want men to do to you, you also do to them likewise."

a. **Just as you want men to do to you, you also do to them likewise**: The negative way of stating this command was known long before Jesus. It had long been said, "You should *not* do to your neighbor what you would *not* want him to do to you." But it was a significant advance for Jesus to put it in the positive to say that we should *do unto others* what we want them to *do unto us*.

i. "The Golden Rule was not invented by Jesus; it is found in many forms in highly diverse settings. About A.D. 20, Rabbi Hillel, challenged by a Gentile to summarize the law in the short time the Gentile could stand on one leg, reportedly responded, 'What is hateful to you, do not do to anyone else. This is the whole law; all the rest is commentary. Go and learn it.' (b. *Shabbath* 31a). Apparently only Jesus phrased the rule positively." (Carson)

ii. In so doing, Jesus made the command much broader. It is the difference between *not* breaking traffic laws and in *doing* something positive like helping a stranded motorist. Under the negative form of the rule, the goats of Matthew 25:31-46 could be found "not guilty." Yet under the positive form of the Golden Rule—Jesus' form—they are indeed found guilty.

b. **You also do to them likewise**: This especially applies to Christian fellowship. If we would experience love and have people reach out to us, we must love and reach out to others.

i. "Oh, that all men acted on it, and there would be no slavery, no war, no swearing, no striking, no lying, no robbing; but all would be justice and love! What a kingdom is this which has such a law!" (Spurgeon)

ii. This makes the law easier to understand, but it doesn't make it any easier to obey. No one has ever consistently done unto others as they would like others to do unto themselves.

4. (32-35) Loving after the pattern of God's love.

"But if you love those who love you, what credit is that to you? For even sinners love those who love them. And if you do good to those who do good to you, what credit is that to you? For even sinners do the

same. And if you lend *to those* from whom you hope to receive back, what credit is that to you? For even sinners lend to sinners to receive as much back. But love your enemies, do good, and lend, hoping for nothing in return; and your reward will be great, and you will be sons of the Most High. For He is kind to the unthankful and evil."

a. **If you love those who love you, what credit is that to you?** We should regard it as no matter of virtue, and no imitation of Jesus, if we merely return the love that is given to us.

i. Remember, Jesus here taught the character of the citizens of His kingdom. We should expect that character to be different from the character seen in the world. There are many good reasons *why* more should be expected from Christians than others:

- They claim to have something that others do not have; they claim to be renewed, repentant, and redeemed by Jesus Christ

- They do in fact have something that others do not have; they are in fact renewed, repentant, and redeemed by Jesus Christ

- They have a power that others do not have; they can do all things through Christ who strengthens them

- They have the Spirit of God dwelling within them

- They have a better future than others do

b. **You will be sons of the Most High**: In doing this, we imitate God, who shows love towards *His* enemies, and **is kind to the unthankful and evil**.

i. "What does God say to us when he acts thus? I believe that he says this: 'This is the day of free grace; this is the time of mercy.' The hour for judgment is not yet, when he will separate between the good and the bad; when he will mount the judgment seat and award different portions to the righteous and to the wicked." (Spurgeon)

ii. This is an *example*—that we also are to love our enemies and bless them if we can. In doing so, we show ourselves to be **sons of the Most High**. "We are made sons by regeneration, through faith in the Son; but we are called to make our calling and election sure—to approve and vindicate our right to that sacred name. We can only do this by showing in word and act that the divine life and principles animate us." (Meyer)

5. (36-38) The principles to follow.

"Therefore be merciful, just as your Father also is merciful. Judge not, and you shall not be judged. Condemn not, and you shall not be condemned. Forgive, and you will be forgiven. Give, and it will be given to

you: good measure, pressed down, shaken together, and running over will be put into your bosom. For with the same measure that you use, it will be measured back to you."

a. **Therefore be merciful, just as your Father also is merciful**: In the Kingdom of Jesus, we have a pattern for the way we should give mercy to others. We should be **merciful** to others the way God has been **merciful** to us. That's a lot of mercy, and would only require *more* mercy from us, not less.

b. **Judge not, and you shall not be judged**: With this command, Jesus warned against passing judgment upon others, because when we do so, we will be **judged** in a similar manner.

i. Among those who seem to know nothing of the Bible, this is the verse that seems to be most popular. Yet most the people who quote this verse don't understand what Jesus said. They seem to think (or hope) that Jesus commanded a universal acceptance of any lifestyle or teaching.

ii. Just a little later in this same sermon (Luke 6:43-45), Jesus commanded us to know ourselves and others by the fruit of their life, and *some* sort of assessment is necessary for that. The Christian is called to show unconditional love, but the Christian is not called to unconditional *approval*. We really *can* love people who do things that should not be approved of.

iii. So while this does not prohibit examining the lives of others, it certainly prohibits doing it in the spirit it is often done. An example of unjust judgment was the disciples' condemnation of the woman who came to anoint the feet of Jesus with oil (Matthew 26:6-13). They thought she wasted something; Jesus said she had done a good work that would always be remembered. They had a rash, harsh, unjust judgment.

- We break this command when we think the worst of others
- We break this command when we only speak to others of their faults
- We break this command when we judge an entire life only by its worst moments
- We break this command when we judge the hidden motives of others
- We break this command when we judge others without considering ourselves in their same circumstances
- We break this command when we judge others without being

mindful that we ourselves will be judged

c. **Condemn not…forgive**: Jesus expanded the idea beyond simply judging others. He also told us to **condemn not** and to freely **forgive**.

d. **Give, and it will be given to you: good measure, pressed down, shaken together, and running over**: Jesus encouraged the freedom to give without fearing that we will become the loser in our giving. He wanted to set us free from the fear of *giving too much*.

> i. This is true and has been tested when it comes to generosity with material resources. Simply said, you can't out-give God. He will return more to you, in one way or another, more than you give to Him. Yet the most pointed application of this in context is not so much the giving of material resources, but with giving love, blessing, and forgiveness. We are never the loser when we give *those* things after the pattern of God's generosity.

> ii. **Put into your bosom**: "The Jew wore a long, loose robe down to the feet and round the waist a girdle. The robe could be pulled up so that the bosom of the robe above the girdle formed a kind of outsized pocket in which things could be carried. So the modern equivalent of the phrase would be, 'People will fill your pocket.'" (Barclay)

e. **With the measure you use, it will be measured back to you**: This is the principle upon which Jesus built the command, "**Judge not, that you be not judged**." God will measure unto us according to the same measure we use for others. This is a powerful motivation for us to be generous with love, forgiveness, and goodness to others. If we want more of those things from God, we should give more of them to others.

> i. We might say that Jesus did not *prohibit* the judgment of others. He only requires that our judgment be completely fair, and that we only judge others by a standard we would also like to be judged.

> ii. When our judgment in regard to others is wrong, it is often not because we judge according to a standard, but because we are hypocritical in the application of that standard—we ignore the standard in our own life. It is common to judge others by one standard and ourselves by another standard—being far more generous to ourselves than others.

> iii. According to the teaching of some rabbis in Jesus' time, God had two measures that He used to judge people. One was a **measure** of *justice* and the other was a **measure** of *mercy*. Whichever **measure** you want God to use with you, you should use that same **measure** with others.

iv. We should only judge another's behavior when we are mindful of the fact that *we ourselves will be judged*, and we should consider how we would want to be judged.

E. The distinction between two ways.

1. (39-42) Illustrations centered around the idea of seeing.

And He spoke a parable to them: "Can the blind lead the blind? Will they not both fall into the ditch? A disciple is not above his teacher, but everyone who is perfectly trained will be like his teacher. And why do you look at the speck in your brother's eye, but do not perceive the plank in your own eye? Or how can you say to your brother, 'Brother, let me remove the speck that *is* in your eye,' when you yourself do not see the plank that *is* in your own eye? Hypocrite! First remove the plank from your own eye, and then you will see clearly to remove the speck that is in your brother's eye."

a. **Can the blind lead the blind?** This is obvious. The **blind** can't **lead the blind**. Therefore we should never look to other blind men to lead us; nor should we try to lead others in our blindness. Instead, we should make Jesus our leader, our teacher, who sees and knows all things.

i. Jesus reminded us that *some supposed leaders are blind*—beware of them. Later Jesus said of some of the religious leaders of His day, *They are blind leaders of the blind. And if the blind leads the blind, both will fall into a ditch* (Matthew 15:14)

ii. "Though the Pharisees and teachers of the law had scrolls and interpreted them in the synagogues, this does not mean that they really understood them…The Pharisees did not follow Jesus; so they did not understand and follow the Scriptures." (Carson)

iii. In these words of Jesus, we see the *guilt* of those who are **blind** leaders **of the blind**. We also see the *responsibility* of followers to make sure their leaders are not blind.

b. **A disciple is not above his teacher**: A **disciple** was much like a student, with the added element of following and patterning after the master or **teacher**. In this way, the disciple would never be greater than the teacher, yet **everyone who is perfectly trained will be like his teacher**. We will become like those we follow, *so we must decide to choose good teachers to follow.*

i. In this perfectly clear and logical truth, Jesus gave a wonderful promise. As we are taught by Him and grow in Him, we will become more like Him. More and more, we are *conformed to the image of His Son* (Romans 8:29) and ultimately, *when He is revealed, we shall be like Him, for we shall see Him as He is* (1 John 3:2).

ii. "The Lord Jesus became like unto us in our low estate, that we should become like Him in his glory…There must ever be the limitation of the creature as compared with Him by whom all things were made. But in our measure there shall be the same perfect beauty—his beauty upon us." (Meyer)

c. **And why do you look at the speck in your brother's eye, but do not perceive the plank in your own eye?** The figures of a speck and a plank are real figures used humorously. Jesus shows that we are generally far more tolerant to our own sin than we are to the sin of others.

i. Though there might be a literal **speck** in one's eye, there obviously would not be a literal **plank** or board in an eye. Jesus used these exaggerated, humorous pictures to make His message easier to understand and more memorable.

ii. It is a humorous picture: A man with a board in his eye trying to help a friend remove a speck from the friend's eye. You can't think of the picture without smiling and being amused by it.

iii. An example of looking for a speck in the eye of another while ignoring the plank in one's own is when the religious leaders brought the woman taken in adultery to Jesus. She had certainly sinned; but their sin was much worse, and Jesus exposed it as such with the statement, *He who is without sin among you, let him throw a stone at her first* (John 8:7).

d. **You yourself do not see the plank that is in your own eye**: Jesus indicates that the one with the **plank in** his **own eye** would not immediately be aware of it. He is blind to his obvious fault. It is the attempt to correct the fault of someone else when we ourselves have the same (or greater fault) that earns the accusation, "**Hypocrite!**"

i. "Jesus is gentle, but he calls that man a '*hypocrite*' who fusses about small things in others, and pays no attention to great matters at home in his own person." (Spurgeon)

ii. Our hypocrisy in these matters is almost always more evident to others than to ourselves. We may find a way to ignore the plank in our own eye, but others notice it immediately. A good example of this kind of hypocrisy was David's reaction to Nathan's story about a man who unjustly stole and killed another man's lamb. David quickly condemned the man, but was blind to his own sin, which was much greater (2 Samuel 12).

e. **First remove the plank from your own eye, and then you will see clearly to remove the speck that is in your brother's eye**: Jesus didn't say that it was wrong for us to help our brother with the speck in his eye. It is a good thing to help your brother with his speck, *but not before* dealing with the plank in your own eye.

2. (43-45) We can only follow Jesus this way if we have been radically changed by Him. If Jesus has touched us, it will show in our lives.

"For a good tree does not bear bad fruit, nor does a bad tree bear good fruit. For every tree is known by its own fruit. For *men* do not gather figs from thorns, nor do they gather grapes from a bramble bush. A good man out of the good treasure of his heart brings forth good; and an evil man out of the evil treasure of his heart brings forth evil. For out of the abundance of the heart his mouth speaks."

a. **A good tree does not bear bad fruit...every tree is known by its own fruit**: This **fruit** is the inevitable result of who we *are*. Eventually—though it may take a time for the harvest to come—the good or bad fruit is evident, revealing what sort of tree we are. *Not every tree is the same.*

i. "Not to have *good fruit* is to have *evil*: there can be no innocent sterility in the invisible tree of the heart. He that brings forth *no* fruit, and he that brings forth *bad* fruit, are both only fit for the *fire*." (Clarke)

ii. "It is not merely the wicked, the bearer of poison berries, that will be cut down; but the neutral, the man who bears no fruit of positive virtue must also be cast into the fire." (Spurgeon)

iii. Just before this, Jesus warned us to judge ourselves first, to look for the speck in our own eye before turning our attention to the beam in our neighbor's eye. Therefore, before asking it of anyone else, we should first ask: "Do I bear fruit unto God's glory?"

b. **A good man out of the good treasure of his heart brings forth good...out of the abundance of the heart his mouth speaks**: Our words reveal our heart. If there is **good treasure** in the heart, it will show; if **evil**, that also will show in time. Our *words say more about us than we think*, and reveal that some are **good** men and some are **evil** men.

3. (46-49) Concluding exhortation: *doing* what Jesus commanded is our foundation.

"But why do you call Me 'Lord, Lord,' and do not do the things which I say? Whoever comes to Me, and hears My sayings and does them, I will show you whom he is like: He is like a man building a house, who dug deep and laid the foundation on the rock. And when the flood arose, the stream beat vehemently against that house, and could not shake it, for it was founded on the rock. But he who heard and did nothing is like a man who built a house on the earth without a foundation, against which the stream beat vehemently; and immediately it fell. And the ruin of that house was great."

a. **But why do you call Me "Lord, Lord," and do not do the things which I say?** Jesus made a distinction between those who merely make a *verbal* profession of faith, and those who actually both **hears** His **sayings and does them**.

    i. We must use the language of "**Lord, Lord**"; we cannot be rescued if we do not. Though hypocrites may say it, we should not be ashamed to say it. Yet it alone is not enough.

    ii. This warning of Jesus applies to people who speak or say things to Jesus or about Jesus, but don't really mean it. It isn't that they believe Jesus is a devil; they simply say the words very superficially. Their mind is elsewhere, but they believe there is value in the bare words and fulfilling some kind of religious duty with no heart, no soul, not spirit—only bare words and passing thoughts.

    iii. This warning of Jesus applies to people who say "**Lord, Lord**"; and yet their spiritual life has nothing to do with their daily life. They go to church, perhaps fulfill some daily religious duties, yet sin against God and man just as any other might. "There are that speak like angels, live like devils; that have Jacob's smooth tongue, but Esau's rough hands." (Trapp)

    iv. Jesus put this in the form of a question: **Why**? "If we are disobedient, why continue the profession of obedience?... Each soul guilty of the wrong referred to must face this 'Why?' alone. All that need be said is, that to do so will inevitably be to discover the unworthiness of the reason." (Morgan)

b. **Whoever comes to Me**: Here in three brief points, Jesus described the one who does follow Him in wisdom and truth, and went on to illustrate the wisdom of that one.

    i. "Carefully note the three-fold condition. 1. 'Every one that cometh to Me,' surrender. 2. 'And heareth My words,' discipleship. 3. 'And doeth them,' obedience." (Morgan)

c. **He is like a man building a house**: In Jesus' final illustration of the two builders, each house looked the same from the outside. The real foundation of life is usually hidden and is only proven in the storm.

    i. "The wise and the foolish man were both engaged in precisely the same avocations, and to a considerable extent achieved the same design; both of them undertook to build houses, both of them persevered in building, both of them finished their houses. The likeness between them is very considerable." (Spurgeon)

d. **When the flood arose**: Jesus warned that the foundations of our lives will be shaken at some time or another, both now (in seasons of difficulty) and in the ultimate judgment before God. It is better that we test the foundation of our life *now*, rather than later at our judgment before God when it is too late to change our destiny.

i. Time and the storms of life will prove the strength of one's foundation, even when it is hidden. We may be surprised when we see who has truly built upon the good foundation. "At last, when Judas betrayed Christ in the night, Nicodemus faithfully professed him in the day." (Trapp)

e. **He who heard and did nothing**: Merely *hearing* God's word isn't enough to provide a secure foundation. It is necessary that we are also *doers* of His word. If we are not, we commit the sin that will surely find us out, the sin of doing nothing (Numbers 32:23)—and **great** will be *our* **ruin**.

i. Yet no one can read this without seeing that they have not, do not, and will not ever completely **do them**. Even if we **do them** in a general sense (in which we should), the revelation of the Kingdom of God in the Sermon on the Mount drives us back again and again as needy sinners upon our Savior.

Luke 7—The Sick Healed, the Dead Raised, the Sinner Forgiven

A. A centurion's servant is healed.

1. (1-5) The centurion's request.

Now when He concluded all His sayings in the hearing of the people, He entered Capernaum. And a certain centurion's servant, who was dear to him, was sick and ready to die. So when he heard about Jesus, he sent elders of the Jews to Him, pleading with Him to come and heal his servant. And when they came to Jesus, they begged Him earnestly, saying that the one for whom He should do this was deserving, "for he loves our nation, and has built us a synagogue."

a. **He entered Capernaum**: After the Sermon on the Plain (Luke 6:20-49), Jesus came to his city of residence (Matthew 4:13, *He came and dwelt in Capernaum*). This means that the location of the Sermon on the Plain was likely not far from **Capernaum**.

b. **A certain centurion's servant, who was dear to him, was sick and ready to die**: This centurion appears as a devout, kind, humble man—yet, all the same he was a *centurion*—not only a Gentile, but a Roman soldier, and an instrument of Israel's oppression.

i. The centurion had an unusual attitude towards his slave. Under Roman law, a master had the right to kill his slave, and it was expected that he would do so if the slave became ill or injured to the point where he could not work.

c. **He sent elders of the Jews to Him, pleading with Him to come and heal his servant**: Apparently, the centurion did not think himself worthy of a personal meeting with Jesus, and perhaps thought Jesus would not *want* to meet with a Gentile like himself, so he sent Jewish leaders as his representatives to Jesus.

d. **The one for whom He should do this was deserving**: The Jewish leaders did this for the centurion because he was a worthy man. In contrast, we can come to Jesus directly without a representative even when we are unworthy; He *justifies the ungodly* (Romans 4:5).

> i. "These considerations suggest that the captain was a God-fearer, a Gentile who embraced Israel's God but who did not undergo circumcision." (Pate)

2. (6-8) The centurion tells Jesus that He need not come, because he knows that Jesus need not be present to do His work.

Then Jesus went with them. And when He was already not far from the house, the centurion sent friends to Him, saying to Him, "Lord, do not trouble Yourself, for I am not worthy that You should enter under my roof. Therefore I did not even think myself worthy to come to You. But say the word, and my servant will be healed. For I also am a man placed under authority, having soldiers under me. And I say to one, 'Go,' and he goes; and to another, 'Come,' and he comes; and to my servant, 'Do this,' and he does *it*."

a. **Then Jesus went with them**: Jesus did not hesitate to go to the centurion's house, and we half wish the centurion would have allowed Him. Would Jesus have entered a Gentile's house? It was completely against Jewish custom, but not against God's law.

> i. Pate cited a rabbinic writing known as *m. Obolot* 18:7: "The dwelling-places of Gentiles are unclean."

b. **Lord, do not trouble Yourself, for I am not worthy that You should enter under my roof**: The centurion knew that it might be a problem for this prominent rabbi to come into his home, so he met Jesus on the way to say that it was not necessary for Him to come all the way to the home.

> i. The centurion was a remarkable man. The elders said he was worthy; he said he was not worthy. They praised him for building a house of worship; he felt unworthy that Jesus would come to his house. They said he was deserving; he felt himself undeserving. Strong faith and great humility are entirely compatible.

> ii. "Two features of character blend in him which do not often meet in such graceful harmony. He won the high opinion of others and yet he held a low estimation of himself." (Spurgeon)

> iii. "Your faith will not murder your humility, your humility will not stab at your faith; but the two will go hand in hand to heaven like a brave brother and a fair sister, the one bold as a lion the other meek as a dove, the one rejoicing in Jesus the other blushing at self." (Spurgeon)

c. **But say the word, and my servant will be healed**: The centurion fully understood that Jesus' healing power was not a magic trick that required the magician's presence. Instead he knew Jesus had true *authority* and could command things to be done and see them completed outside His immediate presence.

> i. The centurion showed great faith in Jesus' *word*. He understood that Jesus could heal with His *word* just as easily as with a *touch*.

d. **For I also am a man placed under authority, having soldiers under me**: The centurion also knew about the military chain of command, and how the orders of one in authority were unquestioningly obeyed. He saw that Jesus had *at least* that much authority.

> i. "He believes that, just as he, a man with authority, is obeyed by his subordinates, just so surely will the authoritative utterance of Christ be fulfilled even though He is not present where the sick person is." (Geldenhuys)

3. (9-10) Jesus heals the servant and marvels at the centurion's faith.

When Jesus heard these things, He marveled at him, and turned around and said to the crowd that followed Him, "I say to you, I have not found such great faith, not even in Israel!" And those who were sent, returning to the house, found the servant well who had been sick.

a. **He marveled at him**: The centurion's understanding of Jesus' spiritual authority made Jesus marvel. His simple confidence in the ability of Jesus' mere word to heal showed a faith that was free of superstitious reliance on merely external things. This was **great faith**, worthy of praise.

> i. Jesus only **marveled** on a few occasions. He did so here at the faith of the centurion, and also at the unbelief of His own people (Mark 6:6). Jesus can be amazed at either our *faith* or our *unbelief*.

b. **I have not found such great faith, not even in Israel!** Jesus considered the faith of this Gentile centurion—a living symbol of Jewish oppression—and thought it greater than any faith He had seen among the people of **Israel**.

> i. As a political entity, there was no **Israel**; there was only a covenant people descended from Abraham, Isaac, and Jacob. Yet Jesus still called them **Israel**.

c. **Found the servant well who had been sick**: Jesus both answered the centurion's unselfish request and proved that He really did have the authority the centurion trusted Him to have.

B. Jesus raises a boy from the dead.

1. (11-13) Jesus comes upon a funeral procession.

Now it happened, the day after, *that* He went into a city called Nain; and many of His disciples went with Him, and a large crowd. And when He came near the gate of the city, behold, a dead man was being carried out, the only son of his mother; and she was a widow. And a large crowd from the city was with her. When the Lord saw her, He had compassion on her and said to her, "Do not weep."

a. **Many of His disciples went with Him, and a large crowd**: The fame and popularity of Jesus continued to grow. Many—more than only the twelve—were disciples of Jesus (in some sense).

i. **Nain** is "a town today located in the Jezreel plain, six miles southwest of Nazareth." (Pate)

b. **A dead man was being carried out**: Any funeral is a tragedy, but this was a special loss. The deceased was **the only son of his mother** and the mother herself was a **widow**. The loss of her only son meant a miserable future for the widow.

i. **A large crowd from the city was with her**: "The procession probably consisted partly of hired mourners and musicians with flutes and cymbals." (Geldenhuys)

c. **Do not weep**: We are specifically told of the **compassion** of Jesus on this occasion. He instantly understood the situation and had sympathy upon the widow, giving her hope despite the tragedy of the situation.

i. **When the Lord saw her**: "Luke uses the absolute form of Lord, 'the Lord' (*kyrios*), which emphasizes Jesus' deity." (Pate)

ii. In a sermon on this passage (*Young Man, Is This For You?*), Spurgeon mentioned a few ways in which this event illustrates spiritual truth:

- The spiritually dead cause great grief to their gracious friends
- For this grief there is only one Helper, but He can truly help

2. (14-17) Jesus raises the young man from the dead.

Then He came and touched the open coffin, and those who carried *him* stood still. And He said, "Young man, I say to you, arise." So he who was dead sat up and began to speak. And He presented him to his mother. Then fear came upon all, and they glorified God, saying, "A great prophet has risen up among us"; and, "God has visited His people." And this report about Him went throughout all Judea and all the surrounding region.

a. **He came and touched the open coffin**: Luke gives the vivid image of an **open coffin**. Jesus looked at the boy and spoke to a dead person as if he were alive.

b. **Young man, I say to you, arise**: Jesus spoke to the dead as if they were alive. Romans 4:17 says that this is what God alone does; to speak to the dead as if they were alive. *God, who gives life to the dead and calls those things which do not exist as though they did* (Romans 4:17).

c. **So he who was dead sat up and began to speak**: On more than one occasion, Jesus broke up funeral processions by raising the dead. This was also true for Jarius' daughter (Luke 8:41-56) and Lazarus (John 11:1-45). Jesus didn't like death, and He regarded it as an enemy that had to be defeated.

> i. This young man was not resurrected, but resuscitated; he rose from the dead only to die again. God promises that we will be *resurrected*, and rise from the dead never to die again.

> ii. "At this point, a famous anecdote comes to mind from the life of D.L. Moody. Mr. Moody was asked to conduct a funeral service, so he decided to study the gospels to find a funeral sermon delivered by Jesus. However, Moody searched in vain, because every funeral Jesus attended He broke up by raising the dead!" (Pate)

C. Jesus and John the Baptist.

1. (18-19) John sends a question to Jesus.

Then the disciples of John reported to him concerning all these things. And John, calling two of his disciples to *him,* sent *them* to Jesus, saying, "Are You the Coming One, or do we look for another?"

a. **Then the disciples of John**: John the Baptist had his own disciples. Some of Jesus' disciples started as John's disciples (such as Andrew and John 1:35-40). It was noted when the disciples of Jesus began to outnumber those of John (John 4:1).

b. **Are You the Coming One, or do we look for another?** John 1:29-36 and other passages indicate that before this, John clearly recognized Jesus as the Messiah. His doubt might be explained because perhaps he himself had misunderstood the ministry of the Messiah. Perhaps John thought that if Jesus were really the Messiah, He would perform works connected with a political deliverance of Israel—or at least the deliverance of John, who was in prison.

> i. It is possible that John made a mistaken distinction between **the Coming One** and the Christ, the Messiah. There is some indication that some Jews of that time distinguished between a prophet to come promised by Moses (Deuteronomy 18:15) and the Messiah. The dominant note here is one of *confusion*; John's long trial in prison had confused him.

ii. "John was already in prison, and things began to appear incomprehensible to him. He had expected that Christ would speedily destroy the powers of darkness and judge the unrighteous. But instead of doing this, He leaves him, His forerunner, helpless in prison." (Geldenhuys)

2. (20-23) Jesus' answer to John the Baptist's disciples: tell John that prophecy regarding the Messiah is being fulfilled.

When the men had come to Him, they said, "John the Baptist has sent us to You, saying, 'Are You the Coming One, or do we look for another?'" And that very hour He cured many of infirmities, afflictions, and evil spirits; and to many blind He gave sight. Jesus answered and said to them, "Go and tell John the things you have seen and heard: that *the* blind see, *the* lame walk, *the* lepers are cleansed, *the* deaf hear, *the* dead are raised, *the* poor have the gospel preached to them. And blessed is *he* who is not offended because of Me."

a. **And that very hour He cured many of infirmities, afflictions, and evil spirits; and to many blind He gave sight**: This was the *real* power of the Messiah in action; yet performed in personal, even humble ways.

i. Most of these miracles fulfill some promise found in Isaiah.

- The blind see (Isaiah 61:1, 35:5)
- The lame walk (Isaiah 35:5)
- The deaf hear (Isaiah 35:5)
- The dead live (Isaiah 26:19)
- The poor hear the good news (Isaiah 61:11)

b. **Go and tell John the things you have seen and heard**: Jesus wanted to assure both John and his disciples that He was the Messiah. But He also reminded them that His power would be displayed mostly in humble acts of service, meeting individual needs, and not in spectacular displays of political deliverance.

i. We might phrase John's question like this: "Jesus, why don't You do more?" Morgan answered this: "To all such restless impatience, He utters the same warning…For the most part, the way of the Lord's service is the way of plodding perseverance in the doing of apparently small things. The history of the Church shows that this is one of the lessons most difficult to learn."

c. **Blessed is he who is not offended because of Me**: Jesus knew that the focus of His ministry was offensive to the expectation of the Jewish people, who longed for political deliverance from Roman domination.

But there was a blessing for those who were **not offended** because of the Messiah who came against the expectation of the people.

i. "The verb rendered *takes offence* is picturesque. It derives from the trapping of birds, and refers to the action that depresses the bait-stick and so triggers off the trap. It is a colourful way of referring to the cause of trouble." (Morris)

ii. "It is remarkable that the same word is predicated of John the Baptist and Israel concerning their response to Jesus—scandalized (*skandalisthe*; cf. Luke 7:23 with Romans 11:9 [cf. 9:33]). Israel was scandalized by Jesus, and we must take Jesus seriously in Luke 7:23 that it was possible for His audience to be offended at His nontraditional role, including John the Baptist." (Pate)

iii. "A friend has turned these words into another beatitude—The blessedness of the unoffended." (Meyer)

3. (24-28) Jesus teaches about John the Baptist.

When the messengers of John had departed, He began to speak to the multitudes concerning John: "What did you go out into the wilderness to see? A reed shaken by the wind? But what did you go out to see? A man clothed in soft garments? Indeed those who are gorgeously appareled and live in luxury are in kings' courts. But what did you go out to see? A prophet? Yes, I say to you, and more than a prophet. This is *he* of whom it is written: 'Behold, I send My messenger before Your face, Who will prepare Your way before You.' For I say to you, among those born of women there is not a greater prophet than John the Baptist; but he who is least in the kingdom of God is greater than he."

a. **What did you go out into the wilderness to see?** Jesus explained that John was a great man of God, one who did not live for his own comfort or the approval of others. John was a chosen prophet of God, not a man-pleaser.

b. **Behold, I send My messenger before Your face, Who will prepare Your way before You**: Jesus quoted the Malachi (Malachi 3:1) passage about the coming of John, because the prophets themselves were not prophesied, but John was, and this was one way that he was greater than all previous prophets.

- John was *steady*, not shaken easily like a reed
- John was *sober*, in that he lived a disciplined life, not in love with the luxuries and comforts of this world
- John was a *servant*, a prophet of God
- John was *sent*, as the special messenger of the Lord

- John was *special,* in that he could be considered the greatest under the Old Covenant

- John was *second* to even the least in the kingdom under the New Covenant

c. **For I say to you, among those born of women there is not a greater prophet than John the Baptist**: Yet, John was greater than all the prophets, mainly because he had the privilege of saying of the Messiah "He is here" instead of "He is coming."

d. **But he who is least in the kingdom of God is greater than he**: Though John was great, he was not born again under the New Covenant. This is because he lived and died before the completion of Jesus' work at the cross and empty tomb. Therefore, he did not enjoy the benefits of the New Covenant (1 Corinthians 11:25, 2 Corinthians 3:6, Hebrews 8:6-13).

i. "As we may say, as a rule, that the darkest day is lighter than the brightest night; so John, though first of his own order, is behind the last of the new or Gospel order. The least in the Gospel stands on higher ground than the greatest under the law." (Spurgeon)

ii. "This is no small comfort to the ministers of the gospel, against the contempts cast upon them by the world. They are somebodies in heaven, whatever men make of them." (Trapp)

4. (29-35) The reaction to the teaching of Jesus.

And when all the people heard *Him,* even the tax collectors justified God, having been baptized with the baptism of John. But the Pharisees and lawyers rejected the will of God for themselves, not having been baptized by him.

a. **And when all the people heard Him, even the tax collectors justified God, having been baptized with the baptism of John**: Those who had repented in preparation for the Messiah by receiving John's baptism found it easy to receive what Jesus said.

b. **But the Pharisees and lawyers rejected the will of God for themselves**: The religious leaders had little use for the demonstration of repentance in John's baptism. Their hearts were hard towards John, so it was no surprise that they were also hard towards Jesus.

5. (31-35) Jesus admonishes those who refuse to be pleased by either His ministry or John's.

And the Lord said, "To what then shall I liken the men of this generation, and what are they like? They are like children sitting in the marketplace and calling to one another, saying: 'We played the flute for you, and you did not dance; we mourned to you, and you did not weep.'

For John the Baptist came neither eating bread nor drinking wine, and you say, 'He has a demon.' The Son of Man has come eating and drinking, and you say, 'Look, a glutton and a winebibber, a friend of tax collectors and sinners!' But wisdom is justified by all her children."

a. **To what then shall I liken the men of this generation**: Jesus considered the nature of His current **generation**, and how they were choosy and uncertain in receiving God's message and His messengers.

b. **We played the flute for you, and you did not dance; we mourned to you, and you did not weep**: The idea was that those who have a heart to criticize will find something to criticize. Many people wouldn't be pleased with *either* John or Jesus.

i. "It is probable that our Lord alludes here to some *play* or *game* among the Jewish children, no account of which is now on record." (Clarke)

ii. The point is clear enough. "If the message is unwelcome, nothing that the messenger can say or do will be right." (Maclaren)

c. **He has a demon**: The religious leaders looked at the ascetic lifestyle of John and concluded that he was mad and demon possessed.

d. **A glutton and a winebibber, a friend of tax collectors and sinners**: The title **friend of tax collectors and sinners** was especially in contrast to the more severe ministry of John the Baptist. Not many people would say that John the Baptist was the **friend of tax collectors and sinners**.

i. "A malicious nick-name at first, it is now a name of honour: the sinner's lover." (Bruce)

ii. Jesus didn't say this of Himself; He told us what the religious leaders said about Him, and for the most part, it was wrong. It wasn't true that John the Baptist had **a demon**. It wasn't true that Jesus was **a glutton and a winebibber**. It wasn't true—at least in the sense that they meant it—that Jesus was **a friend of tax collectors and sinners**. But there was another sense, a glorious sense, in which that last accusation was true.

- He *wasn't* **a friend of tax collectors and sinners** in the sense that He was like them, or in the sense that He helped them commit their sin. This is what the religious leaders meant by their accusation, and it was a false accusation

- He *was* **a friend of tax collectors and sinners** in the sense that He loved them; He did not despise them or push them away. He genuinely wanted to help them and rescue them from the guilt, the shame, the power, and the penalty of their sin

e. **But wisdom is justified by her children**: However, the wise man is proved to be wise by his wise actions (**her children**). Jesus had especially in mind the wisdom to accept *both* Jesus and John for what they were and what they were called to be.

> i. "Probably the *children of wisdom* is a mere Hebraism here for the *products* or *fruits of wisdom*." (Clarke)

> ii. People criticized John, but look at what he *did*—he led thousands of people into repentance, preparing the way for the Messiah. People criticized Jesus, but look at what He *did*—taught and worked and loved and died like no one ever has.

D. Jesus forgives a sinful woman.

1. (36-38) A sinful woman anoints Jesus' feet.

Then one of the Pharisees asked Him to eat with him. And He went to the Pharisee's house, and sat down to eat. And behold, a woman in the city who was a sinner, when she knew that *Jesus* sat at the table in the Pharisee's house, brought an alabaster flask of fragrant oil, and stood at His feet behind *Him* weeping; and she began to wash His feet with her tears, and wiped *them* with the hair of her head; and she kissed His feet and anointed *them* with the fragrant oil.

> a. **Then one of the Pharisees asked Him to eat with him**: This seems to show that relations between Jesus and the religious leaders were not yet totally antagonistic. There were some **Pharisees** who at least wanted a closer, honest look at Jesus.

> b. **And behold, a woman in the city who was a sinner**: Some suppose this was Mary Magdalene, but we have no evidence of this. In John 12:3, Mary of Bethany also anointed Jesus' feet with oil, but this was a separate incident.

>> i. "It ought not to astonish you that there were two persons whose intense affection thus displayed itself; the astonishment should rather be that there were not two hundred who did so, for the anointing of the feet of an honored friend...Loved as Jesus deserved to be, the marvel is that he was not oftener visited with these generous tokens of human love." (Spurgeon)

> c. **Who was a sinner**: This tells us more than that she was a sinner in the sense that all people are. She was a particularly notorious **sinner**—most suppose that she was a prostitute. Her presence in the Pharisee's home showed courage and determination.

>> i. Trapp called her, "A strumpet, a she-sinner...a hussy."

ii. It was bold for a woman with a sinful reputation to come into the house of a Pharisee, but she was willing to do anything to express her love for Jesus.

d. **Brought an alabaster flask of fragrant oil**: Both the container and the contents show that this was an expensive gift she brought to honor Jesus. Since Jesus later announced that her sins were forgiven (Luke 7:48-50), it may be that Jesus forgave her earlier, and would soon publically declare her forgiven.

i. Morris on the **alabaster flask**: "It had no handles and was furnished with a long neck which was broken off when the contents were needed...We may fairly deduce that this perfume was costly. Jewish ladies commonly wore a perfume flask suspended from a cord round the neck, and it was so much a part of them that they were allowed to wear it on the sabbath."

ii. "Her service to Jesus was personal. She did it all herself, and all to him. Do you notice how many times the pronoun occurs in our text? [*she*, three times and *her* twice in Luke 7:37-38]... She served Christ himself. It was neither service to Peter, nor James, nor John, nor yet to the poor or sick of the city, but to the Master himself; and, depend upon it, when our love is in active exercise, our piety will be immediately towards Christ — we shall sing to him, pray to him, teach for him, preach for him, live to him." (Spurgeon)

e. **And stood at His feet behind Him weeping; and she began to wash His feet with her tears**: We can imagine that as the woman anointed Jesus' feet with oil, she was overcome with emotion. With tears flowing from her eyes, she washed His feet with her tears, wiped them clean with her hair, and she kissed His feet repeatedly.

i. "People reclined on low couches at festive meals, leaning on the left arm with the head towards the table and the body stretched away from it. The sandals were removed before reclining." (Morris)

ii. Normally, this oil was used on someone's head. "In all probability, the woman intended to anoint Jesus' head with her perfume. But, because Jesus, like the other participants, reclined with His head toward the table, the closest the woman could get to Jesus was His feet." (Pate)

iii. "O for more of this love! If I might only pray one prayer this morning, I think it should be that the flaming torch of the love of Jesus should be brought into every one of our hearts, and that all our passions should be set ablaze with love to him." (Spurgeon)

iv. "To have her hair flowing would be deemed immodest…[she] kissed fervently, again and again." (Bruce) We can only imagine how awkward this scene was, and how everyone silently watched the woman and her emotional display. No one said anything until Jesus broke the silence in the following verses.

2. (39-40) An objection to what the woman did.

Now when the Pharisee who had invited Him saw *this,* **he spoke to himself, saying, "This man, if He were a prophet, would know who and what manner of woman** *this is* **who is touching Him, for she is a sinner." And Jesus answered and said to him, "Simon, I have something to say to you." So he said, "Teacher, say it."**

a. **When the Pharisee who had invited Him saw this**: The host now became a questioner, possibly a hostile one.

b. **This man, if He were a prophet, would know who and what manner of woman this is who is touching Him, for she is a sinner**: Simon the Pharisee doubted that Jesus was a prophet because he thought that Jesus was unable to see this woman's heart. Jesus will show that He can read the heart of man by exposing Simon's heart.

c. **Simon, I have something to say to you**: Jesus broke the silence—probably a terribly awkward silence—by saying that *He* had something to say, and to say personally to Simon.

i. "When all the philosophers are dumb, and cannot give one word of help or comfort; when learning has no message to inspire or to console the heart; when sympathy hesitates to break the silence…the Lord has something to say." (Morrison)

3. (41-43) Jesus answers with a parable.

"There was a certain creditor who had two debtors. One owed five hundred denarii, and the other fifty. And when they had nothing with which to repay, he freely forgave them both. Tell Me, therefore, which of them will love him more?" Simon answered and said, "I suppose the *one* **whom he forgave more." And He said to him, "You have rightly judged."**

a. **There was a certain creditor who had two debtors**: Jesus used a simple parable to illustrate the point that the more we are forgiven, the more we should love.

i. "Christ tells the supercilious and self-conceited Pharisee by this parable, that himself was a sinner also as well as the woman, and as a debtor to God's judgment, had as much need of his grace in Christ for remission of sin and removal of wrath." (Trapp)

ii. "All men are debtors to God; yet some are greater debtors than others." (Spurgeon)

b. **Which of them will love him more**: Simon seemed to hesitate in his response (**I suppose…**). He probably understood that Jesus set a trap with this story.

4. (44-47) Jesus applies the parable to both Simon and the sinful woman.

Then He turned to the woman and said to Simon, "Do you see this woman? I entered your house; you gave Me no water for My feet, but she has washed My feet with her tears and wiped *them* with the hair of her head. You gave Me no kiss, but this woman has not ceased to kiss My feet since the time I came in. You did not anoint My head with oil, but this woman has anointed My feet with fragrant oil. Therefore I say to you, her sins, *which are* many, are forgiven, for she loved much. But to whom little is forgiven, *the same* loves little."

a. **Do you see this woman**: Simon the Pharisee thought that *Jesus* was the one who could not see her. His thought was, "Jesus, don't you see this shameful woman associating so closely to You?" Jesus turned the thought around on Simon, saying, "**Do you see this woman?** Simon, do you see her love, her repentance, her devotion? That's what I see."

i. Simon the Pharisee did not see the woman as she *was* (a humble sinner seeking forgiveness, pouring out love for Jesus) because he looked at her as she had *been* (a notorious sinner).

ii. "It is not easy for us to blot out a past, and to free ourselves from all prejudice resulting from our knowledge of that past. Yet that is exactly what the Lord does. And He does so, not unrighteously, but righteously. He knows the power of His own grace, and that it completely cancels the past, and gives its own beauty to the soul." (Morgan)

b. **I entered your house; you gave Me no water for My feet**: Simon the Pharisee denied Jesus the common courtesies from a host to a guest—washing the feet, a kiss for a greeting, and anointing the head with oil. Yet, he criticized the woman for giving these courtesies to Jesus.

i. Jesus noticed *neglect* and *appreciated* devotion. He did not reject deeply emotional devotion.

c. **I say to you, her sins, which are many, are forgiven, for she loved much**: She wasn't forgiven *because* of her great love; her great love was evidence that she had been forgiven, probably privately on a prior occasion and now publically.

5. (48-50) Jesus assures the woman of her forgiveness from God.

Then He said to her, "Your sins are forgiven." And those who sat at the table with Him began to say to themselves, "Who is this who even forgives sins?" Then He said to the woman, "Your faith has saved you. Go in peace."

a. **Your sins are forgiven**: Jesus had already said that her sins were *forgiven* (Luke 7:47), yet He also said this directly to the woman. We need the healing power inherent in the words **your sins are forgiven**.

i. It can be so hard for us to truly believe that we are forgiven; often, we must be *persuaded* of it.

b. **Who is this who even forgives sins?** Jesus had the authority to forgive the woman, and He was right to do so. She displayed *humility, repentance, trust,* and *love for* Jesus.

i. "Even the guests began to realize that Jesus was more than a prophet; He was divinely able to forgive an unclean woman." (Pate)

c. **Your faith has saved you**: The key to her forgiveness was **faith**—it was her faith that saved her, because it was her faith that believed the words from Jesus **your sins are forgiven**. Faith enabled her to take the grace God gave to her.

i. Forgiveness is ready from God; there is no hesitation or shortage on His part. Our part is to come with humility and loving submission to Jesus, and to receive the forgiveness He offers by faith.

d. **Go in peace**: The woman came to Jesus in complete humility, with the attitude that she was not worthy to even be in His presence. That was a good way for her to come to Jesus, but He did not want her to *stay* there. He raised her up, acknowledged her love, forgave her sin, and sent her in peace.

i. The word "**go**" was probably not welcome. She liked being at the feet of Jesus. Yet Jesus sweetened the "**go**" by adding, "**in peace.**" She could **go in peace** because she heard from Jesus that her faith had **saved** her.

ii. Of the works done in this chapter, this was the greatest. Healed sickness (as in the centurion's servant), or restored life (as in the widow's son) are not permanent works of healing, because those bodies would one day die again. Sins that are forgiven are forgiven *forever*.

Luke 8—*The Importance and Power of Jesus' Word*

A. The parable of the soils.

1. (1-3) Women who ministered to Jesus.

Now it came to pass, afterward, that He went through every city and village, preaching and bringing the glad tidings of the kingdom of God. And the twelve *were* with Him, and certain women who had been healed of evil spirits and infirmities; Mary called Magdalene, out of whom had come seven demons, and Joanna the wife of Chuza, Herod's steward, and Susanna, and many others who provided for Him from their substance.

a. **He went through every city and village**: This is often thought to be the *second* tour of Jesus through the region of Galilee (the first being described in Luke 4:42-44). Jesus probably went to the same cities and villages more than once in His itinerant preaching work.

i. On this second tour, **the twelve were with Him**. When He started the first tour of Galilee, the twelve disciples had not yet been formally chosen.

b. **Preaching and bringing glad tidings**: This broadly described the theme of Jesus' preaching. He brought good news to the people, news that God's Messiah and King was present with them, announcing His kingdom.

c. **And certain women**: Luke specifically mentioned **certain women** who followed Jesus, because this was unusual. Jesus had a different attitude towards women than the religious leaders and teachers of that day.

i. "The rabbis refused to teach women and generally assigned them a very inferior place." (Morris) It's interesting to note that in the four Gospels, all of Jesus' enemies were men.

ii. One of these women was **Mary called Magdalene**. This Mary had been demon possessed until Jesus freed her. Many also assume that she was given over to immorality, but this isn't said by the biblical text. "The Christian imagination has made free with Mary Magdalene, mostly seeing her as a beautiful woman whom Jesus had saved from an immoral life. There is nothing whatever in the sources to indicate this." (Morris)

iii. **Joanna the wife of Chuza, Herod's steward**: "Herod's *epitropos*. A king had man prerequisites and much private property; his *epitropos* was the official that looked after the king's financial interests…There could be no more trusted and important official." (Barclay)

iv. "It is an amazing thing to find Mary Magdalene, with the dark past, and Joanna, the lady of the court, in the one company." (Barclay)

v. Mary and Joanna were among the first witnesses of Jesus' resurrection (Luke 24:10).

d. **And many others who provided for Him from their substance**: We see the true humble nature of Jesus, who willingly made Himself dependent upon others. He didn't have to; He could have just created all the money or food He needed. Jesus was humble enough and godly enough to receive from others.

i. Many of us are too proud to receive help from others. Sometimes the ability to humbly receive is a better measure of Jesus in our life than the ability to give. Giving sometimes puts us in a higher place, but receiving may put us in a lower place.

ii. "The term used of the women's support of Jesus' mission is *diakonia*, probably because it anticipated the office of deacon, especially the deaconess, created in the early church." (Pate)

2. (4-8) The parable of the soils.

And when a great multitude had gathered, and they had come to Him from every city, He spoke by a parable: "A sower went out to sow his seed. And as he sowed, some fell by the wayside; and it was trampled down, and the birds of the air devoured it. Some fell on rock; and as soon as it sprang up, it withered away because it lacked moisture. And some fell among thorns, and the thorns sprang up with it and choked it. But others fell on good ground, sprang up, and yielded a crop a hundredfold." When He had said these things He cried, "He who has ears to hear, let him hear!"

a. **When a great multitude had gathered**: Jesus taught large groups at one sitting. He certainly didn't despise teaching smaller groups or even individuals, but on many occasions taught large groups. He drew crowds **from every city**.

i. Matthew 13:1-3 and Mark 4:1-2 tell us that this crowd was so large that Jesus taught this from a boat. The crowd pressed in on the shore, and Jesus could use the boat as an effective pulpit.

b. **He spoke by a parable**: The idea behind the word *parable* is "to throw alongside of." It is a story thrown alongside the truth intended to teach. Parables have been called "earthly stories with a heavenly meaning."

i. "The Greek *parabole* is wider than our 'parable'; in the LXX it translates *masal*, which includes proverbs, riddles and wise sayings as well as parables. Matthew uses it for instance for Jesus' cryptic saying about defilement (Matthew 15:10-11, 15), and in Matthew 24:32 ('lesson') it indicates a comparison." (France)

ii. "It had a double advantage upon their hearers: first, upon their memory, we being very apt to remember stories. Second, upon their minds, to put them upon studying the meaning of what they heard so delivered." (Poole)

iii. Parables generally teach *one main point* or principle. We can get into trouble by expecting that they be intricate systems of theology, with the smallest detail revealing hidden truths. "A parable is not an allegory; an allegory is a story in which every possible detail has an inner meaning; but an allegory has to be *read and studied*; a parable is *heard*. We must be very careful not to make allegories of the parables." (Barclay)

c. **A sower went out to sow his seed**: Jesus spoke according to the agricultural customs of His day. In those days seed was scattered first and then it was plowed into the ground. For the most part, you didn't know the quality of the precise piece of ground until after the sowing.

d. **As he sowed, some seed fell by the wayside...some fell on rock... some fell among thorns...others fell on good ground**: In this parable the seed fell on four different types of soil. Though this is commonly called *the parable of the sower*, it could be better called *the parable of the soils*. The difference is never the *seed*, but on the kind of *soil* it lands.

i. **The wayside** was the path where people walked and nothing could grow because the ground was too hard.

ii. **On rock** was where the soil was thin, lying upon a stony shelf. On this ground the seed sprang up quickly because of the warmth of the soil, but the seed was unable to take root because of the rocky shelf.

iii. **Among thorns** described soil that is fertile, perhaps too fertile, because **thorns** grow there as well as grain. The **thorns** choked out the good grain and did not make a productive crop.

iv. **Good ground** described soil that was both fertile and weed-free. A good, productive crop grew in the **good ground**. The crop may be **a hundredfold** increase to what was sown.

e. **He who has ears to hear, let him hear**: This was not a call for all to listen. Rather, it was a call for those who were spiritually sensitive to take special note. This was especially true in light of the next few verses, in which Jesus explained the purpose of parables.

3. (9-10) The purpose of parables.

Then His disciples asked Him, saying, "What does this parable mean?" And He said, "To you it has been given to know the mysteries of the kingdom of God, but to the rest *it is given* in parables, that 'Seeing they may not see, and hearing they may not understand.'"

a. **What does this parable mean?** The meaning of this parable wasn't immediately obvious to the disciples. Apparently Jesus' use of parables wasn't as easy as simple illustrations of spiritual truth.

b. **To you it has been given to know the mysteries of the kingdom of God, but to the rest it is given in parables**: As Jesus used them, parables were more like puzzles or riddles than illustrations. Only those who had the right "key" could understand them. The disciples, who wanted the things of God, were **given to know the mysteries of the kingdom**—they could be spoken to plainly. But often, others were taught **in parables**.

i. **The mysteries of the kingdom of God**: In the Bible, a *mystery* isn't something you can't figure out. It is something that you would never know unless God revealed it to you. In the biblical sense, one might know what the mystery is; yet it is still a mystery, because they would not have known unless God revealed it.

c. **Seeing they may not see, and hearing they may not understand**: By quoting this passage from Isaiah 6:9, Jesus explained that His parables were not illustrations making difficult things clear to all who heard. They were a way of presenting God's message so those who were spiritually sensitive could understand, but the hardened would merely hear a story without heaping up additional condemnation for rejecting God's Word.

i. A parable isn't exactly an *illustration*. A good teacher can illustrate by stating a truth, and then *illustrating* the truth through a story or an analogy. But when Jesus used parables, He didn't start by stating a truth. Instead, the parable was like a doorway. Jesus' listeners stood at the doorway and heard Him. If they were not interested, they stayed on the outside. But if they were interested, they could walk through the doorway, and think more about the truth behind the parable and what it meant to their life.

ii. "So, that their guilt may not accumulate, the Lord no longer addresses them directly in explicit teachings during the period immediately preceding His crucifixion, but in parables." (Geldenhuys)

iii. If you don't understand the *key* to the parable, you don't understand it at all. We can imagine what different people in Jesus' audience might have thought when He taught this parable with no explanation.

- The farmer thought, "He's telling me that I have to be more careful in the way I cast my seed. I guess I have wasted an awful lot."

- The politician thought, "He's telling me that I need to begin a farm education program to help farmers more efficiently cast their seed. This will be a big boost in my reelection campaign."

- The newspaper reporter thought, "He's telling me that there is a big story here about the bird problem and how it affects the farming community. That's a great idea for a series in the newspaper."

- The salesman thought, "He's encouraging me in my fertilizer sales. Why, I could help that farmer more than he knows if he only used my product."

iv. But none of them could understand the *spiritual* meaning until Jesus explained the key to them: *The seed is the word of God* (Luke 8:11). If you miss the key, you miss the whole parable. If you think the seed represents money, you miss the parable. If you think the seed represents love, you miss the parable. If you think the seed represents hard work, you miss the parable. You can only understand it by understanding the key: *The seed is the word of God.*

d. **Seeing they may not see, and hearing they may not understand**: In light of this, how blessed are those who *do* understand the parables of Jesus. Not only do they gain the benefit of the spiritual truth illustrated; they also display some measure of responsiveness to the Holy Spirit.

4. (11-15) Jesus explains the parable.

"Now the parable is this: The seed is the word of God. Those by the wayside are the ones who hear; then the devil comes and takes away the word out of their hearts, lest they should believe and be saved. But the ones on the rock *are those* who, when they hear, receive the word with joy; and these have no root, who believe for a while and in time of temptation fall away. Now the ones *that* fell among thorns are those who, when they have heard, go out and are choked with cares, riches, and pleasures of life, and bring no fruit to maturity. But the ones *that*

fell on the good ground are those who, having heard the word with a noble and good heart, keep *it* and bear fruit with patience."

a. **The seed is the word of God**: Jesus likened the word of God (we could say both spoken and written) to seed. A seed has enormous power in itself for the generation of life and usefulness, if it is received (planted) in the right conditions.

> i. The idea that **the seed is the word of God** is repeated in the Bible. Paul used the idea in 1 Corinthians 3:6, and Peter wrote that we have *been born again, not of corruptible seed but incorruptible, through the word of God which lives and abides forever* (1 Peter 1:23).

> ii. "The preacher of the gospel is like the sower. He does not make his seed; it is given him by his divine Master. No man could create the smallest grain that ever grew upon the earth, much less the celestial seed of eternal life." (Spurgeon)

b. **Those by the wayside are the ones who hear; then the devil comes and takes away the word out of their hearts, lest they should believe and be saved**: As the birds devoured the seed on the wayside (Luke 8:5), so some receive the word with hardened hearts and **the wicked one** quickly **takes away** the sown word. The word has no effect because it never penetrates and is quickly taken away.

> i. The **wayside** soil represented those who never heard the word with understanding. The word of God must be understood before it can truly bear fruit. One of Satan's chief works is to keep men in darkness regarding their understanding of the gospel (2 Corinthians 4:3-4).

> ii. This tells us that Satan is at work during the teaching and preaching of God's word. Satan seems to believe in the power of God's word more than many preachers do; he knows that when it is taught or preached, he needs to be busy against it.

> iii. **Then** comes the devil; he is *punctual* in his work. The devil knows just the right time to come during preaching. He knows how to bring a distraction of some kind at just the right moment—or actually, the wrong moment. Sometimes the preacher himself provides opportunities for distraction. Sometimes accidentally a word or a story in the sermon triggers a distracting association. Sometimes the mind fills with yesterday's and tomorrow's checklist, or the after-church activities. Sometimes a cute child or clever whispered remark from the congregation does the job.

> iv. **The devil comes and takes the word**: Jesus said that he actually does it, not only that he tries to do it. In this regard, the devil has *power*. He sees, he comes, and he conquers. If it were not for the op-

posing work of the Holy Spirit, *nothing* would happen at the preaching of the word.

v. **Takes the word** also shows the devil's *purpose*. He is actually a pretty good theologian, and he knows that faith and salvation come to people who hear the word of God. He works hard to keep salvation and spiritual strength from those who might otherwise hear to good effect.

vi. Satan's strategy gives some wisdom to us if we will receive it—that if a heart *does* stay in contact with the word of God, there is a good chance that repentance and faith will come forth.

c. **But the ones on the rock are those who, when they hear, receive the word with joy; and these have no root, who believe for a while and in time of temptation fall away**: As seed falling on the thin soil on top of the rocky places quickly springs up and then quickly withers and dies (Luke 8:6) so some respond to the word with immediate enthusiasm, yet soon wither away.

i. They had good seed, they had a warm environment, they had a joyful reception of the word, and they received it eagerly. None of those things were the problem; they failed because the seed *lacked moisture* (Luke 8:6) and therefore had no root to endure the **time of temptation**.

ii. There was something that they did not have in connection with the spirit of God, who waters the word. "When we speak of spiritual dew, we refer to the operation of the Holy Spirit. When we talk of the river of the water of life, we mean those sacred things which come streaming down to us from the throne of God through the working of the Spirit of God." (Spurgeon)

iii. Spurgeon detailed some indications of this lack of moisture:

- Doctrine without feeling
- Experience without humiliation
- Practice without heart-love
- Faith without repentance
- Confidence without reservation
- Action without spirituality
- Zeal without communion

iv. "We need the Holy Spirit; and if the Lord does not water us daily from the living springs on the hilltops of glory, we shall certainly die.

So take heed, brothers and sisters, that you do not lack the moisture of the Holy Spirit's gracious influence." (Spurgeon)

d. **Now the ones that fell among thorns are those who, when they have heard, go out and are choked with cares, riches, and pleasures of life, and bring no fruit to maturity**: As seed falling among thorns would grow the stalks of grain among the thorns yet soon be choked out (Luke 8:7), so some respond to the word and grow for a while, but are choked and stopped in their spiritual growth by competition from unspiritual things.

i. This soil represented fertile ground for the word; but the soil was *too* fertile, because it also grew all sorts of other things that choked out the word of God. Namely it grew **the cares, riches, and pleasures of life**.

e. **The ones that fell on the good ground are those who, having heard the word with a noble and good heart, keep it and bear fruit with patience**: Some people are like the good ground, and receive the word **with a good and noble heart**. They **keep** the word, and thus bear fruit, thus fulfilling the purpose of the seed.

i. This soil represented those who received the word, and it brought forth fruit in their soil, and in generous proportion (Luke 8:8).

f. **Bear fruit with patience**: Obviously, this is the desired outcome for both the farmer and the preacher. Yet it is wrong to receive this parable fatalistically as if one said, "That's just the kind of soil you are or I am." Instead, this parable is a challenge for every listener, with God's help, to cultivate the soil of their heart so that the good word of God has the best effect in their life.

i. We benefit from seeing bits of ourselves in all four soils.

- Like the **wayside**, sometimes we allow the word no room at all in our lives
- Like the **stony places**, we sometimes have flashes of enthusiasm in receiving the word that quickly burn out
- Like the soil **among thorns**, the cares of this world and the deceitfulness of riches are constantly threatening to choke out God's word and our fruitfulness
- Like the **good ground**, the word bears fruit in our lives

ii. We notice that the difference in each category was with the soil itself. The sower cast the same seed. You could not blame the differences in results on the sower or on the seed, but only on the soil. "O my dear hearers, you undergo a test today! Peradventure you will be judging the preacher, but a greater than the preacher will be judging you, for the Word itself shall judge you." (Spurgeon)

iii. The parable was also an encouragement to the disciples. Even though it might seem that few respond, God is in control and the harvest will certainly come. This was especially meaningful in light of the rising opposition to Jesus. "Not all will respond, but there will be some who do, and the harvest will be rich." (France)

iv. Even more than describing the mixed progress of the gospel message, the parable of the sower compels the listener to ask, "What kind of soil am I? How can I prepare my heart and mind to be the *right* kind of soil?" This parable invites *action* so that we will receive the word of God to full benefit.

B. The responsibility of those who receive the word.

1. (16-17) Those who receive the word are responsible to expose and publish the truth—that is, the word of God.

"No one, when he has lit a lamp, covers it with a vessel or puts *it* under a bed, but sets *it* on a lampstand, that those who enter may see the light. For nothing is secret that will not be revealed, nor *anything* hidden that will not be known and come to light."

a. **No one, when he has lit a lamp, covers it with a vessel or puts it under a bed, but sets it on a lampstand**: Truth, by its nature is meant to be revealed; and God promised that it will be (**nothing is secret that will not be revealed**).

b. **That those who enter may see the light**: If you have the truth of God, you have a solemn responsibility to spread that truth in whatever way God gives you opportunity, even as someone who has the cure for a life-threatening disease has the moral responsibility to spread that cure. God didn't light your lamp so that it would be **hidden**.

i. One must either spread the word itself, or spread the influence of God's word by bringing others to a place where they will hear it. It's best to do both.

2. (18) Those who receive the word become accountable; so we must take care how we hear.

"Therefore take heed how you hear. For whoever has, to him *more* will be given; and whoever does not have, even what he seems to have will be taken from him."

a. **Therefore take heed how you hear**: It's good to **hear** the word of God; it's much better to take heed to **how you hear**. In this, Jesus warned His listeners to actively prepare the soil of their heart and mind, to judge themselves as hearers, at least as much as they judge the preacher.

i. It is dangerous to **hear** God's word in too passive a way; without engaging the word with the mind, the heart, and the will. To be hearers only of the word, and not to be also doers of the word, means destruction (Luke 6:49).

ii. In his sermon titled *Heedful Hearing*, Charles Spurgeon suggested some ways to heedfully hear the word of God:

- Hear attentively, retentively
- Hear believingly, obediently
- Hear candidly, honestly
- Hear devoutly, sincerely
- Hear earnestly, spiritually
- Hear feelingly, sensitively
- Hear gratefully, prayerfully

b. **For whoever has, to him more will be given**: When we hear the word of God, and receive it with gladness, more will be given to us from God's spiritual riches.

i. **More will be given**: More what? More desire to hear. More understanding of what you hear. More personal possession of the blessings you hear about.

ii. **More will be given**: Jesus reminds us that spiritual growth follows momentum, positive or negative. When we have the godly habits of receiving the word and living it, more is built on to that. When we lose those godly habits, they are extremely difficult to get back.

c. **Even what he seems to have**: Sometimes what people think they have spiritually, they only *seem* to have. The Pharisees were like this; so was the church at Laodicea (Revelation 3:14-22). The Laodiceans said of themselves, "We are rich, wealthy, and need nothing"; but they did not know that they were actually wretched, miserable, poor, blind, and naked.

3. (19-21) We show that we are close to Jesus by hearing and obeying His word.

Then His mother and brothers came to Him, and could not approach Him because of the crowd. And it was told Him *by some,* who said, "Your mother and Your brothers are standing outside, desiring to see You." But He answered and said to them, "My mother and My brothers are these who hear the word of God and do it."

a. **Then His mother and brothers came to Him, and could not approach Him because of the crowd**: We might have expected that Jesus' family would have special privileges before Him; it almost surprises us that they do not.

i. The **brothers** of Jesus never seemed to be supportive of His ministry before His death and resurrection (John 7:5, Mark 3:21).

b. **Brothers…brothers…brothers**: Jesus plainly had many brothers and sisters. The Roman Catholic idea of the perpetual virginity of Mary contradicts the plain meaning of the Bible.

i. "The most natural way to understand 'brothers' is that the term refers to sons of Mary and Joseph and thus to brothers of Jesus on his mother's side." Efforts to make brothers mean something else are "nothing less than farfetched exegesis in support of a dogma that originated much later than the New Testament." (Carson)

ii. "The erudite Catholic scholar Fitzmyer concedes this point. He writes about the supposed perpetual virginity of Mary, 'There is no indication in the New Testament itself about Mary as *aei parthenos*, 'ever virgin.' This belief in one form or another can only be traced to the second century A.D.'" (Pate)

c. **My mother and My brothers are these who hear the word of God and do it**: Jesus indicated that His closest family is made up of those who hear and obey God's word. We draw close to Jesus by hearing His word and doing it. In doing so, we gain a *closer* relationship with Him than even a normally understood family relationship. *This is a startling statement.*

i. One may pray or sing or fast all day long, but if they do not hear His word and do it, they are not really drawing close to God.

ii. The repeated emphasis on **the word of God** is impressive. "How anyone can dream, that either praying, or government, or administering sacraments, or anything else, should be more the work of a minister of Christ than preaching, may justly amaze any thinking soul that ever read the gospel." (Poole)

C. Jesus calms the storm.

1. (22-23) The stormy Sea of Galilee.

Now it happened, on a certain day, that He got into a boat with His disciples. And He said to them, "Let us cross over to the other side of the lake." And they launched out. But as they sailed He fell asleep. And a windstorm came down on the lake, and they were filling *with water*, and were in jeopardy.

a. **Let us cross over to the other side of the lake**: With these words, Jesus made a promise to His disciples. He didn't say, "Let us perish in the middle of the Sea of Galilee." He promised His disciples that they would **cross over to the other side of the lake**.

i. "The Lake of Galilee is 13 miles long at its longest, and 8 miles wide at its widest. At this particular part it was about 5 miles across." (Barclay)

ii. "Jonah ended up in a storm because of his disobedience, but the disciples got into a storm because of their *obedience* to the Lord." (Wiersbe)

b. **As they sailed, He fell asleep**: We are impressed by the fact that He *needed to sleep*, showing His true humanity. He became tired and would sometimes need to catch sleep wherever He was able to, even in unlikely places.

i. "It was the sleep of one worn by an intense life, involving constant strain on body and mind." (Bruce)

ii. We are also impressed by the fact that He *could sleep*. His mind and heart were peaceful enough, trusting in the love and care of His Father in heaven, that He could sleep in the storm.

c. **A windstorm came down on the lake**: The Sea of Galilee is well known for its sudden, violent storms. The severity of this storm is evident in the fact that the disciples (many of whom were experienced fishermen on this very sea) were terrified (Mark 4:40).

2. (24-25) Jesus calms the storm.

And they came to Him and awoke Him, saying, "Master, Master, we are perishing!" Then He arose and rebuked the wind and the raging of the water. And they ceased, and there was a calm. But He said to them, "Where is your faith?" And they were afraid, and marveled, saying to one another, "Who can this be? For He commands even the winds and water, and they obey Him!"

a. **They came to Him and awoke Him, saying, "Master, Master, we are perishing!"** The disciples did not take comfort from the sleeping Jesus and supposed that if He were at rest, all would be fine. They needed His help, so they **awoke Him**.

i. "The 'we' in their cry 'Master, Master, *we* perish,' included Him as well as them. If that boat went down, all went with it—His mission, their hopes, and the great enterprises which He had called them into fellowship with Himself to carry out." (Morgan)

ii. "How often we are over-anxious about the enterprises of our Lord! In the hour of storm we imagine everything is about to perish. Then He ever says to us" 'Where is your faith?'" (Morgan)

b. **He arose and rebuked the wind and the raging of the water**: Jesus didn't merely quiet the wind and the sea; He **rebuked the winds and the sea**. This, along with the disciples' great fear, and what Jesus would confront at their destination, gives the sense that Satan had a significant hand in this storm.

i. Adam Clarke supposed that the storm was "Probably excited by Satan, the prince of the power of the air, who, having got the author and all the preachers of the Gospel together in a small vessel, thought by drowning it, to defeat the purposes of God, and thus to prevent the salvation of a ruined world. What a noble opportunity must this have appeared to the enemy of the human race!"

c. **Where is your faith?** Jesus did not say, "Wow, what a storm." Instead, He asked, "**Where is your faith?**" The storm could not disturb Jesus, but the unbelief of His disciples could and did.

i. Their unbelief was not in that they were afraid of a fearful circumstance, but because Jesus had said *Let us go over to the other side of the lake* (Luke 8:22). Jesus didn't say, "Let's do the best we can and maybe we will all drown."

ii. Difficult circumstances—storms, so to speak—are not evidence of unbelief. Unbelief is the rejection of a promise or a command of God relevant to a particular situation.

iii. The disciples also should have known that God would not allow the Messiah to perish in a boat crossing the Sea of Galilee. It was not possible for the story of Jesus the Messiah to end with Him drowning in the Sea of Galilee.

iv. This account shows the abiding care Jesus has for His people. "There are many Christians today who seem to think the boat is going down! I am tired of the wailing of some of my friends who take that view. The boat cannot go down. Jesus is on board." (Morgan)

d. **And they were afraid, and marveled**: The total calm of the sea should have filled them with peace, but instead, they were just as afraid when He calmed the storm as when they were in the midst of the storm.

i. The disciples were amazed. Such a powerful display over creation led them to ask, "**Who can this be?**" It could only be the LORD, Jehovah, who only has this power and authority: *O LORD God of hosts, who is mighty like You, O LORD? Your faithfulness surrounds You. You rule the raging of the sea; when waves rise, You still them.* (Psalm 89:8-9)

ii. In the span of a few moments, the disciples saw both the complete humanity of Jesus (in His tired sleep) and the fullness of His deity. They saw Jesus for who He is: truly man and truly God.

D. The deliverance of the Gaderene demoniac.

1. (26-29) Description of the demon-possessed man.

Then they sailed to the country of the Gadarenes, which is opposite Galilee. And when He stepped out on the land, there met Him a certain man from the city who had demons for a long time. And he wore no clothes, nor did he live in a house but in the tombs. When he saw Jesus, he cried out, fell down before Him, and with a loud voice said, "What have I to do with You, Jesus, Son of the Most High God? I beg You, do not torment me!" For He had commanded the unclean spirit to come out of the man. For it had often seized him, and he was kept under guard, bound with chains and shackles; and he broke the bonds and was driven by the demon into the wilderness.

a. **To the country of the Gadarenes**: By most estimates, this was on the eastern side of the Sea of Galilee in the mostly Gentile area of the Decapolis, the Gentile cities of the broader region.

b. **There met Him a certain man from the city who had demons for a long time**: This is the most detailed description of a demon-possessed man we have in the Bible. It is the classic profile of demonic possession.

- The man had been demon possessed **for a long time**
- The man **wore no clothes** and lived more like a wild animal than a human being (**nor did he live in a house…driven by the demon into the wilderness**)
- The man lived among the decaying and dead, contrary to Jewish law and human instinct (**in the tombs**)
- The man had supernatural strength (**broke the bonds**)
- The man was tormented and self-destructive (*crying out and cutting himself with stones*, Mark 5:5)
- The man had uncontrollable behavior (*neither could anyone tame him*, Mark 5:4)

  i. Strangely, some Christians think the Holy Spirit works in a similar way; by overwhelming the operations of the body, and making one do strange and grotesque things.

  ii. We can be sure that he did not start out this way. At one time, this man lived among others in the village. But his own irrational, wild behavior convinced the villagers that he was demon possessed, or at least insane. They bound him with chains to keep him from hurting others, but he broke the chains time and again. Finally, they drove him out of town and he lived in the village cemetery, a madman among the tombs, hurting the only person he could—himself.

iii. **Driven by the demon**: "As a horse is by his rider (so the word signifieth) or a ship with oars." (Trapp)

c. **There met Him a certain man**: This means that Jesus did not directly seek out this man, but the man was drawn to Jesus.

d. **He had commanded the unclean spirit to come out of the man**: The man could not, or would not deliver himself, but Jesus had all authority over **the unclean spirit**.

e. **What have I to do with You…I beg You, do not torment me!** This was the demonic spirit within the possessed man, not the man himself. The demon did not want to leave the body he inhabited.

i. Demonic possession is when a demonic spirit *resides* in a human body, and at times will exhibit its own personality through the personality of the host body. Demonic possession is a reality today, though we must guard against either *ignoring* demonic activity or *over-emphasizing* supposed demonic activity.

ii. We are not told specifically how a person becomes demon possessed, other than the inference that it must be by some sort of invitation, whether offered knowingly or not.

iii. Superstition, fortunetelling, so-called harmless occult games and practices, spiritism, New Age deception, magic, drug taking and other things open doors of deception to the believer, and real demonic danger to the unbeliever.

iv. People often get involved in the occult or demonic things because there is something there that seems to *work*. Unfortunately, it is not some*thing* at work, but a some*one* at work—a demonic spirit.

v. We can say that demons want to inhabit bodies for the same reason the vandal wants a spray can, or a violent man wants a gun—a body is a weapon that they can use in their attack against God. Demons also attack men because they hate the image of God in man, so they try to mar that image, by debasing man and making him grotesque.

vi. Demons have the same goal in Christians (to wreck the image of God), but their tactics are restricted; in regard to Christians, demonic spirits were *disarmed* by Jesus' work on the cross (Colossians 2:15), though they can both deceive and intimidate Christians, binding them with fear and unbelief.

vii. **I beg You, do not torment me!** This was an ironic statement, because the man was constantly tormented by the demons overwhelming him in body, mind, and soul. Yet he thought that _Jesus_ might **torment** him.

f. **Jesus, Son of the Most High God**: This is what the demons said _in response_ to Jesus' command to **come out of the man** (**for He said to them, "Come out of the man"**). This was one way they tried to _resist_ the work of Jesus.

> i. In the background of all this was the ancient superstition that you had spiritual power over another if you knew or said their exact name. This is why the unclean spirits addressed Jesus with this full title: **Jesus, Son of the Most High God**. According to the superstitions of the day, this was like a shot fired back at Jesus.

> ii. Therefore in their address of Jesus, they have the right theological facts, but they don't have the right heart. The demons inhabiting him had a kind of "faith" in Jesus. They knew the true identity of Jesus better than the religious leaders did. Yet it was not a faith or knowledge of Jesus that could save (James 2:19).

2. (30-33) Jesus demonstrates His authority over evil spirits.

Jesus asked him, saying, "What is your name?" And he said, "Legion," because many demons had entered him. And they begged Him that He would not command them to go out into the abyss. Now a herd of many swine was feeding there on the mountain. So they begged Him that He would permit them to enter them. And He permitted them. Then the demons went out of the man and entered the swine, and the herd ran violently down the steep place into the lake and drowned.

a. **What is your name?** According to the customs of Jewish exorcists of that time, one had to know the _name_ of the demon in order to gain authority over it and deliver the demon-possessed person. Yet Jesus did not use the name learned in this exchange; He had authority over demons that went far beyond current superstitions.

b. **And he said, "Legion"**: Jesus probably asked the name of the demon so that _we_ would know the full extent of the problem, knowing that the man was filled with **many demons**, not only one. We note that **Legion** is not a name; it was evasive, a threat, and attempt to intimidate.

> i. A Roman legion usually consisted of six thousand men. This does not mean that the man was inhabited with six thousand demons, but that he had many.

> ii. It is also possible that this was the demons' attempt to intimidate Jesus. A cornered animal will often try to make itself seem larger to

the predator that seeks it; these many demons may have made a massive claim in the mistaken idea that they could frighten Jesus. **Legion** says, "There are a lot of us, we are organized, we are unified, we are ready to fight, and we are mighty."

iii. According to the superstitions of the day, the onlookers probably felt that the unclean spirits had the upper hand. They knew and declared a full name of Jesus. They evaded His request for their name. And finally, they hoped to frighten Jesus with their large number. But Jesus didn't buy into these ancient superstitions at all, and easily cast the unclean spirits out of the afflicted man.

c. **They begged Him that He would not command them to go out into the abyss**: The demons inhabiting this man did not want to be imprisoned in the **abyss**, which is the *bottomless pit* described in Revelation 9:11. Apparently, it is some place of imprisonment for certain demonic spirits.

i. These demons did not want to become inactive. "Lo, it is another hell to the devil to be idle, or otherwise than evil-occupied." (Trapp)

d. **The demons went out of the man and entered the swine**: The idea that demons may inhabit the bodies of animals seems strange, but the idea is also shown in Genesis 3. It was also appropriate that these demons be cast into **swine**, being non-kosher animals.

i. Notice that the demons can't even afflict *pigs* without the permission of God. "Since a demon cannot enter even into a *swine* without being *sent* by God himself, how little is the *power* or *malice* of them to be dreaded by those who have God for their portion and protector!" (Clarke)

ii. "Satan would rather vex swine than do no mischief at all. He is so fond of evil that he would work it upon animals if he cannot work it upon men." (Spurgeon)

iii. Jesus allowed this because the time of the total demonstration of His authority over demons had not yet come—it would come at the cross. Colossians 2:15 tells us that at the cross Jesus disarmed demons in their attacks on believers, He made a public spectacle of their defeat, and He triumphed over them in His work on the cross.

e. **The herd ran violently down the steep place into the lake and drowned**: The destructive nature of demonic spirits was shown by their effect on the swine. They were like their leader Satan, whose desire is to *steal, and to kill, and to destroy* (John 10:10).

i. This helps explain *why* Jesus allowed the demons to enter the pigs, because He wanted everyone to know what the real intention of these demons was. They wanted to destroy the man, just as they destroyed the pigs. Because men are made in the image of God, they could not have their way as easily with the man, but their intention was just the same—to completely destroy him.

ii. Some think this was unfair to the owner of the pigs. "'But the owners of the swine lost their property.' Yes, and learn from this how small value temporal riches are in the estimation of God. He suffers them to be lost, sometimes to disengage us from them through *mercy*; sometimes out of *justice*, to punish us for having *acquired* or *preserved* them either by *covetousness* or *injustice*." (Clarke)

iii. Spurgeon had several wise comments on the way the demons affected the swine:

- "*Swine* prefer death to devilry; and if men were not worse than swine, they would be of the same opinion"
- "They run hard whom the devil drives"
- "The devil drives his hogs to a bad market"

3. (34-37) The reaction of the bystanders to the deliverance of the demon-possessed man.

When those who fed *them* saw what had happened, they fled and told *it* in the city and in the country. Then they went out to see what had happened, and came to Jesus, and found the man from whom the demons had departed, sitting at the feet of Jesus, clothed and in his right mind. And they were afraid. They also who had seen *it* told them by what means he who had been demon-possessed was healed. Then the whole multitude of the surrounding region of the Gadarenes asked Him to depart from them, for they were seized with great fear. And He got into the boat and returned.

a. **They were afraid...and they were seized with great fear**: They were more afraid of a free man than a possessed man. When they saw the man **in his right mind** and **sitting at the feet of Jesus, they were afraid**.

i. Part of their fear was found in the fact that their superstitions had been shattered, and they didn't know what to make of it all. According to their superstitions, the demons should have had the upper hand over Jesus—but they didn't at all. They had a hard time accepting this.

b. **Then the whole multitude...asked Him to depart**: They didn't seem to mind having this demon-possessed, tormented man in their midst, but they did mind having Jesus around so they asked Him to leave, *and He did!*

i. The work of Jesus had unified the **whole multitude**, and they had all come out to meet with and to talk to Jesus; but it was not in a good way. "Here was a whole city at a prayer meeting, praying against their own blessing…Horrible was their prayer; *but it was heard*, and Jesus *departed out of their coasts*." (Spurgeon)

ii. When people are more afraid of what Jesus does than what Satan does, they push Jesus away—and He may leave asked to.

4. (38-39) The reaction of the man who had been delivered from demons.

Now the man from whom the demons had departed begged Him that he might be with Him. But Jesus sent him away, saying, "Return to your own house, and tell what great things God has done for you." And he went his way and proclaimed throughout the whole city what great things Jesus had done for him.

a. **The man from whom the demons had departed**: That is a wonderful name. Perhaps for the rest of his life this man would be called by a name that remembered the great work that Jesus did for him.

b. **Begged Him that he might be with Him**: First, this formerly demon-possessed man simply sat at the feet of Jesus (Luke 8:35). But then he just wanted to **be with** Jesus, following Him as a disciple.

i. This man didn't only want what Jesus could do for him; the true change in his heart was shown by the fact that he wanted Jesus Himself.

c. **But Jesus sent him away**: The man's desire to follow Jesus was good, but Jesus did not allow it. Jesus knew that he had a more important ministry with his own family and community.

i. Sometimes we have a hard time understanding the ways of God. The people of the city made an evil request (*asked Him to depart from them*) and Jesus answered their prayer. The man **from whom the demons departed** made a godly request: **that he might be with Him**, and Jesus said "no" to that prayer.

ii. Of course, this was because this man could be a light among the people of these Gentile cities in a way that Jesus and the disciples could not. But it was also to cure the man of any superstitions. He might have thought that he had to stay close to Jesus so the demons would not come back. "Perhaps, too, his prayer was not answered, lest his fear should have been thereby sanctioned. If he did fear, and I feel morally certain that he did, that the devils would return, then, of course, he longed to be with Christ. But Christ take that fear from him, and as good as says to him, 'You do not need to be near me; I have so healed that you will never be sick again'" (Spurgeon).

iii. "So we see it is an old error and weakness for men to be too strongly conceited of Christ's corporeal presence…Christ would not have him depend upon his bodily presence, but upon his Almighty power." (Trapp)

d. **He went his way and proclaimed throughout the whole city what great things Jesus had done for him**: This was a great message to tell, and a message that every follower of Jesus should be able to preach. His story showed the value of *one life* to Jesus, because this was the only reason why Jesus came to this side of the Sea of Galilee. His story also showed that with Jesus, *no one is beyond hope*, because if this man could be changed, then anyone can.

i. Jesus told him to **tell what great things God has done**, and the man spoke to others of **what great things Jesus had done**. There was no contradiction, because Jesus is God.

E. A woman healed, a girl raised from the dead.

1. (40-42) A father's plea that Jesus would heal his only daughter.

So it was, when Jesus returned, that the multitude welcomed Him, for they were all waiting for Him. And behold, there came a man named Jairus, and he was a ruler of the synagogue. And he fell down at Jesus' feet and begged Him to come to his house, for he had an only daughter about twelve years of age, and she was dying. But as He went, the multitudes thronged Him.

a. **The multitude welcomed Him**: Jesus left the Gentile region around the Sea of Galilee, where He met the man possessed by many demons. Now He returned to the Jewish towns on the other side, and the large crowds were **all waiting for Him**.

b. **He was a ruler of the synagogue**: The *ruler of the synagogue* was somewhat like a modern pastor. He managed both the spiritual and the business affairs of the synagogue. Jairus came in desperation to Jesus (**fell down at Jesus' feet and begged**), because his daughter **was dying**.

i. "As synagogue-ruler he was a lay official responsible for supervision of the building and arranging the service." (Lane)

ii. When the centurion came to Jesus in a similar situation (Luke 7:1-10), Jesus didn't even go to the centurion's house to heal the servant—He simply pronounced him healed from a distance.

iii. "Everybody in Capernaum knew Jairus; but no one knew that he believed in Christ until his little daughter was at the point of death. *Then* he confessed it." (Morrison)

c. **But as He went**: Jesus did not demand that Jairus show the same faith as the centurion did. Jesus responded to the faith that Jairus showed and went with him, as the **multitude thronged Him**.

> i. The ancient Greek word here translated **thronged** means, "almost *suffocated him*-so great was the throng about him." (Clarke) The same Greek root word is used to describe the choking of the seed of the word (Luke 8:7).

2. (43-44) A woman healed of her hemorrhage.

Now a woman, having a flow of blood for twelve years, who had spent all her livelihood on physicians and could not be healed by any, came from behind and touched the border of His garment. And immediately her flow of blood stopped.

a. **A woman, having a flow of blood for twelve years**: This woman was in a desperate condition. Her bleeding made her ceremonially and socially unclean, and this would be quite a burden to live under for 12 years.

> i. According to the Jewish ideas of the time, if this woman touched anyone, she imparted her uncleanness to them, an uncleanness that would not allow them to take part in any aspect of Israel's worship (Leviticus 15:19-31).

b. **Who had spent all her livelihood on physicians and could not be healed**: She went to the doctors to get better, but only suffered worse and became poorer. Luke the physician knew how doctor bills could take all that you had.

> i. The ancient rabbis had many different formulas to help a woman afflicted like this. "Rabbi Jochanan says: '*Take of gum Alexandria, of alum, and of corcus hortensis, the weight of a zuzee each; let them be bruised together, and given in wine to the woman that hath an issue of blood.* But if this fail, *Take of Persian onions nine logs, boil them in wine, and give it to her to drink: and say,* Arise from thy flux. But should this fail, *Set her in a place where two ways meet, and let her hold a cup of wine in her hand; and let somebody come behind and affright her, and say,* Arise from thy flux. But should this do no good . . .'" (Clarke)

> ii. When a soul is sick today, they often go to different "doctors" and spend a great deal of time and money, and are **not...healed** by them. A sick soul may go to "Doctor Entertainment," but finds no cure. They may pay a visit to "Doctor Success," but he is no help in the long run. "Doctor Pleasure," "Doctor Self-Help," or "Doctor Religion" can't bring a real cure. Only "Doctor Jesus" can.

c. **Came from behind and touched the border of His garment**: Because this woman's condition was embarrassing, and because she was ceremonially unclean and would be condemned for touching Jesus or even being in a pressing crowd, she wanted to do this secretly. She did not *openly* ask Jesus to be healed.

> i. "The word 'fringe' [**border**] is the Greek word *kraspedon*, the Septuagint term for the tassel which male Jews were to wear on the corners of their outer garments." (Pate)

> ii. The woman approached Jesus with a degree of superstition, thinking there was power in the border of His garment. Yet there was also an element of faith, because there is no evidence that Jesus had ever healed that way before.

> iii. Because even though her faith had elements of error and superstition, she believed in the healing power of Jesus, and the border of His garment served as a point of contact for that faith. There are many things that we could find wrong with this woman's faith. Yet more than anything, her faith was in *Jesus*, and the object of faith was much more important than the quality of faith.

d. **And immediately her flow of blood stopped**: According to the thinking of the day, when this unclean woman touched Jesus, it would make *Him* unclean. But because of the nature of Jesus and the power of God, that isn't how it worked. When she touched His garment, Jesus wasn't made unclean; the woman was made whole. When we come to Jesus with our sin and lay it upon Him, it doesn't make Him a sinner, but it makes us clean.

3. (45-48) Jesus speaks to the healed woman.

And Jesus said, "Who touched Me?" When all denied it, Peter and those with him said, "Master, the multitudes throng and press You, and You say, 'Who touched Me?'" But Jesus said, "Somebody touched Me, for I perceived power going out from Me." Now when the woman saw that she was not hidden, she came trembling; and falling down before Him, she declared to Him in the presence of all the people the reason she had touched Him and how she was healed immediately. And He said to her, "Daughter, be of good cheer; your faith has made you well. Go in peace."

a. **Who touched Me?** This question made no sense to the disciples. Luke told us that *the multitudes thronged Him* (Luke 8:42), and Jesus seemed annoyed that someone touched Him. There were people all about who pressed in on Jesus and who made some kind of contact with Him.

b. **Master, the multitudes throng and press You**: Peter and the disciples didn't understand the difference between *casual contact* with Jesus, and *reaching out to touch Him in faith*.

i. We can imagine someone, who because of the press of the crowd, bumped up against Jesus. When the woman's miracle was revealed, they might say, "I bumped into Jesus, I touched Him—yet I was not healed." But there is a huge difference between bumping into Jesus here and there and reaching out to touch Him in faith. You can come to church week after week and "bump into" Jesus. That isn't the same as reaching out to touch Him in faith.

ii. "It is not every contact with Christ that saves men; it is the arousing of yourself to come near to him, the determinate, the personal, resolute, believing touch of Jesus Christ which saves." (Spurgeon)

iii. "We may be very near Christ, and throng Him, without touching; but no one can touch Him, however lightly, without deriving the very grace needed." (Meyer)

c. **I perceived power going out from Me**: When the woman touched Jesus and was immediately healed, Jesus felt something happen. Jesus had a sense that someone had just been healed.

d. **The woman saw that she was not hidden**: This probably means that Jesus was looking right at her when He said, "**Somebody touched Me**" (Mark 5:32 says, *He looked around her to see her who had done this thing*). The woman *had* to come forward, because Jesus knew who she was. He called her forward, and it embarrassed her, but Jesus' purpose was not to just embarrass her but to bless her.

i. Jesus did it so that *she* would know she was healed. It is true that she felt **she was healed immediately**, but this woman was like any other person. Soon she would begin to doubt and fear that she really was healed. She would wonder when the ailment would return. But Jesus told her, "**Your faith has made you whole**." Jesus called her forward so *she* would absolutely know that she was healed.

ii. Jesus did it so *others* would know she was healed. This woman had an ailment that no one could see and that made her a public outcast. It would sound suspicious to many if she just announced that she was healed. They would think that she made it up just to be considered clean again. Jesus called her forward so *others* would absolutely know that she was healed, and so **she declared to Him in the presence of all the people she had touched Him**.

iii. Jesus did it so that she would know *why* she was healed. When Jesus said, "**Your faith has made you well**," it showed the woman that it really wasn't touching the clothing of Jesus that healed her. Instead, it was her **faith** in Jesus and what He could do for her.

iv. Jesus did it because He didn't want her to think that she *stole* a blessing; that she could never look Jesus in the eye again. She didn't steal anything. She received it by faith, and Jesus wanted her to know that.

v. Jesus did it so *Jairus* could see this woman's faith and be encouraged regarding his daughter. Jesus called her forward to *encourage someone else* in faith.

vi. Jesus did it because He wanted to bless her in a special way. He called her "**Daughter**." Jesus never called any other person by this name. Jesus wanted her to come forth and hear this special name of tenderness. When Jesus calls us forward, it is because He has something special to give us.

vii. Jesus may ask us to do things that seem embarrassing today. He doesn't ask us to do them just because He wants to embarrass us. There is also a higher purpose, even if we can't see it. But if avoiding embarrassment is the most important thing in our life, then pride is our god. We are more in love with ourselves and with our self-image than we are in love with Jesus.

viii. Poor Jairus! During all this, his daughter sits ill at home, her life slipping away. It must have tortured him to see Jesus take time out to minister to this woman while his daughter suffered. God is never slow, but He often *seems* slow to the sufferer.

4. (49-50) Jesus calls Jairus to a radical faith with a radical promise.

While He was still speaking, someone came from the ruler of the synagogue's *house*, saying to him, "Your daughter is dead. Do not trouble the Teacher." But when Jesus heard *it*, He answered him, saying, "Do not be afraid; only believe, and she will be made well."

a. **Your daughter is dead**: We can imagine how Jairus' heart sank when he heard this. He must have thought, "I knew this took too long. I knew Jesus shouldn't waste His time on this silly woman. Now the situation is beyond repair."

b. **But when Jesus heard it, He answered him**: Jesus gave Jairus two things to do. First, He told him, **do not be afraid**. Second, He told him, **only believe**.

i. **Do not be afraid**: It sounds almost cruel for Jesus to say this to a man who just lost his daughter, but Jesus knew that *fear* and *faith* don't go together. Before Jairus could really trust Jesus, he had to *decide* to put away fear.

ii. **Only believe**: Don't try to **believe** and be afraid at the same time. Don't try to **believe** and figure it all out. Don't try to **believe** and make sense of the delay. Instead, **only believe**.

c. **Only believe, and she will be made well**: The *only* thing that Jairus had to believe in was Jesus' word. *Everything* else told him that his daughter was gone forever. This was both the *best place* to be and the *hardest place* to be.

5. (51-56) Jesus raises the little girl from the dead.

When He came into the house, He permitted no one to go in except Peter, James, and John, and the father and mother of the girl. Now all wept and mourned for her; but He said, "Do not weep; she is not dead, but sleeping." And they ridiculed Him, knowing that she was dead. But He put them all outside, took her by the hand and called, saying, "Little girl, arise." Then her spirit returned, and she arose immediately. And He commanded that she be given *something* to eat. And her parents were astonished, but He charged them to tell no one what had happened.

a. **He permitted no one to go in except Peter, James, and John**: Often these three are considered the inner circle of Jesus' disciples. Perhaps the case was that Jesus knew that He had to keep a special eye on these three.

b. **All wept and mourned for her**: In that day it was customary to hire professional mourners to add to the atmosphere of grief and pain at a death. But the professional mourners could only grieve superficially. They quickly turned from weeping to scornful laughter (**they ridiculed Him**).

i. Jesus was often mocked and **ridiculed**. "Men ridiculed His origin. Men ridiculed His actions. Men ridiculed His claims to be Messiah. Not in all history is there such exposure of the cruelty and bestiality of ridicule as in the mocking and taunting at the cross." (Morrison)

ii. Probably even more than in the time of Jesus, we live in an age of mockery and ridicule, when people find it easy to use sneer and snark against anything that seems or claims to be good. "I should like to say also to those who are tempted to see only the ridiculous side of things, that perhaps in the whole gamut of the character there is nothing quite so dangerous as that... When we take to ridiculing all that is best and worthiest in *others*, by that very habit we destroy the power of believing in what is worthiest in *ourselves*." (Morrison)

c. **She is not dead, but sleeping**: Jesus wasn't out of touch with reality when He said this. He did not play make-believe. He said this because He knew a higher reality, a spiritual reality that was more certain and powerful than death itself.

d. **He put them all outside**: Jesus would have nothing to do with these people who didn't believe His promises. He drove them out so that they would not discourage the faith of Jairus.

> i. "It was not a caprice that when Jesus Christ was ridiculed, He turned the mockers out of the miracle-chamber. That is what the Almighty always does when men and women take themselves to mocking. He shuts the door on them, so that they cannot see the miracles with which the universe is teeming, and they miss the best, because in their blind folly they have laughed the Giver of the best to scorn." (Morrison)

e. **Little girl, arise**: Because Jesus is God, He could speak to the girl as if she were alive. Romans 4:17 says that God *gives life to the dead and calls those things which do not exist as though they did*. Jesus spoke to this girl with the power of God, and she was raised from the dead.

f. **He commanded that she be given something to eat**: Perhaps He did this not only for the good of the girl, but also for her mother—to give her something to do, to ease the shock of the moment.

> i. "Though she was raised to life by a miracle, she was not to be preserved by a miracle. Nature is God's great instrument, and he delights to work by it; nor will he do any thing by his sovereign power, in the way of miracle, that can be effected by his ordinary providence." (Clarke)

g. **Her parents were astonished**: Jesus didn't fail Jairus, and He didn't fail the woman who needed healing. But in serving both of them, He needed to stretch the faith of Jairus extra far.

> i. In all this we see how the work of Jesus is different, yet the same among each individual. If Jesus can touch each need this personally, He can touch our needs the same way.

- Jairus had twelve years of sunshine (Luke 8:42) that were about to be extinguished. The woman had twelve years of agony that seemed hopeless to heal

- Jairus was an important man, the ruler of the synagogue. The woman was a nobody. We don't even know her name

- Jairus was probably wealthy, because he was an important man. The woman was poor because she spent all her money on doctors

- Jairus came publicly. The woman came secretly

- Jairus thought Jesus had to do a lot to heal his daughter. The woman thought all she needed was to touch Jesus' garment

- Jesus responded to Jairus after a delay; Jesus responded to the woman immediately

- Jairus' daughter was healed secretly. The woman was healed publicly

Luke 9—The Kingdom of God Preached, Displayed

A. The apostles are sent to preach and heal.

1. (1-2) Jesus calls them and sends them forth.

Then He called His twelve disciples together and gave them power and authority over all demons, and to cure diseases. He sent them to preach the kingdom of God and to heal the sick.

a. **He called His twelve disciples together**: The selection of the disciples was described in Luke 6:12-16. They had been with Him together as a group for some time, and now Jesus delegated some of His work to them.

b. **And gave them power and authority over all demons, and to cure diseases**: Jesus did not only *call* the twelve. He also gave them **power** to do what He had called them to do. The same principle holds true today: whom God calls, God equips. The equipping may not be completely evident before the ministry begins, but it will be evident along the way.

i. Jesus didn't delegate the work without also delegating the **power and authority** to do that work.

ii. "The reader will please to observe: 1. That Luke mentions both *demons* and *diseases*; therefore he was either mistaken, or *demons* and *diseases* are *not* the *same*. 2. The *treatment* of these two was not the *same*: the demons were to be *cast out*, the diseases to be *healed*." (Clarke)

c. **He sent them to preach the kingdom of God**: To **preach** simply means to proclaim, to tell others in the sense of announcing news to them. The disciples were sent with the work of proclaiming that the **kingdom of God** was present, and what the character of that **kingdom** was like.

i. Their work of preaching might happen in open-air settings, such as street corners or marketplaces. It might happen in synagogues, as they found opportunity to speak. It might happen in small group or one-on-one conversations.

ii. Whatever the setting, the message was essentially:

- The King has arrived; Jesus the Messiah is present
- His kingdom is different from what we expected
- He gathers a kingdom community of those who will repent and believe

iii. It's not too much to say that *Jesus used the available media of His day*. They didn't have newspapers or podcasts or internet or any number of other media opportunities we have today. Yet Jesus did use the media that was available to Him, and used it well.

d. **He sent them to preach the kingdom of God and to heal the sick**: Jesus sent the disciples to do more than present a message, but also to do good with supernatural empowering; to bless the whole person, and **to heal the sick**.

i. This **power and authority over all demons, and to cure diseases** was vitally connected with preaching the gospel. The two go together.

ii. "Alluding to a play on words, Luke mentions that Jesus 'sent' (*apostello*) the 'apostles' to preach the kingdom of God and to heal." (Pate)

2. (3-6) The Kingdom to preach is marked by simplicity, urgency, and sincerity.

And He said to them, "Take nothing for the journey, neither staffs nor bag nor bread nor money; and do not have two tunics apiece. Whatever house you enter, stay there, and from there depart. And whoever will not receive you, when you go out of that city, shake off the very dust from your feet as a testimony against them." So they departed and went through the towns, preaching the gospel and healing everywhere.

a. **Take nothing for the journey**: The disciples didn't need sophisticated equipment to preach a simple message. Too many things would get in the way of their urgent message.

i. There was a rule among the rabbis of the day that one could not enter the temple area with a staff, shoes, or moneybag so as to avoid even the appearance of being engaged in any other business than the service of the Lord. The disciples were engaged in such holy work (preaching the gospel and bringing God's healing) that they could not give the impression that they had any other motive.

ii. "He was once again speaking words which were very familiar to a Jew. The *Talmud* tells us that: 'No one is to go to the Temple Mount with staff, shoes, girdle of money, or dusty feet.' The idea was that when a man entered the temple, he must make it quite clear that he had left everything which had to do with trade and business and worldly affairs behind." (Barclay)

iii. Pate notes that Josephus wrote that the Essenes had similar rules about traveling light, trusting for provision along the way (*J. W.* 2.124-125)

b. **Neither staffs nor bag nor bread nor money**: Travelling light also kept them dependent upon God. If they did not take much with them, they had to trust the Lord for everything. If the preacher himself doesn't trust God, how can he tell others to trust Him?

i. "The forbidden *bag* may be the kind frequently used by itinerant philosophers and religious mendicants for begging." (Liefeld)

c. **And whoever will not receive you**: Their job as preachers wasn't primarily to change people's minds. They were to persuasively present the message, but if their listeners didn't receive it, they could leave and **shake the very dust from your feet** as they left.

i. If Jewish people of that time had to go in or through a Gentile city, as they left, they often shook the dust off their feet as a gesture saying, "We don't want to take anything from this Gentile city with us." Essentially, Jesus told His disciples to regard a Jewish city that rejected their message as if it were a Gentile city.

d. **So they departed**: They actually did what Jesus told them to do. They were **preaching the gospel and healing everywhere**, with both the mission given to them by Jesus and the power and authority to fulfill that mission.

3. (7-9) Herod hears of Jesus' ministry and is perplexed.

Now Herod the tetrarch heard of all that was done by Him; and he was perplexed, because it was said by some that John had risen from the dead, and by some that Elijah had appeared, and by others that one of the old prophets had risen again. Herod said, "John I have beheaded, but who is this of whom I hear such things?" So he sought to see Him.

a. **He was perplexed...said by some that John had risen...by some that Elijah had appeared...by others that one of the old prophets had risen again**: There is no indication that **Herod** (Herod Antipas, son of Herod the Great) was a man of sincere spiritual interest. Yet he was interested in Jesus as a famous man, a miracle worker, and perhaps as a rival. Herod absorbed the popular thinking about who Jesus was (as in Luke 9:19).

i. Some thought Jesus was a herald of national repentance, like **John** the Baptist. Some thought Jesus was a famous worker of miracles, like **Elijah** (whose return before the coming of the Messiah was promised in Malachi 4:5-6). Some thought Jesus was **one of the old prophets**, perhaps the one Moses promised would come (Deuteronomy 18:15-19).

ii. The popular rumors about Jesus left Herod **perplexed**, especially because of his guilty conscience over the murder of John the Baptist. A bad conscience brings confusion and perplexity.

b. **It was said by some that John had risen from the dead**: The last time Luke wrote of John the Baptist, he was in prison and wondered if Jesus really was the Messiah (Luke 7:18-23). Now we learn that Herod executed John in prison, because John rebuked Herod about his sin with his brother's wife (Matthew 14:1-12).

c. **So he sought to see Him**: Herod wanted to **see** Jesus, but not as a sincere seeker. He either wanted to indulge idle curiosity or to do the same to Jesus as he had done to His cousin John. Luke noted this to emphasize the increasing danger surrounding the work of Jesus.

i. Luke records a second reference to this Herod. Later, Jesus was told that this Herod wanted to kill Him. Jesus replied, *Go, tell that fox, "Behold I cast our demons and perform cures today and tomorrow, and the third day I shall be perfected."* (Luke 13:32)

ii. Luke also told us that Jesus finally met this Herod on the morning of His crucifixion. Herod was in Jerusalem at the time, and when He heard that Pilate was sending Jesus to him, he got happy and excited—Herod wanted Jesus to perform a miracle for him. Yet Jesus did no miracle for Herod, and when he asked Jesus many questions, Jesus answered him *nothing*. Herod then treated Jesus with contempt, mocked Him with a purple robe, and sent Him back to Pilate.

4. (10) The apostles return.

And the apostles, when they had returned, told Him all that they had done. Then He took them and went aside privately into a deserted place belonging to the city called Bethsaida.

a. **And the apostles**: When they left Jesus in Luke 9:1, they were called *disciples*, that is, "learners." When they came back after their preaching mission, they were called **apostles**, that is, "those sent with authority and a message." They certainly remained disciples, but knew both the message and the authority in a much better way after their work.

b. **Told Him all that they had done**: Jesus wanted to know how they had done. Jesus is concerned with the results of our work for Him.

c. **He took them and went aside privately into a deserted place**: Jesus did this to serve and bless those to whom He delegated His work. Jesus has a special care to bless and serve those who serve Him.

B. The feeding of the 5,000.

1. (11) Jesus serves the multitude.

But when the multitudes knew *it,* **they followed Him; and He received them and spoke to them about the kingdom of God, and healed those who had need of healing.**

a. **When the multitudes knew it, they followed Him**: Jesus had gone to Bethsaida to bless and serve His disciples after their work for Him. They could not keep the **multitudes** away for long; **they followed Him** there, also.

b. **He received them and spoke to them about the kingdom of God, and healed**: Jesus served the seeking, needy multitudes in three ways.

- **He received them**: This speaks of His *attitude.* He didn't run from the crowd or tell them to go away. With love and service, **He received them**

- **Spoke to them about the kingdom of God**: This speaks of His *teaching.* As was the emphasis in His work, Jesus proclaimed a message to the multitudes

- **And healed those**: Jesus did not only give them spiritual instruction, but He also did good among them with supernatural empowering

2. (12-15) Jesus challenges His disciples to provide for the need of the multitude.

When the day began to wear away, the twelve came and said to Him, "Send the multitude away, that they may go into the surrounding towns and country, and lodge and get provisions; for we are in a deserted place here." But He said to them, "You give them something to eat." And they said, "We have no more than five loaves and two fish, unless we go and buy food for all these people." For there were about five thousand men. Then He said to His disciples, "Make them sit down in groups of fifty." And they did so, and made them all sit down.

a. **Send the multitude away**: After the long day (**when the day began to wear away**), the disciples saw the crowd as a bother. Like Jesus, they came to Bethsaida to get away from the multitudes, not to serve them.

i. Actually, it's not entirely fair to criticize the disciples for their recommendation to **send the multitude away**. They probably could not even conceive that Jesus could or would miraculously feed the crowd.

They felt they were doing good for the multitude by sending them away to **lodge and get provisions**.

b. **You give them something to eat**: To the disciples, this request must have sounded strange or even shocking. It was obvious to them that they did not have the resources to feed even a fraction of the multitude. With this statement, Jesus challenged both their faith and their compassion.

i. Both Jesus and the disciples were aware of the **great multitude** and aware of their needs. Yet it was the *compassion* of Jesus (Matthew 14:14) and His awareness of the power of God that led Him to go about feeding the multitude.

- The people are hungry, and the atheists and skeptics try to convince them that they aren't hungry at all

- The people are hungry, and the empty religionist offers them some ceremony or empty words that can never satisfy

- The people are hungry, and the religious showman gives them video and special lighting and cutting-edge music

- The people are hungry, and the entertainer gives them loud, fast action; so loud and fast that they don't have a moment to think

- The people are hungry—and Jesus has the bread of life

c. **Make them sit down in groups of fifty**: Jesus wanted them to do this work in an orderly, organized way, and He also wanted them to *enjoy* the meal. This command suggests that this was more than just putting food in their stomachs; that could be done standing up. The idea was that there was something of a banquet-like atmosphere of enjoyment.

i. Organizing them **in groups of fifty** also made it possible to much more easily count the multitude, giving more reliability to the number of **about five thousand men**.

3. (16-17) The multitude is fed.

Then He took the five loaves and the two fish, and looking up to heaven, He blessed and broke *them*, and gave *them* to the disciples to set before the multitude. So they all ate and were filled, and twelve baskets of the leftover fragments were taken up by them.

a. **He took the five loaves and the two fish**: Jesus took the little that they had (first mentioned in Luke 9:13), and He thanked God for it. It would be easy to think that such a small amount of food was worthless to feed such a large crowd, but Jesus used what He had at hand.

i. In John's account (John 6:8-9), we learn that these **five loaves** and **the two fish** came from a young boy. Even what they had, they borrowed from a young man who brought the food with him.

b. **Looking up to heaven, He blessed and broke them**: When Jesus **blessed** before the meal, He wasn't blessing the food. He blessed God for supplying it. The idea of praying before a meal isn't to bless the food; it is to bless, that is, to *thank* God for blessing us with the food.

i. Though it wasn't much, Jesus blessed the Father for the food that He *did* have. He may have prayed a familiar Jewish prayer before a meal: "Blessed art Thou, Jehovah our God, King of the universe, who bringest forth bread from the earth."

c. **He blessed and broke them, and gave them to the disciples to set before the multitude**: This miracle displayed Jesus' total authority over creation. Yet He insisted on doing this miracle *through* the hands of the disciples. He could have done it directly, but He wanted to use the disciples.

i. No one knew where this bread actually came from. Jesus showed that God can provide out of resources that we cannot see or perceive in any way. It is easier to have faith when we think we know *how* God might provide, but God often provides in unexpected and undiscoverable ways.

d. **So they all ate and were filled**: Jesus miraculously multiplied the loaves and fish, until far more than 5,000 were fed. Seemingly, the miracle happened in the hands of Jesus, not in the hands of the disciples—they simply distributed what Jesus had miraculously provided.

i. If someone left hungry, it was either because they refused the bread from Jesus, or because the apostles didn't distribute the bread to everyone. Jesus *supplied* plenty for everybody.

ii. The assurance that Jesus can provide, even miraculously, for all of our needs should be precious to us; it was to the earliest Christians. On the walls of the catacombs and other places of early Christian art loaves and fish are common pictures.

iii. What we have in ourselves to give others is insignificant, but when we put it in Jesus' hands, He can do great things with our gifts and talents to touch the lives of others.

iv. "In a remarkable way, that feeding is a parabolic illustration of the method by which those who serve Him are to reach the needs of humanity. Their duty is to yield all they have to Him, and then to obey Him, no matter how mere prudence and worldly wisdom may question the method." (Morgan)

B. The kingdom and the cross.

1. (18-20) Peter's understanding of who Jesus is.

And it happened, as He was alone praying, *that* His disciples joined Him, and He asked them, saying, "Who do the crowds say that I am?" So they answered and said, "John the Baptist, but some *say* Elijah; and others *say* that one of the old prophets has risen again." He said to them, "But who do you say that I am?" Peter answered and said, "The Christ of God."

a. **As He was alone praying, that His disciples joined Him**: This scene began with Jesus praying, and the disciples joining Him. We don't really know if they **joined** with Him in prayer, or if they interrupted His time of prayer. When Jesus was done praying, He asked them a question: **Who do the crowds say that I am?**

i. Jesus didn't ask this question because He was ignorant on this point and needed information from His disciples. He asked this question to introduce a more important follow-up question.

ii. G. Campbell Morgan was convinced that the disciples interrupted the prayer of Jesus. "A careful study of the Gospel narratives has led to the justifiable conclusion that our Lord never prayed with His disciples. Often He left them when He would pray. When in their company He prayed, it was not in association with them, but in separation…His praying was on a different plane." (Morgan)

b. **John the Baptist, but some say Elijah; and others say that one of the old prophets has risen again**: People who thought that Jesus was **John the Baptist** didn't know much about Him, because He and John worked at the same time. Both John and **Elijah** were national reformers who stood against the corrupt rulers of their day, and the similarity with the courage and righteousness of Jesus may have suggested the connection.

i. Perhaps in seeing Jesus as John or Elijah, the people hoped for a political messiah, one who would overthrow the corrupt powers that oppressed Israel.

c. **Who do you say that I am?** It was fine for the disciples to know what **the crowds** thought about Jesus. But Jesus had to ask them, as individuals, what *they* believed about Him.

i. Jesus *assumed* that the disciples would have a different opinion of Him from **the crowds**. They didn't just receive the conventional wisdom or the popular opinion. *They* should know who Jesus was.

ii. This is the question placed before all who hear of Jesus; and it is we, not He, who are judged by our answer. In fact, we answer this question every day by what we believe and do. If we really believe Jesus is who He says He is, it will affect the way that we live.

d. **The Christ of God**: Peter knew Jesus better than the crowds did. He knew that Jesus is **the Christ of God**, God's Messiah, the promised redeemer from the Old Testament, the Messiah from the heart of God, *not* the Messiah from the desire of man.

2. (21-22) Jesus reveals the true nature of His mission.

And He strictly warned and commanded them to tell this to no one, saying, "The Son of Man must suffer many things, and be rejected by the elders and chief priests and scribes, and be killed, and be raised the third day."

a. **He strictly warned and commanded them to tell this to no one**: Jesus was pleased that His disciples were coming to know who He was in truth, but He still didn't want His identity popularly known before the proper time. The crowds couldn't understand that Jesus really was the Messiah, yet *had to* suffer—the disciples had to learn this first.

i. "Before they could preach that Jesus was the Messiah, they had to learn what that meant." (Barclay)

b. **The Son of Man must suffer many things**: After hearing what the crowd thought of Him, Jesus then told them what He had really come to do—**suffer**, **be rejected**, **be killed**, and **be raised the third day**. This wasn't what His disciples or the crowds expected or wanted at all.

i. This was an unbelievable shock to all who expected or hoped that Jesus was the national and political messiah. By analogy, we can imagine a presidential candidate announcing towards the end of his campaign that he was going to Washington, but to be rejected and executed.

c. **Must suffer many things**: An important word here is **must**. This wasn't just a plan or an idea or a prediction; this was the fulfillment of what was planned before the world began for our salvation (1 Peter 1:20 and Revelation 13:8).

d. **And be raised the third day**: The resurrection was as much a **must** as any other aspect of His suffering; Jesus *had* to rise from the dead.

3. (23) Jesus calls everyone wanting to follow Him to do what He will do.

Then He said to *them* all, "If anyone desires to come after Me, let him deny himself, and take up his cross daily, and follow Me."

a. **Then He said to them all**: It was bad enough for the disciples to hear that Jesus would suffer, be rejected, and die on a cross. Now He told them that *they* must do the same, or at least have the same intention.

b. **Let him deny himself, and take up his cross daily, and follow Me**: As Jesus spoke these words, everybody knew what Jesus meant. In the Roman world, before a man *died* on a cross, he had to *carry* his cross (or at least the horizontal beam of the cross) to the place of execution.

i. When the Romans crucified a criminal, they didn't just hang him on a cross. They first hung a cross on him.

ii. *Carrying* a cross always led to *death* on a cross. No one carried a cross for fun. The first hearers of Jesus didn't need an explanation of the cross; they knew it was an unrelenting instrument of torture, death, and humiliation. If someone took **up his cross**, he never came back. It was a one-way journey.

iii. In the real-life crosses of the Roman world, no one *took them up* (suggesting a voluntary action). Instead, crosses were pressed upon people, quite apart from their willingness. Here Jesus said that those who follow Him must voluntarily **take up** their cross.

iv. This isn't to suggest that we can *choose* our way to die a living death as followers of Jesus; but as the unchosen circumstances come into life, we choose to bear them as a way to daily die for Jesus' glory.

c. **Let him deny himself, and take up his cross daily**: Jesus made **deny himself** equal with **take up his cross**. The two phrases expressed the same idea. The cross wasn't about self-promotion or self-affirmation. The person carrying a cross knew he couldn't save himself, and that *self* was destined to die.

i. Denying your self means to live as an others centered person. Jesus was the only person to do this perfectly, but we are to follow in His steps.

d. **Take up his cross daily**: Jesus made it clear that He spoke spiritually when He added the word **daily**. No one could be crucified *literally* everyday. **Daily** they *could* have the same attitude as Jesus had.

i. This is following Jesus at its simplest. He carried a cross, so His followers carry one. He walked to His self-death, so must those who would follow Him.

4. (24-27) Why we must take up our cross and follow Jesus.

"For whoever desires to save his life will lose it, but whoever loses his life for My sake will save it. For what profit is it to a man if he gains the whole world, and is himself destroyed or lost? For whoever is ashamed of Me and My words, of him the Son of Man will be ashamed when He comes in His *own* glory, and *in His* Father's, and of the holy angels. But I tell you truly, there are some standing here who shall not taste death till they see the kingdom of God."

a. **For whoever desires to save his life will lose it, but whoever loses his life for My sake will save it**: We must follow Jesus this way because it is the only way that we will ever find life. It sounds strange to say, "You will never live until you walk to your death with Jesus," but that is the idea. You can't gain resurrection life without dying first.

i. *This is a strong and sure promise of the afterlife*. If there is no life after death, then what Jesus said makes no sense; there *is* no reward for either the dying martyr or the living martyr.

ii. You don't *lose* a seed when you plant it, though it seems dead and buried. In truth, you set it free to fulfill its greatest destiny.

b. **For what profit is it to a man if he gains the whole world**: Avoiding the walk to death with Jesus means that we may gain the **whole world**—and end up losing everything.

i. Jesus Himself had the opportunity to gain the whole world by worshipping Satan (Luke 4:5-8), but found life and victory in obedience instead.

ii. Amazingly, the people who live this way before Jesus are the ones who are really, genuinely happy. Giving our lives to Jesus all the way, and living as an others centered person does not take away from our lives, it adds to it.

c. **For whoever is ashamed of Me and My words, of him the Son of Man will be ashamed when He comes in His own glory**: It isn't easy to walk death row with Jesus. It means that we have to associate ourselves with someone who was despised and executed—but if we are ashamed of Him, He will be ashamed of us.

i. *This is a radical call to personal allegiance to Jesus.* He wanted to know if we would be **ashamed of** *Him* or of *His* **words**. If Jesus were not God, this was an invitation to idolatry. Because *He is God*, this is a call to worship.

ii. **Ashamed of Me**: It's no wonder that some were ashamed of Jesus during the days of His earthly ministry; it is astounding that any would be ashamed of Him today.

- Jesus, revealed in the full glory of His sacrificial love
- Jesus, revealed in the full power of His resurrected glory
- Jesus, ascended to heaven and honored
- Jesus, loving and praying for His people from heaven

Who could be ashamed of *that*?

iii. Yet, some are **ashamed**. The ashamed man believes; you can't be ashamed of something you don't believe in. He believes, but doesn't take satisfaction and confidence in his belief.

- Ashamed means you don't want to be seen together in public

- Ashamed means that you don't want to talk about Him

- Ashamed means that you avoid Him when possible

iv. Some are **ashamed** out of fear, some out of social pressure, some out of intellectual or cultural pride. Objectively considered, such shame is a strange phenomenon.

d. **But I tell you truly, there are some standing here who shall not taste death till they see the kingdom of God**: After this extreme call to follow Jesus unto death, He added a promise of significant glory (**till they see the kingdom of God**). Jesus wanted them to know that it wasn't *all* suffering and death; the *end* of it all wasn't death.

C. The Transfiguration.

1. (28-29) Jesus is transfigured before Peter, John, and James.

Now it came to pass, about eight days after these sayings, that He took Peter, John, and James and went up on the mountain to pray. As He prayed, the appearance of His face was altered, and His robe *became* white *and* glistening.

a. **He took Peter, John, and James and went up on the mountain to pray**: What started as a mountaintop prayer meeting, quickly changed into the shining forth of the glory of Jesus, and **as He prayed**, Jesus was transformed right before the eyes of the disciples.

i. "Although Luke does not name the mountain, ever since Origen some have identified it as Mt. Tabor, which is west of the Sea of Galilee. Others, however, equate it with Mt. Hermon, north of Caesarea Philippi, the place of Peter's confession." (Pate)

b. **The appearance of His face was altered**: After carefully setting the context of prayer, Luke explained what happened to Jesus. He changed in His appearance in what has become known as the *transfiguration*.

i. **White and glistening** translates a word that has the idea of "flashing like lightning." Jesus' entire appearance was transformed in a brilliant radiance of light.

ii. Matthew says that Jesus' *face shone like the sun* (Matthew 17:2), and both Matthew and Mark used the word *transfigured* to describe what happened to Jesus. For this brief time, Jesus took on an appearance more appropriate for the King of Glory than for a humble man.

iii. This was not a *new* miracle, but the temporary pause of an ongoing miracle. The real miracle was that Jesus, most of the time, *could keep* from displaying His glory.

c. **The appearance of His face was altered**: This was important at this point in Jesus' ministry because He had just told His disciples that He would go the way of the cross, and that they should follow Him spiritually. It would have been easy for them to lose confidence in Jesus after such a seemingly defeatist statement. Yet in His transfigured radiance, Jesus showed His glory as King over all God's Kingdom.

i. If they would listen, this would give great confidence to the disciples. *Jesus knows what He is doing. He promised that He would suffer, die, and rise again, but He is still the King of Glory.*

ii. Jesus showed in an acted-out way that cross bearers would be glory receivers. The end isn't the cross; the end is the glory of God.

2. (30-31) Moses and Elijah appear with Jesus.

And behold, two men talked with Him, who were Moses and Elijah, who appeared in glory and spoke of His decease which He was about to accomplish at Jerusalem.

a. **Two men talked with Him**: Jesus was not alone in this display of glory. **Two men** also appeared with Him, whom the disciples seemed to immediately recognize as **Moses and Elijah**.

i. Their immediate recognition of these men **who appeared in glory** without prior introduction gives some evidence that we will also be able to immediately recognize others in heaven. There won't be a need for nametags.

ii. They seemed to have a wonderful time together as they **talked with Him**. "Possibly that transfiguration was an example of the way in which Adam and all his race might have passed into heaven, and not death come upon us all through sin." (Meyer)

b. **Moses and Elijah, who appeared in glory**: Many wonder why it was *these* two particular men from the Old Testament, and not two others. It wasn't Abraham or David or Joshua or Joseph or Daniel; it was **Moses and Elijah**.

i. It may be because **Moses and Elijah** represent those who are caught up to God (Jude 9 and 2 Kings 2:11). Moses represents those who die and go to glory, and Elijah represents those who are caught up to heaven without death (as in 1 Thessalonians 4:13-18).

ii. It can also be said that they represent the Law (**Moses**) and the Prophets (**Elijah**). The sum of Old Testament revelation came to meet with Jesus at the Mount of Transfiguration.

iii. **Moses and Elijah** also figure together in prophecy, because they are likely the witnesses of Revelation 11:3-13.

c. **Spoke of His decease which He was about to accomplish at Jerusalem**: Of all the things they might have discussed, they chose this topic. It seems that **Moses and Elijah** were interested in the outworking of God's plan through Jesus; they spoke about what Jesus **was about to accomplish at Jerusalem**.

i. We can almost picture Moses and Elijah asking, "Are You really going to do it?" Moses might say, "I offered to be judged in the place of the people, but God wouldn't have it. Can You go through with this, Jesus?" Elijah might add, "I was persecuted terribly by Ahab and Jezebel, and I hated it—sometimes I went into a deep spiritual depression. Can You go through with this, Jesus?"

ii. **Spoke of His decease**: "Greek, of his exodus; in reference to that expedition or departure of Israel out of Egypt." (Trapp) "The term, in large part, portrayed Jesus' suffering and death as the means to His receiving divine glory." (Pate)

3. (32) The disciples sleep in the presence of Jesus, Moses, and Elijah.

But Peter and those with him were heavy with sleep; and when they were fully awake, they saw His glory and the two men who stood with Him.

a. **Peter and those with him were heavy with sleep**: This leads us to believe that perhaps the disciples saw and heard only a small part of this meeting of Jesus, Moses, and Elijah. It perhaps lasted much longer, and they discussed many more things.

i. "It is very probable that, on this occasion, he had been engaged in earnest prayer for several hours before the transfiguration came, and it is worthy of note that he was transfigured while he was praying. Every blessing comes to the great Head of the Church, and to all the members of his mystical body, through prayer." (Spurgeon)

b. **Heavy with sleep**: It's remarkable to think that one might be in the presence of tremendous glory, yet still be **heavy with sleep**. By analogy, we note that *spiritual sleep* keeps many from seeing or experiencing the glory of God.

c. **When they were fully awake, they saw His glory**: The glory was present all the time, yet they only **saw** it when they awakened. Awake, they

saw His glory—not even mentioning the glory of either Moses or Elijah. Compared to the glory of Jesus, it was as if they weren't even there.

d. **The two men who stood with Him**: In the mental conception many have of this event, they imagine Jesus floating in the air with Moses and Elijah. Instead, the text clearly says that they **stood** together.

4. (33-34) Peter's unwise offer to build three tabernacles.

Then it happened, as they were parting from Him, *that* **Peter said to Jesus, "Master, it is good for us to be here; and let us make three tabernacles: one for You, one for Moses, and one for Elijah"; not knowing what he said. While he was saying this, a cloud came and overshadowed them; and they were fearful as they entered the cloud.**

a. **Master, it is good for us to be here; and let us make three tabernacles**: Like many since, Peter made trouble for himself when he spoke, **not knowing what he said**.

i. **As they were parting from Him** makes it clear that Peter said what he said when Moses and Elijah *began* to leave. Peter didn't want the scene of glory to stop.

ii. Perhaps his thinking went something like this: *This is how it should be! Forget this idea of suffering, being rejected, and crucified; let's build some tabernacles so we can live this way with the glorified Jesus all the time.* Peter's suggestion meant that not only would Jesus avoid the future cross, *but so also would Peter.*

iii. Also, in suggesting **three tabernacles**, Peter made the mistake of putting Jesus on an equal level with Moses and Elijah, with one tabernacle for each of them.

b. **While he was saying this, a cloud came and overshadowed them**: As Peter said this, they were **overshadowed** with the cloud of God's glory called in the Old Testament *the Shekinah.*

i. This is the same idea of *overshadow* in Luke 1:35, when the glory of God came upon Mary and she received the child Jesus.

c. **They were fearful as they entered the cloud**: Peter and the apostles at first felt **it is good for us to be here**, but as the glory intensified, it began to create in them the awe and dread that sinners feel in the presence of God.

i. Peter may not have known what he *said*, but he knew what he *saw*—the cloud of glory was real, and he was wide-awake when he and the apostles saw it.

ii. "We have not dreamt our religion, it has not come to us as a vision of the night; but when we were fully awake, we saw Christ's glory." (Spurgeon)

5. (35-36) The voice from the cloud of glory.

And a voice came out of the cloud, saying, "This is My beloved Son. Hear Him!" When the voice had ceased, Jesus was found alone. But they kept quiet, and told no one in those days any of the things they had seen.

a. **And a voice came out of the cloud, saying, "This is My beloved Son. Hear Him!"** The voice from the cloud of glory made it clear that Jesus was not on the same level as Moses and Elijah. He is the **beloved Son**—so **Hear Him!**

i. Moses and Elijah were great men, and each have an important place in God's unfolding plan of the ages. Yet compared to Jesus the Messiah, to God the Son, they were insignificant—so all the focus and attention should be focused upon Jesus. None of these noble servants can compare to the **beloved Son**, so **Hear Him!**

ii. Peter may not have known what he *said*, but he knew what he *heard* The voice from heaven was real, and he was wide-awake when he and the apostles heard it.

b. **When the voice had ceased, Jesus was found alone**: God made it *impossible* to focus on them any longer. Jesus deserved all the focus.

c. **But they kept quiet, and told no one in those days any of the things they had seen**: After it was all over, Peter, John and James **told no one**—after all, who would believe them?

i. They **told no one in those days**, but they couldn't keep quiet about it. Peter clearly remembered and referred to this event in 2 Peter 1:16-18. John probably referred to it in John 1:14. They remembered this powerful experience that showed Jesus in both His glory and singular role as Messiah, greater than even Moses and Elijah.

ii. As impressive as this experience was, *it in itself did not change the lives of the disciples* as much as being born again did. Being born again by the Spirit of God is the great miracle, the greatest display of the glory of God ever.

D. The glory of God in action.

1. (37-40) The request from the father of a demon-possessed boy.

Now it happened on the next day, when they had come down from the mountain, that a great multitude met Him. Suddenly a man from the multitude cried out, saying, "Teacher, I implore You, look on my son,

for he is my only child. And behold, a spirit seizes him, and he suddenly cries out; it convulses him so that he foams *at the mouth*, and it departs from him with great difficulty, bruising him. So I implored Your disciples to cast it out, but they could not."

a. **When they had come down from the mountain**: Immediately after the radiant glory of the transfiguration, Jesus and the disciples came down from the mountain and were met by demonic trouble and opposition.

i. "There the mountain; now the valley. There glorified saints; here the lunatic. There the King in His heavenly gory; here the representatives of baffled and beaten faith." (Morgan)

b. **Teacher, I implore You, look on my son**: The father felt (rightly so), that all Jesus had to do was **look on** his son, and the compassion of the Savior would lead Him to help the afflicted boy.

c. **A spirit seizes him, and he suddenly cries out; it convulses him so that he foams at the mouth, and it departs from him with great difficulty, bruising him**: The description fits what we would call an epileptic seizure. In this case, Jesus knew (and it was demonstrated) that a demonic force brought it on, not merely physiological causes.

d. **I implored Your disciples to cast it out, but they could not**: The disciples had previously had some success in casting out demons (Luke 9:1). It may be that this was a stronger or more stubborn case of demonic possession.

i. There are ranks of demonic powers (Ephesians 6:12), and evidently, some demons are stronger (more stubborn, resistant) than others. In Matthew 17:21, Jesus said that their failure was due to a lack of prayer and fasting. It isn't that prayer and fasting make us more worthy to cast out demons. The idea is that prayer and fasting draw us closer to the heart of God, and put us more in line with His power.

ii. Their failure was in fact good for them. Their failure taught them.

- It taught them not to get into a rut of mechanical ministry
- It taught them the great superiority of Jesus
- It taught them to wish for the presence of Jesus
- It taught them to come to Jesus with the problem

iii. "They were confounded at their want of success-but not at their want of faith, which was the cause of their miscarriage!" (Clarke)

2. (41-42) Jesus casts out a demon that His disciples were unable to cast out.

Then Jesus answered and said, "O faithless and perverse generation, how long shall I be with you and bear with you? Bring your son here."

And as he was still coming, the demon threw him down and convulsed *him.* **Then Jesus rebuked the unclean spirit, healed the child, and gave him back to his father.**

a. **O faithless and perverse generation, how long shall I be with you and bear with you?** There is a sense that Jesus was frustrated with His disciples. His season of ministry before the cross was coming to an end, and perhaps He felt frustration that the disciples did not have more faith.

b. **As he was still coming, the demon threw him down and convulsed him**: Even when the father brought the boy to Jesus, at first he did not seem to get better, but the problems showed themselves as bad as ever. This was the last, desperate effort of the possessing demon to hold on to the boy and cast the father, the disciples, and all into despair.

i. **The demon threw him down**: "As he was coming to Jesus, the demon *dashed him down.* It is the word used of a boxer dealing a knock-out blow to his opponent or of a wrestler throwing someone." (Barclay)

ii. In a sermon titled *The Devil's Last Throw,* Spurgeon considered how the devil often strikes hard against a person just as they begin to come to the Savior. "I have seen men, just when they were beginning to hear and beginning to think, taken on a sudden with such violence of sin, and so fearfully carried away by it, that if I had not seen the same thing before I should have despaired of them."

iii. Spurgeon considered some of the lies that Satan uses to throw men down just as they are coming to Jesus:

- "You're not elect"
- "You're too big of a sinner"
- "It's too late"
- "There's no use in trying—give it up"
- "This won't work for you"

c. **Jesus rebuked the unclean spirit, healed the child**: Not intimidated by this last display of demonic power, Jesus delivered the demon-possessed boy instantly. What was too hard for the disciples was not too hard for Jesus.

3. (43-45) Jesus reminds His disciples about His mission.

And they were all amazed at the majesty of God. But while everyone marveled at all the things which Jesus did, He said to His disciples, "Let these words sink down into your ears, for the Son of Man is about to be betrayed into the hands of men." But they did not understand

this saying, and it was hidden from them so that they did not perceive it; and they were afraid to ask Him about this saying.

a. **And they were all amazed at the majesty of God**: Jesus had just revealed His glory in two spectacular ways—the transfiguration and the casting out of a difficult demon. Yet, He reminded His disciples that His mission had not changed; He still had come to die on the cross for our sins, and **the Son of Man is about to be betrayed into the hands of men.**

i. **Let these words sink down into your ears**: "To *other* words, you may lend *occasional* attention-but to what concerns my *sufferings* and *death* you must *ever* listen. Let them *constantly* occupy a place in your most serious meditations and reflections." (Clarke)

b. **But they did not understand this saying**: Though they were frequent, the disciples forgot these reminders about Jesus' suffering and resurrection until after His resurrection (Luke 24:6-8).

i. **They did not understand**: "So besotted they were with that carnal conceit of an earthly kingdom." (Trapp)

E. The unusual character of greatness in the Kingdom of God.

1. (46-48) True greatness shows itself in being like a child, and in being the least, not in the popular conceptions of greatness.

Then a dispute arose among them as to which of them would be greatest. And Jesus, perceiving the thought of their heart, took a little child and set him by Him, and said to them, "Whoever receives this little child in My name receives Me; and whoever receives Me receives Him who sent Me. For he who is least among you all will be great."

a. **As to which of them would be greatest**: The disciples were often concerned about the question of greatness. They seem to ask this question thinking that Jesus has already chosen one of them as **greatest**, or as if they wanted Jesus to decide among them.

i. "Long ago the Venerable Bede suggested that this particular quarrel arose because Jesus had taken Peter, John, and James up into the mountain top with him and the others were jealous." (Barclay)

ii. We can imagine the disciples arguing among themselves about which one was the greatest (as they did later again in Luke 22:46 and other places), and then saying, "Let's let Jesus settle this."

iii. They probably thought in terms of position and advancement in the glorious administration of Messiah the King. "He spoke of his abasement, they thought of their own advancement; and that '*at the same time*'." (Spurgeon)

b. **And Jesus, perceiving the thought of their heart, took a little child and set him by Him**: Jesus might have answered the question, "Who is the greatest?" by pointing to Himself. Instead, Jesus drew their attention to His *nature* by having them look at a **little child** as an example.

i. Jesus overheard their conversation, but more importantly He understood **the thoughts of their heart** behind the conversation. He understood their motives and impulses.

ii. The **little child** was the model of greatness. By this act, Jesus said to the disciples, "If you want to be great, learn something from this little child." Especially in that culture, children were of little importance, were not threatening, unconcerned for social status, and not jaded by success and ambition. When we most fulfill the humble place a child had in that culture, we are then on our way to greatness. No one should think that a **little child** shows us *everything* about greatness and the kingdom, but certainly some things, and important things at that.

iii. "The principle being established by Jesus was that in the kingdom of God there is a reversal of values involved. The last will be first; the least will be the greatest." (Pate)

iv. Jesus pointed to a **little child**, and did not point to Peter. If Peter really was to be regarded as the first pope in the way Popes are regarded by Roman Catholic theology and history, Jesus should have declared that *Peter* was **the greatest** among them.

c. **Whoever receives this little child in My name receives Me; and whoever receives Me receives Him who sent Me**: Jesus said that the child was a representation or reflection of *Himself*, and that Jesus is a reflection of His Father in heaven. Using the child as an example, Jesus indirectly pointed to *Himself* as the greatest in the kingdom.

i. We know that one Man was actually the **greatest** among them and among all—Jesus Christ. This means that Jesus Himself was humble like a little child. He wasn't concerned about His own status. He didn't have to be the center of attention. He could not deceive, and He didn't have an intimidating presence.

ii. Since the nature of Jesus is like one of these little children, how we treat those who are humble like children (**whoever receives this child in My name receives Me**) shows what we think of the nature of Jesus.

iii. "There is a tradition that the child grew to be Ignatius of Antioch, who in later days became a great servant of the Church, a great writer, and finally a martyr for Christ." (Barclay) Clarke indicates that this tradition came from the Christian writer Nicephorus, who wrote that

Ignatius was killed by Trajan in AD 107. Yet Clarke also wrote of Nicephorus, that he "is not much to be depended on, being both weak and credulous."

iv. We can contrast what the devil does with children (Luke 9:39) and what Jesus does with children.

d. **For he who is least among you all will be great**: Jesus then challenged His followers to be the **least**. The desire to be praised and to gain recognition should be foreign to a follower of Jesus. Jesus wants His followers to embrace **least** as a choice, allowing others to be preferred, and not because we are forced to be **least**.

i. It is easy to actually *despise* humble people. They are the losers; the kind who will never make it in our competitive and aggressive and get-ahead world. Yet when we despise humble people, we actually despise Jesus.

ii. This aspect of humility and giving preference to others in the Christian faith has been often derided and despised. Nietzsche and others glorified the *will to power* and looked down on Jesus and His followers as weak and worthy of disregard. Yet Nietzsche is gone and largely discredited; Jesus and His followers live and transform lives and cultures through the power exemplified (in some ways) by a child.

2. (49-50) True greatness isn't cliquish.

Now John answered and said, "Master, we saw someone casting out demons in Your name, and we forbade him because he does not follow with us." But Jesus said to him, "Do not forbid *him*, for he who is not against us is on our side."

a. **Master, we saw someone casting out demons in Your name, and we forbade him because he does not follow with us**: This must have been frustrating to the disciples, because it showed that other followers of Jesus were able to cast out demons when they sometimes were not able (Luke 9:40). No wonder John wanted them to stop!

b. **Do not forbid him, for he who is not against us is on our side**: Jesus taught them to have a more generous spirit. There are many that are wrong in some aspect of their presentation or teaching, yet they still set forth Jesus in some manner. Let God deal with them. Those who are not against a Biblical Jesus are still **on our side**, at least in some way.

i. Paul saw many men preaching Christ from many motives, some of them evil motives—yet he could rejoice that Christ was being preached (Philippians 1:15-18).

3. (51-53) True greatness is marked by steadfast determination.

Now it came to pass, when the time had come for Him to be received up, that He steadfastly set His face to go to Jerusalem, and sent messengers before His face. And as they went, they entered a village of the Samaritans, to prepare for Him. But they did not receive Him, because His face was *set* for the journey to Jerusalem.

a. **When the time had come for Him to be received up**: This is the beginning of a new section of the Gospel of Luke. Jesus was on His way to Jerusalem **to be received up**.

- He would be **received up** to the higher-elevation city of Jerusalem
- He would be **received up** on a cross
- He would be **received up** to heaven in a glorious Ascension

b. **He steadfastly set His face to go to Jerusalem**: Jesus undertook this final journey towards Jerusalem with steadfastness fitting the difficulty of the task ahead of Him.

    i. Isaiah 50:7 speaks prophetically of the Messiah, the Great Servant: *For the Lord GOD will help Me; therefore I will not be disgraced; therefore I have set My face like a flint, and I know that I will not be ashamed.* This is Jesus, who **steadfastly set His face**, like a flint, as Isaiah wrote, going to Jerusalem to suffer and die.

    ii. Jesus hardened His face; not in the sense of becoming a hard or angry man, but in the sense of having *focus*, and having focus through a difficult time.

    iii. There are two kinds of courage—the courage of moment, which requires no previous thought; and a planned courage, which sees the difficulty ahead and **steadfastly** marches toward it. Jesus had this kind of courage; He saw the cross on the horizon, but still **steadfastly set His face to go to Jerusalem**.

    iv. Spurgeon had a wonderful sermon on Isaiah 50:7 text titled, *The Redeemer's Face Set like a Flint.* In it, he considered how severely the steadfast resolve of Jesus was tested.

- By offers from the world
- By the persuasions of His friends
- By the unworthiness of His clients
- By the ease at which He could have backed out if He had wished to
- By the taunts of those who mocked Him
- By the full stress and agony of the cross

v. **Sent messengers before His face**: "*Angels*, literally; but this proves that the word *angel* signifies a messenger of any kind, whether Divine or human. The messengers in this case were probably *James* and *John*." (Clarke)

c. **They entered a village of the Samaritans, to prepare for Him. But they did not receive Him**: Because Jesus went to Jerusalem, these particular Samaritans did not welcome Jesus. They didn't have good relations with the Jews, and were prejudiced against them. We may also see this as the opposition (knowingly or not) that comes the way of all who set their face steadfastly to do God's will.

i. "The origin of the Samaritan people seem to have been the inter-marrying of Jews from the Northern Kingdom with imported non-Jewish colonists after the conquest of 722 b.c. (2 Kings 17:24). These mixed Jews-Gentiles developed their own translation of the Penta-teuch (Samaritan Pentateuch), built their own temple of worship on Mt. Gerazim (see John 4:20), which was later destroyed by John Hyr-canus (128 b.c.), and celebrated their own Passover." (Pate)

ii. "For Jesus to take that way to Jerusalem was unusual; and to at-tempt to find hospitality in a Samaritan village was still more un-usual." (Barclay)

4. (54-56) True greatness is marked by mercy, not judgment

And when His disciples James and John saw *this*, they said, "Lord, do You want us to command fire to come down from heaven and consume them, just as Elijah did?" But He turned and rebuked them, and said, "You do not know what manner of spirit you are of. For the Son of Man did not come to destroy men's lives but to save *them.*" And they went to another village.

a. **Lord, do You want us to command fire to come down from heaven and consume them, just as Elijah did?** James and John, outraged by the poor reception Jesus received among the Samaritans, offered to destroy the city in spectacular judgment for Jesus' sake.

i. It's interesting and perhaps amusing that James and John were so confident that they could do this, especially after their recent failure with the demon-possessed boy. Their angry reaction shows why Jesus sometimes called them *Boanerges*, meaning *Sons of Thunder* (Mark 3:17).

ii. "It were to be wished that we would first consult with Christ in his word, ere we stir hand or foot to revenge." (Trapp)

b. **He turned and rebuked them**: Their offence—even on behalf of Jesus—was not appreciated. The determination of Jesus mentioned in the previous verses did not mean that He was tough or angry.

> i. They saw the flint-face of Jesus and thought it meant *mean* or *tough*. They didn't understand that it meant *focus* and being more focused on *love* than ever before. That flint-like face will end up on the cross in the ultimate demonstration of love, not the ultimate demonstration of anger.

> ii. "I resolved to use every possible method of preventing...a narrowness of spirit, a party zeal...that miserable bigotry which makes many so unready to believe that there is any work of God but among ourselves." (Wesley, cited in Barclay)

c. **You do not know what manner of spirit you are of. For the Son of Man did not come to destroy men's lives but to save them**: Jesus explained their failing at this point came in two ways.

> i. *They didn't know themselves.* Perhaps they thought they were being like Jesus, or showing the character of God. They were mistaken, and did not represent God and His heart. *He loved the Samaritans and wanted them to repent and be saved.*

> ii. *They didn't know Jesus and His mission.* He came to save the lost, not to burn them up with fire from heaven.

> iii. Following Jesus means being merciful to others, instead of harsh with them. Especially, we should remember that God says *Vengeance is Mine, I will repay, says the Lord* (Romans 12:19). "The disciples of that Christ who died for his enemies should never think of *avenging* themselves on their persecutors." (Clarke)

5. (57-58) True greatness is shown in sacrifice.

Now it happened as they journeyed on the road, *that* someone said to Him, "Lord, I will follow You wherever You go." And Jesus said to him, "Foxes have holes and birds of the air *have* nests, but the Son of Man has nowhere to lay *His* head."

a. **Lord, I will follow You wherever You go**: With the miracles associated with the ministry of Jesus, following Him might have seemed more glamorous than it really was. Jesus perhaps received many spontaneous offers like this.

b. **Foxes have holes and birds of the air have nests, but the Son of Man has nowhere to lay His head**: Jesus didn't tell the man "No, you can't follow Me." But He told him the truth, without painting a glamorized version of what it was like to follow Him. This is the *opposite* of techniques used by many evangelists today, but Jesus wanted the man to know what it would really be like.

    i. "In the immediate context of Jesus' ministry, the saying does not mean that Jesus was penniless but homeless; the nature of his mission kept him on the move and would keep his followers on the move." (Carson)

    ii. The reason this man turned away from Jesus was because Jesus lived a very simple life by faith, trusting His Father for every need and without reserves of material resources. *This is just the kind of thing that would make Jesus more attractive to a truly spiritual man.* "Here is a man who lives completely by faith and is satisfied with few material things; I should follow Him and learn from Him."

    iii. "We have good evidence here that he knew how to shut the door as well as to open it. He knew as well how to warn the pretentious as to accept the penitent." (Spurgeon)

6. (59-60) True greatness means that we give Jesus the top priority in our lives.

Then He said to another, "Follow Me." But he said, "Lord, let me first go and bury my father." Jesus said to him, "Let the dead bury their own dead, but you go and preach the kingdom of God."

    a. **He said to another, "Follow Me"**: The man described in Luke 9:57-58 offered to follow Jesus. In contrast, Jesus asked this man to **follow** Him.

    b. **Lord, let me first go and bury my father**: Actually, this man did not ask for permission to dig a grave for his deceased father. He wanted to remain in his father's house and care for him until the father died. This was obviously an indefinite period, which could drag on and on.

    i. "He was not torn between the right and wrong. He was torn between the right and right. He hesitated between two rival claims, both of them stamped with the seal of the divine." (Morrison)

    ii. The man wanted to follow Jesus, *but not just yet*. He knew it was good and that he should do it, but he felt there was a good reason why he could not do it *now*. The previous man was too quick to follow Jesus; this man was too slow.

    c. **Let the dead bury their own dead, but you go and preach the kingdom of God**: Jesus pressed the man to follow Him *now*, and clearly stated the principle that family obligations, or any other obligation, must not be put ahead of following Jesus. Jesus must come first.

    i. Jesus was not afraid to discourage potential disciples. Unlike many modern evangelists, He was interested more in *quality* than in *quan-*

tity. In addition, Jesus was merely being *honest*. This is what it meant to follow Him, and He wanted people to know it at the beginning.

7. (61-62) True greatness means that we follow Jesus wholeheartedly, without delay.

And another also said, "Lord, I will follow You, but let me first go *and* bid them farewell who are at my house." But Jesus said to him, "No one, having put his hand to the plow, and looking back, is fit for the kingdom of God."

a. **Lord, I will follow You, but let me first go and bid them farewell who are at my house**: The previous man offered to follow Jesus after an indefinite, perhaps long delay. This man offered to follow Jesus after a relatively short delay.

i. "O young man, when you are thinking of leaving the world, be afraid of these farewells! They have been the ruin of hundreds of hopeful people. They have been almost persuaded; but they have gone to their old companions just to give them the last kiss, and the last shake of the hand, and we have not seen anything more of them." (Spurgeon)

b. **No one, having put his hand to the plow, and looking back, is fit for the kingdom of God**: Jesus stressed to this man the commitment necessary to follow Him. One must have a similar determination as a farmer plowing a field, who must do it with all his strength and always looking forward.

i. In plowing a field in that day, a farmer kept the rows straight by focusing on an object in front and in the distance (such as a tree). If the farmer started to plow and kept looking behind, he would never make straight rows and do a good job plowing. In following Jesus, we are to keep our eyes on Jesus, and never take our eyes off Him. "No ploughman ever ploughed a straight furrow looking back over his shoulder." (Barclay)

ii. Plowmen also do something else of great importance: *they hold on*. A plowman who lets go is no plowman at all. "Ploughmen are not usually learned persons, nor are they often poets in disguise. But there is one virtue they possess pre-eminently, and that is the virtue of quietly holding to it." (Morrison)

ii. More than anyone else, Jesus lived this; He *steadfastly set His face to go to Jerusalem* (Luke 9:51).

Luke 10—The Sending of the Seventy

A. Instructing the seventy disciples at their departure.

1. (1-3) Seventy disciples are appointed and sent out.

After these things the Lord appointed seventy others also, and sent them two by two before His face into every city and place where He Himself was about to go. Then He said to them, "The harvest truly *is* great, but the laborers *are* few; therefore pray the Lord of the harvest to send out laborers into His harvest. Go your way; behold, I send you out as lambs among wolves."

a. **After these things the Lord appointed seventy others also**: Jesus knew that the time was short before His crucifixion, and that there were still many villages that had not yet heard His message. Jesus turned to this larger group of His disciples to be His messengers, to prepare these places ahead of Him (**where He Himself was about to go**).

i. This reminds us that there was a larger group of interested followers of Jesus beyond the twelve He chose as disciples and apostles. From among this larger group Jesus **appointed seventy others** to do His work. There are a few reasons why He chose **seventy**.

- Perhaps seventy was simply the wise number that made the most effective use of the people at hand

- Perhaps seventy suggested a connection with the seventy elders who went up with Moses on Sinai and saw the glory of God (Exodus 24:1, 9)

- Perhaps seventy suggested a connection with the seventy members of the Sanhedrin, and Jesus showed He was establishing a new order, a new leadership

- Perhaps seventy suggested a connection with the seventy translators of the Hebrew Bible into Greek, the *Septuagint*, that these were the ones to "translate" His word into everyday life

ii. "Better to be one of the unnamed seventy, who did their work and were very happy in it, and whose names are only known to God. Better: perhaps *safer* too. There was a Judas in the twelve: we never read of one among the seventy." (Morrison)

iii. **Sent them two by two**: "These Christ sent by *two* and *two*: 1. To teach them the necessity of *concord* among the ministers of righteousness. 2. That in the mouths of two witnesses every thing might be established. And, 3. That they might comfort and support each other in their difficult labour." (Clarke)

iv. **Where He Himself was about to go**: "What a mercy it is when the preacher knows that his Master is coming after him, when he can hear the sound of his Master's feet behind him! What courage it gives him! He knows that, though it is very little that he can do, is be the thin end of the wedge preparing the way for One who can do everything." (Spurgeon)

b. **The harvest truly is great**: Using the analogy of a ripe field of grain, Jesus explained *why* He felt an increased urgency about His work. He considered the multitude of humanity to be like a harvest field ready for gathering. He thought of the greatness of human need, and saw it as an *opportunity*.

i. Using the picture suggested by Jesus, we can say that the *field itself* is large, and the *ready harvest* is also large. This wasn't the only time Jesus said this; some time before and at a different place Jesus said basically the same thing (Matthew 9:37-38). Perhaps this was almost a proverbial statement of Jesus, something He observed and said often.

ii. This is *still* true. If we believe that it is but a short time until Jesus comes back, we should make the principles of Jesus' commission to the seventy our own.

iii. "Can you picture the distress of a farmer when he sees his fields golden with harvest, and there are no servants to gather that harvest in? It was such an agony that filled the heart of Jesus as He looked out on *His* harvest field." (Morrison)

c. **The laborers are few**: This means not only that there must be more workers, but also that those engaged in the work must have appropriate focus on their work. When there is a lot of work and few workers, one must be busy about the work.

i. This is a harvest that needs **laborers**. The good of a harvest can go to waste if there are no **laborers** to take advantage of the bounty. Jesus warned us that opportunities to meet human need and bring people into His kingdom may wasted because of a shortage of **laborers**.

d. **Therefore pray the Lord of the harvest**: Jesus commanded them to **pray**; the work before them was great and could not be accomplished without much prayer. Specifically, they were to ask **the Lord of the harvest to send out laborers into His harvest**. This speaks powerfully to:

- The need for prayer in the work of evangelism (**therefore pray**)
- The maker of the harvest (**the Lord of the harvest**)
- The need for workers in the work of evangelism (**laborers**)
- The calling of God for the work of the harvest (**to send out**)
- The nature of harvest participation, *work* (**laborers**)
- The need to recognize Whom the harvest belongs to (**His harvest**)

i. We are to pray that the Lord would **send out laborers**: "Now the Greek is much more forcible, it is that he would push them forward, and thrust them out; it is the same word which is used for the expulsion of a devil from a man possessed. It takes great power to drive a devil out, it will need equal power from God to drive a minister out to his work." (Spurgeon)

e. **Go your way**: Jesus commanded them to **go**, because God would use them to answer their own prayers. Praying, "Lord, send out workers to Your harvest" is just the kind of prayer that builds a harvest-interest within the one who prays.

f. **I send you out as lambs among wolves**: Jesus commanded them to go with a certain kind of heart, trusting God and not seeking to abuse and manipulate others. Going **as lambs among wolves** doesn't sound very attractive; yet, it was exactly how Jesus was sent, and how the power of God worked through Him mightily.

i. "After all, the mission of sheep to wolves is a hopeful one, since we see in the natural world that the sheep, though so feeble, by far outnumber the wolves who are so fierce. The day will come when persecutors will be as scarce as wolves, and saints as numerous as sheep." (Spurgeon)

2. (4-8) Specific guidelines for their ministry.

"Carry neither money bag, knapsack, nor sandals; and greet no one along the road. But whatever house you enter, first say, 'Peace to this house.' And if a son of peace is there, your peace will rest on it; if not, it will return to you. And remain in the same house, eating and drinking such things as they give, for the laborer is worthy of his wages. Do not go from house to house. Whatever city you enter, and they receive you, eat such things as are set before you."

a. **Carry neither money bag, sack, nor sandals**: First Jesus told them to pray; then He told them to go; then He told them *how* to go. Jesus gave the seventy specific instructions that were to display a particular attitude for their work in representing Jesus and His message.

- They were not to be distracted either by material concerns (**Carry neither money bag, sack, nor sandals**)

- They were not to be distracted by tedious ceremonies of etiquette (**greet no one along the road**)

    i. "In the East greetings are so tedious, so full of flattery, so certain to lead on to wayside gossip, that men who are out on a work of life and death must run the risk of seeming unsocial sometimes." (Morrison)

b. **Whatever house you enter, first say, "Peace to this house"**: The customs of that time meant that they would likely stay in the home of hospitable people (inns, if available, were often houses of prostitution and unsuitable for godly messengers). They were instructed to bring a blessing of peace to each house, if the home would receive it.

    i. **If a son of peace is there**: "In the Jewish style, a man who has any *good* or *bad* quality is called *the son* of it...*Son of peace* in the text not only means a *peaceable, quiet* man, but one also of *good report* for his *uprightness* and *benevolence*. It would have been a dishonour to this mission, had the missionaries taken up their lodgings with those who had not a good report among them who were without." (Clarke)

c. **And remain in the same house, eating and drinking such things as they give**: They were to trust that God would provide for them through the generosity of others, and they were to thankfully receive what was offered to them, without begging from **house to house**.

d. **For the laborer is worthy of his wages**: Jesus told His disciples to not regard the support given to them as charity, but as proper payment for their work on behalf of God's kingdom.

3. (9) What Jesus wanted the seventy to do: to heal and to preach.

"And heal the sick there, and say to them, 'The kingdom of God has come near to you.'"

a. **And heal the sick**: The healing was important because it showed that though the Kingdom of God had come with power (as everyone expected it would), and the power was evident in acts of mercy and kindness (which was not expected).

b. **Say to them, "The kingdom of God has come near to you"**: This meant that the healing was a part of their preaching. As part of healing the sick, they described what the kingdom of God was about from what Jesus had taught and shown them.

i. **Come near to you**: According to Pate, this ancient Greek word *engiken* can mean "arrived" in the sense of already present, or it can mean "drawn near" in the sense of about to appear. It may be that the remarkable display of God's power in the work of the seventy was meant to prepare people for the ultimate revelation of God's power and kingdom in the soon death and resurrection of Jesus.

4. (10-16) What would happen to those who would reject the message of the seventy.

"But whatever city you enter, and they do not receive you, go out into its streets and say, 'The very dust of your city which clings to us we wipe off against you. Nevertheless know this, that the kingdom of God has come near you.' But I say to you that it will be more tolerable in that Day for Sodom than for that city. Woe to you, Chorazin! Woe to you, Bethsaida! For if the mighty works which were done in you had been done in Tyre and Sidon, they would have repented long ago, sitting in sackcloth and ashes. But it will be more tolerable for Tyre and Sidon at the judgment than for you. And you, Capernaum, who are exalted to heaven, will be brought down to Hades. He who hears you hears Me, he who rejects you rejects Me, and he who rejects Me rejects Him who sent Me."

a. **The very dust of your city which clings to us we wipe off against you**: Jesus told His disciples to publicly say this in the streets of any city that rejected the seventy messengers and their message. It was important that those cities knew the *price* of rejecting Jesus and His kingdom.

b. **Nevertheless know this, that the kingdom of God has come near you**: Their message and the evidence of the kingdom's power was to be clear enough that they could say this publicly to a city that rejected them.

i. A sad commentary on much work that is done among Christian people today is that they could not credibly say to those who might reject them and their message, "**Nevertheless know this, that the kingdom of God has come near you.**"

c. **It will be more tolerable in that Day for Sodom than for that city**: The cities of **Sodom** and **Tyre and Sidon** were notoriously sinful. Jesus said that the cities that rejected His message were in more trouble before God than these, because they saw a greater work of God than any of those sinful cities did; yet they still rejected Him.

i. The more we hear God's truth and the more we see Him move, the more we are accountable for. Since the people of **Chorazin** and **Beth-**

saida and **Capernaum** had received such convincing signs, they were held to greater account for what they had seen.

ii. **They would have repented long ago, sitting in sackcloth and ashes**: The cities of **Chorazin** and **Bethsaida** and **Capernaum** received much but repented little. It is a great mystery why some receive so many chances and such clear help, yet refuse to repent.

iii. **Capernaum** especially was **exalted to heaven**, because it was the adopted home of Jesus during the days of His Galilean ministry, hearing much of His teaching to seeing many of His miracles.

iv. Jesus said that it would be **more tolerable** for some in the day of judgment than for others. This leads us to believe that on that day, some will receive worse judgment than others. No one will have it good in hell, but some will have it worse than others.

v. The Bible never specifically mentions Jesus' miracles in **Chorazin**. This is an indication that the Gospels give us sketches of Jesus' life, not full biographies. The Apostle John admitted this, saying it would be impossible to recount everything Jesus did (John 21:25).

d. He who hears you hears Me, he who rejects you rejects Me, and he who rejects Me rejects Him who sent Me: As He sent His seventy disciples with the anticipation that some would reject them, Jesus also encouraged them with the thought that they were *His* representatives, and should not take their rejection (or acceptance) too personally. If others rejected the messengers, they rejected Jesus, and also rejected His Father (**Him who sent Me**).

i. It is helpful for all servants of God not to hold either praise or rejection too tightly. If they truly represent their Master, the success or rejection of their work is due more to Him than to them. Their greatest concern should not be with success or rejection, but with properly representing Jesus, their Master.

B. Joy at the return of the seventy.

1. (17-20) The joy of the seventy and Jesus' warning.

Then the seventy returned with joy, saying, "Lord, even the demons are subject to us in Your name." And He said to them, "I saw Satan fall like lightning from heaven. Behold, I give you the authority to trample on serpents and scorpions, and over all the power of the enemy, and nothing shall by any means hurt you. Nevertheless do not rejoice in this, that the spirits are subject to you, but rather rejoice because your names are written in heaven."

a. **The seventy returned with joy**: This was a good day. The disciples and followers of Jesus endured their share of confusion and hardship, but they also enjoyed some wonderful blessings of effective service.

i. All **seventy** returned. "Not one of the lambs had been eaten by the wolves." (Spurgeon)

b. **Even the demons are subject to us in Your name**: A careful look at the instructions Jesus gave these seventy (Luke 10:9) shows that Jesus had not originally commissioned them to cast out demons (as He did the twelve disciples in Luke 9:1-2). Therefore, we might regard this as an unexpected blessing of their ministry.

i. These seventy disciples learned that when we boldly do what Jesus tells us to do, we can anticipate that He will bless us in ways beyond our expectation.

ii. **In Your name** shows they didn't take the credit to themselves. They knew it was the power and authority of Jesus. "Be sure to rely, not on numbers or organization, but on the name of Jesus, used not as a charm, but as representing his living and ascended might." (Meyer)

c. **I saw Satan fall like lightning from heaven**: The success of these commissioned disciples, especially their authority over demonic spirits, caused Jesus to speak of the **fall** of Satan, when he fell as quick and dramatic as **lightning from heaven**.

i. The Bible actually mentions four falls of Satan:

- From glorified to profane (Ezekiel 28:14-16)
- From having access to heaven (Job 1:12, 1 Kings 22:21, Zechariah 3:1) to restriction to the earth (Revelation 12:9)
- From the earth to bondage in the bottomless pit for 1,000 years (Revelation 20:1-3)
- From the pit to the lake of fire (Revelation 20:10)

ii. Here Jesus spoke of Satan's first fall, from glorified to profane. **Fall like lightning from heaven** doesn't mean that Satan fell *from* heaven, but that his fall was as dramatic and sudden as a bolt of **lightning from heaven**. According to Job 1:12, 1 Kings 22:21, and Zechariah 3:1, Satan still has access to heaven. Yet the success of the disciples against demonic spirits was confirmation that Satan had fallen from his place of authority and power, and though was still powerful, was in an inferior place.

iii. Satan's **fall** was God's immediate judgment upon that rebellious spirit (though not complete judgment, which still awaits). Every time the kingdom of Jesus is presented in truth and power, it is like another judgment upon Satan and all who share his rebellious spirit. "So, where the gospel is preached with divine power, Satan comes down from his throne, in human hearts and human minds, as rapidly as the lightning-flash falls from heaven; and when we see his kingdom shaken, then, like Jesus, we rejoice in spirit." (Spurgeon)

iv. In remembering the fall of Satan, Jesus also warned them against pride. After all, if Satan could **fall like lightning** from his place of high spiritual status and privilege, so could they. "In the most holy work there always lurks this danger of the glorification of the self-life." (Morgan)

d. **Behold, I give you the authority**: Because Satan was fallen and the disciples were messengers of Jesus and His kingdom, they enjoyed the superior power of God over Satan.

i. "If you dare to live in the risen Christ, you share His empire and all the fruits of His victory over Satan." (Meyer)

e. **Nevertheless do not rejoice in this, that the spirits are subject to you**: Jesus warned them to rejoice in what God had done for them (**because your names are written in heaven**), more than in what they had done for God (**that the spirits are subject to you**).

i. It wasn't wrong for them to rejoice in the success of their service but they must have a greater joy in a greater miracle, the promise of their own salvation. "He did not mean in the present instance to censure their joy in their success, but only to make it subordinate to another rejoicing, and to prevent its growing to excess." (Spurgeon)

ii. Some people get emotionally intoxicated after successful service or the display of spiritual power. After God uses them in some way, they are arrogantly impressed with all *they did* for God. God wants us to always see that what He did for us always is far greater than what we could ever do for Him. It's good for us to be moderate in the joy we have over our *talents*, our *gifts*, and our *success*.

iii. **Your names are written in heaven**: "That you are enrolled burgesses of the new Jerusalem. Paul by his privilege of being a Roman escaped whipping; we by this escape damnation." (Trapp)

iv. *All* God's people share in this joy. By earth's estimation some service is more successful than others, but this joy unites all believers.

2. (21-22) The joy of Jesus as He sees the work of God in His people.

In that hour Jesus rejoiced in the Spirit and said, "I thank You, Father, Lord of heaven and earth, that You have hidden these things from *the* wise and prudent and revealed them to babes. Even so, Father, for so

it seemed good in Your sight. All things have been delivered to Me by My Father, and no one knows who the Son is except the Father, and who the Father is except the Son, and *the one* to whom the Son wills to reveal *Him.*"

a. **In that hour Jesus rejoiced in the Spirit**: Jesus was genuinely excited. Literally, the ancient Greek says He was *thrilled with joy*. This singular specific example of Jesus rejoicing was over the work of His servants. God *delights* in using the weak and foolish things of this world to confound the wise (1 Corinthians 1:27-29).

i. This is the only occasion in the gospels where it is specifically said that Jesus rejoiced. It stands alone; yet we should not think that Jesus never rejoiced other times. "We do not hear that he laughed, though it is thrice recorded that he wept; and here for once, as quite unique, we find the inspired assurance that he rejoiced." (Spurgeon)

ii. Geldenhuys says that the ancient Greek word for **rejoiced** is "referring to exceptional rejoicing and exultation." Jesus rejoiced *strongly*, but He also rejoiced *deeply* (**in the Spirit**).

iii. "This Man of Sorrows was often very joyful, but never more than in His friends' success…Jesus *exults* when His nameless children prosper." (Morrison)

iv. One reason Jesus was so happy is because *every victory is important.* "There is no victory won anywhere by an lonely disciple, or handful of disciples, that does not react on the entire battlefield." (Meyer)

b. **I thank You, Father**: Jesus' joy made Him break out into prayer. He praised God the Father for His wisdom, for His plan, and for His own unique relationship with God the Father.

- Jesus thanked the Father, not praising His own work
- Jesus thanked the Father for His wise, sometimes unexpected plan
- Jesus thanked the Father for the fellow servants in His midst
- Jesus thanked the Father for the simplicity of His servants

i. Jesus spoke of His unity with the Father (**All things have been delivered to Me by My Father**).

ii. Jesus spoke of His special relationship with the Father (**no one knows who the Son is but the Father, and who the Father is but the Son**).

iii. Jesus spoke of how God allows us to have some part in that special relationship (**and the one to whom the Son wills to reveal Him**).

c. **That You have hidden these things from the wise and prudent and revealed them to babes**: Jesus rejoiced that *unlikely* people were taught of God and used by Him. The **babes** were the seventy, simple believers who received real wisdom from the revelation of God.

- He had to send the simple, because the wise of this world would never go out as lambs among wolves

- He had to send the simple, because they would not change the message

- He had to send the simple, because He wanted to reach the simple

- He had to send the simple, because they would do the work in His name

- He had to send the simple, because they would rejoice over the work

- He had to send the simple, because they would give the praise to Jesus

3. (23-24) Jesus tells the disciples of the unique blessing they have.

Then He turned to *His* disciples and said privately, "Blessed *are* the eyes which see the things you see; for I tell you that many prophets and kings have desired to see what you see, and have not seen *it*, and to hear what you hear, and have not heard *it*."

a. **Blessed are the eyes which see the things you see**: The disciples lived in a unique time, and it was good for them to realize that it was a special blessing for them to be part of the work of the Messiah.

i. "Jesus was the peak to which history had been climbing, the goal to which it had been marching, the dream which had ever haunted men of God." (Barclay)

ii. "There is a similar saying to this among the rabbins, in *Sohar. Genes.*, where it is said, 'Blessed is that generation which the earth shall bear, when the King Messiah cometh.'" (Clarke)

b. **Many prophets and kings have desired to see what you see, and have not seen it**: The great men of the Old Testament would have longed to see Jesus' ministry and to minister for Him. One may consider how King David would have loved to see Jesus do the things He did, and how Isaiah would have longed to hear what Jesus said.

i. Our own age has special privileges, and it is good to see the blessings of our current time.

ii. Considering the work of the seventy disciples as described in Luke 10 shows ways that we can go forth to serve Jesus and spread His message.

- *The harvest is great*: We do the work knowing how big the job is
- *The laborers are few*: We do the work knowing that we have a key job
- *Pray the Lord of the harvest*: We do the work with a lot of prayer
- *Go your way*: We are to actually go and do the work
- *Like lambs among wolves*: We do the work making ourselves vulnerable, letting God be our strength
- *Carry neither*: We do the work without reliance upon anything except the gospel and power of God
- *Greet no one*: We do the work not allowing social obligations to hinder our work
- *Whatever house you enter*: We do the work expecting that God will bring help and provision
- *Eating and drinking such things as they give*: We do the work not being hung up on minor points
- *Heal the sick*: We do the work looking to minister to the whole person with the power of God
- *Say to them, "The kingdom of God has come near to you"*: We do the work preaching that the King and His kingdom are here
- *But whatever city you enter, and they do not receive you, go out into its streets*: As we do the work, we don't waste our time on those who reject the gospel
- *He who hears you hears Me, he who rejects you rejects Me*: We do the work remembering whom we represent
- *The seventy returned with joy*: We do the work expecting God to do more than we expect
- *Jesus rejoiced in the Spirit*: We do the work knowing that Jesus has so much joy when we do His work

C. The story of the Good Samaritan.

1. (25-29) A lawyer asks a question.

And behold, a certain lawyer stood up and tested Him, saying, "Teacher, what shall I do to inherit eternal life?" He said to him, "What is written in the law? What is your reading *of it*?" So he answered and said, "'You shall love the LORD your God with all your heart, with all your soul, with all your strength, and with all your mind,' and 'your neighbor as yourself.'" And He said to him, "You have answered right-

ly; do this and you will live." But he, wanting to justify himself, said to Jesus, "And who is my neighbor?"

a. **A certain lawyer stood up and tested Him**: The **lawyer** (an expert in the Jewish Mosaic and rabbinical law) **tested** Jesus. The idea behind the ancient Greek word for **tested** isn't necessarily mean or evil. This may have been a sincere question from a sincere seeker.

b. **What shall I do to inherit eternal life?** The Biblical understanding of **eternal life** doesn't necessarily refer to *duration* of life, because every person is immortal, either in heaven or hell. It doesn't refer to a life that begins only when we die. **Eternal life** is a particular quality of life; a life that comes from God, and a life we can have *right now*.

c. **What is written in the law?** Jesus pointed the lawyer back to the commandments of God. If the question was "**What shall I do to inherit eternal life**," then the answer was simple: keep the **law** of God, and keep it perfectly.

> i. "The first part seemed mildly sarcastic, 'What does the Law say?' In other words, 'You are the lawyer who interprets the Law; you tell me what it says.'" (Pate)

d. **"You shall love the Lord your God with all your heart, with all your soul, with all your strength, and with all your mind," and "your neighbor as yourself"**: The lawyer was wise enough to know this was the essence of the law. Knowing the requirements of the law, now all he had to do was *live it*: **do this and you will live**.

> i. It is clear enough what it means to *love God* with all we are, though it is impossible to do completely. But there has been much confusion about what it means to love **your neighbor as yourself**. This doesn't mean that we must love ourselves before we can love anyone else; it means that in the same way we take care of ourselves and are concerned about our own interests, we should take care and have concern for the interests of others.

e. **But he, wanting to justify himself, said to Jesus, "And who is my neighbor?"** The lawyer measured himself against both commandments. He figured that he obeyed the first commandment well enough, but his keeping of the second commandment depended on how one defined "**neighbor**."

> i. His first and perhaps greatest mistake was in assuming that he had fulfilled the first commandment. When we really consider what the words mean, then who among us has loved God with **all your heart, with all your soul, with all your strength, and with all your mind**?

It is easy for us to be distracted in any one of these areas, even when we worship God; even more so in our daily living.

ii. His second mistake was in thinking that he could fulfill the commandment to love God with all he had and still possibly not fulfill the commandment to love his neighbor. *If someone says, "I love God," and hates his brother, he is a liar; for he who does not love his brother whom he has seen, how can he love God whom he has not seen? And this commandment we have from Him: that he who loves God must love his brother also.* (1 John 4:20-21)

iii. His third mistake was in the way that he wanted to narrowly define **neighbor**. If only our friends and those who are easy to love are our neighbors, then perhaps this man fulfilled it in an imperfect way. It all depends on how broad the definition is. The Jews in Jesus' day did believe that you had to love your **neighbor**; but it was also taught among them that it was a duty before God to *hate your enemy*. It all depends on who your **neighbor** is and who your enemy is.

2. (30-35) Jesus defines *neighbor* with an illustration.

Then Jesus answered and said: "A certain *man* went down from Jerusalem to Jericho, and fell among thieves, who stripped him of his clothing, wounded *him,* and departed, leaving *him* half dead. Now by chance a certain priest came down that road. And when he saw him, he passed by on the other side. Likewise a Levite, when he arrived at the place, came and looked, and passed by on the other side. But a certain Samaritan, as he journeyed, came where he was. And when he saw him, he had compassion. So he went to *him* and bandaged his wounds, pouring on oil and wine; and he set him on his own animal, brought him to an inn, and took care of him. On the next day, when he departed, he took out two denarii, gave *them* to the innkeeper, and said to him, 'Take care of him; and whatever more you spend, when I come again, I will repay you.'"

a. **A certain man went down from Jerusalem to Jericho, and fell among thieves**: The road from Jerusalem to Jericho was infamous for crime and robbery. It wasn't surprising to Jesus' listeners that He set the story on this particular road.

i. "That road was famous for its lurking dangers, especially robbers (see Josephus, *J. W.* 2.451-75)." (Pate)

ii. "He was an obviously reckless and foolhardy character. People seldom attempted the Jerusalem to Jericho road alone if they were carrying goods or valuables. Seeking safety in numbers, they travelled in convoys or caravans. This man had no one but himself to blame for the plight in which he found himself." (Barclay)

b. **Now by chance a certain priest came down that road**: The **priest** and the **Levite** (both categories of religious officials) saw their Jewish brother lying in his terrible condition, but neither of them did anything. They both **passed by on the other side**.

> i. "*Priest* and *Levite* are mentioned here, partly because they were the most frequent travellers on this road, and partly to show that these were the persons who, from the nature of their office, were most obliged to perform works of mercy; and from whom a person in distress had a right to expect immediate succour and comfort; and their inhuman conduct here was a flat breach of the law." (Clarke)

> ii. Think of all the excuses that they could have used:
> - "This road is too dangerous for me to stop and help the man"
> - "He might be a decoy for an ambush"
> - "I've got to get to the temple and perform my service for the Lord"
> - "I've got to get home and see my family"
> - "Someone really should help that man"
> - "If I'm going to serve at the temple, I can't get my clothes bloody"
> - "I don't know first aid"
> - "It's a hopeless case"
> - "I'm only one person; the job is too big"
> - "I can pray for him"
> - "He brought it on himself; he should have never been alone on such a dangerous road"
> - "He never asked for help"

> ii. But all of these are simply excuses. "I never knew a man refuse to help the poor who failed to give at least one admirable excuse." (Spurgeon)

c. **But a certain Samaritan, as he journeyed, came where he was. And when he saw him, he had compassion**: When Jesus' listeners heard about the priest and the Levite, they probably expected Jesus to say next that a common Jewish man came and helped. Then this story would be another way Jesus showed that the corruption of the religious leaders were in his day. But Jesus shocked them by saying that the man who helped was a **Samaritan**.

d. **A certain Samaritan**: Generally speaking, Jews and Samaritans despised each other, both racially and religiously. The culture gave the Samaritan plenty of reasons to hate this Jewish man and pass him by.

i. Some rabbis taught that a Jew was forbidden to help a Gentile woman who was in distress giving birth, because if they succeeded, all they did was to help one more Gentile come into the world. They often thought that Samaritans were *worse* than other Gentiles were.

e. **He had compassion. So he went to him and bandaged his wounds, pouring on oil and wine; and he set him on his own animal, brought him to an inn, and took care of him**: Instead of passing by, the Samaritan loved him sacrificially. He didn't wait to be asked; to see the need right in front of him was enough to make him do something. He also gave freely of both his time and his resources.

i. The **wine**, containing alcohol, had an antiseptic effect on the man's wounds. The **oil** helped to soothe the wounds, easing the pain. To **set him on his own animal** meant that the Samaritan himself walked.

ii. **He took out two denarii, gave them to the innkeeper**: It seems that **two denarii** would provide for the man's needs in the inn for at least two or three weeks.

iii. There are many ways that the Samaritan was like Jesus.

- The Samaritan was an outsider, despised by many
- The Samaritan came after others failed to meet the need
- The Samaritan came before it was too late
- The Samaritan came with everything necessary
- The Samaritan came right to the afflicted man
- The Samaritan gave tender care
- The Samaritan provided for future needs

3. (36-37) Jesus applies the parable.

"So which of these three do you think was neighbor to him who fell among the thieves?" And he said, "He who showed mercy on him." Then Jesus said to him, "Go and do likewise."

a. **Which of these three do you think was neighbor**: According to the thinking of the day, the priest and the Levite were **neighbor** to the man who had been beaten and robbed. But they didn't act like neighbors at all.

i. "We are arrested by the fact that He completely shifted the ground of the question, and by this reply said, in effect, that the question as to who is a neighbor was not so important as the question to whom he was a neighbor." (Morgan)

b. **He who showed mercy on him**: The lawyer knew who the true **neighbor** was, yet he could not bring himself to say the name "Samaritan." We might have expected him to be an enemy, but he was instead a neighbor **who showed mercy on him**.

i. Obviously, the lawyer knew that he could no longer justify himself. He did not have this kind of love, a love that went beyond what he wanted to think of as "neighbor."

c. **Go and do likewise**: Jesus allowed the parable to answer the lawyer's question and guide the application. I am to love my neighbor, and my neighbor is the one who others might consider my enemy. My neighbor is the one with a need right in front of me.

i. Spurgeon wrote that, "When we see innocent persons suffering as the result of the sin of others our pity should be excited." He then gave examples of situations that should provoke pity in the believer:

- Children sick and starving because of a drunken father
- Wives overworked and burdened because of lazy and cruel husbands
- Workers oppressed in wages and working conditions, just to survive
- Those afflicted from accidents and disease

ii. This doesn't mean running after every need that might present itself. After all, the Samaritan didn't establish a hospital for unfortunate travelers. But it does mean a concern for the ones plainly before us, in both social and spiritual needs. "The world would be a changed place if every Christian attended to the sorrows that are plain before him." (Maclaren)

iii. Many, even most, people don't have this kind of love for God or others. How then will they receive eternal life?

- First, by refusing to inherit eternal life by *doing*. Instead, believe on Jesus; trust God that Jesus paid the penalty you deserve for every time you have fallen short of loving God or loving others the way you should
- Then, having received *eternal life*—God's kind of life in you— God will give you the resources to love Him and other people in

a much better way. You can't do it apart from having His life in you

iv. "Let it never be forgotten that what the law demands of us the gospel really produces in us." (Spurgeon)

D. Mary and Martha.

1. (38-40) Martha's appeal to Jesus.

Now it happened as they went that He entered a certain village; and a certain woman named Martha welcomed Him into her house. And she had a sister called Mary, who also sat at Jesus' feet and heard His word. But Martha was distracted with much serving, and she approached Him and said, "Lord, do You not care that my sister has left me to serve alone? Therefore tell her to help me."

a. **A certain woman named Martha welcomed Him into her house**: Martha and Mary, along with their brother Lazarus, were two dear friends of Jesus who lived in Bethany. It's easy to imagine that Martha wanted everything perfect when Jesus came to visit.

i. "If this village was Bethany, where Martha and Mary lived, at less than two miles' distance from Jerusalem." (Clarke)

b. **Mary, who also sat at Jesus' feet and heard His word**: Martha didn't get the help she wanted from her sister Mary. It wasn't that Mary was lazy—she prepared as well as Martha—but Mary *also* sat at Jesus' feet.

i. "This was the posture of the Jewish scholars, while listening to the instructions of the rabbins. It is in this sense that St. Paul says he was *brought up at the FEET of Gamaliel*, Acts 22:3." (Clarke)

c. **Martha was distracted with much serving**: Martha did nothing wrong in working hard for Jesus, that was good. Her problem was that she became **distracted with much serving**. She was distracted from Jesus.

i. There are many people who become crabby and irritable in their service for the Lord like Martha was. It is easy to look at all we do and to criticize those who don't seem to do as much. But Martha's real problem wasn't Mary; it was Martha. She had become distracted and had taken her eyes off Jesus.

ii. Martha's frustration is typical of those who diligently serve with good intent, but forget to *also* sit at Jesus' feet. "The Martha spirit says, if the work is done, is not that all? The Mary spirit asks whether Jesus is well pleased or no? All must be done in his name and by his Spirit, or nothing is done." (Spurgeon)

2. (41-42) Jesus' reply to Martha.

And Jesus answered and said to her, "Martha, Martha, you are worried and troubled about many things. But one thing is needed, and Mary has chosen that good part, which will not be taken away from her."

a. **Martha, Martha**: We can almost sense the love in Jesus' voice as He said this. Martha did good, she wanted to serve Jesus, but she had not added the **one thing** [that] **is needed**. The Bible speaks of **one thing**.

> i. *One thing have I desired of the LORD, that I will seek: that I may dwell in the house of the LORD all the days of my life, to behold the beauty of the LORD, and to inquire in His temple.* (Psalm 27:4)

> ii. *When Jesus heard these things, he said to him, "You still lack one thing…come, follow Me."* (Luke 18:22)

> iii. *Brethren, I do not count myself to have apprehended; but one thing I do, forgetting those things which are behind and reaching forward to those things which are ahead, I press toward the goal for the prize of the upward call of God in Christ Jesus.* (Philippians 3:13-14)

> iv. "The one thing needful evidently is that which Mary chose — that good part which should not be taken away from her. Very clearly this was to sit at Jesus' feet, and hear his word." (Spurgeon)

> - To sit at the feet of Jesus implies readiness to accept and obey what Jesus teaches
> - To sit at the feet of Jesus implies submission to Jesus; rebellion is done with
> - To sit at the feet of Jesus implies faith in who Jesus is
> - To sit at the feet of Jesus implies discipleship
> - To sit at the feet of Jesus implies love

> v. "If we would be strong for service in the strength that prevents distraction and unrest, we must know what it is to find time amid all the duties of life to sit at His feet as disciples." (Morgan)

> vi. "The way to get the revival is to begin at the Master's feet; you must go there with Mary and afterwards you may work with Martha." (Spurgeon)

b. **Mary has chosen the good part, which will not be taken away from her**: Mary's **good part** was her simple devotion to Jesus, loving Him by listening to His word. This was Mary's chosen focus.

> i. "Imagine not that to sit at Jesus' feet is a very small, unmeaning thing. It means peace, for they who submit to Jesus find peace through his precious, blood. It means holiness, for those who learn

of Jesus learn no sin, but are instructed in things lovely and of good repute. It means strength, for they that sit with Jesus, and feed upon him, are girded with his, strength; the joy of the Lord is their strength. It means wisdom, for they that learn of the Son of God understand more than the ancients, because they keep his statutes. It means zeal, for the love of Christ fires hearts that live upon it, and they that are much with Jesus become like Jesus, so that the zeal of the Lord's house eats them up." (Spurgeon)

- People say we need revival; *we need to sit at the feet of Jesus and hear His word*

- People say we need unity; *we need to sit at the feet of Jesus and hear His word*

- People say we need to win arguments; *we need to sit at the feet of Jesus and hear His word*

- People way we need to reach the world; *we need to sit at the feet of Jesus and hear His word*

ii. One might say that this account from the life of Jesus shows us three types of those who say they follow Jesus Christ.

- There are people like Mary: Those who know how to serve and *also sit at Jesus' feet*

- There are people like Martha: Those who diligently, and with the best intention serve God, but without adding the *one thing*—a continued focus on Jesus—and it results in great frustration

- There are people who don't do either. They are not even in the house with Jesus, for they are too busy with their own pursuits

Luke 11—Jesus Teaches and Warns

A. Teaching on prayer.

1. (1) A request from the disciples: **Lord, teach us to pray**.

Now it came to pass, as He was praying in a certain place, when He ceased, *that* **one of His disciples said to Him, "Lord, teach us to pray, as John also taught his disciples."**

a. **As He was praying in a certain place**: Jesus prayed as was His custom, but a request came **when He ceased**—the disciples allowed Jesus to finish praying. They stood there and watched Him, drinking in the power of His prayer, until He was finished.

b. **Lord, teach us to pray**: There was something about watching Jesus pray that made them want to learn how to pray as Jesus prayed. There was something magnetic about the prayer life of Jesus, and the way He prayed showed something of His relationship with God the Father.

i. Just as the disciples, we need Jesus to teach us to pray. Prayer is so simple that the smallest child can pray, but it is so great that the mightiest man of God cannot be said to truly have mastered prayer.

ii. "It is on prayer that the promises wait for their fulfillment, the kingdom for its coming, the glory of God for its full revelation... Jesus never taught His disciples how to preach, only how to pray. He did not speak much of what was needed to preach well, but much of praying well. To know how to speak to God is more than knowing how to speak to man. Not power with men, but power with God is the first thing." (Murray)

c. **Lord, teach us to pray**: Most directly, their request was not to learn *how to* pray, but *to pray*. Our greatest difficulty is not with mastering a specific technique or approach in prayer (though that may be good and helpful); our greatest need is simply **to pray** and **to pray** more and more.

i. As the Apostle Paul would later write in Ephesians 6:18: *Praying always with all prayer and supplication in the Spirit, being watchful to this end with all perseverance and supplication for all the saints.*

ii. Apparently, John the Baptist had **taught his disciples** something of how to pray; the disciples wanted to learn more from their teacher.

2. (2-4) Pray after this pattern.

So He said to them, "When you pray, say: Our Father in heaven, hallowed be Your name. Your kingdom come. Your will be done on earth as *it is* in heaven. Give us day by day our daily bread. And forgive us our sins, for we also forgive everyone who is indebted to us. And do not lead us into temptation, but deliver us from the evil one."

a. **When you pray, say**: On a previous occasion Jesus taught this same basic prayer (Matthew 6:9-13). The fact that He repeats it here shows how important it is. The fact that He did not repeat it the exact same way as in Matthew shows that it is not to be used as a precise ritual or magic formula for prayer.

i. This prayer is notable for its simplicity and brevity; it is a marvel of powerful prayer put in simple terms. The Rabbis had sayings like: "Whoever is long in prayer is heard" and "Whenever the righteous make their prayer long, their prayer is heard." One famous Jewish prayer began: "Blessed, praised, and glorified, exalted, and honored, magnified and lauded be the name of the Holy One."

ii. When we try to impress God with our many words, we deny that God is a loving, yet holy Father. Instead, we should follow the counsel of Ecclesiastes 5:2: *God is in heaven, and you are on earth; therefore let your words be few.*

b. **Our Father in heaven**: The model prayer shows us to come to God as a **Father in heaven**. It rightly recognizes whom we pray to, coming with a privileged title that demonstrates a privileged relationship. It was very unusual for the Jews of that day to call God "**Father**" because it was considered too intimate.

i. "There is no evidence of anyone before Jesus using this term to address God." (Carson)

ii. It is true that God is the mighty sovereign of the universe, who created, governs, and will judge all things—but He is also to us a **Father**.

iii. He is our **Father**, but He is our **Father in heaven**. When we say "**in heaven**," we remember God's holiness and glory. He is **our Father**, but our Father **in heaven**. To say that God is in heaven says:

- He is a God of majesty and dominion: *O LORD God of our fathers, are You not God in heaven, and do You not rule over all the kingdoms of the nations, and in Your hand is there not power and might, so that no one is able to withstand You?* (2 Chronicles 20:6)

- He is a God of power and might: *But our God is in heaven; He does whatever He pleases* (Psalm 115:3)

- He sees everything: *The LORD's throne is in heaven; His eyes behold, His eyelids test the sons of men* (Psalm 11:4)

iv. This is a prayer focused on *community*; Jesus said "**Our Father**" and not "My Father." "The whole prayer is social. The singular pronoun is absent. Man enters the presence of the Father, and then prays as one of the great family." (Morgan)

c. **Hallowed be Your name**: **Hallowed** means *set apart*. It is to say that there is no one like God, He is completely unique—not just a super person or a better person. **Name** means that God's whole character, His whole person, is set apart.

i. "The *name* in antiquity stood for far more than it does with us. It summed up a person's whole character, all that was known or revealed about him." (Morris)

d. **Hallowed be Your name. Your kingdom come. Your will be done on earth as it is in heaven**: The model prayer shows us passion for God's glory and agenda. His **name**, **kingdom** and **will** have the top priority.

i. Everyone wants to guard their own name and reputation. But we must resist the tendency to protect and promote ourselves first and instead put God's **name**, **kingdom** and **will** first. This shows that prayer isn't a tool to get what we want from God. It is a way to get God's will accomplished in us and all around us.

ii. Jesus wanted us to pray with the desire that the **will** of God would **be done on earth as it is in heaven**. In heaven there is no disobedience and there are no obstacles to God's will; on earth there is disobedience and there are at least apparent obstacles to His will. The citizens of Jesus' kingdom will want to see His will done as freely **on earth as it is in heaven**.

iii. A man can say, "**Your will be done**" in different ways and moods. He may say it with fatalism and resentment. "You will do your will and there is nothing I can do about it anyway. Your will wins, but I don't like it." Or he may say it with a heart of perfect love and trust: "Do Your will, because I know it is the best. Change me where I don't understand or accept Your will."

iv. "He that taught us this prayer used it himself in the most unrestricted sense. When the bloody sweat stood on his face, and all the fear and trembling of a man in anguish were upon him, he did not dispute the decree of the Father, but bowed his head and cried. 'Nevertheless, not as I will, but as thou wilt.'" (Spurgeon)

v. One might rightly wonder why God wants us to pray that *His* will would be done, as if He were not able to accomplish it Himself. God is more than able to do His will without our prayer or cooperation; yet He invites the participation of our prayers, our heart, and our actions in seeing His **will be done on earth as it is in heaven**.

vi. "In heaven God's will is obeyed by all, spontaneously, with the deepest joy and in a perfect manner without a shadow of unfaithfulness. And the believer must pray that such a condition should also prevail on earth." (Geldenhuys)

vii. Some see the Trinity in these requests. The *Father* is the source of all holiness; *Jesus* brings the kingdom of God to us; and the *Holy Spirit* accomplishes God's will in us and among us.

viii. Some see the three greatest things in these three requests. To pray **Our Father** requires *faith*, because he who comes to God must believe that He is. To pray **Your kingdom come** requires *hope*, because we trust it is to come in fullness. To pray **Your will be done** requires *love*, because love is the incentive to obey all of God's will.

e. **Give us day by day our daily bread**: The model prayer shows us to freely bring our needs to God. This will include needs for daily provision, forgiveness, and strength in the face of temptation.

i. When Jesus spoke of **bread**, He meant real bread, as in the sense of daily provisions. Early theologians allegorized this, because they couldn't imagine Jesus speaking about an everyday thing like bread in such a majestic prayer like this. So they thought bread referred to *communion*, the Lord's Supper. Some have thought it referred to Jesus Himself as the bread of life. Others have thought it speaks of the word of God as our daily bread. Calvin rightly said of such interpretations, which fail to see God's interest in everyday things: "This is exceedingly absurd." God *does* care about everyday things, and we should pray about them.

ii. Yet it is a prayer for **daily bread**, not a warehouse of bread. "The prayer is for our needs, not our greeds. It is for one day at a time, reflecting the precarious lifestyle of many first-century workers who were paid one day at a time and for whom a few days' illness could spell tragedy." (Carson)

f. **And forgive us our sins, for we also forgive everyone who is indebted to us**: Just as real as the need for daily bread is the need for daily forgiveness. We often *feel* the need for food more, but the need for forgiveness is real whether it is felt or not.

i. "As bread is the first need of the body, so forgiveness for the soul." (Murray)

ii. Jesus represented **sins** with the idea of being **indebted**. *The sinner owes a debt to God.* "Sin is represented here under the notion of a *debt*, and as our sins are *many*, they are called here *debts*. God made man that he might live to his glory, and gave him a law to walk by; and if, when he does any thing that tends not to glorify God, he contracts a debt with Divine Justice." (Clarke)

iii. **For we also forgive** *assumes* that the forgiven one will show forgiveness to others.

g. **And do not lead us into temptation, but deliver us from the evil one**: **Temptation** literally means a *test*, not always a solicitation to do evil. God has promised to keep us from any testing that is greater than what we can handle (1 Corinthians 10:13).

i. "God, while he does not 'tempt' men to do evil (James 1:13), does allow his children to pass through periods of testing. But disciples, aware of their weakness, should not desire such testing, and should pray to be spared exposure to such situations in which they are vulnerable." (France)

ii. "The man who prays 'Lead us not into temptation,' and then goes into it is a liar before God...'Lead us not into temptation,' is shameful profanity when it comes from the lips of men who resort to places of amusement whose moral tone is bad." (Spurgeon)

iii. If we truly pray, **lead us not into temptation**, it will be lived out in several ways. It will mean:

- Never boast in your own strength
- Never desire trials
- Never go into temptation
- Never lead others into temptation

iv. Andrew Murray thought of this prayer as a "school of prayer," and wrote along that theme in his book *With Christ in the School of Prayer*. In that book he has a wonderful prayer for new students in Jesus' school of prayer:

"Blessed Lord! Who ever lives to pray, You can teach me to pray, me to ever live to pray. In this You love to make me share Your glory in heaven, that I should pray without ceasing, and ever stand as a priest in the presence of my God.

"Lord Jesus! I ask You this day to enroll my name among those who confess that they do not know how to pray as they ought, and specially ask You for a course in teaching in prayer. Lord! Teach me to wait with You in the school and give You time to train me. May a deep sense of my ignorance, the wonderful privilege and power of prayer, of the need of the Holy Spirit as the Spirit of prayer, lead me to cast away my thoughts of what I think I know, and make me kneel before You in true teachableness and poverty of spirit.

"And fill me, Lord, with the confidence that with a teacher like You I shall learn to pray. In the assurance that I have as my teacher, Jesus, who is ever praying to the Father, and by His prayer rules the destinies of His Church and the world, I will not be afraid. As much as I need to know of the mysteries of the prayer-world, You will fold for me. And when I may not know, You will teach me to be strong in faith, giving glory to God.

"Blessed Lord! You will not put to shame Your student who trusts You, nor, by Your grace, would he put You to shame either. Amen."

3. (5-8) Pray with boldness and persistence.

And He said to them, "Which of you shall have a friend, and go to him at midnight and say to him, 'Friend, lend me three loaves; for a friend of mine has come to me on his journey, and I have nothing to set before him'; and he will answer from within and say, 'Do not trouble me; the door is now shut, and my children are with me in bed; I cannot rise and give to you'? I say to you, though he will not rise and give to him because he is his friend, yet because of his persistence he will rise and give him as many as he needs."

a. **Which of you shall have a friend, and go to him at midnight**: In the custom of that day, a whole family lived together in a one-room house. On one side of the house was a raised platform where they all slept; down on the ground were all their animals—a cow, perhaps some sheep and goats and so forth. There was no way the man could come to the door without disturbing the whole household.

b. **Yet because of his persistence he will rise and give him as many as he needs**: It took a lot of boldness for the man in the story to so shamelessly ask his friend in the middle of the night; he really *wanted* and *needed* the bread.

i. God often waits for our passionate persistence in prayer. It isn't that God is reluctant and needs to be persuaded. Our persistence doesn't change God; it changes us, developing in us a heart and passion for what God wants.

4. (9-13) Pray with a childlike confidence.

"So I say to you, ask, and it will be given to you; seek, and you will find; knock, and it will be opened to you. For everyone who asks receives, and he who seeks finds, and to him who knocks it will be opened. If a son asks for bread from any father among you, will he give him a stone? Or if *he asks* for a fish, will he give him a serpent instead of a fish? Or if he asks for an egg, will he offer him a scorpion? If you then, being evil, know how to give good gifts to your children, how much more will *your* heavenly Father give the Holy Spirit to those who ask Him!"

> a. **Ask, and it will be given to you; seek, and you will find; knock, and it will be opened to you**: We are told to *keep on* asking, seeking and knocking. "All three verbs are continuous: Jesus is not speaking of single activities, but of those that persist." (Morris)
>
>> i. These descriptions speak of an earnestness and intensity. All too often, our prayers are merely wishes cast up to heaven, and this is not real prayer.
>
> b. **If a son asks for bread from any father among you, will he give him a stone?** Any human father loves to bless his children, and would never answer a simple request for something good with something evil. If that is the case with us, **how much more** will God answer us, though sometimes it doesn't seem so!
>
> c. **How much more will your heavenly Father give the Holy Spirit to those who ask Him!** God especially loves to give **the Holy Spirit to those who ask Him**. We never need doubt God's desire to pour out His Spirit. The problem is in our receiving, not in God's desire to give.

B. Jesus answers controversy about demons and signs.

1. (14-16) Some accuse Jesus of being in partnership with Satan; others request a sign from Him.

And He was casting out a demon, and it was mute. So it was, when the demon had gone out, that the mute spoke; and the multitudes marveled. But some of them said, "He casts out demons by Beelzebub, the ruler of the demons." Others, testing *Him,* sought from Him a sign from heaven.

> a. **He was casting out a demon, and it was mute**: The Jews in Jesus' day had their own exorcists, who sought to cast demons out of people. But

they believed that they had to make the demon reveal his name, or they had no authority over the demon to cast it out.

b. **When the demon had gone out, that the mute spoke; and the multitudes marveled**: This is why **the multitudes marveled** when Jesus cast out a demon that caused muteness. According to the Jewish thinking of that day, the demon was impossible to cast out because he made the man unable to speak, and unable to reveal the name of the demon.

c. **But some of them said, "He casts out demons by Beelzebub, the ruler of the demons"**: When people saw this great work, there were two reactions. Some attributed the working of Jesus to Satan (**Beelzebub, the ruler of the demons**), and some wanted to see more miracles before they would believe (**testing Him, sought a sign from heaven**).

> i. **Beelzebub** is a difficult name to analyze. It may come from a similar sounding word that means, "Lord of the Flies." It was a harsh accusation. "It is by no means uncommon for people to resort to slander when honest opposition is helpless." (Barclay)

2. (17-19) Jesus answers those who attribute His working to Satan.

But He, knowing their thoughts, said to them: "Every kingdom divided against itself is brought to desolation, and a house *divided* against a house falls. If Satan also is divided against himself, how will his kingdom stand? Because you say I cast out demons by Beelzebub. And if I cast out demons by Beelzebub, by whom do your sons cast *them* out? Therefore they will be your judges."

a. **But He, knowing their thoughts**: It is possible that Jesus here displayed the gift of the Holy Spirit Paul would later describe as a *word of knowledge* (1 Corinthians 12:8). It is likewise possible that Jesus knew this through experience and intuition. The point is that Jesus did not have to access His divine privilege to know their thoughts.

b. **Every kingdom divided against itself is brought to desolation**: Jesus logically answered that if He were an agent of Satan, and worked against Satan, then civil war had come to Satan's kingdom, and Satan's kingdom would therefore not stand. The point was that Satan would not work *against* himself and His accusers had to answer how *Satan* benefited from the work Jesus had just done.

> i. "Satan may be wicked, He says in effect, but he is not a fool." (Bruce) "Whatever fault the devils have, they are not at strife with each other; that fault is reserved for the servants of a better Master." (Spurgeon)

c. **And if I cast out demons by Beelzebub, by whom do your sons cast them out?** At the same time, Jesus observed that the Jewish leaders themselves also had exorcists. Did His accusers accuse them also?

3. (20-23) Jesus proclaims His strength over all demonic forces.

"But if I cast out demons with the finger of God, surely the kingdom of God has come upon you. When a strong man, fully armed, guards his own palace, his goods are in peace. But when a stronger than he comes upon him and overcomes him, he takes from him all his armor in which he trusted, and divides his spoils. He who is not with Me is against Me, and he who does not gather with Me scatters."

a. **But if I cast out demons with the finger of God, surely the kingdom of God has come upon you**: With this, Jesus answered the charge that He was in partnership with the Devil. He said, "I'm not under Satan; instead, I'm proving that I am stronger than he is."

i. Jesus did not suggest the slightest doubt when He said, "**If I cast out demons**." As Pate suggests, the idea is more *since* than *if.* "Thus, '*since* by the finger of God I cast out demons, *then* the kingdom of God has come upon you.'" (Pate)

b. **But when a stronger than he comes upon him and overcomes him**: In the picture Jesus used, Satan is the **strong man** who guards what belongs to him. Jesus' ministry, both in the case of casting the demon out of the man who was mute and in the broader sense, did the work of defeating this **strong man**.

c. **But when a stronger than he comes**: Jesus is the One who is **stronger than he** (Satan, the **strong man** of Luke 11:21). Jesus spoke about His work in overcoming Satan on several different stages:

i. **He comes upon him**: Jesus engaged Satan in battle, even on the ground of what seemed to belong to Satan (such as demon-possessed people).

ii. **And overcomes him**: Jesus simply defeated this strong man, showing to everyone that He is **stronger than he**. Jesus made it clear that He was the *stronger man* who was not captive under the **strong man**. His message was, "I'm not under Satan's power. Instead, I'm proving that I am stronger than he is by casting him out of those he has possessed."

iii. **He takes from him all his armor in which he trusted**: Jesus not only defeated Satan on our behalf, He also disarmed him. As Colossians 2:15 says, *Having disarmed principalities and powers, He made a public spectacle of them, triumphing over them in it* [the cross].

iv. **And divides his spoils**: Satan will never get to keep or enjoy the battle-spoil from his momentary victory. Jesus' victory over the **strong man** is complete. Jesus looks at every life delivered from Satan's domination and says, "I'm plundering the kingdom of Satan one life at a time." There is *nothing* in our lives that *must* stay under Satan's domination. The One who binds the strong man and **divides his spoils** is our risen Lord.

d. **He who is not with Me is against Me, and he who does not gather with Me scatters**: If Jesus is **stronger than** Satan, then each person is confronted by a decision: with whom will they partner? Will we be **with** Jesus or will we be **against** Him? Will we work for Jesus or will we work against Him?

i. "In the conflict against the powers of darkness there is no room for neutrality." (Geldenhuys)

ii. In this sense, to be undecided is to be decided. There is no neutral ground; we are either with Jesus or against Him. There is no luxury of guarded neutrality.

iii. If Satan is the **strong man**, and Jesus is **stronger than** Satan is, there are two strong forces at work, trying to win our allegiance. We will embrace one or the other, intentionally or unintentionally.

4. (24-26) Jesus tells more about the dynamics of demonic possession.

"When an unclean spirit goes out of a man, he goes through dry places, seeking rest; and finding none, he says, 'I will return to my house from which I came.' And when he comes, he finds *it* swept and put in order. Then he goes and takes with *him* seven other spirits more wicked than himself, and they enter and dwell there; and the last *state* of that man is worse than the first."

a. **When an unclean spirit goes out of a man**: This is the picture of a person delivered from a demon, but not yet filled with Jesus. It is a picture of a person who tries to be neutral. They say they are not for Satan, but they are also not for Jesus. Jesus shows us that this is impossible.

b. **I will return to my house from which I came**: Apparently, demons regard *vacant* places as opportunities. For some reason they want to inhabit bodies. We can suppose that this is for the same reason why the vandal wants a spray can, or a violent man wants a gun—a body is a weapon a demon can use in their attack against God.

i. "It is probably implied that the house was unoccupied…the context of Luke 11:25 seems to assume that the reason the demon could return to the house was because it was vacant." (Pate)

c. **The last state of that man is worse than the first**: Jesus revealed the danger of delivering a person from demonic possession without filling their life with Jesus. They can end up worse than before.

i. The heart of man has a vacuum-like nature to it. It has to be filled. If we empty our hearts from evil without filling them with Jesus and His good, evil will rush in again to fill them—and sometimes worse evil than before.

ii. Therefore, in answering those who accused Him of working by the power of Satan, Jesus told them that He had not merely come to fight against evil, but to bring God's good into our hearts. He did not come to merely empty the house, but to fill it with Himself.

5. (27-28) Jesus reveals the truly blessed.

And it happened, as He spoke these things, that a certain woman from the crowd raised her voice and said to Him, "Blessed *is* the womb that bore You, and *the* breasts which nursed You!" But He said, "More than that, blessed *are* those who hear the word of God and keep it!"

a. **Blessed is the womb that bore You**: This was a seemingly spontaneous cry from a **certain woman** in the crowd who wanted to honor Jesus and His family. The sense seems to be, "Jesus, You are so wonderful that Your mother must be a very blessed woman."

b. **More than that, blessed are those who hear the word of God and keep it**: While not *dishonoring* His mother, Jesus pointed out the greater and more important connection between Himself and those who hear the word of God and keep it. *This* is a more blessed and important relationship to Jesus than even being the mother who bore Him.

i. This does not demean Mary; but it does honor and bless the one who hears and keeps God's word. *This* is the blessed place. "His disciples were more blessed in hearing Christ than his mother in bearing him." (Trapp)

6. (29-32) Jesus answers those who seek for a sign.

And while the crowds were thickly gathered together, He began to say, "This is an evil generation. It seeks a sign, and no sign will be given to it except the sign of Jonah the prophet. For as Jonah became a sign to the Ninevites, so also the Son of Man will be to this generation. The queen of the South will rise up in the judgment with the men of this generation and condemn them, for she came from the ends of the earth to hear the wisdom of Solomon; and indeed a greater than Solomon *is* here. The men of Nineveh will rise up in the judgment with this generation and condemn it, for they repented at the preaching of Jonah; and indeed a greater than Jonah *is* here."

a. **This is an evil generation. It seeks a sign**: Jesus said this to the thick crowd, rebuking their inclination to seek and value signs. Jesus just mentioned the blessedness of being one who heard and did God's word; the contrast is the one who **seeks a sign**.

i. According to William Barclay, about fifteen years after Jesus' time on earth, a man named Theudas arose among the Jews and claimed to be the Messiah. He persuaded people to follow him with the promise that he would part the Jordan River in two. He tried, he failed, and the Romans dealt severely with him. But he knew what kind of sign the people wanted to see. Jesus told us that hearing and keeping the Word of God are more important than signs.

ii. Ironically, Jesus had given *many* remarkable signs, just not the kind they wanted to see. They wanted to see signs leading to military resistance and the political independence of the Jesus people from the occupying Romans.

iii. Jesus condemned their seeking after a sign, especially when countless signs had already happened before their eyes. It is easy to overestimate the power of miraculous signs to change the heart of doubters and skeptics.

b. **No sign will be given to it except the sign of Jonah the prophet**: Jesus told us that Jonah **became a sign**, and Jesus would be a similar sign to His generation. Jonah gave his life to appease the wrath of God coming upon others. But death did not hold him; after three days and nights of imprisonment, he was alive and free (Jonah 1-2).

i. *This* is the sign that Jesus promised. Jesus is that sign, both to His present generation and to ours. Jesus *Himself* is the sign; we are to believe in Him, not a sign.

c. **The queen of the South will rise up in the judgment with the men of this generation and condemn them**: The **queen of the South** came to Solomon in 1 Kings 10. When she saw the great works that God did for and through Solomon, she praised the God of Israel. She didn't say, "Show me more and maybe I'll believe."

i. The **queen of the South came from the ends of the earth to hear the wisdom of Solomon**. She sought after God's word with a tenacity that shames us. The people who asked Jesus for a sign saw His work right there in their own neighborhood, and didn't believe.

ii. The point is clear: the **queen of the South** and the **men of Nineveh** were both Gentiles, but they had a more open heart to the things of God than the religious people of Jesus' day, who would not believe and receive the work of God right before their eyes.

iii. "The irony is biting: the Ninevites and the Queen of Sheba accepted the messengers of God. But Jesus' audience rejected God Himself." (Pate)

d. **A greater than Solomon is here**: Solomon was the son of David, and one of the great messianic titles of Jesus is "Son of David." Jesus was a much **greater** Son of David than Solomon was.

i. We again are impressed by the greatness of Jesus' self-claim. To stand in front of these religious leaders and claim to be **greater** than Israel's richest and wisest king was audacious. Yet the seeming audacity of Jesus was well justified.

e. **Indeed a greater than Jonah is here**: Jesus repeatedly brought the focus back upon Himself. He was and is greater than all previous prophets; He should become the focus of faith and trust from His people. His **greater** light brought a greater accountability to His hearers.

i. Adam Clarke described several ways that the witness of Jesus was **greater than Jonah**.

- "Christ, who preached to the Jews, was infinitely greater than Jonah, in his nature, person, and mission"

- "Jonah preached repentance in Nineveh only *forty* days, and Christ preached among the Jews for several years"

- "Jonah wrought no miracles to authorize his preaching; but Christ wrought miracles every day, in every place where he went, and of every kind"

- "Notwithstanding all this, the people of Judea did not repent, though the people of Nineveh did"

C. Jesus' warnings to hypocrites.

1. (33-36) Jesus warns about inner darkness.

"No one, when he has lit a lamp, puts *it* in a secret place or under a basket, but on a lampstand, that those who come in may see the light. The lamp of the body is the eye. Therefore, when your eye is good, your whole body also is full of light. But when *your eye* is bad, your body also *is* full of darkness. Therefore take heed that the light which is in you is not darkness. If then your whole body *is* full of light, having no part dark, *the* whole *body* will be full of light, as when the bright shining of a lamp gives you light."

a. **No one, when he has lit a lamp, puts it in a secret place or under a basket, but on a lampstand**: Just as a lamp should be displayed out in the open so that all can benefit from its light, so the word and work of God should be displayed. Yet when Jesus displayed *His* word and works, the religious people of His day would not accept them.

i. This section has application to both what went before it (Jesus answers those who thought His miracles were the work of Satan and those who wanted to see more), and what comes after it (Jesus deals with hypocrisy).

ii. Some saw His brightness, some did not, and others thought the light wasn't bright enough and demanded to see more. "Our Lord's constant answer was, to go shining on. He was meant to be observed; even as a lamp is intended to be seen." (Spurgeon)

b. **The lamp of the body is the eye**: Even as a bad eye will make a person blind, so bad hearts will make one spiritually blind. One must be spiritually blind to attribute Jesus' miracles to Satan and to ignore the work of Jesus right before the eyes or to live as a hypocrite.

i. When one lives in darkness, there are two possible reasons why. There may be no light source, or the darkness may be within—the inability to *perceive* light. When Jesus warned, **take heed that the light which is in you is not darkness**, He warned against the darkness within.

ii. "We see by life and character, by all that we have made ourselves, by every secret sin that we have cherished, by every battle we have fought and won." (Morrison)

iii. "If you do not see Jesus, it is not because he has hidden himself in darkness, but because your eyes are blinded." (Spurgeon)

iv. "If any of my readers are like that—if they see the Carpenter but cannot see the Lord—let me ask them, tenderly and quietly, *What kind of life have you been living?*" (Morrison)

v. If the darkness comes from within a man and prevents him from seeing the light of Jesus, *it doesn't matter how bright and glorious Jesus is*—he can't see it. "A man without an eye might as well be without the sun, so far as light is concerned." (Spurgeon)

vi. "Do you wonder that our Lord seemed to hold up his hands in astonishment as he said, 'If the light that is in thee be darkness, how great is that darkness!' If that which should lead misleads, how misled you will be! If your better part turns out to be evil, how evil must you be!" (Spurgeon)

c. **If then your whole body is full of light, having no part dark, the whole body will be full of light**: When the light of God's word shines;

when the word and work of Jesus is understood, then one does not walk in the darkness of spiritual blindness.

> i. "He saw the Kingdom in a mustard-seed, and the adoring woman in a harlot. He saw the solid rock in Simon, and the lover in the son of thunder. He saw in a child the citizen of heaven, in a bit of bread His broken body, in a cup of common wine His sacred blood.... Never was a vision such as this, because never was there a nature such as this." (Morrison)

2. (37-41) Jesus rebukes the Pharisees for concern only for external things.

And as He spoke, a certain Pharisee asked Him to dine with him. So He went in and sat down to eat. When the Pharisee saw *it,* he marveled that He had not first washed before dinner. Then the Lord said to him, "Now you Pharisees make the outside of the cup and dish clean, but your inward part is full of greed and wickedness. Foolish ones! Did not He who made the outside make the inside also? But rather give alms of such things as you have; then indeed all things are clean to you."

a. **So He went in and sat down to eat**: Though Jesus experienced increasing conflict and opposition from the religious leaders, He didn't hate them in return. Jesus accepted this invitation to **eat** with **a certain Pharisee**.

> i. Based on the words Jesus said in his home, it is possible that the Pharisee regretted his invitation to Jesus.

b. **He marveled that He had not first washed before dinner**: Jesus was not unhygienic when **He had not first washed before dinner**. He did not follow the extremely technical and rigid requirements of ceremonial washing practiced by many pious Jews.

> i. "This the Pharisees deemed as great a sin as to commit fornication." (Trapp)

> ii. For these ceremonial washings, Barclay described how special stone vessels of water were kept because ordinary water might be ceremonially unclean. In performing the washing, one started with at least enough of this water to fill one and one-half eggshells. One began by pouring the water over the hands, starting at the fingers and running down towards the wrist. Then each palm was cleansed by rubbing the fist of the other hand into it. Water was poured over the hands again, this time from the wrist towards the fingers.

> iii. A *really* strict Jew would do this not only before the meal, but also between each course through the meal. The rabbis were deadly serious about this, saying that bread eaten with unwashed hands was no better than excrement. A rabbi who once failed to do this was considered excommunicated. Another rabbi was imprisoned by the Romans and

used his ration of water for ceremonial cleansing instead of drinking, nearly dying of thirst—but being regarded as a great hero.

iv. If these religious leaders were as concerned about cleansing their hearts as they were about their hands, they would be more godly men. We often want to look to a ceremony or a ritual to cleanse us, instead of the sacrificial work of God on our behalf.

c. **Now you Pharisees make the outside of the cup and dish clean, but your inward part is full of greed and wickedness**: These Pharisees were careful to maintain the *appearance* of righteousness, but not the inner *reality* of it. They were **foolish ones** because they could be outwardly clean while actually being dirty on the inside.

3. (42-44) Woes to the scribes and Pharisees.

"But woe to you Pharisees! For you tithe mint and rue and all manner of herbs, and pass by justice and the love of God. These you ought to have done, without leaving the others undone. Woe to you Pharisees! For you love the best seats in the synagogues and greetings in the marketplaces. Woe to you, scribes and Pharisees, hypocrites! For you are like graves which are not seen, and the men who walk over *them* are not aware *of them*."

a. **But woe to you…Woe to you…Woe to you**: Jesus spoke harshly here, yet this was not the language of personal irritation but of divine warning and condemnation. He seems to speak in the tone and rhythm of the Old Testament prophets (Isaiah 5:8-23, Habakkuk 2:6-19).

b. **For you tithe mint and rue and all manner of herbs, and pass by justice and the love of God**: Their tithing was meticulous and noteworthy, but hypocritical because it served to sooth the guilt of their neglect of the **justice and love of God**. It is both possible and common to be distracted with relatively trivial matters while a lost world perishes.

i. The Pharisees were so careful in their outward obedience that they would literally tithe from their herb gardens, counting out seeds and leaves, and giving a tenth of each to God.

ii. Legalism of this sort assumes that people will only know we follow God if we do all these things associated with rules and regulations. Instead, Jesus said that the real mark of a believer is the love they have for others in God's family.

iii. But the Jewish leaders saw it differently. "The Mishna lays it down that it is more important to observe the scribal interpretations than the Law itself (*Sanhedrin* 11:13)." (Morris)

iv. It was as if a solider did great in marching drills and put all their emphasis there, but wasn't any good in battle. This would not be a good soldier. Being good at all the *outward* things of Christianity doesn't mean you are necessarily a good Christian.

c. **These you ought to have done, without leaving the others undone**: Jesus did not say that their tithing was wrong. Instead, what was wrong was what they did *not* do—**leaving the others undone**.

d. **You love the best seats in the synagogues and greetings in the marketplaces**: The **best seats in the synagogues** were the seats up front facing the congregation. This is where the leaders and prominent people sat. These people thought it was no good to walk right with God if others didn't *know* they walked right with God.

i. The **best seats** and honored **greetings in the marketplaces** were wonderful to religious leaders who wanted to be celebrities, who thought that being spiritual was a great way to become famous. Jesus severely rebuked this attitude and proclaimed a **woe** to any who held it.

e. **Scribes and Pharisees, hypocrites**: Literally, the word "**hypocrites**" refers to an actor, someone playing a part. Jesus exposed the corruption that was covered by the spiritual image of the **scribes and Pharisees**.

f. **For you are like graves which are not seen, and the men who walk over them are not aware of them**: These religious leaders loved giving the impression that they were ever so spiritual, but they actually defiled everyone they came in contact with. Walking over a grave ceremonially defiled a Jewish person, even if they didn't know it was there.

i. According to Numbers 19:16, everyone who touched a grave was ceremonially unclean for seven days. For this reason, the Jews sought to mark graves clearly, usually using whitewash, so everyone would know where they were and would avoid them.

4. (45-46) Jesus rebukes the lawyers for their oppressive religious system.

Then one of the lawyers answered and said to Him, "Teacher, by saying these things You reproach us also." And He said, "Woe to you also, lawyers! For you load men with burdens hard to bear, and you yourselves do not touch the burdens with one of your fingers."

a. **Teacher, by saying these things You reproach us also**: The lawyer would have done better to keep quiet, but since he drew attention to himself, Jesus addressed him also.

i. **One of the lawyers** meant the man was an expert in the interpretation and application of the Law of Moses.

b. **For you load men with burdens hard to bear, and you yourselves do not touch the burdens with one of your fingers**: Because of the way that they interpreted the law, these experts in the Mosaic law laid heavy burdens on people—yet with elaborate evasions and loopholes.

i. For example, they taught that on the Sabbath, a man could not carry something in his right hand or in his left hand, across his chest or on his shoulder; but you could carry something with the back of your hand, with your foot, with your elbow, or in your ear, your hair, or in the hem of your shirt, or in your shoe or sandal.

ii. On the Sabbath it was forbidden to tie a knot, except a woman could tie a knot in her girdle. So if a bucket of water had to be raised from a well, you could not tie a rope to the bucket, but a woman could tie her girdle to the bucket and raise it from the well.

iii. Another example is how ancient rabbis took the command to respect proper sanitation in the army camp of Israel (Deuteronomy 23:12-14) and applied it to Jerusalem, considering it the "camp of the Lord." When this interpretation was combined with Sabbath travel restrictions, it resulted in a prohibition against going to the bathroom on the Sabbath.

iv. It is possible to wrongly use the Scriptures as a tool of control and oppression, all while evading one's true responsibility before God. To do so puts one under this same woe and condemnation of Jesus.

5. (47-51) The religious leaders only admired dead prophets.

"Woe to you! For you build the tombs of the prophets, and your fathers killed them. In fact, you bear witness that you approve the deeds of your fathers; for they indeed killed them, and you build their tombs. Therefore the wisdom of God also said, 'I will send them prophets and apostles, and *some* of them they will kill and persecute,' that the blood of all the prophets which was shed from the foundation of the world may be required of this generation, from the blood of Abel to the blood of Zechariah who perished between the altar and the temple. Yes, I say to you, it shall be required of this generation."

a. **For you build the tombs of the prophets, and your fathers killed them**: They professed to venerate dead prophets, but they rejected living prophets. In doing so, they showed that they really were the children of those who murdered the prophets in the days of old (**you approve of the deeds of your fathers**).

i. We express the same thought when we think that we would have trusted Jesus more than His disciples did, or been more faithful to Him.

b. **I will send them prophets and apostles, and some of them they will kill and persecute**: Jesus prophesied that these leaders would complete the rejection of the prophets their fathers began by persecuting His disciples, whom He would send to them.

c. **That the blood of all the prophets which was shed from the foundation of the world may be required of this generation**: This was a remarkable condemnation from Jesus, saying that those who rejected Him and His apostles and prophets would face a greater and unique accountability.

i. "No amount of argument can rob these words of their terrible import. They stand upon the page for evermore speaking to us of 'the wrath of the Lamb.'" (Morgan)

d. **From the blood of Abel to the blood of Zechariah**: Jesus here spoke of *all* the righteous martyrs of the Old Testament. **Abel** was clearly the first, and in the way that the Hebrew Bible was arranged, **Zechariah** was the last. 2 Chronicles is the last book of the Hebrew Bible, and Zechariah's story is found in 2 Chronicles 24.

i. Abel's blood cried out (Genesis 4:10), and Zechariah asked that his blood be remembered (2 Chronicles 24:22).

ii. "One can almost feel the withering force of His strong and mighty indignation—indignation directed, not against the people, but against their false guides. And yet behind it all is His heart, and the 'woes' merge into a wail of agony, the cry of a mother over her lost child." (Morgan)

6. (52) Their most terrible crime—keeping others from God.

"Woe to you lawyers! For you have taken away the key of knowledge. You did not enter in yourselves, and those who were entering in you hindered."

a. **For you have taken away the key of knowledge**: Their legalistic approach had **taken away** understanding and knowledge. By giving the people a list of rules by which they could supposedly save themselves, they didn't help them at all.

b. **You did not enter in yourselves, and those who were entering in you hindered**: It is bad for someone to not enter into heaven themselves; but it is far worse to hinder another person from entering in.

i. "The idea is that the scribes' encrustation of the Word of God with the traditions of men keeps people from encountering the revelation of God." (Pate)

7. (53-54) The reaction of Jesus' enemies.

And as He said these things to them, the scribes and the Pharisees began to assail *Him* vehemently, and to cross-examine Him about many things, lying in wait for Him, and seeking to catch Him in something He might say, that they might accuse Him.

a. **The scribes and the Pharisees began to assail Him vehemently**: They did not receive Jesus' correction. They preferred to stay in their own sinful thinking and habits rather than to repent and learn from Jesus' rebuke. Their reaction was strong and violent in words, if not action (**assail Him vehemently**).

b. **That they might accuse Him**: The religious leaders responded the way many do when they are faced with the correction and the truth of God. Instead of humbly receiving the correction, they responded with outraged accusations.

i. Proverbs tells us what those who refuse correction do. First, they hate those who correct them (Proverbs 9:8, Proverbs 15:12). Second, they do not listen to the one correcting them (Proverbs 13:1). Third, they despise their own soul (Proverbs 15:32).

ii. Proverbs also tells us the character of those who refuse correction. They are stupid (Proverbs 12:1) and they are foolish (Proverbs 15:5).

Luke 12—Attitudes for Followers of Jesus

A. The kind of attitude those who will face persecution should have.

1. (1-3) A warning to beware of hypocrisy.

In the meantime, when an innumerable multitude of people had gathered together, so that they trampled one another, He began to say to His disciples first *of all,* "Beware of the leaven of the Pharisees, which is hypocrisy. For there is nothing covered that will not be revealed, nor hidden that will not be known. Therefore whatever you have spoken in the dark will be heard in the light, and what you have spoken in the ear in inner rooms will be proclaimed on the housetops."

a. **When an innumerable multitude of people had gathered**: As Jesus continued in the general direction towards Jerusalem, vast multitudes came to hear Him. The crowds were so large that some were injured (**so that they trampled one another**).

b. **Beware of the leaven of the Pharisees, which is hypocrisy**: Jesus spoke this primarily to His disciples (**He began to say to His disciples**), warning them against the great danger of **hypocrisy**, likening it to **leaven**.

i. Hypocrisy is like *leaven* in the sense that it only takes a little bit of it to affect a great mass. A little bit of hypocrisy can be like a little bit of arsenic. In light of their tremendous popularity, it was *especially* important for the disciples to remember this. The temptation to hypocrisy is often strongest to those who enjoy some measure of outward success.

ii. "Such is hypocrisy, which also, as leaven, is: 1. spreading; 2. swelling; 3. souring the meal." (Trapp)

iii. Some think that the only way to avoid being a hypocrite is to never aspire to a higher standard. But this is dangerous both for ourselves and for society. We should aspire to a high standard, yet be honest about our difficulty in fulfilling that standard.

c. **For there is nothing covered that will not be revealed, nor hidden that will not be known**: The art of being a hypocrite depends on concealment, but one day all will be revealed. We can only be hypocrites before men, but never before God. He sees through the actor's mask.

i. In 1985, a nationally known evangelist and preacher wrote a book condemning sin in America, especially sexual sin and pornography. Just a short time later, he tearfully confessed years of involvement in these very sins, and promised repentance—but was arrested for similar crimes again a few years down the road. His hypocrisy may have surprised many people, but not God. God knew all along.

2. (4-5) Do not fear persecution.

"And I say to you, My friends, do not be afraid of those who kill the body, and after that have no more that they can do. But I will show you whom you should fear: Fear Him who, after He has killed, has power to cast into hell; yes, I say to you, fear Him!"

a. **I say to you, My friends**: It's difficult to know if Jesus said this to His disciples (as in Luke 12:1-3) or to the multitude. Given the context, it is probably best to think that Jesus spoke to His disciples, but in the plain hearing of the crowd.

i. The connection to His previous words may be that hypocrites will always despise the faithful, so the followers of Jesus must be ready to face persecution.

b. **Do not be afraid of those who kill the body**: When Jesus spoke to these disciples of His about martyrdom and persecution, He knew that all of them—except John—would die martyrs' deaths for Him. He also knew of His own coming suffering.

i. Given the recent display of opposition to Jesus (Luke 11:53-54), it is reasonable to think that the disciples felt the increasing stress and anxiety leading up to the crucifixion. They needed to gain the same peace Jesus had, and put fear into perspective.

c. **After that have no more that they can do**: All persecutors can do is kill, and God has ultimate power over the life and death of the believer. Therefore, we shouldn't fear our persecutors, but have a healthy respect for God that makes us more concerned with obeying Him than any man.

i. "A man has but one life to lose, and one soul to save; and it is madness to sacrifice the salvation of the soul to the preservation of the life." (Clarke)

d. **Fear Him who, after He has killed, has power to cast into hell**: The word translated **hell** is *Gehenna*. It is derived from the words *Valley of*

Hinnom, which was located on the south and west sides of Jerusalem. In the Old Testament, it was a place of child-sacrifice to Molech (2 Chronicles 28:3, Jeremiah 7:30-31, 19:1-6, 32:35). The reforming King Josiah stopped child sacrifice in the Valley of Hinnom (2 Kings 23:10), and it became a garbage dump, a stench with continually smoldering fires. In the days of Jesus it became associated with eternal, fiery punishment—what is called *the lake of fire* in other passages (Revelation 19:20, 20:1-3).

e. **Yes, I say to you, fear Him!** There are literally millions of examples of people standing strong for Jesus through persecution, of those who honored God more than honoring man. Following is the particular story of an Englishman named Rowland Taylor.

i. In a book first printed in 1890, John Ryle describes the death of Rowland Taylor, who was executed in England because he believed that priests could marry and that the bread and wine of communion did not become the actual, literal body and blood of Jesus.

ii. On the last day of January 1555, Taylor appeared with two others before the Bishop of Winchester, and was charged with heresy and dividing the church. When they refused to change their minds, they were condemned to death. When condemned, they replied back to the Bishop, "We know that God, the righteous Judge, will require our blood at your hands, and the proudest of all of you shall repent this receiving again of Antichrist, and of the tyranny you now show against the flock of Christ."

iii. On February 4, Taylor was kicked out of the priesthood, and that night his wife and son were permitted to eat dinner with him. After dinner, they left with much affection and tears. The next day, he was led out to Hadleigh to be executed, so that he would be burned to death in the city where he served as a pastor and in front of his congregation.

iv. When they left the London jail on the morning of February 5, it was still dark. Taylor's wife suspected he might be taken that morning, so she waited with her two daughters outside the jail. When she called out to him, the sheriff allowed her to come with her daughters for one last meeting with her husband. Rowland Taylor took his little daughter Mary up in his arms, while Elizabeth knelt with him and said the Lord's Prayer. They prayed together, then kissed and hugged, and Taylor said to his wife: "Farewell, my dear wife: be of good comfort, for I am quiet in my conscience. God shall raise up a father for my children." He kissed his daughter Mary and said, "God bless you, and make you His servant"; and, kissing Elizabeth, he said, "God bless you. I pray you all stand strong and steadfast to Christ and His

Word." As he was led away, his wife called out, "God be with you, dear Rowland: I will, with God's grace, meet you at Hadleigh."

v. The journey from London to Hadleigh took several days, and all along on the trip, Rowland Taylor was joyful and merry, as if he were going to a banquet or a party. But on February 9, 1555, they came into Hadleigh. When they were still two miles from town, Taylor leapt off his horse and started on foot—but he was walking fast, almost as if he were dancing. The sheriff asked him how he felt, and he said, "Well, God be praised, good master sheriff, never better; for now I know I am almost at home...even at my Father's house...O good Lord, I thank You! I shall yet once before I die, see my flock whom You, Lord, know I have most heartily loved and most truly taught. Good Lord, bless them, and keep them steadfast in Thy Word and truth."

vi. When they came into Hadleigh, they put a hood over his head and came over a bridge. At the foot of the bridge was a poor man with five children, who cried out, "O dear father and good shepherd, Dr. Taylor, God help you, as you have many a time helped me and my poor children." The streets were crowded on both sides with people who wanted to see him; when they saw him being led to death, they cried and wept with all their strength. People cried out, "Ah, good Lord, there goes our good shepherd from us, that so faithfully has taught us, so fatherly has cared for us, and so godly has governed us. O merciful God! What shall we poor scattered lambs do? What shall come of this most wicked world? God Lord, strengthen him and comfort him." Taylor answered back, "I have preached to you God's Word and truth, and am come this day to seal it with my blood."

vii. When they came to the town square, he heard a great multitude and asked where they were. When they told him they were at the place he would be executed, he said "Thank God, I am even at home," and he took the hood from his head. When the people saw his face, there was an outpouring of emotion. They wept and cried out, "God save you, good Dr. Taylor! Jesus Christ strengthen you; the Holy Spirit comfort you," and many other such things. Taylor wanted to speak to the people one last time, but as soon has he opened his mouth, a guard put a spear right up to his open mouth, and made him stop.

viii. He started giving away his clothes—first his boots, then his coat and jacket, till all he had left was his pants and shirt. He then cried out with a loud voice, "Good people, I have taught you nothing but God's Holy Word, and those lessons that I have taken out of God's blessed Book, the Holy Bible; and I am come here today to seal it with my blood." But then one of the guards clubbed him over the head and said, "Is that keeping your promise of silence, you heretic?" So, seeing he could not speak, he knelt down to pray. A poor woman came to kneel beside him and pray, and the guards tried to push her away but she would not go.

ix. When he had prayed, he came to the stake he would be tied to and he kissed it, stepped into a barrel, and stood with his hands folded in prayer and his eyes towards heaven as they tied him to the stake. After some agonizing delays, they finally lit the fire and Rowland Taylor prayed out loud: "Merciful Father of heaven, for Jesus Christ my Saviour's sake, receive my soul into Your hands." Then he stood perfectly still as the fires arose around him, without crying or moving, until a guard clubbed him on the head and his brains fell out, and his dead corpse fell into the fire. A marker was left that simply said, *1555: Dr. Taylor, in defending that which was good, at this place left his blood.*

3. (6-7) Realize your great value to God.

"Are not five sparrows sold for two copper coins? And not one of them is forgotten before God. But the very hairs of your head are all numbered. Do not fear therefore; you are of more value than many sparrows."

a. **Not one of them is forgotten before God**: If God remembers the **sparrows**, He will not forget you—so don't lose heart. There are few things worse than the sense of being **forgotten**; Jesus assured every believer that their life was precious and remembered before God.

i. Before he left London to be executed, Rowland Taylor wrote his final thoughts in a book and presented them to his son: "I say to my wife and to my children, the Lord gave you unto me, and the Lord has taken me from you and you from me: blessed be the name of the Lord! I believe that they are blessed which die in the Lord. God cares for sparrows, and for the hairs of our heads. I have ever found Him more faithful and favourable than is any father or husband. Trust, therefore, in Him by means of our dear Savior Christ's merits. Believe, love, fear, and obey Him: pray to Him, for He has promised to help. Count me not dead, for I shall certainly live and never die. I go before, and you shall follow after to our long home."

b. **The very hairs of your head are all numbered**: It has been said that a redhead has about 90,000 hairs; a dark-haired person has about 120,000 hairs, and a blonde has about 145,000. Yet God knows *exactly* how many hairs you have. If He knows that about you, He also knows all the important things.

c. **You are of more value than many sparrows**: Those who are persecuted are tempted to give in to the feeling that they are worthless and no one cares for them. Yet a loving God in heaven values each one.

i. Matthew 10:29 tells us that one could buy two sparrows for one copper coin. Here we learn that five sparrows cost two copper coins. There was a discount for buying more, from .5 copper coin per sparrow to .4 copper coin per sparrow.

4. (8-10) The importance of a good confession.

"Also I say to you, whoever confesses Me before men, him the Son of Man also will confess before the angels of God. But he who denies Me before men will be denied before the angels of God. And anyone who speaks a word against the Son of Man, it will be forgiven him; but to him who blasphemes against the Holy Spirit, it will not be forgiven."

a. **Whoever confesses Me before men, him the Son of Man also will confess before the angels of God**: Jesus comforted the faithful, explaining that the suffering Christian will be given the reward of allegiance and honor before the throne of God (the idea being that **the angels of God** surround His throne).

i. Among early Christians, the *confessors* had special honor. They were those who endured suffering for Jesus, yet were spared death.

b. **He who denies Me before men will be denied before the angels of God**: Even as there was an honorable reward for the faithful, there is a terrible penalty for the faithless. They would be denied and disgraced before the throne of God.

i. Jesus did not say, *denies Me in their heart* or *denies me in their mind*; He said, **denies Me before men**. There is a real and important place for a *public* declaration of allegiance to Jesus. For many, this is the most difficult thing of all, usually because of the fear of man, the exact thing Jesus warned against in His previous words (Luke 12:4-7).

ii. The test to either confess or deny Jesus before men may come in many ways, but it will always come. It is helpful to be determined in heart and mind *before* the test comes.

iii. Jesus clearly called His listeners to a *choice*. As before in Luke 11:23, the choice is to either be *with* Jesus or *against* Him. Here the choice is to *confess* Jesus or *deny* Him.

c. **Speaks a word against the Son of Man**: This probably refers to a moment of weakness (especially in public testimony), which could be forgiven. In contrast, he who **blasphemes against the Holy Spirit** is in a settled rejection of God's truth, which **will not be forgiven**.

i. Jesus said this when it seemed He was more popular than ever (Luke 12:1). Yet Jesus knew that being regarded as popular wasn't the same as truly being confessed and trusted. Even as He called His hearers to make a choice, He warned against making the wrong choice.

ii. The Holy Spirit's main ministry is to testify of Jesus (*He will testify of Me*, John 15:26). When that testimony of Jesus is fully and finally rejected, one has truly blasphemed the Holy Spirit and essentially called Him a liar in respect to His testimony about Jesus. Those who reject Jesus, in a settled sense, are guilty of this sin.

d. **It will not be forgiven**: The eternal consequences of this sin force us to regard it seriously. How can one know if they have in fact blasphemed the Holy Spirit? The fact that one desires Jesus *at all* shows that they are not guilty of this sin. Yet continued rejection of Jesus makes us more hardened against Him and puts us on the path of a full and final rejection of Him.

i. Some people, as a joke or a dare, *intentionally* say words they suppose commit the sin of **blasphemy against the Spirit**. They think it a light thing to joke with eternity. Yet true **blasphemy against the Spirit** is more than a formula of words; it is a settled disposition of life that rejects the testimony of the Holy Spirit regarding Jesus. Even if someone has intentionally said such things, they can still repent and prevent a *settled* rejection of Jesus.

ii. The blasphemy of the Holy Spirit will never be forgiven—not because it is a sin too big for God to forgive, but because it is an attitude of heart that cares nothing for God's forgiveness. It never *has* forgiveness because it never *wants* forgiveness God's way. It may want forgiveness on its own terms, but never God's way.

iii. The way to *not* blaspheme the Holy Spirit is to receive Jesus Christ, and to put one's loving trust upon Him today. It means to stop rejecting the work of the Holy Spirit in bringing us to Jesus.

5. (11-12) Don't worry about what to say—the Holy Spirit will help you.

"Now when they bring you to the synagogues and magistrates and authorities, do not worry about how or what you should answer, or what you should say. For the Holy Spirit will teach you in that very hour what you ought to say."

a. **Now when they bring you to the synagogues and magistrates and authorities**: Jesus also warned them that men would persecute them in the civic arena (**magistrates**) and religious arena (**synagogues**). They could expect opposition from both city hall and the halls of religion.

i. Jesus spoke these words to men who would face this exact challenge. Thousands upon thousands since them have faced this challenge and received God's sustaining grace in it.

b. **Do not worry about how or what you should answer, or what you should say**: Jesus' disciples could have perfect trust in God in such moments of great testing, knowing that the Holy Spirit would speak through them even if they were unprepared.

i. "It was not the humiliation which early Christians dreaded, not even the cruel pain and the agony. But many of them feared that their own unskilfulness in words and defence might injure rather than commend the truth. It is the promise of God that when a man is on trial for his faith, the words will come to him." (Barclay)

ii. "Alice Driver, martyr, at her examination, put all the doctors to silence, so that they had not a word to say, but looked upon another. Then she said, Have ye no more to say? God be honored; you be not able to resist the Spirit of God in me, a poor woman…So the chancellor condemned her, and she returned to the prison as joyful as the bird of the day." (Trapp) She was burned at the stake two weeks before the end of Queen Mary's reign (Bloody Mary).

iii. The word **answer** in Luke 12:11 is the ancient Greek word *apologeomai*—"apology." It means to make a defense or give an adequate answer. We get the modern term *apologetics* from just this word and idea.

c. **For the Holy Spirit will teach you in that very hour what you ought to say**: This gave them confidence that the **Holy Spirit** would speak to and through them at the necessary moment, even if they were not prepared with a statement.

i. This isn't a justification of poor preparation in teaching and preaching God's Word, but it is a promise of strength and guidance for the persecuted that have an opportunity to testify of Jesus.

B. Attitudes in regard to material possessions.

1. (13-15) The overall principle regarding material things.

Then one from the crowd said to Him, "Teacher, tell my brother to divide the inheritance with me." But He said to him, "Man, who made Me a judge or an arbitrator over you?" And He said to them, "Take heed and beware of covetousness, for one's life does not consist in the abundance of the things he possesses."

a. **Teacher, tell my brother to divide the inheritance with me**: Jesus had just taught on our great value to God and on the importance of standing for Him. In the midst of this teaching, a man interrupted Jesus to ask that He take his side in a financial dispute.

i. According to the law of the day, the elder brother received two-thirds of the inheritance and the younger brother received one-third (Barclay). This man did not ask Jesus to listen to both sides and make a righteous judgment; he asked Jesus to take sides with him against his brother ("**Tell my brother to divide the inheritance**").

ii. Obviously, Jesus' previous words about the need for full commitment and God's care for us didn't penetrate this man's heart. He felt he needed to fight for what was his.

iii. "If each of them learned the real meaning of life, and sought as its chief endeavor to be 'rich toward God,' the question of possessions would settle itself. The one would be eager to share, while the other would be careless about receiving." (Morgan)

b. **Man, who made Me a judge or an arbitrator over you?** It wasn't that Jesus was unconcerned about justice, but He was all too aware that this man's covetousness would do him more harm than not having his share of the inheritance.

i. We may fight and fight for what is ours by right; and in the end, having it may be worse for us than if we had let it go and let God take care of the situation.

ii. Jesus did not feel it was His responsibility to judge every matter and solve every problem. There were some disputes that He refused to become entangled in.

ii. Here is where the deceptive nature of the heart is such a challenge. We often mask our covetousness by claiming we are on a righteous crusade.

c. **Take heed and beware of covetousness**: Jesus used the man's request to speak to him and the crowd about **covetousness**. Perhaps the man's passionate request for justice really had a low motive; perhaps he was more animated by **covetousness** than by justice.

i. "Actually *beware* scarcely does justice to the force of *phylassesthe*, which is rather 'guard yourselves.'" (Morris) The idea is that we all are under attack from covetousness, and we must protect ourselves from it.

ii. "Great possessions are generally accompanied with *pride*, *idleness*, and *luxury*; and these are the greatest enemies to salvation." (Clarke)

iii. "To divide property between covetous men is to prepare for future strife. To make men free from covetousness, is to make peace." (Morgan)

d. **One's life does not consist in the abundance of the things he possesses**: This is the overall principle that Jesus will develop in the following teaching on material things. When we live with the attitude that our life *does* consist in what we posses, we live in **covetousness**, and *covetousness is idolatry* (Colossians 3:5).

i. "Covetous men by gaping after more lose the pleasure of that they posses, as a dog at his master's table swalloweth the whole meat he casteth him without any pleasure, gaping still for the next morsel." (Trapp)

2. (16-21) The parable of the rich fool.

Then He spoke a parable to them, saying: "The ground of a certain rich man yielded plentifully. And he thought within himself, saying, 'What shall I do, since I have no room to store my crops?' So he said, 'I will do this: I will pull down my barns and build greater, and there I will store all my crops and my goods. And I will say to my soul, "Soul, you have many goods laid up for many years; take your ease; eat, drink, *and* be merry."' But God said to him, 'Fool! This night your soul will be required of you; then whose will those things be which you have provided?' So *is* he who lays up treasure for himself, and is not rich toward God."

a. **The ground of a certain rich man yielded plentifully**: The man in Jesus' parable was blessed with fertile ground. We can assume that by adding hard work to the fertile ground, he was a financial success. He was so successful that he had trouble managing his resources (**I have no room to store my crops**).

i. His trouble and anxiety were reflected by the words, "**What shall I do?**" "When we are young we think that to be rich means to be free from anxiety altogether…But *this* rich man was just as full of cares as the beggar without a sixpence in the world." (Morrison)

b. **I will do this**: With a wealth of resources, the man in the parable had his life confidently planned. He would build to better manage his wealth, and then enjoy life to the fullest.

c. **But God said to him, "Fool! This night your soul will be required of you"**: In one night, all the man's accomplishments and plans were ruined. He made business plans and life plans, but could not control the day of his death—and all his accomplishments and plans were instantly nothing.

i. The man was a **fool**, not because he was rich, but because he lived without any awareness of and preparation for *eternity*.

ii. **Your soul will be required of you** is the language of *obligation*. This man owed his life, his livelihood, and his wealth to God; but most of all he owed his **soul** to God, and it would be **required** of him. It was obligated to God every day of his life, but would **be required** on the day of his death.

iii. Everyone would think the man in the parable was a great success, but God said he was a **fool**. Eternity proved the man a fool, and his story showed that it isn't only sin to give material things too high a place in your life—it is also stupid.

d. **Whose will those things be which you have provided?** In a sense, **those things** did not belong to God, because the man never surrendered those things to God. They did not belong to the rich fool, because he could not take **those things** with him. Perhaps they only belonged to the devil.

i. "Poorer than the poorest beggar he had to leave this world." (Geldenhuys)

e. **So is he who lays up treasure for himself:** The rich man in the parable thought it was all for him. He said, *my* **crops**, *my* **barns**, *my* **goods**, *my* **soul**. Everything was about him, and nothing was about God. It was proved in the end that nothing was his—even his own soul was subject to God. He didn't have any **crops**, any **barns**, any **goods**, and his **soul** was dead.

f. **So is he who lays up treasure for himself, and is not rich toward God:** The man's problem was not in that he had treasure on earth, but that he was not **rich toward God**.

i. We may become **rich toward God** by sacrificial giving to those in need (Luke 12:33, 18:22; 1 Timothy 6:17-19). Also, by trusting in Jesus for every necessary thing (Revelation 3:17-18).

ii. We can't obscure the fact that earthly riches often keep us from going after heavenly riches as we should. Paul wrote: *But those who desire to be rich fall into temptation and a snare, and into many foolish and harmful lusts which drown men in destruction and perdition.* (1 Timothy 6:9) Most of us are afraid of poverty; we should be afraid of wealth.

iii. John Wesley taught and lived wisely regarding riches. He said that you should earn as much as you can, save as much as you can, and give as much as you can. He himself lived on £28 British pounds a year and gave the rest away, even when his salary went from £30 to £60 to £90 to £120 over his lifetime.

3. (22-28) A warning against worry.

Then He said to His disciples, "Therefore I say to you, do not worry about your life, what you will eat; nor about the body, what you will put on. Life is more than food, and the body *is more* than clothing."

a. **Therefore I say to you, do not worry about your life**: Greed and worry are closely connected. Greed can never *get* enough; worry is afraid it will never *have* enough—neither have their eyes on Jesus.

i. "You can be as unfaithful to God through care as well as through covetousness." (Bruce)

ii. **Do not worry** is a loving command. We often fail to appreciate what damage worry does in our lives. Research clearly shows that stress deteriorates our immune systems; people under constant or high stress show lower T cell counts, essential for immune response. Stress has a definite effect on fertility. Prolonged stress has been shown to affect the brain, making a person less able to respond to future stress. And stress also is related to sudden heart failure.

b. **Do not worry**: There is a difference between a godly sense of responsibility and an ungodly, untrusting worry. However, an ungodly, untrusting sense of worry usually masquerades as responsibility.

c. **Life is more than food**: The worry Jesus spoke of brings man down to the level of an animal that is merely concerned with physical needs. Your life is **more**, and you have eternal matters to pursue.

4. (24-28) Reasons not to worry.

"Consider the ravens, for they neither sow nor reap, which have neither storehouse nor barn; and God feeds them. Of how much more value are you than the birds? And which of you by worrying can add one cubit to his stature? If you then are not able to do *the* least, why are you anxious for the rest? Consider the lilies, how they grow: they neither toil nor spin; and yet I say to you, even Solomon in all his glory was not arrayed like one of these. If then God so clothes the grass, which today is in the field and tomorrow is thrown into the oven, how much more *will He clothe* you, O *you* of little faith?"

a. **Consider the ravens...God feeds them**: God provides for the birds, and He takes care of them. Therefore, we should expect that God would take care of us.

i. Yet take careful note: the birds don't *worry*, but they do *work*. Birds don't just sit with open mouths, expecting God to fill them.

b. **Of how much more value are you than the birds?** The worry many people have over the material things of life is rooted in a low understanding of their **value** before God. They don't comprehend how much He loves and cares for them.

c. **Which of you by worrying can add one cubit to his stature?** Worry accomplishes nothing; we can **add** nothing to our lives by worrying. There may be greater sins than worry, but there are none more self-defeating and useless.

i. **Can add**: The ancient Greek may mean *adding to life* instead of *adding to height*, but the thought is the same. Indeed, instead of *adding* to our life, we can actually harm ourselves through worry. Stress is one of the great contributors to disease and poor health.

d. **If God so clothes the grass**: God even takes care of the **grass**, so He will also certainly take care of you. We are confident of the power and care of a loving heavenly Father.

i. God cares for the flowers, but that means that every day for the flowers is not sun and sweetness. If every day was sunny, and there were never clouds and rain, the flowers would die quickly.

ii. **You of little faith**: " '*Little faith*' is not a little fault; for it greatly wrongs the Lord, and sadly grieves the fretful mind. To think the Lord who clothes the lilies will leave his own children naked is shameful. O little faith, learn better manners!" (Spurgeon)

5. (29-31) God's intention is that your attention be on His kingdom and His treasure, not the kingdom and treasure of this world.

"And do not seek what you should eat or what you should drink, nor have an anxious mind. For all these things the nations of the world seek after, and your Father knows that you need these things. But seek the kingdom of God, and all these things shall be added to you."

a. **Do not seek what you should eat or what you should drink, nor have an anxious mind**: Jesus' good news is simple. You don't have to hold on to the things of this world with a death grip. Jesus let go of everything heaven itself held and was happy with a simple trust in God.

i. **Anxious mind** translates the ancient Greek word *meteorizesthe*, with the root word *meteor*. Trapp thought the sense was, "Hang not in suspense, as meteors do in the air, not certain whether to hang or fall to the ground."

ii. "The original of the text is not easy to explain, for the word translated 'doubtful' [**anxious**] is not used anywhere else in the New Testament. It appears to have something to do with meteors, so that the passage might be rendered, 'Neither be ye of meteoric mind.'" (Spurgeon)

b. **For after all these things the nations of the world seek**: Jesus contrasted the life of those who do not know God and are separated from Him with those who do know God and receive His loving care. Those who know God should **seek** after other things.

i. "You say again that you cannot help being anxious. Then, my dear friend, I must very solemnly ask you what is the difference between you and the man of the world?" (Spurgeon)

c. **But seek first the kingdom of God**: This must be the rule of our lives when ordering our priorities. Yet it is wrong to think that this is just another priority to fit onto our list of priorities—and to put at the top. Instead, in everything we do, we **seek first the kingdom of God**.

i. For example, we rarely have to choose between honoring God and loving our wives or being good workers. We honor God and **seek first the kingdom of God** by being good husbands and good workers.

ii. We should also remember this statement in its immediate context. Jesus reminds us that our physical well-being is not a worthy object to devote our lives unto. If you think it is worthy that your god is mammon, then your life is cursed with worry, and you live life too much like an animal lives, concerned mostly with physical needs.

iii. Jesus didn't just tell them to stop worrying; He told them to *replace* worry with a concern for the kingdom of God. A habit or a passion can only be given up for a greater habit or passion.

d. **And all these things shall be added to you**: If you put God's kingdom first, and do not think that your physical well-being is a worthy object to live your life for, you then may enjoy **all these things**. He promises heavenly treasure, rest in divine provision, and fulfillment of God's highest purpose for man—fellowship with Him, and being part of His kingdom.

i. This choice—to **seek first the kingdom of God**—is the fundamental choice everyone makes when they first repent and are converted. Yet every day after that, our Christian life will either reinforce that decision or deny it.

6. (32-34) Trust in God's provision builds generosity in the followers of Jesus.

"Do not fear, little flock, for it is your Father's good pleasure to give you the kingdom. Sell what you have and give alms; provide yourselves money bags which do not grow old, a treasure in the heavens that does not fail, where no thief approaches nor moth destroys. For where your treasure is, there your heart will be also."

a. **Do not fear, little flock**: The original uses a double diminutive, as in *little, little flock* (Trapp, Clarke). It was to this small and unlikely flock that the Father would give the kingdom unto. It was a little flock, but it was His flock.

i. They were little, but they were a **flock**—meaning they have a Shepherd. Better a little flock with the Good Shepherd than a big flock with a hireling.

b. **It is your Father's good pleasure to give you the kingdom**: This was true in a personal sense for the disciples, because they enjoyed the presence of King Jesus and the benefits of His reign among them. It was also true in another sense; Jesus would ascend to heaven and in a sense, leave **the kingdom** in the hands of these disciples. Such a great calling was also a promise of great blessings, protection, and provision.

i. Jesus gave them confidence when He said **your Father** instead of saying "*My Father.*"

c. **Sell what you have and give alms**: The command to give away what we have is a *test* of discipleship, and it is also a *tool* to train us as disciples. It points to *giving* as an antidote or cure to *covetousness*.

i. "Readiness to respond to the call of renunciation is a sign of genuine conversion, a sign of undivided loyalty to Jesus, a sign of unwavering faith in Him." (Pate)

d. **For where your treasure is, there your heart will be also**: The correlation between where your heart is and the location of your treasure isn't a suggestion; it is a simple fact. If you regard your material possessions as your treasure, then your heart is set here on this earth.

i. "If a person's primary interests are earthbound, that is where his or her commitment will be." (Pate)

ii. We should not forget that this teaching about riches and greed came from the man who interrupted Jesus' sermon with the request to settle a dispute between he and his brother. To this man (and to all), Jesus warned about the location of his treasure and his heart.

C. Attitudes in regard to Jesus' return.

1. (35-40) Be ready and waiting for your Master's return.

"Let your waist be girded and *your* lamps burning; and you yourselves be like men who wait for their master, when he will return from the wedding, that when he comes and knocks they may open to him immediately. Blessed *are* those servants whom the master, when he comes, will find watching. Assuredly, I say to you that he will gird himself and have them sit down *to eat,* and will come and serve them. And if he

should come in the second watch, or come in the third watch, and find *them* so, blessed are those servants. But know this, that if the master of the house had known what hour the thief would come, he would have watched and not allowed his house to be broken into. Therefore you also be ready, for the Son of Man is coming at an hour you do not expect."

a. **And you yourselves be like men who wait for their master**: If the followers of Jesus are to not be greedy or worried, they are to put their focus on the return of Jesus. This is something *worth* putting our lives into.

i. "These words of the Saviour are closely linked up with the previous warnings not to be worldly minded but heavenly minded." (Geldenhuys)

b. **Let your waist be girded and your lamps burning**: The idea behind this phrase is well expressed in the NIV: *Be dressed ready for service and keep your lamps burning.*

i. We are also reminded that *Your word is a lamp to my feet and light to my path* (Psalm 119:105). One may have an inner willingness to serve God (your **waist** is **girded**), but not have the illumination needed to serve Him well (the light of God's word burning brightly).

c. **I say to you that he will gird himself and have them sit down to eat, and will come and serve them**: The ready servants will be served by their Master and blessed; there is rich reward in living a life ready and expectant for Jesus to return.

i. "Those servants who are alert to their master's return will be blessed. So blessed are they, in fact, that the lord will reverse the roles and serve them by girding up his loins and seating them at the table and serving them." (Pate)

d. **Therefore you also be ready, for the Son of Man is coming at an hour you do not expect**: We all know the embarrassment of being called on when unprepared. Jesus told everyone to be prepared for His coming, which is the most important thing anyone could ever be ready for.

i. A thief never announces his coming; he comes at a time when you would not expect him. The way to be on guard against a thief is to live in constant readiness, and the way to be ready for Jesus' return is to live in constant readiness.

2. (41-48) Be good stewards in your Master's absence.

Then Peter said to Him, "Lord, do You speak this parable *only* to us, or to all *people*?" And the Lord said, "Who then is that faithful and wise steward, whom *his* master will make ruler over his household, to give

them their portion of food in due season? Blessed *is* that servant whom his master will find so doing when he comes. Truly, I say to you that he will make him ruler over all that he has. But if that servant says in his heart, 'My master is delaying his coming,' and begins to beat the male and female servants, and to eat and drink and be drunk, the master of that servant will come on a day when he is not looking for *him,* and at an hour when he is not aware, and will cut him in two and appoint *him* his portion with the unbelievers. And that servant who knew his master's will, and did not prepare *himself* or do according to his will, shall be beaten with many *stripes.* But he who did not know, yet committed things deserving of stripes, shall be beaten with few. For everyone to whom much is given, from him much will be required; and to whom much has been committed, of him they will ask the more.

a. **Peter said to Him, "Lord, do You speak this parable only to us, or to all people?"** Jesus answered Peter, saying that He spoke to every one, that all should be like a **faithful and wise steward** (manager). In a sense Jesus said "I speak this parable to all who will live their lives in readiness, even as **faithful and wise stewards.**"

i. All who are servants of Jesus must be ready for His return, but those who are ministers among His servants must all the more be ready. "Ignorance of the Divine shall not wholly excuse the sinner, he shall be beaten, but his stripes shall be few, his damnation shall be gentle compared with a minister's, that knows his Master's will but does it not; teaches it to others, but does it not himself…God looks upon wicked, loose, and scandalous and mischievous ministers as the greatest transgressors, and he will deal with them as such." (Poole)

b. **But if that servant says in his heart, "My master is delaying his coming"**: A poor steward lives without the expectation of his master's return, and it shows in several areas of life.

- He mistreats the master's other servants (**begins to beat the male and female servants**)

- He is excessively given to the pleasures of this world (**to eat and drink**)

- He is given to intoxication (**and be drunk**)

i. Jesus here clearly connected the readiness for His return to a life of love, spiritual focus, and self-control. Likewise, the heart that says, **"My master is delaying his coming"** is connected to this kind of low and fruitless life.

ii. Some get *weary* of waiting for His return, or *cynical* about the return of Jesus because it hasn't happened yet. *This is exactly the at-*

titude Jesus warned against here. If, in the perception of some, Jesus **is delaying his coming**, it is to rescue more people from the judgment to come upon the world in the very last days.

c. **The master of that servant will come on a day when he is not looking for him**: Ready or not, one day the master *will* come. When He comes, He will punish those who were not ready and denied His coming, and will reward the ready.

d. **And that servant who knew his master's will, and did not prepare himself or do according to his will, shall be beaten with many stripes. But he who did not know, yet committed things deserving of stripes, shall be beaten with few**: When the master comes, He will let the punishment match the offence. Those who *knew* how to be ready and yet were not will be punished worse than those who did not know and were not ready.

3. (49-53) Jesus brings purifying fire and division.

"I came to send fire on the earth, and how I wish it were already kindled! But I have a baptism to be baptized with, and how distressed I am till it is accomplished! Do *you* suppose that I came to give peace on earth? I tell you, not at all, but rather division. For from now on five in one house will be divided: three against two, and two against three. Father will be divided against son and son against father, mother against daughter and daughter against mother, mother-in-law against her daughter-in-law and daughter-in-law against her mother-in-law."

a. **I came to send fire on the earth, and how I wish it were already kindled!** One might regard this **fire** in a few possible ways.

- It may be that the **fire** Jesus spoke of was judgment to come upon the Jewish people in the following decades. "In Jewish thought fire is almost always the symbol of *judgment*. So, then, Jesus regarded the coming of his kingdom as a time of judgment" (Barclay)

- It may be that the **fire** Jesus spoke of is the power of the Holy Spirit that could only come after He had accomplished His work on the cross (**I have a baptism to be baptized with**)

- It may be that the **fire** Jesus spoke of is the spread of the good news and the coming expansion of the work of His kingdom across the globe, which could not happen until He had accomplished His work on the cross

  i. The fact that Jesus spoke of His suffering as **a baptism** is meaningful. He wasn't sprinkled with suffering; He was immersed in agony. In the same way, we are to be baptized into Jesus Christ and baptized with the Holy Spirit, immersed and overflowing.

b. **How distressed I am till it is accomplished!** Jesus was **distressed** until His work on the cross was **accomplished**, because He knew all the good that would come of it. *Who for the joy that was set before Him endured the cross, despising the shame* (Hebrews 12:2).

c. **Father will be divided against son and son against father, mother against daughter and daughter against mother**: This may be the price one must pay for being a faithful steward. When you follow Jesus faithfully, there may very well be division for His sake.

i. "His coming would inevitably mean division; in point of fact it did. That was one of the great reasons why the Romans hated Christianity—it tore families in two." (Barclay)

4. (54-56) The urgency to discern the times.

Then He also said to the multitudes, "Whenever you see a cloud rising out of the west, immediately you say, 'A shower is coming'; and so it is. And when you see the south wind blow, you say, 'There will be hot weather'; and there is. Hypocrites! You can discern the face of the sky and of the earth, but how *is it* you do not discern this time?"

a. **You can discern the face of the sky and of the earth, but how is it you do not discern this time?** Jesus rebuked the people of His day because they did not **discern this time**. They should have understood more about the prophecies regarding the first coming of Jesus and appreciate the obvious signs confirming Jesus as the promised Messiah.

i. Jesus' listeners knew that when clouds formed in the west over the Mediterranean Sea, rain was on the way. They knew that when the warm wind blew south from the Arabian Desert, a heat wave was coming.

b. **He also said to the multitudes**: Jesus spoke this to the **multitudes**, not only to His disciples. Jesus wanted everyone to **discern this time** and be ready for His return.

i. In our present times, there are many reasons to believe that Jesus is coming soon, adding to our sense of urgency as we hope to **discern this time**.

- The stage is set for a rebuilt temple, necessary to fulfill the prophecies of the abomination of desolation (Matthew 24:15, Mark 13:14, 2 Thessalonians 2:3-4). Since 1948 Israel is a nation again, and hopes of a rebuilt temple continue to rise among a minority of Jews

- The stage is set for the sort of world-dominating confederation of nations, heir to the Roman Empire to arise (Daniel 2:36-

45, Revelation 13:1-8, Revelation 17:10-14). It will likely be connected to the modern European Community, arising out of the goals of their leaders and the chaos of the times

- The stage is set for a political and economic world leader to arise, the sort of single political leader who will lead this world-dominating confederation of nations (2 Thessalonians 2:3-12, Revelation 13:4-7)

- The stage is set for the kind of false religion the Bible says will characterize the very last days (2 Thessalonians 2:4, 2 Thessalonians 2:9-12, Revelation 13:11-15, Revelation 17:1-6)

- The stage is set for the kind of economic system predicted for the very last days (Revelation 13:15-17). The technology is available, and the need is present

ii. None of these *guarantees* that the return of Jesus is soon. It is possible that in the wisdom of God, the time is not soon—yet, if that were the case, God would have to allow the same kind of circumstances that mark our present age to assemble again at a later time.

5. (57-59) Knowing the times, get right with God now.

"Yes, and why, even of yourselves, do you not judge what is right? When you go with your adversary to the magistrate, make every effort along the way to settle with him, lest he drag you to the judge, the judge deliver you to the officer, and the officer throw you into prison. I tell you, you shall not depart from there till you have paid the very last mite."

a. **Why, even of yourselves, do you not judge what is right?** Jesus asked His listeners to think it through for themselves. Anyone who can **judge what is right** can see the importance and good of getting right with God *before* we come before Him as Judge. If one waits until they will stand before His throne of judgment, the time will then be too late.

b. **Make every effort along the way to settle with him**: In the illustration Jesus used, it made sense to settle before appearing before the judge. By analogy, we can say that in light of the work of Jesus at the cross, God offers a settlement out of court (before judgment) with God, by putting our trusting love in who Jesus is and what He did for us on the cross.

c. **You shall not depart from there till you have paid the very last mite**: Jesus reminded them (and us) of the great *penalty* of not settling with God before the Day of Judgment. All of this presses upon us the urgency to get right with God now, and to live in readiness and anticipation of the return of Jesus.

i. Jesus here alluded to the idea that there is a *price to be paid* in hell (**till you have paid the very last mite**). This helps to explain the fearful yet Biblical truth that hell is eternal, because *payment* for sins is required, and imperfect humanity can't make a perfect payment, required by a perfect God.

ii. The coin Jesus referred to here was "The *Lepton*; *lepton* means the *thin one*; it was the smallest coin." (Barclay)

iii. The punishment of hell is eternal, just as life is eternal in heaven (Matthew 25:46, 2 Thessalonians 1:9). The torment of hell is forever (Revelation 14:11), and the fires of hell are not quenched, burning forever (Mark 9:48). The unjust have their own resurrection, presumably with bodies suited to endure the punishment of hell (John 5:29, Acts 24:15).

Luke 13—Repentance, False Religion and the True Way

A. The importance of repentance.

1. (1-5) Jesus uses two recent disasters to explain the urgency of repentance.

There were present at that season some who told Him about the Galileans whose blood Pilate had mingled with their sacrifices. And Jesus answered and said to them, "Do you suppose that these Galileans were worse sinners than all *other* Galileans, because they suffered such things? I tell you, no; but unless you repent you will all likewise perish. Or those eighteen on whom the tower in Siloam fell and killed them, do you think that they were worse sinners than all *other* men who dwelt in Jerusalem? I tell you, no; but unless you repent you will all likewise perish."

a. **The Galileans whose blood Pilate had mingled with their sacrifices**: We don't have a record in secular history about the specific incident mentioned here. According to Barclay, there is a similar incident before the ministry of Jesus. Pilate wanted to build an aqueduct from the Pools of Solomon to the city of Jerusalem. To pay for it, he demanded money from the temple treasury, money that had been dedicated to God—and this outraged the priests and the people. When the Jews sent a delegation to beg for their money back, Pilate sent into the crowd soldiers dressed as common people, and at a certain signal they took out daggers and attacked the people asking for the money.

i. This doesn't seem to be the same incident mentioned here, but it shows how completely consistent it was with the character of Pilate to slaughter a group of Galilean Jews on their way to sacrifice to the Lord in Jerusalem.

b. **Do you suppose that these Galileans were worse sinners than all other Galileans**: Jesus mentioned two disasters that were well known in

His day. One was an evil done by the hand of man, and the other was seemingly a natural disaster (**eighteen on whom the tower in Siloam fell and killed them**).

> i. We normally think of some people as good and some people as bad and find it easy to believe that God should allow good things to happen to good people and bad things to bad people. Jesus corrected this thinking.

> ii. But Jesus' point was not that the Galileans in question were innocent; His point was that they were simply not *more* guilty than the others. All were and are guilty.

> iii. "It is true, the wicked man sometimes falls dead in the street; but has not the minister fallen dead in the pulpit? It is true that a pleasure-boat, in which men were seeking their own pleasure on the Sunday, has suddenly gone down; but is it not equally true that a ship which contained none but godly men, who were bound upon an excursion to preach the gospel, has gone down too?" (Spurgeon)

c. **Unless you repent you will all likewise perish**: In analyzing the issue, Jesus turned His focus *from* the question, "Why did this happen?" and turned it *to* the question, "What does this mean to me?"

> i. It means that we all may die at any time, so repentance must be a top priority. Those who died in both of these instances did not think they would die soon, but they did, and we can suppose that most of them were not ready.

d. **Unless you repent....unless you repent**: By noting the ancient Greek grammar, we see that Jesus here mentioned two kinds of repentance, and both are essential. Luke 13:5 (**unless you repent**) described a *once and for all* repentance. The verb tense in Luke 13:3 (**unless you repent**) described a *continuing* repentance.

> i. Jesus' warning that they must repent or perish had an immediate, chilling fulfillment. Within a generation, those citizens of Jerusalem who had not repented and turned to Jesus perished in the destruction of Jerusalem.

> ii. "We cannot say that individual suffering and sin are inevitably connected but we can say that national sin and suffering are so connected. The nation which chooses the wrong ways will in the end suffer for it." (Barclay)

2. (6-9) Jesus illustrates some principles regarding God's judgment.

He also spoke this parable: "A certain *man* had a fig tree planted in his vineyard, and he came seeking fruit on it and found none. Then he

said to the keeper of his vineyard, 'Look, for three years I have come seeking fruit on this fig tree and find none. Cut it down; why does it use up the ground?' But he answered and said to him, 'Sir, let it alone this year also, until I dig around it and fertilize *it*. And if it bears fruit, *well*. But if not, after that you can cut it down.'"

a. **He came seeking fruit**: After the warning *unless you repent you will all likewise perish*, Jesus used this parable to illustrate principles of God's judgment. The first point was simple: *God looks for fruit.*

i. The fruit of our lives shows what kind of person we really are. An apple tree will bring forth apples, not watermelons. If Jesus Christ has truly touched our lives, it will show in the fruit we bear—even if it takes a while for the fruit to come forth.

ii. What fruit is God looking for? It certainly has to begin with the fruit of the Spirit, mentioned in Galatians 5:22-23: *But the fruit of the Spirit is love, joy, peace, longsuffering, kindness, goodness, faithfulness, gentleness, self-control.*

b. **Look, for three years I have come seeking fruit...let it alone this year**: The farmer in the parable illustrated the *patience* of God in judgment. He waited **three years** and gave it a second chance.

i. The farmer, illustrating God, did not leave the tree alone. He gave it special care. When God shows special care for someone, it may feel to them like they are surrounded by manure, but He is nourishing and preparing it for fruit-bearing to come.

c. **If not, after that you can cut it down**: The farmer, illustrating God, was also *just* in His judgment. There finally would come the day of reckoning. It was not just an endless string of threats.

i. "There is a time for felling fruitless trees, and there is an appointed season for hewing down and casting into the fire the useless sinner." (Spurgeon)

ii. Barclay drew several wise points of application from this:

• Uselessness invites disaster

• If something only takes, it can not survive

• God gives second chances

• There is a final chance

B. The healing of a woman in a synagogue.

1. (10-13) The healing of a woman in a synagogue.

Now He was teaching in one of the synagogues on the Sabbath. And behold, there was a woman who had a spirit of infirmity eighteen years,

and was bent over and could in no way raise *herself* up. But when Jesus saw her, He called *her* to *Him* and said to her, "Woman, you are loosed from your infirmity." And He laid *His* hands on her, and immediately she was made straight, and glorified God.

a. **He was teaching in one of the synagogues**: Though the opposition against Jesus continued to rise, He was apparently, even at the late time in His ministry, still welcomed into some **synagogues**.

b. **A spirit of infirmity**: Apparently, this woman's physical condition (**bent over and could in no way raise herself up**) was due to some spiritual cause. We are foolish to think that spiritual issues cause *all* physical problems, but we are also foolish to think spiritual issues can *never* cause physical problems.

i. **Bent over and could in no way raise herself up**: "A situation equally painful and humiliating; the *violence* of which she could not support, and the *shame* of which she could not conceal." (Clarke)

ii. "The physical cause of her inability to straighten up has been examined by J. Wilkinson, who identified the paralysis as the result of *spondylitis ankylopoietica*, which produces the fusion of the spinal bones." (Pate)

iii. She was in this condition for **eighteen years**. "For eighteen years she had not gazed upon the sun; for eighteen years no star of night had gladdened her eye; her face was drawn downward towards the dust, and all the light of her life was dim: she walked about as if she were searching for a grave, and I do not doubt she often felt that it would have been gladness to have found one." (Spurgeon)

iv. This woman is sometimes used as an example of a believer who can be demon possessed. Yet as godly as she may have been, she was not *born again by the Spirit of God*, because the work of Jesus had not yet been accomplished on the cross. We believe that Christians cannot be demon possessed; not because they are good, church-going people, but because they are new creatures in Jesus Christ, and off limits to demonic possession and control.

v. "He must have bound her very cunningly to make the knot hold all that time, for he does not appear to have possessed her. You notice in reading the evangelists that our Lord never laid his hand on a person possessed with a devil. Satan had not possessed her, but he had fallen upon her once upon a time eighteen years before, and bound her up as men tie a beast in its stable, and she had not been able to get free all that while." (Spurgeon)

c. **Woman, you are loosed from your infirmity**: Jesus spoke a word of both compassion and authority to the woman. He also **laid His hands on her**, giving a compassionate touch.

i. The woman went to synagogue for 18 years and remained in bondage, until she finally met Jesus at the synagogue.

d. **He laid His hands on her, and immediately she was made straight, and glorified God**: Jesus showed His complete mastery of illness and disease and deformity, no matter if the cause were spiritual or physical. The woman was happy she decided to go to the synagogue on that Sabbath day.

i. "He might have called to her from a distance, and said, 'Be healed,' but he did not, for he wished to show his special sympathy with such a sad case of suffering." (Spurgeon)

2. (14) The indignation of the synagogue ruler.

But the ruler of the synagogue answered with indignation, because Jesus had healed on the Sabbath; and he said to the crowd, "There are six days on which men ought to work; therefore come and be healed on them, and not on the Sabbath day."

a. **The ruler of the synagogue answered with indignation**: It may surprise that the ruler of the synagogue was so upset at such a wonderful miracle, but it is important to remember how strongly many of the Jewish people held to their Sabbath laws and customs. He was angry **because Jesus had healed on the Sabbath**.

i. "It would seem as if the demon who had left the *woman's body* had got into *his heart*." (Clarke)

b. **There are six days on which men ought to work; therefore come and be healed on them, and not on the Sabbath day**: The ruler of the synagogue did not have the ability or the authority to heal on *any* day of the week, yet he objected that Jesus did this **on the Sabbath day**.

i. **He said to the crowd**: "He had not even have the courage to speak directly to Jesus. He addressed his protest to the waiting people, although it was meant for Jesus." (Barclay)

3. (15-17) Jesus responds to the angry ruler of the synagogue.

The Lord then answered him and said, "Hypocrite! Does not each one of you on the Sabbath loose his ox or donkey from the stall, and lead *it* away to water it? So ought not this woman, being a daughter of Abraham, whom Satan has bound; think of it; for eighteen years, be loosed from this bond on the Sabbath?" And when He said these things, all

His adversaries were put to shame; and all the multitude rejoiced for all the glorious things that were done by Him.

a. **Hypocrite!** Jesus did not respond with gentleness. With authority He confronted the ruler of the synagogue who valued extreme extensions of Biblical commands more than the compassionate and life-changing power of Jesus to heal a long-afflicted woman.

i. "Thou *hypocrite* to pretend zeal for God's glory, when it is only the workings of thy malicious, unfeeling, and uncharitable heart." (Clarke)

b. **Does not each one of you on the Sabbath loose his ox or donkey from the stall, and lead it away to water it?** Jesus' reply was simple—if you can help an animal on the Sabbath, why can't you also help a suffering person on the Sabbath?

i. "The word 'loose,' as referring to the untying of the livestock, anticipates a play on words in v. 16; the woman 'was loosed' (*lythenai*) from her sickness." (Pate)

c. **So ought not this woman**: Jesus gave several compelling reasons why it was appropriate to show her mercy, and more appropriate than helping a distressed animal.

- She was a **woman**—made in the image of God, and because a woman and not a man, worthy of more care and concern

- She was **a daughter of Abraham**, a Jewish woman, with a covenant connection to Abraham. This may also indicate that she was a woman of *faith*, as well as her attendance at synagogue

- She was one **whom Satan had bound**, and every day is a good day to oppose the work of Satan and to set free his captives

- She was afflicted **for eighteen years**, long enough to suffer greatly and to draw forth the compassion of Jesus and others

d. **So ought not this woman...be loosed from this bond on the Sabbath?** Jesus used a strong word in the ancient Greek language; the idea was more that she *must* be loosed than she **ought** to be loosed.

i. "Nobody had told him that she had been eighteen years bound, but he knew all about it,—how she came to be bound, what she had suffered during the time, how she had prayed for healing, and how the infirmity still pressed upon her. In one minute he had read her history and understood her case." (Spurgeon)

e. **All His adversaries were put to shame; and all the multitude rejoiced**: The woman was so obviously healed, and the ruler of the synagogue was so obviously wrong, that all **rejoiced** in Jesus' victory.

C. Two parables warn of corruption in God's kingdom.

2. (18-19) The parable of the mustard seed tree.

Then He said, "What is the kingdom of God like? And to what shall I compare it? It is like a mustard seed, which a man took and put in his garden; and it grew and became a large tree, and the birds of the air nested in its branches."

a. **What is the kingdom of God like?** The traditional and often more familiar explanation of this parable is that it describes the growth and spreading influence of the church. Yet in light of both the parable itself and the context of the parables both before and after, this should be regarded as another description of *corruption* in the kingdom community.

b. **It grew and became a large tree**: Many or even most regard this as a beautiful picture of the church growing so large that it provides refuge for all of the world. But this **mustard seed** plant grew unnaturally large, and it harbored **birds**, which in some previous parables, were emissaries of Satan (Matthew 13:4, 13:19).

i. **Became a large tree**: The mustard plant customarily never grows beyond what one would call a bush, and at its normal size would be an unlikely place for birds' nests. The **large tree**-like growth from this **mustard seed** describes something unnatural.

ii. Additionally, trees are sometimes used in the Bible to describe human governments, and evil governments at that. In fact, this tree reminds us of the one Nebuchadnezzar saw in his vision (Daniel 4:10-16).

iii. "Close study of birds as symbols in the Old Testament and especially in the literature of later Judaism shows that birds regularly symbolize evil and even demons or Satan (cf. b. *Sanhedrin*, 107a; cf. Revelation 18:2)." (Carson)

iv. This parable accurately describes what the kingdom community became in the decades and centuries after the Christianization of the Roman Empire. In those centuries, the church grew abnormally large in influence and dominion, and was a nest for much corruption. "Birds lodging in the branches most probably refers to elements of corruption which take refuge in the very shadow of Christianity." (Morgan)

2. (20-21) The parable of the leaven in the measures of meal.

And again He said, "To what shall I liken the kingdom of God? It is like leaven, which a woman took and hid in three measures of meal till it was all leavened."

a. **It is like leaven**: Jesus used a surprising picture here. Many, if not most, regard this as a beautiful picture of the kingdom of God working its way through the whole world. Yet **leaven** is consistently used as a picture of sin and corruption (especially in the Passover narrative of Exodus 12:8, 12:15-20). Both the content and the context point towards this being a description of corruption in the kingdom community.

i. "There would be a certain shock in hearing the Kingdom of God compared to leaven." (Barclay)

b. **Leaven, which a woman took and hid in three measures of meal till it was all leavened**: This was an unusually large amount of meal. It was much more than any normal woman would prepare, and again suggests the idea of massive or unnatural size.

i. "*Three measures of meal* would be about 40 litres, which would make enough bread for a meal for 100 people, a remarkable baking for an ordinary *woman*." (France)

c. **Hid in it**: The idea of hiding leaven in **three measures of meal** would have offended any observant Jew. This certainly isn't a picture of the church gradually influencing the whole world for *good*. Even as the recent experience in the synagogue showed religious corruption of some sort, Jesus announced that His kingdom community would also be threatened by corruption and impurity.

i. G. Campbell Morgan wrote that the leaven represents "paganizing influences" brought into the church. "The parable of the tree, teaches the growth of the Kingdom into a great power; and the second, the parable of the leaven, its corruption." (Morgan)

C. The first and the last.

1. (22-24a) Jesus responds to a question about salvation.

And He went through the cities and villages, teaching, and journeying toward Jerusalem. Then one said to Him, "Lord, are there few who are saved?" And He said to them, "Strive to enter through the narrow gate"

a. **He went through the cities and villages, teaching, and journeying toward Jerusalem**: As Luke described it, Jesus came closer and closer to His appointed work in **Jerusalem**. In Luke's description, Jesus doesn't arrive to Jerusalem until chapter 19, but He continues on the way.

b. **Lord, are there few who are saved?** Like these who asked Jesus, many people wonder about the salvation of *others*. But in His reply (**Strive to enter through the narrow gate**), Jesus pointed back to the only person's salvation we can really know, asking, "Are you yourself **saved?**"

> i. "The question seems to reflect a debate that existed among Jews at the time of Christ." (Pate) Pate then cited two rabbis, one who said that all Jews would be saved, and another that said only a few. Yet Jesus would not be drawn into that debate. His only question was, "Are *you* saved?"

> ii. "A question either of *impertinence* or *curiosity*, the answer to which can profit no man. The grand question is, *Can I be saved?*" (Clarke)

c. **Strive to enter through the narrow gate**: Because the way is **narrow**, it takes effort and purpose to enter into it. A **narrow gate** also implies that we can't bring with us unnecessary things. Therefore, we must **strive** (the word is literally "*agonize*") in order to lay these things aside and come in. The Greek word for *strive* has "the idea of a struggle or prize-fight." (Bruce)

> i. Many come to the gate, but then decide they don't like it for some reason. It's too wide, it's too narrow, it's too fancy, it's too plain. You can criticize the gate all you want, but it's a terrible thing to refuse to enter into it.

> ii. "Strive even to an agony; or as they did for the garland in the Olympic games, to which the word *agonizomai*, here used, seemeth to allude." (Trapp)

> iii. **Strive to enter through the narrow gate** isn't a call to save yourself by good works. Good works aren't the right **gate**. One may strive to enter all life long, but if it isn't at the right **gate**, it makes no difference. Jesus Himself is the gate; He is the door.

> iv. It is necessary to **strive to enter** because there are many obstacles in the way. The *world* is an obstacle. The *devil* is an obstacle. Probably the worst obstacle is our own *flesh*.

2. (24b-27) The reason why it is important to strive in entering.

"For many, I say to you, will seek to enter and will not be able. When once the Master of the house has risen up and shut the door, and you begin to stand outside and knock at the door, saying, 'Lord, Lord, open for us,' and He will answer and say to you, 'I do not know you, where you are from,' then you will begin to say, 'We ate and drank in Your presence, and You taught in our streets.' But He will say, 'I tell you I do not know you, where you are from. Depart from Me, all you workers of iniquity.'"

a. **Will seek to enter and will not be able. When once the Master of the house has risen up and shut the door**: The punctuation supplied by translators in Luke 13:24-25 is poor. It could better read *will not be able when once the Master of the house has risen up and shut the door.* The point is that there will come a time when it is too late to enter; that is why one must have an urgency to enter *now*.

i. "You will see a considerable difference between seeking and striving. You are not merely advised to seek; you are urgently bidden to strive." (Spurgeon)

ii. Jesus previously spoke of the *narrow door*; here He warned of the **shut...door**. Jesus "showed that there are limits to the divine mercy, that there will be those who will not be able to enter in." (Morgan)

b. **You begin to stand outside and knock at the door, saying, "Lord, Lord, open for us"**: Many will seek to enter (in the sense of *wishing* to enter), but they will not be able to. When the door is open, it is open; when it is shut, it is shut.

i. There is a real difference between a mere *seeking* and *striving* to enter. A casual wish to be saved isn't enough, because there are too many obstacles on the way.

c. **Then you will begin to say, "We ate and drank in Your presence, and You taught in our streets"**: In speaking of those who are excluded from God's presence, Jesus said they would protest that they knew something of Jesus and had heard something of His teaching.

d. **I tell you I do not know you, where you are from. Depart from Me, all you workers of iniquity**: Jesus warned that it wasn't enough to know something of Jesus and have some association with Him; *He had to know and recognize them.*

i. Of course Jesus knew them in a sense; He knew who they were and of their lives. Yet He did not know them in the sense of relationship, of the vital connection of faith. His words stress the importance of *relationship* (**I do not know you**) that affects the *manner of living* (**you workers of iniquity**).

3. (28-30) The destiny of those who *don't* strive to enter.

"There will be weeping and gnashing of teeth, when you see Abraham and Isaac and Jacob and all the prophets in the kingdom of God, and yourselves thrust out. They will come from the east and the west, from the north and the south, and sit down in the kingdom of God. And indeed there are last who will be first, and there are first who will be last."

a. **There will be weeping and gnashing of teeth**: In speaking of those excluded from the Kingdom of God, Jesus said that they would be in hell (the place of **weeping and gnashing of teeth**), and that they would see that others enter instead of them.

i. One woman protested to an evangelist that **weeping and gnashing of teeth** could not apply to those who had lost their teeth. The preacher solemnly replied, "Teeth will be provided!"

ii. More seriously, "The definite articles with 'weeping' and 'gnashing' (cf. Greek) emphasize the horror of the scene: *the* weeping and *the* gnashing. . . . Weeping suggests suffering and gnashing of teeth despair." (Carson)

iii. We see that Jesus was unafraid to speak of hell, and in fact did so more than any other in the Bible. "There are some ministers who never mention anything about hell. I heard of a minister who once said to his congregation—'If you do not love the Lord Jesus Christ you will be sent to that place which it is not polite to mention.' He ought not to have been allowed to preach again, I am sure, if he could not use plain words." (Spurgeon)

b. **They will come from the east and the west, from the north and the south, and sit down in the kingdom of God**: Jesus told His astonished audience that there would be many from all over the world—from many nations—together with God in His **kingdom**. This was a shock to the many Jewish people of His day that had been taught that salvation was only for the Jews, and *not* for the Gentiles.

i. This was a radical idea to many of the Jewish people in Jesus' day; they assumed that this great Messianic Banquet would have no Gentiles, and that all Jews would be there. Jesus corrected both mistaken ideas.

ii. These few words of Jesus tell us a little something of what heaven is like.

- It is a place of rest; we **sit down** in heaven

- It is a place of good company to sit with; we enjoy the friendship of **Abraham, Isaac, and Jacob** and **all the prophets** in heaven

- It is a place with people from all over the earth; **from the east and the west, from the north and the south** they will come to heaven

- It is a certain place; Jesus said **they will come**, and when Jesus says it **will** happen, it will happen

iii. "But ye shall hear those loved voices again; ye shall hear those sweet voices once more, ye shall yet know that those whom ye loved have been loved by God. Would not that be a dreary heaven for us to inhabit, where we should be alike unknowing and unknown? I would not care to go to such a heaven as that. I believe that heaven is a fellowship of the saints, and that we shall know one another there." (Spurgeon)

c. **And you yourselves thrust out**: Jesus reminded his Jewish listeners that just as the Gentile's racial identity was no automatic barrier to the kingdom, so also *their* racial identity was no guarantee of the kingdom.

i. "There could hardly be a more radical statement of the change in God's plan of salvation inaugurated by the mission of Jesus." (France)

d. **Indeed there are last who will be first, and there are first who will be last**: Jesus reminded them that those who are in the kingdom, or out of the kingdom, may be different than what they or others expected. This was not intended as a universal law; Jesus did not say, "All who are last will be first" or "All who are first will be last." Yet some will, and it will surprise many.

i. "There will be surprises in the kingdom of God. Those who are very prominent in this world may have to be very humble in the next; those whom no one notices here may be the princes of the world to come." (Barclay)

ii. Spurgeon said that **there are last that shall be first** was a *wonder* [miracle] *of grace*, and that **there first that shall be last** was a *wonder of sin*.

4. (31-33) Jesus continues His work despite a threat from Herod.

On that very day some Pharisees came, saying to Him, "Get out and depart from here, for Herod wants to kill You." And He said to them, "Go, tell that fox, 'Behold, I cast out demons and perform cures today and tomorrow, and the third *day* I shall be perfected.' Nevertheless I must journey today, tomorrow, and the *day* following; for it cannot be that a prophet should perish outside of Jerusalem."

a. **Some Pharisees came... "Get out and depart from here, for Herod wants to kill You"**: This shows that not all the Pharisees opposed Jesus. These wanted to protect Him from the plotting of Herod.

i. According to William Barclay, the Talmud described seven different types of Pharisees:

- The *Shoulder Pharisee*, who wore all his good deeds and righteousness on his shoulder for everyone to see

- The *Wait-a-Little Pharisee*, who always intended to do good deeds, but could always find a reason for doing them later, not now

- The *Bruised* or *Bleeding Pharisee*, who was so holy that he would turn his head away from any woman seen in public—and was therefore constantly bumping into things and tripping, thus injuring himself

- The *Hump-Backed Pharisee*, who was so humble that he walked bent over and barely lifting his feet—so everyone could see just how humble he was

- The *Always-Counting Pharisee*, who was always counting up his good deeds and believed that he put God in debt to him for all the good he had done

- The *Fearful Pharisee*, who did good because he was terrified that God would strike him with judgment if he did not

- The *God-Fearing Pharisee*, who really loved God and did good deeds to please the God he loved

ii. "But Jesus, in fact, would leave Galilee, not because He was afraid of Herod but because He was moving according to a divine schedule." (Pate)

b. **Go, tell that fox**: According to some (such as Geldenhuys), the idea behind calling someone a **fox** was to describe them as a "cunning but weak ruler." It was used as a contrast with a majestic animal like a lion.

i. "To the Jew the fox was a symbol of three things. First it was regarded as the slyest of animals. Second, it was regarded as the most destructive of animals. Third, it was the symbol of a worthless and insignificant man." (Barclay)

ii. Herod was also an example of one of those *first* who would be *last*, mentioned in Luke 13:30. At the time he sat in power and authority, but it would not last long.

c. **Behold, I cast out demons and perform cures today and tomorrow, and the third day I shall be perfected**: Jesus wanted Herod to know that He would continue His work, even to its conclusion. Jesus wasn't afraid of Herod, and He wanted him to know it.

i. **Be perfected** actually has the idea of "to reach the goal." Jesus knew that before long, He would reach the goal on the third day—resurrection would be His.

ii. "I shall then have *accomplished* the purpose for which I came into the world, leaving nothing *undone* which the counsel of God designed me to *complete*." (Clarke)

iii. "Looking back, as we are able to do, we know that the 'third day' was the way of the Cross and all that issued from it." (Morgan)

d. **It cannot be that a prophet should perish outside of Jerusalem**: Jesus probably spoke with a touch of irony. Of course there were times when a prophet died **outside of Jerusalem**, but there was special irony in the fact that the Messiah of Israel would be rejected and executed in Jerusalem.

i. "Probably this was a proverb amongst the Jews, which our Savior used and endorsed. For many years Jerusalem had been stained with the blood of prophets." (Spurgeon)

ii. Morgan said of these words, "They reveal His own undisturbed outlook upon His work, and the quiet intrepidity of His devotion."

5. (34-35) Jesus laments over the city that will reject Him.

"O Jerusalem, Jerusalem, the one who kills the prophets and stones those who are sent to her! How often I wanted to gather your children together, as a hen *gathers* her brood under *her* wings, but you were not willing! See! Your house is left to you desolate; and assuredly, I say to you, you shall not see Me until *the time* comes when you say, 'Blessed is He who comes in the name of the Lord!'"

a. **O Jerusalem, Jerusalem**: Jesus spoke with special feeling, repeating the name for emphasis and depth. When God repeats a name twice, it is to display deep emotion, but not necessarily anger (as in the *Martha, Martha* of Luke 10:41 and the *Saul, Saul* of Acts 9:4).

i. This deep love Jesus had for Jerusalem was with full knowledge of the city's sins: **the one who kills the prophets and stones those who are sent to her**. Despite that, He still pleaded with the city to turn from the destruction that would come upon it.

b. **How often I wanted to gather your children together, as a hen gathers her brood under her wings**: Jesus wanted to protect, nourish, and cherish His people the Jews, even as a mother bird protects the young chicks.

i. "The image of a *hen* (Greek is simply 'bird') protecting its young is used in the Old Testament for God's protection of his people (Psalm 17:8; 91:4; Isaiah 31:5; *etc.*)." (France)

ii. "When the hen sees a beast of prey coming, she makes a noise to assemble her chickens, that she may cover them with her wings from the danger. The Roman *eagle* is about to fall upon the Jewish state—nothing can prevent this but their conversion to God through Christ—Jesus cries throughout the land, publishing the gospel of *reconciliation*—they would not *assemble*, and the *Roman eagle* came and destroyed them." (Clarke)

iii. This picture of **a hen** and **her brood** tells us something about what Jesus wanted to do for these who rejected Him.

- He wanted to make them safe

- He wanted to make them happy

- He wanted to make them part of a blessed community.

- He wanted to promote their growth

- He wanted to them to know His love

- This could only happen if they came to Him when He called

iv. G. Campbell Morgan called this a display of "the Mother heart of God."

v. The words **how often I wanted** are a subtle indication that Luke knew Jesus had visited Jerusalem many times before (as clearly recounted in the Gospel of John), even though he only mentions this last visit.

c. **But you were not willing!** The problem was not the willingness of Jesus to rescue and protect them; the problem was that they **were not willing**. Therefore the predicted destruction would come upon them.

i. **Your house is left to you desolate**: These words "Seem to predict the coming destruction of Jerusalem by the Roman army in A.D. 70." (Pate)

d. **You shall see Me no more till you say, "Blessed is He who comes in the name of the Lord!"** Jesus here revealed something of the conditions surrounding His Second Coming. When Jesus comes again, the Jewish people will welcome Him as the Messiah saying, "**Blessed is He who comes in the name of the Lord!**"

i. "Till after the fulness of the Gentiles is brought in, when the word of life shall again be sent unto you; then will ye rejoice, and bless, and *praise* him *that cometh in the name of the Lord*, with full and final salvation for the lost sheep of the house of Israel." (Clarke)

ii. It will take a great deal to bring Israel to that point, but God will do it. It is promised that Israel will welcome Jesus back even as the Apostle Paul said in Romans 11:26: *And so all Israel will be saved.*

Luke 14—Feasts and Invitations

A. Healing on the Sabbath.

1. (1) Jesus eats in a Pharisee's home.

Now it happened, as He went into the house of one of the rulers of the Pharisees to eat bread on the Sabbath, that they watched Him closely.

a. **He went into the house of one of the rulers of the Pharisees to eat bread on the Sabbath**: Even though Jesus had some of His greatest disputes with the Pharisees, He still associated with them—not to be one of them, but to love them and show them a godly example.

b. **They watched Him closely**: Jesus was under constant observation. People wanted to know what He would do in different situations, and they formed their opinions about Jesus (and His God) based on what they saw.

i. **Watched Him closely**: "The word used for *watching* is the word used for 'interested and sinister espionage.' Jesus was under scrutiny." (Barclay) As John Trapp wrote, "They watched as intently as a dog doth for a bone."

ii. In 2 Corinthians 3:2-3, Paul explained that we are letters from Jesus, that all men read; and that the letters are not written with ink, but with the Holy Spirit, and not on paper, but on our own hearts. *We* are the only kind of Bible many will ever read.

2. (2-4) In front of His critics, Jesus heals an afflicted man.

And behold, there was a certain man before Him who had dropsy. And Jesus, answering, spoke to the lawyers and Pharisees, saying, "Is it lawful to heal on the Sabbath?" But they kept silent. And He took *him* and healed him, and let him go.

a. **And behold, there was a certain man before Him who had dropsy**: Because this was in the home of one of the rulers of the Pharisees (Luke 14:1), this man was an invited guest. Some believe that he was invited simply to provoke Jesus into doing something that they could accuse Him regarding.

> i. "Probably the insidious Pharisee had brought this dropsical man to the place, not doubting that our Lord's eye would affect his heart, and that he would instantly cure him; and then he could most plausibly accuse him for a breach of the Sabbath. If this were the case, and it is likely, how deep must have been the perfidy and malice of the Pharisee!" (Clarke)

> ii. The man was afflicted with **dropsy**, which is an "abnormal accumulation of serous fluid in the tissues of the body" (Liefeld), "A disease that swells up the body due to fluids forming in the cavities and tissue." (Barclay) The word for **dropsy** here comes from the Greek words for "water" and "face" or "countenance," because the disease often made a person look bloated in the face.

> iii. **And Jesus, answering**: "The arresting word is the word 'answering.' These men had said nothing, yet He answered them." (Morgan) Jesus answered them with both a *question* and an *action*.

b. **Is it lawful to heal on the Sabbath?** The issue was not about the healing directly, but on healing **on the Sabbath**. When Jesus healed the man, His accusers believed that He *worked* on the Sabbath, and violated God's command, *but that wasn't true*. With this question, Jesus reminded them that there *was no command against healing on the Sabbath*.

> i. Jesus never broke the commandments of God, but He often offended man's traditions that surrounded and extended the commandments of God. The commandments of God are enough, and we should never make the traditions of man—even good traditions—equal to the commandments of God (Mark 7:8-9).

> ii. **But they kept silent**: Notably, *Jesus' accusers had no answer for this question*.

c. **He took him and healed him, and let him go**: We notice that there seems to be no ceremony or hocus-pocus in the healing ministry of Jesus. He simply *did it*, and the man was completely well. Additionally, since the man's affliction (**dropsy**) affected the man's appearance, it should be understood that the man's appearance immediately was transformed, indicating health. This was a remarkable miracle.

3. (5-6) Jesus explains why He can heal on the Sabbath.

Then He answered them, saying, "Which of you, having a donkey or an ox that has fallen into a pit, will not immediately pull him out on the Sabbath day?" And they could not answer Him regarding these things.

a. **Which of you, having a donkey or an ox that has fallen into a pit, will not immediately pull him out on the Sabbath day?** Jesus' logic was simple and impossible to dispute. If it was allowed to help animals on the Sabbath, how much more was it right to heal *people* who are made in God's image?

> i. "If they said no, they would reveal themselves for what they really were—inhuman religious leaders. If they said yes, they would be breaking their own laws governing the Sabbath." (Pate)

b. **They could not answer Him regarding these things**: One reason they could not answer was that in using this analogy, Jesus appealed to something good in His accusers. "You aren't brutal and cruel men. You will help your animals in need. Now, extend that same common-sense kindness to needy people."

> i. "Thus, while our Lord rebuked the wrong attitude and temper of these men, He did so by appealing to the best within them and calling them to be true to it. His purpose is not that of shaming men, but that of saving them." (Morgan)

B. Jesus teaches on pride and humility.

1. (7) The setting for this teaching.

So He told a parable to those who were invited, when He noted how they chose the best places, saying to them:

a. **So He told a parable**: What follows is a **parable**, a real-life illustration set alongside a Biblical truth to give an example. Parables are not *fables*; Jesus didn't tell fanciful stories with morals. He took real-life situations familiar to all, and used them to bring forth God's truth, especially for those open to hear His truth.

b. **When He noted how they chose the best places**: At the home of the Pharisee, Jesus noticed how people strategically placed themselves so as to be in **the best places**; that is, the places of most honor.

> i. In Jesus' day, the seating arrangement at a dinner showed a definite order of prestige or honor. The most honored person sat in a particular seat, the next most honored person in another seat, and so on down the line.

2. (8-9) What not to do: don't take the highest place on your own initiative.

"When you are invited by anyone to a wedding feast, do not sit down in the best place, lest one more honorable than you be invited by him; and he who invited you and him come and say to you, 'Give place to this man,' and then you begin with shame to take the lowest place."

a. **When you are invited by anyone to a wedding feast**: A wedding party was the most important social occasion in Jewish life at that time. The seating arrangement at the table indicated one's standing in the community.

b. **Do not sit down in the best place**: If one takes the most honored seat for himself, he may be asked to be removed if the host would rather have someone else sit there.

i. We don't have the same exact customs illustrating social standing by the seating arrangements at a wedding. Yet there are constant occasions in modern life where one can display their own sense of self-importance, pride, and high opinion of one's self.

c. **And then you begin with shame to take the lowest place**: Jesus reminded them of the **shame** that often comes with self-exaltation. When we allow others (especially God) to promote and lift us up, then we don't have the same danger of being exposed as someone who exalted himself.

i. The Bible reminds us that we should not play the self-promotion game. We should do our work hard and unto the Lord, and let God raise us up. *For exaltation comes neither from the east nor from the west nor from the south, but God is the Judge: He puts down one, and exalts another* (Psalm 75:6-7).

3. (10-11) What to do: take a lower place, and let God move you up.

"But when you are invited, go and sit down in the lowest place, so that when he who invited you comes he may say to you, 'Friend, go up higher.' Then you will have glory in the presence of those who sit at the table with you. For whoever exalts himself will be humbled, and he who humbles himself will be exalted."

a. **Go and sit down in the lowest place**: When we are at the lower place, we aren't there just to be noticed so we can go up higher. Nor are we miserable there, and letting everyone know by our facial expressions that we really don't belong there. There is something wonderful in being content in whatever place God allows you to have.

i. Jesus wasn't merely teaching good manners, but a lifestyle that *in lowliness of mind esteems others better than himself.* (Philippians 2:3)

b. **"Friend, go up higher." Then you will have glory in the presence of those who sit at the table with you**: Instead, we joyfully embrace the lower place; we aren't filled with such a high opinion of ourselves that we think we don't belong there. If the master of the feast were to raise us to a more prominent place, then it would be all the more satisfying (**you will have glory in the presence of those who sit at the table**).

i. Especially in Christian service, there is something wonderful about knowing that *God* has raised you up, instead of you raising *yourself* up, to prominence of some sort.

c. **For whoever exalts himself will be humbled, and he who humbles himself will be exalted**: When we seek to take honor to ourselves, we will always be humbled—if not on earth, then for all of eternity. The promise of exaltation for the humble and humiliation for the proud is one ultimately fulfilled in eternity.

i. We don't have the same cultural situation for wedding feasts today, but we certainly do have the desire to grasp for a certain position or status. And we even learn how to do our grasping with a spiritual veneer.

ii. We may choose the low place, and act meek and humble, so that others may notice how humble we are. This is a subtle form of spiritual pride that is very dangerous.

iii. When we get our own position, either through outward or subtle pride, we can even *say*, "It was the Lord, it was the Lord"—but in our heart of hearts we know it was us, our own calculation, our own schemes, our own grasping. We should remember the words of George MacDonald: *In whatever man does without God, he must fail miserably—or succeed more miserably.*

d. **Whoever exalts himself will be humbled, and he who humbles himself will be exalted**: Jesus was the perfect One to teach on this subject, because He fulfilled it perfectly. He is the ultimate example of someone who *deserved* the highest seat, but *took* the lowest seat, and was *granted* the highest seat. (Philippians 2:5-11)

4. (12-14) Jesus warns His host about the danger of pride when it comes to the guest list.

Then He also said to him who invited Him, "When you give a dinner or a supper, do not ask your friends, your brothers, your relatives, nor rich neighbors, lest they also invite you back, and you be repaid. But when you give a feast, invite *the* poor, *the* maimed, *the* lame, *the* blind. And you will be blessed, because they cannot repay you; for you shall be repaid at the resurrection of the just."

a. **When you give a dinner or a supper, do not ask your friends**: Jesus spoke this specifically **to him who invited Him**. Jesus saw that His host chose his guests from a sense of exclusion and pride, lacking love to others. Jesus told him to not ask only those who could repay something to the host.

i. **Do not ask** is more properly "do not habitually ask" (Geldenhuys). It isn't wrong to ever invite **your friends, your brothers**, and so on; but it is wrong to *only* invite such people.

b. **Lest they also invite you back, and you be repaid**: It is wrong to only associate with people who can advance us or give something to us. It is easy for us to limit our friends to a few comfortable, easy people, instead of reaching out to others.

i. Jesus here told us to not associate with people only on the basis of what they could do for us. That is self-centered living; we are called to follow Jesus, and He showed others-centered living.

ii. There is something *wonderful* in giving a gift that can never be **repaid**. This is some of the *more blessing* Jesus spoke of when He said, *It is more blessed to give than to receive* (Acts 20:35). This helps to explain some of the pleasure of God in giving the gift of salvation and blessing to His people.

c. **You shall be repaid at the resurrection of the just**: This kind of living will cost us something, yet we will be **repaid** with the full repayment coming **at the resurrection of the just**. Here again, Jesus shows how important it is to live with an *eternal* perspective.

i. **You shall be repaid** reminds us that we will *never* be the loser when we give after the pattern of God's generosity.

C. The guests of the Messiah's Banquet.

1. (15) An exclamation about the Messiah's Banquet.

Now when one of those who sat at the table with Him heard these things, he said to Him, "Blessed *is* he who shall eat bread in the kingdom of God!"

a. **Now when one of those who sat at the table**: Still at the dinner given by one of the rulers of the Pharisees (Luke 14:1), Jesus had just spoken strongly warning them against traditionalism, pride, and exclusivity. Perhaps this **one of those** thought to break the tension with these words.

b. **Blessed is he who shall eat bread in the kingdom of God!** The man spoke of the goodness and blessedness of the great banquet with the Messiah that was spoken of many times in the Old Testament, and is known in the New Testament as the marriage supper of the Lamb: *Blessed are those who are called to the marriage supper of the Lamb!* (Revelation 19:9)

2. (16-20) The parable of the great feast: Invitations and excuses.

Then He said to him, "A certain man gave a great supper and invited many, and sent his servant at supper time to say to those who were invited, 'Come, for all things are now ready.' But they all with one *accord*

began to make excuses. The first said to him, 'I have bought a piece of ground, and I must go and see it. I ask you to have me excused.' And another said, 'I have bought five yoke of oxen, and I am going to test them. I ask you to have me excused.' Still another said, 'I have married a wife, and therefore I cannot come.'"

a. **A certain man gave a great supper and invited many**: Jesus told a parable about a man who gave a great feast, a large banquet, inviting many people to come. Normally, this was just the sort of occasion that people would be thrilled to attend, and be quite happy to be invited.

b. **Come, for all things are now ready**: In an age before the clock, the *date* of the banquet was announced long before, but the *exact time* was only announced the very day.

i. This means that many accepted the invitation when it was first given; yet when the actual time of the banquet came, they were of a different mind. "To accept the invitation beforehand and then to refuse it when the day came was a grave insult." (Barclay)

ii. By analogy, we can say that God has made it so **all things are now ready** for men to come and receive from Him. We come to God and find that He has been **ready** for us.

c. **But they all with one accord began to make excuses**: Central to this parable are the excuses that were offered. The excuses are different, but really all the same—**they all *with one accord* began to make excuses**.

i. Excuses are *made*. They are fashioned for convenience and are clung to in desperation. Hope doesn't begin until excuses end. "Excuses are curses, and when you have no excuses left there will be hope for you." (Spurgeon)

ii. The excuses begin to explain why such a wonderful invitation was rejected. This answers an important question asked by many: If Christianity is so true and so good, why don't more embrace it? Why don't more accept the invitation?

d. **I have bought a piece of ground...I have bought five yoke of oxen**: The first two excuses had to do with material things and were foolish excuses. Only a fool first buys a piece of land, and *then* goes to check it. Only a fool buys ten oxen and is only interested in testing them *after* the purchase.

i. When we buy something new, we are almost always preoccupied by it. Preoccupation with material things and experiences is a common excuse for not following Jesus.

e. **I have married a wife**: The third excuse had to do with a man who put his family before everything. The best thing we can show to our family is that they are not first in our lives, but that Jesus Christ is.

i. These excuse makers condemned themselves; their excuses were only a thin veil hiding the fact that they did not *want* to come. "Back of an excuse is a lack of desire." (Morgan) There is no *rational* reason why someone would not want to be part of this feast; they just didn't *want* to.

ii. **I cannot come**: "In saying, 'I cannot come,' the man intended, as it were, to dismiss the matter. He wished to be understood as having made up his mind, and he was no longer open to argument. He did not parley; he did not talk; but he just said, off-hand, 'I want no more persuading; I cannot come, and that settles it.'" (Spurgeon)

3. (21-24) The parable of the great feast: Filling the feast.

"So that servant came and reported these things to his master. Then the master of the house, being angry, said to his servant, 'Go out quickly into the streets and lanes of the city, and bring in here *the* poor and *the* maimed and *the* lame and *the* blind.' And the servant said, 'Master, it is done as you commanded, and still there is room.' Then the master said to the servant, 'Go out into the highways and hedges, and compel *them* to come in, that my house may be filled. For I say to you that none of those men who were invited shall taste my supper.'"

a. **So that servant came and reported these things to his master**: The master of the feast must have been surprised at the response; he was certainly **angry**. It was strange and offensive that so many made excuses when given such a wonderful invitation.

b. **Go out quickly into the streets and lanes of the city, and bring in here the poor and the maimed and the lame and the blind**: If those first invited to the feast refused, there would still be a feast, because the master would not prepare a banquet in vain.

i. We see that Jesus responded to the man's exclamation *Blessed is he who shall eat bread in the kingdom of God!* (Luke 14:15) by asking, "You admire the Messianic Banquet; yet are *you* ready to receive the invitation to come? Will you make excuses?"

ii. This is an especially relevant question when one considers the sort of people who will also be at the feast: redeemed sinners and **the maimed and the lame and blind**.

c. **Compel them to come in, that my house may be filled**: The master of the feast was determined that *some* would enjoy what he had prepared. If those originally invited made excuses, the master commanded his servants to use all persuasion (**compel them to come**) to fill the feast.

i. Jesus said **compel** to indicate God's great desire to fill His house, and because these wanderers and outcasts needed to be *convinced* that they were welcome, compelled by love.

ii. "So if we are to have many sinners saved, we must go out of our own quiet haunts, and go forth into frequented places. We must preach in the street, or at the market-place, or on the village green." (Spurgeon)

iii. Tragically, Augustine and others used the phrase **compel them to come in** as a justification to coerce people into Christianity, sometimes using persecution and torture. "It was taken as a command to coerce people into the Christian faith. It was used as a defence of the inquisition, the thumb-screw, the rack, the threat of death and imprisonment, the campaigns against heretics, all those things which are the shame of Christianity." (Barclay)

iv. Even John Trapp (1601-1669) agreed with this idea: "This may be meant (saith Mr Perkins) of the Christian magistrate; for that is the magistrate's duty in respect of the outward profession."

v. Bruce on **compel**: "Reflects in the first place the urgent desire of the master to have an absolutely full house, in the second the feeling that pressure will be needed to overcome the incredulity of country people as to the invitation to them being meant seriously. They would be apt to laugh in the servant's face."

vi. "As the commentators well recognize, the veiled reference is to the Gentiles who would soon be invited to enter the kingdom of God through faith in Christ." (Pate)

D. The cost of receiving the invitation.

1. (25-26) Disciples must put Jesus first.

Now great multitudes went with Him. And He turned and said to them, "If anyone comes to Me and does not hate his father and mother, wife and children, brothers and sisters, yes, and his own life also, he cannot be My disciple."

a. **Now great multitudes went with Him**: As Jesus continued toward Jerusalem, many went with Him. He then spoke an appropriate word to these **great multitudes (He turned and said to them)**.

b. **He cannot be My disciple**: Jesus clearly spoke about the kind of person who *could not be* His **disciple**. The word **disciple** simply means "learner." A disciple is someone who is a student, a learner of Jesus.

i. Previously, Jesus said that coming to God was like accepting an invitation (Luke 14:16-24). Jesus was careful to add that there is more to being His follower than simply accepting an invitation.

c. **If anyone comes to Me and does not hate his father and mother, wife and children, brothers and sisters, yes, and his own life also, he cannot be My disciple**: Jesus boldly said that the true disciple comes to Him without reservation, setting Jesus first. Other relationships are definitely of lower priority than faithfulness and obedience to Jesus.

i. *This was an audacious demand.* None of the prophets or apostles asked for such *personal* commitment and devotion. If Jesus was not and is not God, this would be idolatry and probably madness.

ii. Napoleon understood this principle when he said, "I know men; and I tell you that Jesus Christ is no mere man. Between him and every other person in the world there is no possible term of comparison. Alexander [the Great], Caesar, Charlemagne, and I have founded empires. But on what did we rest the creations of our genius? Upon force. Jesus Christ founded his empire upon love; and this hour millions of men would die for him." (Barclay)

d. **And does not hate**: Repeatedly in the Bible we see that Jesus founded a way of *love*, not hate. Yet Jesus used the strong word **hate** to show how great the difference must be between our allegiance to Jesus and our allegiance to everyone and everything else.

i. "It is only in a comparative sense, and not literally, that the term can possibly be used; and to make this very clear, Christ said that we are to hate our own life." (Spurgeon)

ii. Normally, being a follower of Jesus makes someone a better and more beloved family member; being a follower of Jesus doesn't automatically divide families. Yet it certainly sometimes divides, and more so among non-Christian or anti-Christian cultures.

iii. The greatest danger of idolatry comes not from what is bad, but from what is *good*, such as love in family relationships. The greatest threat to the *best* often comes from *second best*.

2. (27) Disciples must count themselves as dead; they must go all the way.

"And whoever does not bear his cross and come after Me cannot be My disciple."

a. **And whoever**: We remember that Jesus spoke this to the *great multitudes*, instructing them on what it meant to be His **disciple**, especially that it is more than accepting an invitation.

b. **Bear his cross and come after Me**: Here Jesus said to the *great multitudes* something very similar to what He said privately to all His disciples in Luke 9:23—that being a follower of Jesus is something like bearing a cross.

i. *This probably horrified His listeners.* As Jesus spoke these words, everybody knew what He meant. In the Roman world, before a man *died* on a cross, he had to *carry* his cross (or at least the horizontal beam of the cross) to the place of execution. When the Romans crucified a criminal, they didn't just hang him on a cross. They first hung a cross on him.

ii. *Everyone* knew this. "When the Roman general, Varus, had broken the revolt of Judas in Galilee [4 BC], he crucified two thousand Jews, and placed the crosses by the wayside along the roads to Galilee." (Barclay)

iii. *Carrying* a cross always led to *death* on a cross. No one carried a cross for fun. The first hearers of Jesus didn't need an explanation of the cross; they knew it was an unrelenting instrument of torture, death, and humiliation. If someone took up **his cross**, he never came back. It was a one-way journey.

c. **His cross**: Jesus chose this phrasing instead of saying, "The cross" or "A cross." The idea is that there is a cross suited to each individual, and one person's experience of the cross may not look just like another person's experience of the cross.

i. "The general idea that these words of Jesus about *bearing the cross* refer to passive submission to all kinds of afflictions, like disappointments, pain, sickness and grief that come upon man in life, is totally wrong . . . only a person who for the sake of His service surrenders all self-seeking and abandons all striving after his own interests can be His disciple." (Geldenhuys)

d. **And come after Me**: Jesus made it clear that the one who bore his own cross would follow the life and pattern of Jesus. Jesus here recognized that He would bear His own cross; that He would go *before*.

i. This is following Jesus at its simplest. He carried a cross, so His followers carry one. He walked to His self-death, so must those who would follow Him.

ii. "When Jesus said this he was on the road to Jerusalem. He knew that he was on the way to the cross; the crowds who were with him thought that he was on his way to an empire." (Barclay)

e. **Cannot be My disciple**: Jesus made it clear that only cross-bearers can be His disciples. Therefore we sometimes may understate the demands of

Jesus when we present the gospel. We can give them the impression that coming to Jesus is only to believe some facts instead of to yield a life.

> i. "It is possible to be a follower of Jesus without being a disciple; to be a camp-follower without being a soldier." (Barclay)

3. (28-33) Carefully measuring the cost of following Jesus.

"For which of you, intending to build a tower, does not sit down first and count the cost, whether he has *enough* to finish *it*; lest, after he has laid the foundation, and is not able to finish, all who see *it* begin to mock him, saying, 'This man began to build and was not able to finish.' Or what king, going to make war against another king, does not sit down first and consider whether he is able with ten thousand to meet him who comes against him with twenty thousand? Or else, while the other is still a great way off, he sends a delegation and asks conditions of peace. So likewise, whoever of you does not forsake all that he has cannot be My disciple."

a. **Sit down first and count the cost**: In the parable of the tower Jesus said, "Sit down and see if you can afford to follow Me."

b. **Sit down first and consider whether he is able with ten thousand to meet him who comes against him with twenty thousand**: In the parable of the king Jesus said, "Sit down and see if you can afford to refuse My demands."

> i. Jesus perhaps alluded to the idea that the work of His kingdom was like *building* and *battle*. Each of these are usually more costly than one thinks before beginning.

c. **Whoever of you does not forsake all that he has cannot be My disciple**: We have a difficult challenge in understanding and communicating the gospel here; there are two extremes to avoid.

> i. We can *never* give people the impression that they have to clean up their lives before they come to Jesus; that is like washing up before you take a bath.

> ii. Yet likewise, we can *never* give people the impression that Jesus won't want to clean up their lives with their cooperation after they come to Him.

> iii. It is important for every potential disciple—those of the great multitudes that followed and heard Jesus (Luke 14:25)—to consider the cost of being a disciple of Jesus. Yet those who choose to reject and resist God should count *that* cost as well. What possible good can come from opposing God? It costs something to be the disciple of Jesus; it costs *more* to reject Him.

d. **Forsake all that he has**: This ancient Greek phrase had the idea, "To say goodbye to." Jesus told us to say goodbye to everything we have, entrusting it to Jesus.

4. (34-35) Given the demands of discipleship, don't be a lukewarm follower of Jesus.

"Salt *is* good; but if the salt has lost its flavor, how shall it be seasoned? It is neither fit for the land nor for the dunghill, *but* men throw it out. He who has ears to hear, let him hear!"

a. **If the salt has lost its flavor**: Salt that loses its "saltiness" is of no use. A professed believer who through corruption or assimilation loses distinctiveness, flavor, or preservative value is of no use as a follower of Jesus.

b. **It is neither fit for the land nor for the dunghill**: Salt is only useful when it has the nature of salt. A Christian is only useful when he or she has the nature of Christ.

5. (15:1) The reaction of the multitude to the strong call of allegiance to Jesus.

Then all the tax collectors and the sinners drew near to Him to hear Him.

a. **Then all the tax collectors and the sinners**: Among the great multitude described in Luke 14:25, the most notoriously sinful **drew near** to Jesus in response to His strong words about discipleship.

i. The strong call to discipleship was consistent with the love of Jesus; it was the result of His love.

b. **Drew near to Him to hear Him**: They did not necessarily give Jesus their trusting love and allegiance immediately; but they did want to **hear** more. Sinners and outcasts saw the love prompting the bold call to discipleship, and they responded.

i. People respond to a challenging gospel if the truth is spoken in love. We do a great disservice when we appear to soften the demands of the gospel, either for others or for ourselves.

Luke 15—The Joy of Finding the Lost

A. The lost sheep, the lost coin.

1. (1-3) Jesus responds to an accusation from the Pharisees.

Then all the tax collectors and the sinners drew near to Him to hear Him. And the Pharisees and scribes complained, saying, "This Man receives sinners and eats with them." So He spoke this parable to them, saying:

a. **Then all the tax collectors and the sinners drew near to Him to hear Him**: In speaking to a large number of people (Luke 14:25), Jesus strongly challenged them regarding discipleship and commitment. His strong challenge did not drive people away; it attracted them to Jesus.

b. **So He spoke this parable to them, saying**: This, one of the most beloved chapters in the Bible, is made up of parables spoken in response to the accusation, "**This man receives sinners and eats with them.**"

i. The following parables were spoken to **the Pharisees and scribes** who **complained**. The religious leaders of Jesus' day divided humanity into two classes: the unclean and the righteous. They decided to live, as much as possible, in complete separation from the unclean. Some rabbis of Jesus day took this idea so seriously that they refused to teach the unclean God's word (Morris).

ii. "Let not a man associate with the wicked, not even to bring him the law." (*m. Mek. Ex.* 18:1, cited in Pate)

iii. The following parables were spoken to **the Pharisees and scribes**, but in the hearing of the multitude of **tax collectors and sinners** who **drew near to Him to hear Him**.

2. (4-7) Finding a lost sheep.

"What man of you, having a hundred sheep, if he loses one of them, does not leave the ninety-nine in the wilderness, and go after the one which is lost until he finds it? And when he has found *it*, he lays *it* on

his shoulders, rejoicing. And when he comes home, he calls together *his* friends and neighbors, saying to them, 'Rejoice with me, for I have found my sheep which was lost!' I say to you that likewise there will be more joy in heaven over one sinner who repents than over ninety-nine just persons who need no repentance."

a. **If he loses one of them**: It isn't strange that a sheep would be lost or that a shepherd would seek the sheep. It does seem strange that a shepherd would endanger 99% of his flock for the sake of 1%. Either the safety of the 99% was assumed, or the point of this parable is in the *rejoicing*, not in the neglect of 99% for the sake of 1%.

i. "No creature strays more easily than a sheep; none is more heedless; and none so incapable of finding its way back to the flock, when once gone astray: it will bleat for the flock, and still run on in an opposite direction to the place where the flock is: this I have often noticed." (Clarke)

b. **Go after the one which is lost until he finds it**: The lost sheep would never save himself, or find the shepherd himself. If the shepherd did not take action, the sheep was doomed.

i. Many rabbis of that time believed that God received the sinner who came to Him the right way. But in the parable of the shepherd and the sheep, Jesus taught that God actively *seeks out* the lost. He does not grudgingly receive the lost; instead, He searches after them. God finds the sinner more than the sinner finds God.

ii. "A great Jewish scholar has admitted that this is the one absolutely new thing which Jesus taught men about God—that he actually searched for men." (Barclay)

c. **He lays it on His shoulders**: When Jesus finds His people, He also carries them. *For when we were still without strength, in due time Christ died for the ungodly.* (Romans 5:6)

d. **Rejoicing…Rejoice with me…more joy in heaven**: The emphasis in this parable is not on the proportion, but on the *joy* of finding the lost. This was the error of the Pharisees and scribes who complained. They were not joyful when tax collectors and sinners drew near to Jesus.

e. **Over one sinner who repents than over ninety-nine just persons who need no repentance**: Though the sheep does nothing to rescue himself or repent, Jesus mentioned the need for repentance in the last few words of this brief story. It's almost as if He said, "The sheep doesn't repent, but you need to when God finds you."

3. (8-10) Finding a lost coin.

"Or what woman, having ten silver coins, if she loses one coin, does not light a lamp, sweep the house, and search carefully until she finds *it*? And when she has found *it*, she calls *her* friends and neighbors together, saying, 'Rejoice with me, for I have found the piece which I lost!' Likewise, I say to you, there is joy in the presence of the angels of God over one sinner who repents."

a. **Or what woman, having ten silver coins, if she loses one coin**: If the shepherd was interested in one in a hundred, it makes sense that the woman would be interested in one in ten. She did not just count the coin as lost and care nothing about it.

i. Bruce suggested that possibly this coin was held with several others on a silver chain worn round the head as a mark of a married woman. It was a precious ornament to the woman, and made the loss all the more severely felt.

ii. In a sense the lost belong to God, whether they know it or not. "The piece of silver was lost *but still claimed*. Observe that the woman called the money, '*my* piece which was lost.' When she lost its possession she did not lose her right to it; it did not become somebody else's when it slipped out of her hand and fell upon the floor." (Spurgeon)

b. **Light a lamp, sweep the house, and search carefully**: The woman in the story first brought light; then swept and cleaned the house, all along searching for the coin **carefully** and with deliberate intent. She kept looking until she found the coin.

i. This is how the church, led by the Holy Spirit, will search for lost souls. First they will put forth the **light** of God's word, then **sweep** and clean their own place, then **search carefully** for the lost.

ii. "One of the first things to arrest us powerfully is *the worth of single souls*. It was one sheep the shepherd went to find. It was for one coin the woman searched the house." (Morrison)

c. **Rejoice with me**: When the coin was finally found, the woman was naturally happy. In the same way, God is *happy* when sinners repent, in contrast to the religious leaders who complained when the tax collectors and sinners drew near to Jesus to hear Him.

i. We don't often think of God as rejoicing, but this passage tells us that He does, and in what circumstances. *As the bridegroom rejoices over the bride, so shall your God rejoice over you* (Isaiah 62:5). *The LORD your God in your midst, The Mighty One, will save; He will rejoice over you with gladness, He will quiet you with His love, He will rejoice over you with singing* (Zephaniah 3:17).

ii. According to Barclay, many of the religious people of Jesus' day believed differently and even had a saying: "There will be joy in heaven over one sinner who is obliterated before God." Christians today must be careful that they do not give the same impression, especially in their often-appropriate zeal to speak out against culturally popular sins.

d. **Over one sinner who repents**: Lost coins find it impossible to repent, so Jesus added this so that both the religious leaders and the sinners who heard Him knew that repentance is important for lost *people*.

B. Finding the lost son.

1. (11-16) How the son came to be lost.

Then He said: "A certain man had two sons. And the younger of them said to *his* father, 'Father, give me the portion of goods that falls *to me.*' So he divided to them *his* livelihood. And not many days after, the younger son gathered all together, journeyed to a far country, and there wasted his possessions with prodigal living. But when he had spent all, there arose a severe famine in that land, and he began to be in want. Then he went and joined himself to a citizen of that country, and he sent him into his fields to feed swine. And he would gladly have filled his stomach with the pods that the swine ate, and no one gave him *anything*."

a. **A certain man had two sons**: The majority of this third parable speaks of the younger of the two sons, but the older brother is clearly and importantly addressed at the end of the parable.

b. **Give me the portion of goods that falls to me**: In those days a father could either grant the inheritance before or after his death, but it was usually done *after* (Geldenhuys). The younger son asked for a special exception, motivated by foolishness and greed.

i. The father clearly illustrates God's love. His love allowed rebellion, and in some sense respected human will. The father knew that the son made a foolish and greedy request, yet allowed him to go his course nonetheless.

c. **Journeyed to a far country, and there wasted his possessions with prodigal living**: The son left the area to become independent of the father and lived a **prodigal** (reckless, foolish, extravagant) life. No doubt it was fun while it lasted.

d. **When he had spent all, there arose a severe famine in the land**: The son was completely to blame for the wasteful, foolish living and spending. He was not to blame for the **severe famine**, but was afflicted by it nevertheless.

e. He began to be in want…he sent him into his fields to feed swine: Driven by hunger and need, the son accepted work that was unacceptable and offensive to any righteous Jewish person because swine were unclean under the law (Leviticus 11:7).

f. No one gave him anything: The misery of the prodigal son moves our sympathy. Yet his misery drove him to the good resolution described in the following verse.

2. (17-19) The lost son's decision to return to his father.

"But when he came to himself, he said, 'How many of my father's hired servants have bread enough and to spare, and I perish with hunger! I will arise and go to my father, and will say to him, "Father, I have sinned against heaven and before you, and I am no longer worthy to be called your son. Make me like one of your hired servants."'"

a. **But when he came to himself**: In his misery, the prodigal son was finally able to think clearly. Before it might be said that he wasn't really himself and thought as another man; then **he came to himself**.

i. In his rebellion and disobedience, he wasn't **himself**. "In his years of riot he was not himself. It was not the prodigal who was the real man. The real man was the penitent, not the prodigal." (Morrison)

ii. In his clear thinking, he didn't think of how to improve conditions in the pigpen. He didn't blame his father, his brother, his friends, his boss, or the pigs. He recognized his misery without focusing on it, and instead focused on his **father**.

b. **I will arise and go to my father**: Jesus didn't say that the man thought of his village or his home, but of his **father**. When the son returned to the father, he also came back to the village and to the house; but his focus was on returning to his **father**.

i. That is how we need to come back to God—to come back to *Him* first and foremost, before coming back to church or coming back to Christian friends.

c. **Father, I have sinned against heaven and before you, and I am no longer worthy to be called your son. Make me like one of your hired servants**: In his prepared speech to his father, the son showed his complete sense of unworthiness and an honest confession of sin. He would not even ask to be treated as a son, but as a hired servant.

i. "**I have sinned against heaven and before you**" shows a complete change of thinking. He didn't think like this before. Now he made no attempt to justify or excuse his sin.

ii. "The ordinary slave was in some sense a member of the family, but the hired servant could be dismissed at a day's notice. He was not one of the family at all." (Barclay)

iii. The lost son *demonstrated* the repentance Jesus specifically spoke of in the previous parables of the lost sheep and the lost coin. After his misery, he thought completely differently about his father, himself, and his home. The son asked for two things: First, "Father, *give me*"; then, "Father, *make me*." Only the second request brought joy.

3. (20-24) The father joyfully receives the lost son.

"And he arose and came to his father. But when he was still a great way off, his father saw him and had compassion, and ran and fell on his neck and kissed him. And the son said to him, 'Father, I have sinned against heaven and in your sight, and am no longer worthy to be called your son.' But the father said to his servants, 'Bring out the best robe and put *it* on him, and put a ring on his hand and sandals on *his* feet. And bring the fatted calf here and kill *it,* and let us eat and be merry; for this my son was dead and is alive again; he was lost and is found.' And they began to be merry."

a. **And he arose and came to his father**: The prodigal first *thought*, but he didn't stop at thinking. He didn't just feel sorry and think about repenting; he actually did it.

i. "Some of you whom I now address have been thinking, and thinking, and thinking, till I fear that you will think yourselves into perdition. May you, by divine grace, be turned from thinking to believing, or else your thoughts will become the undying worm of your torment." (Spurgeon)

ii. "He did not go back to the citizen of that country and say, 'Will you raise my wages? If not, I must leave.' Had he parleyed he had been lost; but he gave his old master no notice, he concerned his indentures by running away. I would that sinners here would break their league with death, and violate their covenant with hell, by escaping for their lives to Jesus, who receives all such runaways." (Spurgeon)

b. **But when he was still a great way off, his father saw him and had compassion**: The father's love waited and never forgot. It was a love that fully received, not putting the son on probation. This was especially remarkable because the son had disgraced the family by his prodigal living.

i. "The depth of the son's repentance is matched only by the depth of the father's love." (Pate)

c. **Ran and fell on his neck and kissed him**: The intensity of the father's reception was indicated by the fact that he **ran** (unusual for grown men in those cultures) and that he repeatedly **kissed him** (indicated by the original grammar, according to Morris).

d. **Father, I have sinned against heaven and in your sight**: The son began to recite his prepared speech; yet it seemed that the father didn't even hear it. Instead, he commanded that the prodigal youth be treated like a son, and not like a servant.

e. **Bring out the best robe and put it on him, and put a ring on his hand and sandals on his feet. And bring the fatted calf here and kill it**: None of the four things brought to the repentant prodigal were necessities; they were all meant to honor the son and make him know he was loved. The father did much more than merely meet the son's needs.

f. **And they began to be merry**: It was a happy thing to find the lost sheep and the lost coin. It was much more happy to find the lost son. They had a wonderful party with special clothing, jewelry, and food. It wasn't just finding a lost son; it was as if he were back from the **dead**.

4. (25-32) The bitterness and resentment of the older son.

"Now his older son was in the field. And as he came and drew near to the house, he heard music and dancing. So he called one of the servants and asked what these things meant. And he said to him, 'Your brother has come, and because he has received him safe and sound, your father has killed the fatted calf.' But he was angry and would not go in. Therefore his father came out and pleaded with him. So he answered and said to *his* father, 'Lo, these many years I have been serving you; I never transgressed your commandment at any time; and yet you never gave me a young goat, that I might make merry with my friends. But as soon as this son of yours came, who has devoured your livelihood with harlots, you killed the fatted calf for him.' And he said to him, 'Son, you are always with me, and all that I have is yours. It was right that we should make merry and be glad, for your brother was dead and is alive again, and was lost and is found.'"

a. **His older son was in the field**: The older son never lived a prodigal life and was hard at work **in the field**, even as the younger son came home. Drawn by the sound of the party (**music and dancing**), he learned from a servant that his younger brother had come home.

b. **But he was angry and would not go in**: The older son was not happy that the brother was so joyfully received. He complained and felt it was an insult to his own obedience and faithfulness.

i. **I never transgressed…you never gave**: These exaggerations are common for those who hold on to bitterness. The older son finally showed this bitterness to the father, but only after it had done its damage in his heart over many years.

ii. The older brother was unappreciative of all he *did* have. "Every day he had his father's company, and the blessed society of home. His father's love was round about him constantly, and everything the father had was his." (Morrison) Yet, "The proud and the self-righteous always feel that they are not treated as well as they deserve." (Morris)

iii. There was a sense in which the older son was obedient, yet far from his father's heart. In this sense, he was a perfect illustration of the religious leaders who were angry that Jesus received tax collectors and sinners. "His story reveals the possibility of living in the father's house and failing to understand the father's heart." (Morgan)

c. **Therefore his father came out and pleaded with him…Son, you are always with me**: The father also loved the older son, and earnestly appealed to him.

i. "The father did not call him *son*. He called him *child*—so it is in the Greek—and child is a word of tenderest affection." (Morrison)

d. **It was right that we should make merry and be glad**: This answered the complaint of the religious leaders that began the chapter. They had no reason to complain and every reason to be happy.

i. In each of the parables, the message to the tax collectors and sinners was clear: repent, come home to the father. The message to the religious leaders was also clear: be happy when the lost are found, when they repent and come home to the father.

ii. As a whole, we might say that these three parables suggest the searching, seeking work of the Shepherd Son, the Holy Spirit (working through the church), and the Heavenly Father.

iii. "The truth here taught is just this: that mercy stretches forth her hand to misery, that grace receives men as sinners, that it deals with demerit, unworthiness and worthlessness; that those who think themselves righteous are not the objects of divine compassion, but the unrighteous, the guilty and the undeserving, are the proper subjects for the infinite mercy of God; in a word, that salvation is not of merit but of grace." (Spurgeon)

Luke 16—Money and Righteousness

A. The story of the dishonest steward.

1. (1-8) What the dishonest steward did.

He also said to His disciples: "There was a certain rich man who had a steward, and an accusation was brought to him that this man was wasting his goods. So he called him and said to him, 'What is this I hear about you? Give an account of your stewardship, for you can no longer be steward.' Then the steward said within himself, 'What shall I do? For my master is taking the stewardship away from me. I cannot dig; I am ashamed to beg. I have resolved what to do, that when I am put out of the stewardship, they may receive me into their houses.' So he called every one of his master's debtors to *him,* and said to the first, 'How much do you owe my master?' And he said, 'A hundred measures of oil.' So he said to him, 'Take your bill, and sit down quickly and write fifty.' Then he said to another, 'And how much do you owe?' So he said, 'A hundred measures of wheat.' And he said to him, 'Take your bill, and write eighty.' So the master commended the unjust steward because he had dealt shrewdly. For the sons of this world are more shrewd in their generation than the sons of light."

a. **He also said to His disciples**: This seems to be a different occasion than the previous chapter. Here Jesus taught **His disciples**, not the multitude mentioned in Luke 15:1-2. However, as Jesus taught **His disciples**, a group of Pharisees also listened (Luke 16:14).

b. **There was a certain rich man who had a steward**: A **steward** was a manager, especially a manager of money or property. In the story Jesus told, the steward's boss (the **rich man**) heard that his steward had cheated him (**wasting his goods**), and he called him to account.

i. "The steward had followed a career of embezzlement." (Barclay)

ii. "**Give an account of your stewardship**" are words that everyone will hear, both sinner and saint. All will have to give **account** in some way, and we will give account to God. Spurgeon once noted that each of us will have to give account of our stewardship regarding our *time*, our *talents*, our *substance*, and our *influence*.

iii. For each of us, our stewardship will one day come to an end. The preacher's voice, mental faculties, and strength will not last forever. The wealth of this world may not last even in this life. A mother's stewardship over her children changes and diminishes greatly. If Jesus does not come first, we *all* will die and pass from this life to the next.

c. **What shall I do? For my master is taking the stewardship away from me**: When the steward knew that he would be called to account, he knew his poor management would be exposed. He also knew that other options were unattractive to him (**I cannot dig; I am ashamed to beg**).

d. **So he called every one of his master's debtors to him**: So the steward made friends with his master's debtors by settling their accounts for less than they actually owed. Therefore the steward, knowing he would be called to account, used his present position to prepare him for the next stage of his life.

e. **So the master commended the unjust steward because he had dealt shrewdly**: While not approving his conduct, the master did in fact approve the steward's *shrewdness*. Jesus added the thought that the businessmen of his day (**sons of this world**) were more wise, bold, and forward-thinking in the management of what they had (**more shrewd**) than the people of God were with managing what they had (**the sons of light**).

i. Some consider this to be one of Jesus' most difficult parables, because it seems that Jesus used an obviously dishonest man as an example for His disciples. Yet God sometimes uses evil things familiar to us with which to illustrate a particular point, without praising the thing itself. Other examples of this principle are when Paul used things like war and slavery as illustrations of the Christian life.

ii. Yet the dishonest steward was a good example on several points. First, he knew he would be called to account for his life, and he took that seriously. Christians should take seriously the idea that they will be called to account, and that idea can be a *joy* if we are properly about our Master's business. Second, he took advantage of his present position to arrange a comfortable future.

iii. Jesus' assessment is still true: **the sons of this world are more shrewd in their generation than the sons of light**. If we pursued the Kingdom of God with the same vigor and zeal that the children of this world pursue profits and pleasure, we would live in an entirely different world. It could be said that it is to the shame of the Church that Coca-Cola is more widely distributed than the gospel of Jesus Christ. Simply, it is because **the sons of this world are more shrewd in their generation than the sons of light**.

iv. "Go to the men of the world, thou Christian, and do not let it be said that the devil's scholars are more studious and earnest than Christ's disciples." (Maclaren)

2. (9) Using money now with an eye to eternity.

"And I say to you, make friends for yourselves by unrighteous mammon, that when you fail, they may receive you into an everlasting home."

a. **Make friends for yourselves by unrighteous mammon**: Jesus transferred the principle of the parable, reminding us that we need to use our present resources to plan ahead for eternity.

i. **Unrighteous mammon**: "The word 'mammon' is from the Aramaic word *mammon*, which originally meant, 'that in which one puts one's trust,' hence wealth." (Pate)

ii. Jesus called it **unrighteous mammon** because "Riches *promise* MUCH, and *perform* NOTHING: they excite *hope* and *confidence*, and *deceive* both: in making a man *depend* on them for *happiness*, they *rob* him of the salvation of God and of eternal glory." (Clarke)

b. **That when you fail, they may receive you into an everlasting home**: The world is filled with financial planners and advisers, and it is good for Christians to learn how to use their money wisely. But when most Christians talk about wise money management, they forget to practice the most important kind of long-term investing—investing with an eye to *eternity*, an **everlasting home**.

i. The important thing is to invest your resources for the Lord *now*. Most of us wait until the day when we think we will have enough.

ii. In a survey taken long ago (1992), people were asked how much money they would have to make to have "the American dream." Those who earn $25,000 or less a year thought they would need around $54,000. Those in the $100,000 annual income bracket said that they could buy the dream for an average of $192,000 a year. These figures indicate that we typically think we must double our income in order to find the good life—instead of finding it *now*.

3. (10-12) Faithfulness in the little things shows how one will be faithful in the large things.

"He who *is* faithful in *what is* least is faithful also in much; and he who is unjust in *what is* least is unjust also in much. Therefore if you have

not been faithful in the unrighteous mammon, who will commit to your trust the true *riches*? And if you have not been faithful in what is another man's, who will give you what is your own?"

a. **He who is faithful in what is least is faithful also in much**: In these words of Jesus, money is considered to be one of the **least** things. Therefore, if a person cannot be faithful in managing the things that are **least**, they should not be trusted to be faithful in handling the things that are **much**.

i. If one is false and unfaithful in everyday life, it doesn't matter if he knows how to project a Christian image; they are also false and unfaithful in the spiritual life—and no one should entrust them with **true riches** (spiritual riches).

b. **If you have not been faithful in the unrighteous mammon, who will commit to your trust the true riches?** In this sense, those who are leaders among God's people must be good managers of their own money. If a person can't be faithful before God with the money He gives, how can he be faithful with the care of people?

i. This certainly does not mean that leaders in the church have to be wealthy or make a lot of money. It is an issue of how they *manage* the resources God has given to them, not how great their resources are.

ii. Unfortunately, when it comes to the question **who will commit to your trust the true riches**, far too many Christians are willing to entrust their spiritual care to a person who can't even care for the things of **unrighteous mammon**.

c. **If you have not been faithful in what is another man's**: Here, Jesus seems to refer to the fact that all our riches belong to God, and we must see that we are managing *His* resources. Faithfulness in this will result in blessing that is our own (**who will give you what is your own**).

i. "So God is testing men by giving them money, that He may know how far to trust them in the mart of the New Jerusalem." (Meyer)

4. (13) No one can be faithful to more than one master.

"No servant can serve two masters; for either he will hate the one and love the other, or else he will be loyal to the one and despise the other. You cannot serve God and mammon."

a. **No servant can serve two masters**: Having **two masters** is not like working two jobs. Jesus has the master and slave relationship in view. A slave can't belong to two masters at the same time.

i. Jesus states that serving two masters is a simple impossibility. If you think that you are successfully serving two masters, you are deceived.

One can *have* both money and God, but one cannot *serve* both money and God.

ii. Certainly, Jesus spoke about the *heart* here. Many people would *say* they love God, but their service of money shows that in fact they do not. How can we tell Who or what we serve? One way is by this principle: *You will sacrifice for your God.* If you will sacrifice for the sake of money, but will not sacrifice for the sake of Jesus, don't deceive yourself—money is your God.

iii. On a Friday afternoon in 1990, a businessman staggered to the steps of his Los Angeles office. Before he died of the gunshot wound to his chest, he called out the names of his three children. But he still had his $10,000 Rolex watch clutched in his hand. He was the victim of a rash of Rolex robberies—and was killed as a sacrifice to his god.

iv. A 1992 story in the *Los Angeles Times* told about Michelle, a successful writer and editor, who fears the day her husband might discover her secret stash of credit cards, her secret post office box or the other tricks she uses to hide how much money she spends shopping for herself. "I make as much money as my husband . . . If I want a $500 suit from Ann Taylor, I deserve it and don't want to be hassled about it. So the easiest thing to do is lie," she explains. Last year, when her husband forced her to destroy one of her credit cards, Michelle went out and got a new one without telling him. "I do live in fear. If he discovers this new VISA, he'll kill me."

v. In the same story, a school teacher explained more: "Men just don't understand that shopping is our drug of choice," she joked, even while admitting that some months her salary goes exclusively to paying the minimum balance on her credit cards. "Walking through the door of South Coast Plaza is like walking though the gates of heaven. God made car trunks for women to hide shopping bags in."

vi. A young professional named Mary continued and explained, "Shopping is my recreation. It's my way of pampering myself. When you walk into [a mall] and you see all the stores, it's like something takes over and you get caught up in it."

b. **You cannot serve God and mammon**: Some think that just because they are not rich, they are not a slave to money (**mammon**). But you don't have to be rich to serve **mammon**. The poor have just as much potential for greed and covetousness as the rich.

i. "When God is served, Mammon is used beneficently. When Mammon is served, the claims of God are ignored." (Morgan)

ii. "The worldling's wisdom (as the ostrich's wings) to make him out-run others upon earth, and in earthly things; but helps him never a wit toward heaven." (Trapp)

iii. "Money possessing a man is the direst curse, for it hardens his heart and paralyzes his noblest powers. The money of a God-possessed man is a blessing, for it becomes the means of his expressing his sympathy with his fellows." (Morgan)

5. (14-15) Jesus responds to the Pharisees' derision.

Now the Pharisees, who were lovers of money, also heard all these things, and they derided Him. And He said to them, "You are those who justify yourselves before men, but God knows your hearts. For what is highly esteemed among men is an abomination in the sight of God."

a. **And they derided Him**: The derision of the Pharisees was based on their own self-interest. They **were lovers of money**. Often we reject the message of Jesus because it hits too close to home.

i. **Derided**: "The word literally means that they turned up their noses at him." (Barclay)

b. **You are those who justify yourselves before men, but God knows your hearts**: It is one thing to **justify yourselves before men**, because smooth words and a "loving" smile can deceive men. **But God knows your hearts**—when you serve another master, it is impossible to be justified before God, no matter what men think.

i. For some people the idea **God knows your hearts** is *comfort*; for others it is a *curse*.

c. **For what is highly esteemed among men is an abomination in the sight of God**: God judges our hearts with a different set of values. Men may honor someone because of their wealth or their public display of spirituality, but God sees who they really are.

6. (16-18) The unchanging nature of God's law.

"The law and the prophets *were* until John. Since that time the kingdom of God has been preached, and everyone is pressing into it. And it is easier for heaven and earth to pass away than for one tittle of the law to fail. Whoever divorces his wife and marries another commits adultery; and whoever marries her who is divorced from *her* husband commits adultery."

a. **The law and the prophets were until John**: Jesus indicated that the ministry of John the Baptist marked the end of one great aspect of God's work. **Since that time** (the time ending with John's ministry) the good news of a new covenant is presented, with an order that is different from the law, yet it fulfills the law.

b. **The kingdom of God has been preached, and everyone is pressing into it**: In Jesus' day, there were hundreds of revolutionaries willing to use violence to bring in the kingdom of God. While we do not imitate their violence, we do imitate their dedication, their willingness to sacrifice, and their passion to see the Messiah reign. In a sense, we are also *at war*.

> i. Pate suggested that **pressing into it** does not describe the appropriate effort and zeal necessary to pursue the kingdom of God. Instead he thought it described the attempt of demonic powers (and their human agents) to forcefully enter and disrupt or destroy the work of God's kingdom, describing *opposition* to the work of Jesus. Certainly in a sense, both are true.

c. **It is easier for heaven and earth to pass away than for one tittle of the law to fail**: As Jesus spoke of a new aspect of God's work beginning after the ministry of John the Baptist, He didn't want any to think that the new aspect of God's work ignored or neglected **the law**.

> i. But the new order that we must press into is not an order of rebellion; it is a new order of submission and obedience to God. His new order fulfills the law.

d. **Whoever divorces his wife and marries another commits adultery**: For example, the law concerning marriage is still binding—no matter how some rabbis tried to explain it away. Some Rabbis taught that if a woman burned her husbands breakfast, it was grounds for divorce. Others considered finding a prettier woman was an acceptable reason to divorce.

> i. Jesus here taught the ideal regarding marriage and divorce, and it is dangerous for us to establish doctrine on isolated statements of Jesus without taking into account the whole counsel of His teaching.

> ii. Jesus also taught that sexual immorality was acceptable grounds for divorce (Matthew 5:31-32, 19:7-9), and later the Apostle Paul added that desertion by an unbelieving spouse was also an acceptable reason (1 Corinthians 7:15). Because of those two clear allowances, we must regard Jesus' command here to refer to the one who **divorces his wife** *without Biblical cause* **and marries another**; that *this one* **commits adultery**.

> iii. Again, Jesus emphasized the point: Under the new covenant (since the ministry of John the Baptist), God still cares about His law and our obedience.

B. The story of Lazarus and the rich man.

1. (19-21) Lazarus and the rich man on earth.

"There was a certain rich man who was clothed in purple and fine linen and fared sumptuously every day. But there was a certain beggar named Lazarus, full of sores, who was laid at his gate, desiring to be fed with the crumbs which fell from the rich man's table. Moreover the dogs came and licked his sores."

a. **There was a certain rich man**: Jesus did not present this story as a *parable*, and in no other parable did Jesus actually name an individual (as the poor man is here named). We have every reason to believe that Jesus gave us an actual case history, one He knew from His eternal perspective.

b. **Clothed in purple and fine linen and fared sumptuously every day**: The rich man's wealth was evident by his **fine linen** clothing (luxurious and expensive), and by his excess with food (most people in that culture **fared sumptuously** only a few times a year).

  i. **Fared sumptuously**: "The word used for feasting is the word that is used for a gourmet feeding on exotic and costly dishes. He did this *every day*." (Barclay)

  ii. The rich man is unnamed, but was traditionally given the name *Dives*, which is simply Latin for *rich*.

c. **A certain beggar named Lazarus, full of sores, who was laid at his gate, desiring to be fed with the crumbs**: Not far from the rich man—at **his gate**—was a desperately poor and sick man. The rich man didn't *do* anything against Lazarus, except neglect and ignore him.

  i. "Here are two men, and day after day there is not the space of twenty yards between them, yet a distance like the sea divides the two." (Morrison)

  ii. "The name is the Latinized form of Eleazar and means *God is my help*." (Barclay)

  iii. **Fed with the crumbs which fell from the rich man's table**: "Food was eaten with the hands and, in very wealthy houses, the hands were cleaned by wiping them on hunks of bread, which were then thrown away. This is what Lazarus was waiting for." (Barclay)

  iv. **The dogs came and licked his sores**: Jesus described the misery of the beggar in these strong, nauseating details.

2. (22-23) Lazarus and the rich man in Hades.

"So it was that the beggar died, and was carried by the angels to Abraham's bosom. The rich man also died and was buried. And being in torments in Hades, he lifted up his eyes and saw Abraham afar off, and Lazarus in his bosom."

a. **So it was that the beggar died…The rich man also died and was buried**: Both men eventually died. Lazarus did not even have the honor of a burial in this life, yet heaven honored him, being **carried by the angels to Abraham's bosom**. The rich man had the honor of a burial, but no angelic escort or pleasant destination.

> i. It would seem obvious that when the beggar was **carried by the angels**, it was his *soul* or *spirit* that was carried; the immaterial and eternal aspect of his being. Except for the angels' carrying work, the same was true of the rich man. His body was **buried** and remained on earth, but *he* was **in torments in Hades**.

> ii. "The idea of Abraham's bosom can be explained in one of three ways." (Pate)

> - The idea that in death, the righteous are gathered to the patriarchs in the faith (Genesis 15:15, 25:8)

> - The thought of a parent's love and care, as in John 1:18 (*The only begotten Son, who is in the bosom of the Father…*)

> - The idea of sitting at the place of honor at a banquet, as in John 13:23

> iii. We should not think that Lazarus was saved by his poverty, any more than we should think that the rich man was damned by his wealth. Lazarus must have had a true relationship of faith with the true God, and the rich man did not. Their life circumstances made that faith easier or more difficult, but did not create it.

b. **And being in torments in Hades, he lifted up his eyes and saw Abraham afar off, and Lazarus in his bosom**: The rich man was not far from Lazarus; yet he was a world apart. His place was full of torment and pain, while Lazarus enjoyed the comfort and care of Abraham.

> i. "Having punishment without pity, misery without mercy, sorrow without succor, crying without compassion, mischief without measure, torments without end, and past imagination." (Trapp)

c. **Being in torments in Hades**: In this story, Jesus described a place He called **Hades**, which seems to have been the common abode of the dead. The rich man and Lazarus were not in the same place, but they were not far from each other. It may be best to say that they were in two areas of the same place (Hades), one a place of torments and the other a place of comfort (**the bosom of Abraham**).

> i. From this story of Jesus, we find some hints regarding the world beyond as it existed in the past and as it exists now. From Jesus' description, one may say that at that time—*before* the finished work of

Jesus on the cross—that the spirit or soul of the human dead went to a place called Hades. Some in Hades rested in comfort; others suffered under torments of fire.

ii. **Hades** is a Greek word, but it seems to carry much the same idea as *Sheol*, a Hebrew word with the idea of the "place of the dead." *Sheol* has no direct reference to either torment or eternal happiness. The idea of *Sheol* is often simply "the grave" and the understanding of the afterlife in the Old Testament is much less clear than in the New Testament.

iii. **Hades** is technically not *hell*, or what is also known as the *Lake of Fire*. That place is called *Gehenna*, a Greek word borrowed from the Hebrew language. In Mark 9:43-44, Jesus spoke of *hell* (*gehenna*), a Greek translation of the Hebrew "Valley of Hinnom," a place outside Jerusalem's walls, desecrated by Molech worship and human sacrifice (2 Chronicles 28:1-3; Jeremiah 32:35). It was also a garbage dump where rubbish and refuse were burned. The smoldering fires and festering worms of the Valley of Hinnom made it a graphic and effective picture of the fate of the damned. This place is also called the "lake of fire" in Revelation 20:13-15, prepared for the devil and his angels (Matthew 25:41).

iv. **Hades** is something of a waiting place until the day of final judgment (Revelation 20:11-13). Yet since Jesus' finished work on the cross, there is no waiting for believers who die; they go directly to heaven, the presence of the Lord (2 Corinthians 5:6-8). It is reasonable to think that when Jesus visited **Hades** as part of His redemptive work (Acts 2:24-27, Acts 2:31), and when Jesus preached in Hades (1 Peter 3:18-19), that Jesus set the captives in Hades free (Ephesians 4:8-9, Isaiah 61:1). Jesus' work and preaching offered salvation for those like Lazarus, who in faith awaited it (Hebrews 11:39-40), and it also sealed the condemnation of the wicked and unbelieving.

3. (24-26) The rich man's plea.

"Then he cried and said, 'Father Abraham, have mercy on me, and send Lazarus that he may dip the tip of his finger in water and cool my tongue; for I am tormented in this flame.' But Abraham said, 'Son, remember that in your lifetime you received your good things, and likewise Lazarus evil things; but now he is comforted and you are tormented. And besides all this, between us and you there is a great gulf fixed, so that those who want to pass from here to you cannot, nor can those from there pass to us.'"

a. **Father Abraham, have mercy on me**: The rich man was a descendant of Abraham, and the great father of faith did not disown him. Yet having

Abraham as father was not enough to escape his torment in the life to come. Now the rich man was the beggar, pleading with Abraham.

i. Again, the rich man was not in torment because he was rich; but because he lived a life apart from love and trust in God, and this was demonstrated by his life. Abraham himself was richer than the man in this story of Jesus.

b. **Send Lazarus that he may dip the tip of his finger in water and cool my tongue**: Even in the afterlife, the rich man thought of himself as superior and Lazarus as his servant. This shows that death did not take away his sense of entitlement and station in life.

i. "And he could not plead he was ignorant of Lazarus, for he recognized him at once in Abraham's bosom. It was not want of *knowledge*, then, but want of *thought* that was the innermost secret of his tragedy." (Morrison)

ii. Death also did not take away the rich man's sense of *desire*, only the fulfillment of that desire. This was true torment, and he was desperate for even a *drop* of relief.

c. **Son, remember that in your lifetime you received your good things**: Through his earthly life, the rich man enjoyed all the good things of life, yet did not share them or use them to prepare for the life to come.

i. The rich man is therefore a *contrast* to the previous parable of the unjust steward (Luke 16:1-12). The unjust steward used his present position to prepare for his next position; the rich man did not.

d. **Between us and you there is a great gulf fixed, so that those who want to pass from here to you cannot**: Though the rich man could see and speak with Abraham, he wasn't close to him at all. There was a **great gulf fixed** between them, and their destinies were fixed for all time.

i. We remember that all this happened to the rich man's spirit or soul, the immaterial part of his being. His body was still buried, yet he did not cease or suspend existence or awareness.

ii. We see no idea of soul sleep or annihilation; not of spiritual progression or reincarnation. Also, "There is no hint here of purgatory or remedial cleansing. The chasm was fixed, it is assumed, by God." (Pate)

4. (27-31) The rich man thinks of his brothers.

"Then he said, 'I beg you therefore, father, that you would send him to my father's house, for I have five brothers, that he may testify to them, lest they also come to this place of torment.' Abraham said to him, 'They have Moses and the prophets; let them hear them.' And he said,

'No, father Abraham; but if one goes to them from the dead, they will repent.' But he said to him, 'If they do not hear Moses and the prophets, neither will they be persuaded though one rise from the dead.'"

a. **I beg you therefore, father**: It is again emphasized that now the *rich man* is the beggar, not Lazarus.

b. **Send him to my father's house, for I have five brothers, that he may testify to them**: It is again seen that the rich man *still* thought of Lazarus as a servant to him. He asked Abraham to send Lazarus on another assignment (perhaps in a dream or vision), this time for the benefit of his **five brothers**.

> i. Obviously, the rich man remembered and cared about his relatives even when he passed from earth to the life to come. His memory was not wiped clean or given a new consciousness.

c. **Lest they also come to this place of torment**: *Now* the rich man cared about others not going to **torment**. He lived his life utterly unconcerned of this, either for himself or for others. If he himself could go to his brothers, he would; but he seemed to understand that this was also impossible, so much so that he did not even ask for it.

> i. The mention of the five brothers is the first indication that the rich man thought about anyone except himself. Unfortunately, his concern for others came when it was too late to do any good.

d. **They have Moses and the prophets, let them hear them**: Abraham pointed out that the rich man's brothers had all the necessary information to escape the torment of Hades. Listening to **Moses and the prophets** and doing what they said to do was enough.

> i. **Abraham said to him**: "Luke uses the historic present tense for Abraham's reply: 'Abraham *says*, "They have Moses and the prophets. Let them listen to them." (Pate)

> ii. "When God's whole creation having been ransacked by the hand of science, has only testified to the truth of revelation—when the whole history of buried cities and departed nations has but preached out the truth that the Bible was true—when every strip of land in the far-off East has been an exposition and a confirmation of the prophecies of Scripture; if men are yet unconvinced, do ye suppose that one dead man rising from the tomb would convince them?" (Spurgeon)

> iii. "If the Holy Scripture be not in the hands of God enough to bring you to the faith of Christ, then, though an angel from heaven, then, though the saints from glory, then, though God himself should descend on earth to preach to you, you would go on unwed and unblest." (Spurgeon)

e. **No, father Abraham; but if one goes to them from the dead, they will repent**: The rich man immediately objected, knowing that his family did not take **Moses and the prophets** seriously. He desperately hoped that if someone came from the dead, it would be more convincing than the Word of God. Yet it would not be more convincing, because if they would not believe because of God's Word, **neither will they be persuaded though one rise from the dead**.

i. The rich man knew what his brothers must do, and what he *did not* do: **repent**. He mistakenly hoped that a spectacular appearance of one from the dead would persuade them, but Abraham knew it would not. After all, the unbeliever thinks the Bible *already* speaks too much of judgment and hell; they don't want to hear more of it, even if the messenger came from the world beyond.

ii. Of course, Jesus did rise from the dead; yet many did not believe then. Additionally, a man named Lazarus also came back from the dead (John 11:38-44), and the religious leaders did not believe him; they tried to kill him (John 12:9-10).

iii. With this story, Jesus showed the weakness of trusting in signs to bring people to faith. It is easy to think that if people saw a spectacular enough sign, they would be *compelled* to believe. But what creates faith unto salvation is hearing the Word of God (Romans 10:17); a sign may or may not have a role in that work. God, working through His word, has power unto salvation. "He declares that the sacred writings are in themselves as powerful as anything like the delivery of their message by one risen from the dead." (Morgan)

iv. "Although a churchyard should start into life, and stand up before the infidel who denies the truth of Christianity; I declare I do not believe there would be enough evidence in all the churchyards in the world to convince him. Infidelity would still cry for something more." (Spurgeon)

v. "I do believe that Lazarus from Abraham's bosom would not be so good a preacher as a man who has not died, but whose lips have been touched with a live coal from off the altar." (Spurgeon)

vi. The rich man wasn't lost because he was rich; he was lost because he did not listen to the law and the prophets. Many will also be lost for the same reason.

vii. In one way, the rich man of Jesus' story was very different from the religious leaders, the Pharisees. He lived a life of gourmet excess and indulgence, and the Pharisees were rigid and disciplined and super self-controlled. Yet they shared this with the rich man: *they cared noth-*

ing for the needy around them, and despised them with neglect. That's why they were so offended when Jesus taught and cared for tax collectors and sinners (Luke 15:1-2). "A hundred miles may separate two rivers, but for all that, they flow from the same lake." (Morrison)

Luke 17—Duty, Thankfulness and the Kingdom

A. Forgiveness, faith and duty.

1. (1-2) The danger of stumbling another.

Then He said to the disciples, "It is impossible that no offenses should come, but woe *to him* through whom they do come! It would be better for him if a millstone were hung around his neck, and he were thrown into the sea, than that he should offend one of these little ones."

a. **Then He said to the disciples**: Jesus, through the account of Lazarus and the rich man, has made it clear that eternity is for real, and no one from beyond will come back to warn us. It is all the more imperative how we live and show Jesus to others on this side of eternity, because right now counts forever.

b. **It is impossible**: It is inevitable that people be offended, but woe to the person through whom those offenses come. It is important to understand what Jesus meant when He spoke of **offenses**.

i. The ancient Greek word used here for **offenses** is *skandalon*, and it comes from the word for a bent-stick—the stick that springs the trap or sets the bait. It also was used for a stumbling block, something that people trip over.

ii. In the Bible sometimes a *skandalon* is good, such as the way that people "trip" over Jesus, and are offended at the gospel (Romans 9:33, 1 Corinthians 1:23, Galatians 5:11).

iii. But among brothers in Jesus, a *skandalon* is bad. It can be false counsel (Matthew 16:23), and it can be leading a brother into sin by your "liberty" (Romans 14:13). Division and false teaching brings a *skandalon* among God's people (Romans 16:17).

c. **Woe to him through whom they do come**: Essentially, Jesus said: "People are going to take the bait—but woe to you if you offer the hook.

People are going to trip up—but woe to you if you set the stumbling block in their way."

> i. It would **better** for the offending one to die a horrible death, such as having a millstone hung around your neck and being thrown into the sea.
>
> ii. This is a lesson that the church learned the hard way in trying to help God to curse the Jewish race for their rejection of the Messiah; the curse came back on the church worse than ever. If someone seems ripe for the judgment or discipline of God, let God do it. Get out of the way. God doesn't need you as an instrument of His judgment, only as an instrument of His love
>
> iii. 1 John 2:10 explains the solution to being a *skandalon* to others—love: *He who loves his brother abides in the light, and there is no cause for stumbling in him.* If we love our brother, we will not bring an offense into their life.

2. (3-4) If someone stumbles you, deal with it and forgive them.

"Take heed to yourselves. If your brother sins against you, rebuke him; and if he repents, forgive him. And if he sins against you seven times in a day, and seven times in a day returns to you, saying, 'I repent,' you shall forgive him."

> a. **If your brother sins against you, rebuke him**: When someone sins against you, you should not pretend that it never happened. You need to **rebuke** that brother in love.
>
> > i. Love is the rule here. We obviously can't walk around keep a record of every little offense committed against us. One aspect of the fruit of the Spirit is *longsuffering* (Galatians 5:22), and we need to be able to suffer long with the slights and petty offenses that come our way in daily living. Ephesians 4:2 says that we should love *with longsuffering, bearing with one another in love.* Don't be too sensitive; bear with one another.
> >
> > ii. But in love, when we are sinned against in a significant way, we must follow Ephesians 4:15 as the pattern: we need to speak the truth in love. Love isn't going to *other* people about it; love isn't bottling it up inside of you. Love is getting it straight with the person who sinned against you.
>
> b. **If he repents, forgive him**: This is the challenge from Jesus. There is no other option given. When the person who offended you repents, you must **forgive** them.

i. What do we do with the person who has never repented? Do we forgive them? Even if the relationship cannot be restored because no common mind is arrived at, we can still choose to forgive them on our part, and wait for a work of God in their life for the restoration of relationship.

ii. Clearly—especially in light of the words that follow—Jesus did not intend here to *narrow* our focus of forgiveness. If anything, His intent was to *broaden* our work of forgiveness. He wasn't giving us a reason to *not* forgive or to be *less* forgiving.

c. **And if he sins against you seven times in a day, and seven times in a day returns to you, saying, "I repent," you shall forgive him**: This indicates that we are not permitted to judge another's repentance. If someone had sinned against me **seven times in a day**, and kept asking me to forgive them, I might think that they were not really sincere. Yet Jesus commands me to still forgive them and restore them.

3. (5-6) Great faith is needed to get along with people like this.

And the apostles said to the Lord, "Increase our faith." So the Lord said, "If you have faith as a mustard seed, you can say to this mulberry tree, 'Be pulled up by the roots and be planted in the sea,' and it would obey you."

a. **Increase our faith**: On this occasion, the disciples were extremely perceptive. They recognized that great faith in God is needed to get along with people in this forgiving, non-offending way. If Jesus' point in the previous passage was to *narrow* forgiveness, they didn't need this faith.

i. "This work of pardoning *every* offence of *every* man, and that *continually*, seemed so difficult, even to the *disciples* themselves, that they saw, without an extraordinary degree of faith, they should never be able to keep this command." (Clarke)

b. **If you have faith as a mustard seed**: We usually think of faith as being exercised with dramatic, miraculous works. That may be true, but the greatest miracles of faith have to do with the restoration of relationships.

i. According to Geldenhuys, the roots of the **mulberry tree** were thought to be extraordinarily strong; it was thought that this tree could stay rooted for six hundred years.

ii. You may have unforgiveness and bitterness that is deeply rooted within you; it may be like one of those trees that send down deep, strong roots. But through faith, Jesus can rip those roots clean out; it can **be pulled up by the roots and be planted in the sea**.

iii. "No duty required of men and women more grates upon flesh and blood than this of forgiving injuries, nothing that the most of people find harder to put in practice; so as indeed where there is not a root of faith, this fruit will not be found." (Poole)

c. **As a mustard seed**: The faith that we must have is a faith that has more to do with what *kind* of faith it is than with *how much* faith there is. A small amount of faith—as much **as a mustard seed** (a very small seed)—can accomplish great things, if that small amount of faith is placed in a great and mighty God.

i. Little faith can accomplish great things; but great faith can accomplish even greater things. What matters most is what our faith is in, the *object* of our faith. "The eye cannot see itself. Did you ever see your own eye? In a mirror you may have done so, but that was only a reflection of it. And you may, in like manner, see the evidence of your faith, but you cannot look at the faith itself. Faith looks away to itself to the object of faith, even to Christ." (Spurgeon)

ii. When ice-skating, it is far better to have small faith on thick ice than great faith on thin ice. Our small faith in so great a Savior can accomplish great things.

4. (7-10) We can't put God into debt to us; anything we do for Him is small repayment for His work in our life.

"And which of you, having a servant plowing or tending sheep, will say to him when he has come in from the field, 'Come at once and sit down to eat'? But will he not rather say to him, 'Prepare something for my supper, and gird yourself and serve me till I have eaten and drunk, and afterward you will eat and drink'? Does he thank that servant because he did the things that were commanded him? I think not. So likewise you, when you have done all those things which you are commanded, say, 'We are unprofitable servants. We have done what was our duty to do.'"

a. **Having a servant plowing or tending sheep**: Jesus had just spoken to His disciples about great works possible by great faith. Here Jesus added some words meant to work against the pride that often rises when God uses someone.

i. Jesus speaks of those who *really* serve. **Plowing** is hard work; it exhausts the strength and endurance of the plowman. It is hard work in farming, and it is hard work in spiritual ministry. **Tending sheep** can also be hard work, requiring a lot of patience, attention to detail, and a caring heart.

ii. It is helpful to remember that these words were not given to the multitude; the chapter began, *Then He said to the disciples* (Luke 17:1). "Mark you, he was not laying down the way of salvation, but pointing out a path of service for those who were already saved." (Spurgeon)

b. **Prepare something for my supper, and gird yourself and serve me till I have eaten and drunk, and afterward you will eat and drink**: Jesus pictured a servant coming in from a hard day of work, either **plowing or tending sheep**. When the servant arrives home, the master does not compliment, or feed, or serve, or massage the servant. The master expected the servant to keep serving because there was still work to do.

i. There is always *something* we can do to serve our Master, and there is always *some way* we can do it. "If you cannot go out ploughing, you shall go down into the kitchen, and do some cooking; and if you cannot feed the cattle, you shall bring up a dish of food for your Master. This is a change of work for you; but you are to keep on as long as you live." (Spurgeon)

ii. In the context of the preceding words of Jesus, we can say there are still people to forgive; there are still great works of faith to do.

iii. These works are hard, but in this mini-parable Jesus gave us the right attitude. His pleasure before our own. His people preferred before ourselves. His name before our own name.

c. **Does he thank that servant because he did the things that were commanded him?** Of course the master does not thank the servant for such things; in that pre-Christian culture, such kindness was unthinkable.

i. Therefore, we don't serve Jesus inwardly demanding that He thank us or praise us.

- It seems strange that Jesus would thank us, in light of all He has done for us

- It seems strange that He would thank us, considering all we have left undone

- It seems strange, considering all we have done has come from Him as a gift and an empowering anyway

ii. "What have we done for him compared with what he has done for us? Our service put beside Christ's is like one single grain of dust put in comparison with the mighty orb of the sun." (Spurgeon)

iii. Yet strangely, *He will thank us and reward us*. Though we don't deserve it, He will look at the work of each of His servants and to the faithful ones He will say, "*Well done, good and faithful servant.*" (Matthew 25:21, 23)

d. **We are unprofitable servants**: The kind of attitude Jesus spoke of is not a false humility, the kind of attitude that says, "I'm no good at anything." It is not an admission that we do nothing good or pleasing to God. It simply recognizes that He has done so much more for us than we could ever do for Him.

e. **We have done what was our duty to do**: This attitude understands that our Master has done more and greater things for us than we could ever do for Him. What He did for us was out of pure *love*; what we do for Him is out of proper gratitude and **duty**.

i. This is why it is so important for Bible teachers to emphasize what the Bible itself emphasizes—what God has done for us. When we realize all that God has done for us in Jesus, we *want* to serve Him out of gratitude. Think of the great work of forgiveness Jesus did for us; think of the great mountains He moved by faith. The greatest works of faith and forgiveness by us are mere **duty** in comparison.

ii. When our hearts are right, we live and act as if we are happy to have the *privilege* of being *allowed* to serve God.

iii. Not enough Christians have this attitude today. Instead, many today often want to project a "super-Christian" image that makes them seem to be anything but **unprofitable servants**. We only think that we are better than others when we look to man, not Jesus.

iv. "Growing saints think themselves nothing; full-grown saints think themselves less than nothing." (Spurgeon)

v. "An old rabbinic saying reveals a similar thought, 'If you learned much in the Torah, claim not merit for yourself; for this purpose were you created' (*m. Abot* 2:8)." (Pate)

B. The cleansing of ten lepers.

1. (11-14) The healing of the lepers.

Now it happened as He went to Jerusalem that He passed through the midst of Samaria and Galilee. Then as He entered a certain village, there met Him ten men who were lepers, who stood afar off. And they lifted up *their* voices and said, "Jesus, Master, have mercy on us!" So when He saw *them,* He said to them, "Go, show yourselves to the priests." And so it was that as they went, they were cleansed.

a. **As He entered a certain village, there met Him ten men who were lepers**: It was not unusual for these lepers to congregate with one another. They were outcasts from society at large, and had no company other than other lepers, so they **stood afar off**.

i. **Who stood afar off**: "They kept at a distance, because forbidden by law and custom to come near to those who were sound, for fear of infecting them. See Leviticus 13:46; Numbers 5:2; 2 Kings 15:5." (Clarke)

ii. **Passed through the midst of Samaria and Galilee**: "The words *dia meson* are best translated 'through the middle of,' or 'between,' referring to Jesus' travel along the border between Samaria and Galilee." (Pate)

b. **And they lifted up their voices and said, "Jesus, Master, have mercy on us!"**: They came to Jesus together and they prayed together, even though they were a mixed group of Jews and Samaritans (Luke 17:15-16). Bonded by their misery, their national and other prejudices vanished as they came together in prayer.

i. "A common misfortune had broken down the racial and national barriers. In the common tragedy of their leprosy they had forgotten they were Jews and Samaritans and remembered only they were men in need." (Barclay)

c. **Go, show yourselves to the priests**: It was remarkable that Jesus asked them to go to the priests while they were still lepers. This was truly stepping out in faith, as in putting on the new man even when we still look and feel like the old man.

i. "The one condition of healing was obedience. Ordered, they must obey. If He was master as they had cried He was, then let them prove their faith by their obedience." (Morrison)

ii. "God highly honours this kind of faith, and makes it the instrument in his hand of working many miracles. He who will not believe till he receives what *he* calls *a reason for it*, is never likely to get his soul saved. The highest, the most sovereign *reason*, that can be given for *believing*, is that *God* has *commanded* it." (Clarke)

d. **And so it was that as they went, they were cleansed**: Just as God blessed the faith of the lepers to step out as the new man even when they feel like the old, so will He bless our faith.

i. "It is as we go on the commanded road that we experience the commanded blessing. Let the Church obey the command of the Lord Jesus, and with enthusiasms evangelise the nations, and, *as she goes*, she will be healed." (Morrison)

2. (15-19) Only one out of ten of the lepers return to give thanks.

And one of them, when he saw that he was healed, returned, and with a loud voice glorified God, and fell down on *his* face at His feet, giving

Him thanks. And he was a Samaritan. So Jesus answered and said, "Were there not ten cleansed? But where *are* the nine? Were there not any found who returned to give glory to God except this foreigner?" And He said to him, "Arise, go your way. Your faith has made you well."

a. **And one of them, when he saw that he was healed, returned, and with a loud voice glorified God**: Only one came back to give thanks, and he was the *unlikely* one, **a Samaritan**. And, though he was the only one, at least he was very **loud** about his thanks.

i. All ten were willing to do a religious ceremony; that is go to the priest. Only one was filled with true praise and thanksgiving. "External religious exercises are easy enough, and common enough; but the internal matter, the drawing out of the heart in thankful love, how scarce a thing it is! Nine obey ritual where only one praises the Lord." (Spurgeon)

b. **Were there not ten cleansed? But where are the nine?** Jesus *missed* the nine who did not return to give thanks. He wondered where they were. Jesus also notices our lack of gratitude.

i. "The question was asked, and it at once proves the value He sets upon the service of praise...One wonders whether it is not so that our Lord has been asking this question very constantly." (Morgan)

ii. "Christ keeps count how many favours men receive from him, and will call them to a particular account thereof." (Trapp)

iii. We can always find reason for gratitude before God. Matthew Henry, the famous Bible commentator, was robbed of his wallet once. He wrote in his diary that night all the things he was thankful about:

- First, that he had never been robbed before
- Second, that though they took his wallet, they did not take his life
- Third, because even though they took it all, it wasn't very much
- Finally, because he was the one who was robbed and not the one who did the robbing

iv. "Lastly, if we work for Jesus, and we see converts, and they do not turn out as we expected, do not let us be cast down about it. If others do not praise our Lord, let us be sorrowful, but let us not be disappointed. The Savior had to say, 'Where are the nine?' Ten lepers were healed, but only one praised him. We have many converts who do not join the church; we have numbers of persons converted who do not come forward to baptism, or to the Lord's Supper. Numbers get a blessing, but do not feel love enough to own it." (Spurgeon)

c. **Your faith has made you well**: There was an extra healing for this tenth leper. When Jesus said this, He likely meant God's work within the man's heart. The other lepers had whole bodies, but sick hearts.

C. The coming of the kingdom.

1. (20-21) If you want to know about Jesus' kingdom, get to know the King.

Now when He was asked by the Pharisees when the kingdom of God would come, He answered them and said, "The kingdom of God does not come with observation; nor will they say, 'See here!' or 'See there!' For indeed, the kingdom of God is within you."

a. **When He was asked by the Pharisees when the kingdom of God would come**: We may just imagine a hostile Pharisee coming to Jesus, and demanding Him to either "put up" and produce the Kingdom of the Messiah, or to "shut up" and stop claiming He was the Messiah.

i. In Jesus' day, just like our own, people longed for the coming of the Messiah. They knew the prophesies in the Old Testament which spoke of the glory of the coming Messiah; they wanted that kind of life and earth *now*.

ii. "WHILE the Lord was yet on earth the days of the Son of man were but lightly esteemed. The Pharisees spoke of them with a sneer, and demanded when the kingdom of God should come. As much as to say, 'Is this the coming of thy promised kingdom? Are these fishermen and peasants thy courtiers? Are these the days for which prophets and kings waited so long?'" (Spurgeon)

b. **The kingdom of God does not come with observation**: Jesus made it clear to the Pharisee asking the question that the **kingdom of God** won't be found through a hostile questioning of Jesus. The ancient Greek word translated **observation** is better translated *hostile examination*. Jesus told the Pharisees that their hostile, doubting eyes were unable to see or receive the kingdom of God.

i. According to Geldenhuys, the verb from which the word **observation** comes from is used often in the New Testament and in the Septuagint; it means "hostile observation."

c. **For indeed, the kingdom of God is within you**: Jesus told them that the kingdom was right in their midst. **Within you** could be better translated *in your midst* or *among you*. The kingdom of God was among them because the King was among them.

i. This was not a mystical revelation by Jesus that in some seed form, the Kingdom of God is within everyone in a New Age sense. After all, Jesus would not have told Pharisees that the kingdom of God was within *them*. The statement of Jesus called attention to Himself, not to man.

ii. Like many today, the Pharisees *said* they wanted the Kingdom of God to come; but you can't want the Kingdom and reject the King. "The Pharisees asked Him when the Kingdom of God would appear, while it was right in their midst because the King Himself was there." (Morgan)

2. (22-24) Jesus' kingdom won't come immediately in the disciples' day.

Then He said to the disciples, "The days will come when you will desire to see one of the days of the Son of Man, and you will not see *it*. And they will say to you, 'Look here!' or 'Look there!' Do not go after *them* or follow *them*. For as the lightning that flashes out of one *part* under heaven shines to the other *part* under heaven, so also the Son of Man will be in His day."

a. **The days will come when you will desire to see one of the days of the Son of Man, and you will not see it**: Now speaking **to the disciples**, Jesus told them that when He left this earth, the days would come when Jesus' disciples—both near and far off—would long for the Messiah's return.

b. **And they will say to you, "Look here!" or "Look there!"** Satan would know how to take advantage of that longing; there would be many who claimed to be the Messiah who would come before Jesus actually returned. It is essential that these false Messiahs do not deceive us.

c. **Do not go after them or follow them**: In the centuries since Jesus spoke these words, there have been many who have claimed to be the Messiah, and some have had significant followings. Jesus solemnly warned us to **not go after them or follow them**; instead we should disregard them.

i. Dr. Charles Feinberg, a noted Jewish-Christian scholar, said that in the course of Israel's history since the time of Jesus, sixty-four different individuals have appeared claiming to be the Messiah.

ii. In the not very distant past, men like David Koresh, Jim Jones, Sun Myung Moon, and many, many others have all claimed to be the Messiah. Many Orthodox Jews thought (and still think) that a Brooklyn Rabbi named Mendel Schneerson was the Messiah. Even more have been regarded as messiah in some sense without necessarily being in the Judeo-Christian framework (such as Stalin or Mao).

d. **For as the lightning that flashes**: In **His day**, the day of the Messiah's triumph, all will see it even as everyone notices **lightning that flashes** across the sky. Those who claim that Jesus has returned or will return **in His day**, in some secret sense, are mistaken.

3. (25) Jesus' kingdom cannot come until He finishes His work on earth.

But first He must suffer many things and be rejected by this generation.

a. **But first He must suffer**: There is a tendency in many followers of Jesus to skip the cross and go straight to the Kingdom of God, but the Kingdom of God could not come until the King went to the cross.

i. Why should it be Jesus who rules and reigns? Because He has fulfilled His own word, and we are called to follow Him in the same way. Jesus said, *If anyone desires to be first, he shall be last of all and servant of all.* (Mark 9:35) He also said, *Whoever desires to become great among you, let him be your servant.* (Matthew 20:26)

ii. We might say that Jesus can only come again in glory because He came first in humility and submission unto death.

b. **Must suffer many things and be rejected**: The strength, certainty, and intensity of this statement is striking.

- Jesus **must** suffer and be rejected
- Jesus must **suffer** and be **rejected**
- Jesus must suffer **many things**, not just a few

c. **By this generation**: Sadly, though the full triumph of Jesus' kingdom would wait, His suffering would come soon, at the hands of **this generation**.

4. (26-30) The coming of the King will be a great surprise.

"And as it was in the days of Noah, so it will be also in the days of the Son of Man: They ate, they drank, they married wives, they were given in marriage, until the day that Noah entered the ark, and the flood came and destroyed them all. Likewise as it was also in the days of Lot: They ate, they drank, they bought, they sold, they planted, they built; but on the day that Lot went out of Sodom it rained fire and brimstone from heaven and destroyed *them* all. Even so will it be in the day when the Son of Man is revealed."

a. **And as it was in the days of Noah**: By showing the similarity to Noah's day, Jesus described a world continuing in the normal routines of life. People **ate, drank…married wives, they were given in marriage**.

i. "All things continued as normal, that is until Noah and his family entered the ark, at which time the Deluge (*kataklysmos*) came and destroyed all the people (see Genesis 7:7, 10, 21; 1 Peter 3:20)." (Pate)

b. **Likewise as it was also in the days of Lot**: The destruction that came upon Sodom and Gomorrah in the days of Lot came in the morning (Genesis 19:15-25). The day before seemed much like any other day to the men of Sodom.

c. **Even so will it be in the day when the Son of Man is revealed**: Even as the world seemed to continue in the normal routines of life before the flood and the judgment of Sodom and Gomorrah, Jesus said there will be some sense of normalcy in the world when He is **revealed**.

i. Jesus didn't say that all would be *good* in the world, or that there would be no crises. Conditions before the flood and before the judgment of Sodom and Gomorrah were terrible, but the wickedness was accepted as *normal* and *routine*.

ii. Significantly, there are other passages of Scripture that seem to show that Jesus will return to an earth that will be anything *but* business as usual. These include:

- *For then there will be great tribulation, such as has not been since the beginning of the world until this time, no, nor shall ever be.* (Matthew 24:21)

- *And the kings of the earth, the great men, the rich men, the commanders, the mighty men, every slave and every free man, hid themselves in the caves and in the rocks of the mountains, and said to the mountains and rocks, "Fall on us and hide us from the face of Him who sits on the throne and from the wrath of the Lamb!* (Revelation 6:15-16)

iii. Because the conditions of the world before the revealing of Jesus are described in such different terms, it is reasonable to say that there will be two distinct phases or aspects of Jesus' coming, separated by some period of time.

iv. Just as in the days of Noah and Lot, when Jesus comes, some will be taken out of the way (escaping judgment), and others will remain and be judged.

5. (31-33) Prepare for the coming of the King by not being attached to this world.

"In that day, he who is on the housetop, and his goods *are* in the house, let him not come down to take them away. And likewise the one who is in the field, let him not turn back. Remember Lot's wife. Whoever

seeks to save his life will lose it, and whoever loses his life will preserve it."

a. **In that day, he who is on the housetop, and his goods are in the house, let him not come down to take them away**: When Noah's flood came, one could imagine people trying to vainly keep their possessions safe while they themselves perished. Even so, if one is ready for Jesus' coming, he will not be concerned about the material things left behind. The heart must not be on what is **in the house**, but what is in *heaven.*

b. **Let him not turn back. Remember Lot's wife**: Because she disobeyed God and looked back on Sodom—presumably with regret and perhaps with longing—Lot's wife was turned into a pillar of salt as she and her family escaped judgment. Jesus here cautioned His followers to not look back at a perishing world, ripe for judgment, but to set their eyes on the deliverance God sets before them.

i. **Remember Lot's wife**: "The word Jesus used for 'remember' … means to pay heed to; to learn a lesson from." (Pate) We see the sin of Lot's wife in at least three ways:

- *Lot's wife lingered behind.* Moses made the point that Lot's wife *looked back behind him, and she became a pillar of salt* (Genesis 19:26). Before she looked back, she lingered *behind him*, as Lot and his daughters sought to escape the judgment of Sodom

- *Lot's wife did not trust and obey the divine word.* The angel specifically told them to escape with urgency, not to lag behind—and especially, to not look back (Genesis 19:17)

- *Lot's wife looked at what she was told to turn away from.* After lingering and doubting, she then looked. "She did look back, and thus proved that she had sufficient presumption in her heart to defy God's command, and risk her all, to give a lingering love-glance at the condemned and guilty world. By that glance she perished" (Spurgeon)

ii. **Lot's wife**, "Who either out of curiosity or covetousness turned her back, and she was turned. We are as hardly drawn off the world as a dog from a fat morsel." (Trapp)

iii. Spurgeon remembered a further tragedy regarding Lot's wife: she *almost* made it. "*Doom befell her at the gates of Zoar.* Oh, if I must be damned, let it be with the mass of the ungodly, having always been one of them; but to get up to the very gates of heaven, and to perish there, will be a most awful thing!" (Spurgeon)

6. (34-36) When Jesus comes, some will be taken suddenly and others will be left behind.

"I tell you, in that night there will be two *men* in one bed: the one will be taken and the other will be left. Two *women* will be grinding together: the one will be taken and the other left. Two *men* will be in the field: the one will be taken and the other left."

a. **In that night there will be two men in one bed: the one will be taken and the other will be left**: This passage is often applied to the rapture, a term applied to Jesus' coming for His people at a time when the world seems to run in the normal routines of life (Luke 17:26-30).

i. The New Testament passage that most clearly describes this event and gives the name *rapture* from the Latin translation of the passage is 1 Thessalonians 4:16-18: *For the Lord Himself will descend from heaven with a shout, with the voice of an archangel, and with the trumpet of God. And the dead in Christ will rise first. Then we who are alive and remain shall be caught up together with them in the clouds to meet the Lord in the air. And thus we shall always be with the Lord. Therefore comfort one another with these words.*

ii. These words of Jesus (**one will be taken and the other will be left**) seem to describe this phenomenon of being *caught up…in the clouds to meet the Lord in the air* as described in 1 Thessalonians 4:16-18.

b. **One will be taken and the other left**: Because this will happen during the normal course of life (while one sleeps in **bed**, while another is **grinding** grain, and while another works **in the field**), the emphasis is on readiness. Jesus will come suddenly and at an unexpected moment.

i. This connects with the prior illustrations of Noah and Lot. "Noah and Lot were taken and, therefore, saved from judgment while the rest were left for destruction." (Pate)

c. **Two men in one bed…Two women will be grinding together**: These words of Jesus may indicate that it will be day in one part of the world while it is night in another; at the same time some sleep, others work in a field. Jesus will come for His people all over the earth at one moment.

i. "Verse 36 is not in the best Greek manuscripts…and is an addition to the biblical text. It was probably added by a scribe because of Matthew 24:40." (Pate)

7. (37) All this will happen at the time when judgment is ripe.

And they answered and said to Him, "Where, Lord?" So He said to them, "Wherever the body is, there the eagles will be gathered together."

a. **Where, Lord?** The disciples wanted to know more about this revelation of Jesus, presumably both **where** the deliverance and judgment might take place. As they came nearer to Jerusalem, perhaps they wondered if these events would take place soon, as they arrived at the City of Zion.

b. **Wherever the body is, there the eagles will be gathered together**: This is a difficult statement. It was probably a figure of speech with the idea, "When judgment is ripe, it will surely come."

i. "That simply meant that a thing would happen when the necessary conditions were fulfilled." (Barclay) "Where that which is ripe for judgment is present, there also will the judgment take place." (Geldenhuys)

ii. Some wonder if the conditions are ready in the present day for this revelation of Jesus, both in delivering His people and judgment upon a world that rejects Him. We may say this with some confidence: The Bible describes certain political, economic, spiritual, social, and military characteristics regarding what the world will be like before His return. It is fair to say that the conditions exist today, and the stage is set.

Luke 18—Prayer, Humility and Discipleship

A. A parable about persistence in prayer.

1. (1) The purpose of the parable: that we might not lose heart in prayer.

Then He spoke a parable to them, that men always ought to pray and not lose heart,

a. **That men always ought to pray**: Man is created with a spiritual instinct (Ecclesiastes 3:11), so prayer often comes naturally. Yet obstacles come in the way of effective and constant prayer, so Jesus knew we needed to be both taught and encouraged **always . . . to pray**.

i. Jesus did not mean that we should always have our knees bent and eyes closed in prayer, but we must always be in what is sometimes called *the spirit of prayer*. Paul mentioned this idea in 1 Thessalonians 5:17 when he wrote, *pray without ceasing*. It's hard to measure how much good such constant prayer would do, and how much bad it would keep us from.

b. **And not lose heart**: Often we fail in praying because we **lose heart**. We become discouraged, and then no longer pray as we should.

i. It is easy to **lose heart** in prayer, because prayer is hard work that we too often approach lightly. In Colossians 4:12, Paul praised a man named Epaphras because he was *always laboring fervently . . . in prayers*. Paul knew that prayer was hard work that required fervent labor. Morrison tried to explain why prayer was difficult, because three parts of the human being are engaged in prayer: "There is the understanding, by which we work intelligently; there is the heart, by which we labour willingly, there is the will by which we labour doggedly." (Morrison)

ii. It is easy to **lose heart** in prayer because the Devil hates prayer. If prayer were powerless, it would be easy.

iii. It is easy to **lose heart** in prayer because we are not always convinced of the reality of the power of prayer. Too often, prayer becomes a last resort instead of a first resource.

iv. Remember that Jesus lived a prayerful life, and He lives on to pray for His people (Hebrews 7:25). We must therefore not **lose heart** in prayer.

- The woman of Canaan kept praying though she was first denied
- Jacob refused to let go even when his leg was crippled
- Rachel said to Jacob, "Give me children, or else I die!"

2. (2-8) The parable of the widow and the unjust judge.

Saying: "There was in a certain city a judge who did not fear God nor regard man. Now there was a widow in that city; and she came to him, saying, 'Get justice for me from my adversary.' And he would not for a while; but afterward he said within himself, 'Though I do not fear God nor regard man, yet because this widow troubles me I will avenge her, lest by her continual coming she weary me.'" Then the Lord said, "Hear what the unjust judge said. And shall God not avenge His own elect who cry out day and night to Him, though He bears long with them? I tell you that He will avenge them speedily. Nevertheless, when the Son of Man comes, will He really find faith on the earth?"

a. **A judge who did not fear God nor regard man**: The judge was ungodly, both as a man and a judge. Yet in the end, he answered the woman's request. The only reason he gave her what she wanted was because the woman wouldn't stop bothering him.

i. Barclay points out that this would not have been a Jewish judge, because disputes in the Jewish world were brought to the elders. "This judge was one of the paid magistrates appointed either by Herod or the Romans. Such judges were notorious." (Barclay)

ii. When he complained the woman would **weary me**, it really means, "*Stun me*. A metaphor taken from boxers, who *bruise* each other." (Clarke) "Although the word *hypopiaze* literally means 'to give a black eye' (cf. 1 Corinthians 9:27), the figurative rendering is preferable here." (Pate)

b. **Though I do not fear God nor regard man, yet because this widow troubles me I will avenge her**: The unjust judge only reluctantly answered the woman's request. Jesus did not give this parable to say that God was *like* the unjust judge, but *unlike* him. God *loves* to answer our prayers, and He even helps us when we pray. God is *on your side* when you pray, not against you (as the unjust judge was against the widow).

i. The woman had to overcome the judge's reluctance to help. We often *feel* that we must do the same when we pray—use our persistence to overcome God's reluctance. This misses the point of the parable entirely. Jesus did not say *that men always ought to pray and not lose heart* because God is reluctant, but because He *isn't*, and that is our encouragement to prayer.

ii. Sometimes it does seem to us that God is reluctant to answer our prayers. Yet the delays in prayer are not needed to change God, but to change us. Persistence in prayer brings a transforming element into our lives, building into us the character of God Himself. It is a way that God builds into us a heart that cares about things the same way He does. "Too many prayers are like boy's runaway knocks, given, and then the giver is away before the door can be opened." (Spurgeon)

iii. Both Jesus (Mark 14:39) and Paul (2 Corinthians 12:8) prayed repeatedly for the same thing. However, we must guard against a persistence of *unbelief*—repeating prayer with the attitude that God never heard us the first time.

iv. There are several contrasts between this judge and the God who hears prayer.

- The judge was unfair; God is fair
- The judge had no personal interest in the widow; God loves and cares for those who petition Him
- The judge answered the widow's cry out of pure self-interest; God loves to bless His people for their good also

c. **Shall God not avenge His own elect who cry out day and night to Him**: Jesus probably had in mind the prayers of persecuted believers, who long for justice and **who cry out day and night** for God to **avenge** them and deal with their persecutors.

i. Those in the fire of persecution need special grace to persevere and to not lose heart in prayer. They need to be assured that God is not like the unjust judge, so we should keep praying to the Lord who will resolve all things righteously.

ii. Our God is a righteous, wonderful Judge:

- We come to a Judge of perfect, good character
- We come to a Judge who loves to care for His children
- We come to a Judge who is kind and gracious
- We come to a Judge who *knows* us
- We come to this Judge with an advocate, a friend who will plead our case before the Judge

- We come to the Judge with promises to encourage us
- We come to the Judge with the right of constant access, to a Judge who has a personal interest in our case

d. **When the Son of Man comes, will He really find faith on the earth?** This ties Jesus' thought to His words about His coming at the end of the previous chapter. Unless we know who God is (being *not* like the unjust judge), and unless we are people who pray without losing heart, we don't yet have the kind of faith Jesus will look for when He returns.

B. Lessons on humility.

1. (9-14) A parable to rebuke the self-righteous.

Also He spoke this parable to some who trusted in themselves that they were righteous, and despised others: "Two men went up to the temple to pray, one a Pharisee and the other a tax collector. The Pharisee stood and prayed thus with himself, 'God, I thank You that I am not like other men; extortioners, unjust, adulterers, or even as this tax collector. I fast twice a week; I give tithes of all that I possess.' And the tax collector, standing afar off, would not so much as raise *his* eyes to heaven, but beat his breast, saying, 'God, be merciful to me a sinner!' I tell you, this man went down to his house justified *rather* than the other; for everyone who exalts himself will be humbled, and he who humbles himself will be exalted."

a. **To some who trusted in themselves that they were righteous, and despised others**: The connection between those who **trusted in themselves that they were righteous** and those who **despised others** is almost inevitable. If I credit myself for a supposed great and spiritual walk with God, then it is an easy thing to despise another for their supposed low and carnal walk with God.

b. **Two men went up to the temple to pray**: In this parable, both men prayed, but both men did not come to God the same way. The Pharisee went up to the temple to pray, but he did not pray. He spoke with himself, not with God.; he **prayed thus with himself**, and in his short prayer he repeated the word "**I**" five times.

i. It is entirely possible to address your words to God, but actually be praying to yourself, because your focus is on yourself, not on God. Your passion is for your agenda, not God's. Your attitude is *my will be done* and not *Thy will be done*. The man was full of praise, but he rejoiced "not for who God was but rather for who he was!" (Pate)

c. **God, I thank You that I am not like other men**: In his (so-called) prayer, the Pharisee praised himself, and compared himself to **other men**.

It isn't hard to have such a high opinion of self when you compare yourself to other people; it often is not difficult to find someone worse.

i. **Even as this tax collector**: "The demonstrative pronoun 'this' (*houtos*) pejoratively distinguishes the Pharisee from his counterpart in the temple." (Pate)

ii. One ancient rabbi (Rabbi Simeon, the son of Jochai) was an example of this kind of Pharisaical pride when he said: "If there were only thirty righteous persons in the world, I and my son would make two of them; but if there were but twenty, I and my son would be of the number; and if there were but *ten*, I and my son would be of the number; and if there were but *five*, I and my son would be of the five; and if there were but *two*, I and my son would be those two; and if there were but *one*, myself should be that *one*." (Clarke)

iii. **I fast twice a week**: In those days many Jews fasted on the second and fifth days of each week, because they believed that Moses went up on Mount Sinai to receive the law on the fifth day of the week, and that he came down with the law on the second day of the week. "Those who wished to gain special merit fasted also on Mondays and Thursdays. It is noteworthy that these were the market days when Jerusalem was full of country people. Those who fasted whitened their faces and appeared in disheveled clothes, and those days gave their piety the biggest possible audience." (Barclay)

iv. "I am not as this publican, No, for thou art worse; yea for this, because thou thinkest thee better." (Trapp)

v. "What the Pharisee said about himself was true. His trouble was not that he was not far enough along the road, but that he was on the wrong road altogether." (Morris)

d. **The tax collector, standing afar off, would not so much as raise his eyes to heaven, but beat his breast, saying, "God, be merciful to me a sinner!"** The Pharisee relied on his own power and deeds before God, but the tax collector relied on the mercy and compassion of God. He recognized that he was a **sinner**, who needed the mercy of God.

i. We can imagine the Pharisee praying with eloquent words and flowing, spiritual style; anyone who heard him pray would say that he was a spiritual man. In contrast, we imagine the tax collector praying awkwardly, with halting phrases and fear; but his prayer pleased God.

ii. **But beat his breast**: The idea behind this was that one was so aware of the sin and heart corruption that one hit at their own heart as a punishment. According to Morris, the verb tense of **beat his breast** describes a continual action; he kept on doing it. "The original does not say that he smote upon his breast once, but he smote and smote again. It was a continuous act. He seemed to say—Oh, this wicked heart! He would smite it. Again and again he expressed his intense grief by this Oriental gesture, for he did not know how else to set forth his sorrow." (Spurgeon)

iii. The Pharisee thought he was not like other men; that he was better than them. The tax collector also thought that he was not like other men; that he was *worse* than them. "He actually prayed, 'O God be merciful to me—*the* sinner,' as if he was not merely *a* sinner, but *the* sinner *par excellence*." (Barclay) "If there was not another sinner in the world, he was one; and in a world of sinners he was a prominent offender—the sinner of sinners. Emphatically he applies to himself the guilty name." (Spurgeon)

iv. The ancient Greek word translated **be merciful** is *hilaskomai*; it is actually the word for an atoning sacrifice. The fullest sense of what the tax collector said was, "God, be merciful to me through Your atoning sacrifice for sins, because I am a sinner." The only other place this word is used in the New Testament is in Hebrews 2:17, where it is translated *propitiation*.

v. "In the original Greek the words are even fewer than in the English. Oh, that men would learn to pray with less of language and more of meaning! What great things are packed away in this short petition! God, mercy, sin, the propitiation, and forgiveness." (Spurgeon)

e. **This man went down to his house justified rather than the other**: The justification of the tax collector was immediate. He humbly came to God on the basis of His atoning sacrifice and was justified. He didn't earn his justification, and he didn't have a probationary period; he was simply **justified**.

i. He was justified because as a sinner, he humbly prayed for *mercy*, and mercy in the sense of atoning sacrifice. He prayed, "O God, be satisfied with the atoning sacrifice, and forgive me."

- He didn't say, "God, be merciful to me, I'm not a Pharisee."
- He didn't say, "God, be merciful to me, a repentant sinner."
- He didn't say, "God, be merciful to me, a praying sinner."
- He didn't say, "God, be merciful to me, I'm only human."
- He didn't say, "God, be merciful to me, I'll try to do better."
- He simply prayed; praying body, soul, and spirit, **"God, be merciful to me a sinner!"**

f. **Everyone who exalts himself will be abased, and he who humbles himself will be exalted**: Essentially, the Pharisee saw prayer and his spiritual life as a way to be exalted, but the tax collector approached God in humility.

i. True humbleness is simply seeing things the way they *are*. The Pharisee saw himself as something great when he wasn't, and the tax collector saw himself as a sinner needing God's mercy, which he was.

ii. We gain nothing by coming to God in the lie of pride. The principle *God resists the proud, but gives grace to the humble* is so important, God repeated it three times (Proverbs 3:34, James 4:6, 1 Peter 5:5).

2. (15-17) Jesus uses children as examples of humility.

Then they also brought infants to Him that He might touch them; but when the disciples saw *it*, they rebuked them. But Jesus called them to *Him* and said, "Let the little children come to Me, and do not forbid them; for of such is the kingdom of God. "Assuredly, I say to you, whoever does not receive the kingdom of God as a little child will by no means enter it."

a. **They also brought infants to Him that He might touch them**: Children love to come to Jesus, and it says something about our Savior that children loved Him and that He loved children. Jesus was not a mean, sour man; because children don't love mean, sour people.

i. "It was the custom for mothers to bring their children to some distinguished Rabbi on the first birthday that he might bless them." (Barclay)

b. **That He might touch them**: Jesus knew that these **infants**, though they did not understand speech or Jesus' eloquent teaching, could respond to a touch. Jesus knows how to communicate in the way we need.

i. Matthew 19:13 says specifically *that He might put His hands on them and pray*. With this, Jesus blessed the children. The laying on of hands is used Biblically as a way to bestow blessing on another (Acts 6:6, Acts 8:17, Acts 9:17, 1 Timothy 5:22, 2 Timothy 1:6).

ii. "He did not baptize them, but he did bless them." (Spurgeon)

c. **Let the little children come to Me**: Because children love to come to Jesus, we should never block the way—or fail to provide them a way. We know more about Jesus than the women of Judea did; so there is no good reason for us to keep our children from Jesus.

d. **For of such is the kingdom of God**: Children receive the blessing of Jesus without trying to make themselves worthy of it, or pretending they don't need it. We need to receive God's blessings the same way.

i. "Not only did Jesus welcome these little human beings as members of the kingdom of God; He also extolled them as model citizens of the same, because of their capacity to trust and love." (Pate)

C. Riches and true discipleship.

1. (18-19) A rich young ruler comes to Jesus.

Now a certain ruler asked Him, saying, "Good Teacher, what shall I do to inherit eternal life?" So Jesus said to him, "Why do you call Me good? No one *is* good but One, *that is,* God."

a. **Now a certain ruler**: This man is commonly known as the *rich young ruler*, because he is described as a **ruler** (Luke 18:18), as *rich* (Luke 18:23), and as *young* (Matthew 19:23). We don't know if his authority was in the world of politics or in the world of religion.

b. **Good Teacher**: This was an impressive and perhaps surprising way to address Jesus. "**Good Teacher**" was a title never applied to other rabbis in that day, because it implied being without sin and *complete* goodness. Jesus, and everyone else, recognized that **Good Teacher** was a unique title.

i. "There is no instance in the whole Talmud of a rabbi being addressed as 'Good Master'" (Plummer, cited in Geldenhuys). They insisted on calling God alone "good."

c. **What good thing shall I do to inherit eternal life?** This question demonstrates that this man, like all people by nature, had an orientation towards *earning* eternal life. He wanted to know what good work or noble deed he should **do to inherit eternal life**.

d. **Why do you call Me good?** In this, Jesus did not deny His own goodness. Instead He asked the man, "Do you understand what you are saying when **you call Me good?** Because **no one is good but One, that is, God.**"

i. It was as if Jesus said, "You come to Me asking about what good thing you can do to inherit eternal life, but what do you really know about goodness?" "The argument is clear: either Jesus was *good*, or he ought not to have called him good; but as there is *none good but God*, Jesus who is good must be God." (Spurgeon)

ii. We might say that the ruler did not really know who Jesus was. If he did, he would humble himself as the tax collector did in the story Jesus told earlier in the chapter (Luke 19:10-14). The following verses show that the ruler also did not really know who *he* was.

2. (20-21) Jesus asks the ruler about his life.

"You know the commandments: 'Do not commit adultery,' 'Do not murder,' 'Do not steal,' 'Do not bear false witness,' 'Honor your father

and your mother.'" And he said, "All these things I have kept from my youth."

    a. **You know the commandments**: This *ruler* was an educated Jew of his day, so of course he knew the **commandments**. Jesus could appeal to the man on this common knowledge.

        i. Modern men and women may not have the same knowledge and exact agreement with the **commandments** as Jesus referred to them here. Yet in general they agree with them, because God also speaks to men through creation and conscience (Romans 1:19-20, 2:14-15).

        ii. Though many people today know the commandments, either through instruction or intuition, far fewer people are interested in the basic question, *how may I inherit eternal life?*

    b. **You shall not murder**: Jesus asked the man about the commandments relevant to man's relation to man. In response, the young man claimed, **"All these things I have kept from my youth,"** thus claiming to fulfill all of God's commands regarding how we must treat other people.

    c. **All these things I have kept from my youth**: It is fair to ask if this man really had kept these commandments. It is likely that he actually did keep them in a way that made him righteous in the eyes of men, in the sense that Paul could say *concerning the righteousness which is in the law, blameless* in Philippians 3:6. But he certainly did not keep them in the full and perfect sense in which Jesus spoke of in the Sermon on the Mount.

        i. "The time span involved in the ruler's mind may have begun with his *bar mitzvah* ('son of the Law'), the time when a youth became an adult at the age of thirteen, and therefore obligated to fulfill the Mosaic Law." (Pate)

3. (22-23) Jesus instructs the ruler.

So when Jesus heard these things, He said to him, "You still lack one thing. Sell all that you have and distribute to the poor, and you will have treasure in heaven; and come, follow Me." But when he heard this, he became very sorrowful, for he was very rich.

    a. **So when Jesus heard these things**: Jesus spoke these words to this one man, in light of who the man was and what he had said. This was a specific word for a specific man, yet in principle it has application for all.

        i. Mark's account adds something here. Mark wrote: *Then Jesus, looking at him, loved him, and said to him* (Mark 10:21). The response of Jesus to this man was said in love—no doubt, because Jesus perceived that he was misguided and empty. One might say that this man had climbed to the top of the ladder of success, only to find his ladder leaned against the wrong building.

b. **You still lack one thing**: Though the man had everything—riches, an outwardly righteous life, respect, and prestige—Jesus could still say to him, "**You still lack one thing**." The man had *everything*, but knew that he did not have eternal life, so he really had *nothing*.

c. **You still lack one thing. Sell all that you have and distribute to the poor, and you will have treasure in heaven; and come, follow Me**: Instead of challenging the man's fulfillment of the law (which Jesus had every right to do), Jesus pointed him to what is commonly called the *first* table of the law—the laws having to do with our relationship with God. Jesus challenged him to put God first; to fulfill the law to *love the LORD your God with all your heart, with all your soul, and with all your strength* (Deuteronomy 6:5).

> i. In saying, "**Sell all that you have and distribute to the poor, and you will have treasure in heaven; and come, follow Me**," Jesus challenged the man to love God more than money and material things. The man failed this challenge. Essentially, this man was an idolater: he loved money and material things more than God. This shows than *both* tables of the law will test men.

> ii. Jesus asked the ruler to give up his money, because He could see money was an idol. He asked him to give it to the **poor**, because He could see that he didn't love others the way he should.

d. **Sell all that you have and distribute to the poor, and you will have treasure in heaven; and come, follow Me**: The call to forsake everything and follow Jesus is a call to put God first in all things. It is full obedience to the first table of the law, which dealt with a man's relation to God.

> i. We may make two mistakes here. The one is to believe this applies to *everyone*, when Jesus never made this a general command to all who would follow Him, but especially to this one rich man whose riches were clearly an obstacle to his discipleship. Instead, many rich people can do *more good* in the world by continuing to make money and using those resources for the glory of God and the good of others. The second mistake is to believe this applies to *no one*, when there are clearly those today for whom the best thing they could do for themselves spiritually is to radically forsake the materialism that is ruining them. Francis of Assisi was a notable one who heard Jesus speak these words to *him*, and gave away all he had to follow Jesus.

> ii. Yet we notice that Jesus simply called this man to be His disciple, in saying, "**Follow Me**." He used similar language in calling many of His

disciples (Matthew 4:19; 8:22; 9:9; Mark 2:14). Jesus simply called this man to be His follower; but for *this* man it meant leaving behind the riches he had set his heart upon.

iii. "Think not, therefore, as many do, that there is no other hell but poverty, no better heaven than abundance." (Trapp)

e. **He became very sorrowful, for he was very rich**: The other gospels note that the man *went away* (Matthew 19:22, Mark 10:22). Luke noticed his expression, his emotional response: **very sorrowful**. When he heard Jesus' radical call to discipleship he said, *I can't do that. I can't make that sacrifice. I guess I'm going to hell.*

i. **Very sorrowful** and **very rich** is a tragic combination, yet common enough in those who make an idol out of riches.

ii. The principle remains: God may challenge and require an individual to give something up for the sake of His kingdom that He still allows to someone else. There are many who perish because they will not forsake what God tells them to.

iii. **Very sorrowful, for he was very rich**: "And what were these in comparison of peace of conscience, and mental rest? Besides, he had unequivocal proof that these contributed nothing to his comfort, for he is now miserable even *while* he possesses them! And so will every soul be, who puts worldly goods in the place of the supreme God." (Clarke)

4. (24-27) The problem of riches.

And when Jesus saw that he became very sorrowful, He said, "How hard it is for those who have riches to enter the kingdom of God! For it is easier for a camel to go through the eye of a needle than for a rich man to enter the kingdom of God." And those who heard it said, "Who then can be saved?" But He said, "The things which are impossible with men are possible with God."

a. **When Jesus saw**: Jesus didn't change the demands of discipleship when the rich man walked away. He did use the man's sorrow as an occasion to teach His disciples and all who would hear.

b. **How hard it is for those who have riches to enter the kingdom of God!** Riches are a problem, because they tend to make us satisfied with this life, instead of longing for the age to come. As well, sometimes riches are sought at the expense of seeking God.

i. Clearly, Jesus said that *riches are an obstacle to the kingdom of God.* We usually only think of *poverty* as a problem. Jesus told us that riches may present a much more serious problem.

ii. We often excuse ourselves from what Jesus says here, because we don't consider ourselves rich. Yet very few among us would *not* be considered richer than this rich young ruler was.

c. **For it is easier for a camel to go through the eye of a needle than for a rich man to enter the kingdom of God**: With this humorous image, Jesus illustrated the difficulty riches present to entering the kingdom of God. We immediately think of this as being impossible.

i. "Attempts have been made to explain Jesus' words about the *camel* and the *eye of a needle* in terms of a camel shuffling through a small postern gate, or by reading *kamilon* 'cable' for *kamelon* 'camel'. Such 'explanations' are misguided. They miss the point that Jesus is using a humourous illustration." (Morris)

ii. "Quite often the rabbis talked of an elephant trying to get through the eye of a needle as a picture of something fantastically impossible." (Barclay) Perhaps Jesus took this well-known proverb and softened it a bit from its common telling. A **camel** *is* smaller than an elephant, though obviously bigger than the eye of a needle.

d. **Who then can be saved?** The response from those who heard this is true to human nature. We also find it hard to see how riches can hinder us from the kingdom of God. We think only of the blessing and good riches might bring.

i. They had probably hoped that their following of Jesus would make them rich and influential, and prominent leaders in His Messianic government. "In a culture where wealth was regarded as a sign of God's blessing and where a religious teacher was therefore expected to be at least moderately wealthy, the lifestyle of Jesus and his disciples was conspicuously different." (France)

ii. We remember what Paul said to Timothy: *But those who desire to be rich fall into temptation and a snare, and into many foolish and harmful lusts which drown men in destruction and perdition. For the love of money is a root of all kinds of evil, for which some have strayed from the faith in their greediness, and pierced themselves through with many sorrows* (1 Timothy 6:9-10).

e. **The things which are impossible with men are possible with God**: It is **possible** for the rich man to be saved. God's grace is enough to save the rich man; we have the examples of people like Zaccheus, Joseph of Armithea, and Barnabas. These all were rich men still able to put God first, not their riches.

i. "Jesus is not saying that all poor people and none of the wealthy enter the kingdom of heaven. That would exclude Abraham, Isaac, and

Jacob, to say nothing of David, Solomon, and Joseph of Arimathea." (Carson)

ii. "Man is ever attempting to personally and socially enter into the Kingdom of God by endeavours with men, and this never succeeds. With God the thing is possible." (Morgan)

5. (28-30) Our reward and the solution to the problem of riches.

Then Peter said, "See, we have left all and followed You." So He said to them, "Assuredly, I say to you, there is no one who has left house or parents or brothers or wife or children, for the sake of the kingdom of God, who shall not receive many times more in this present time, and in the age to come eternal life."

a. **See, we have left all and followed You**: In contrast to the rich young ruler, the disciples *did* give up everything (or most everything) to follow Jesus. Peter wondered what reward would be promised to them who obeyed where the rich young ruler disobeyed.

i. There is a special honor for these disciples. They have a special place in judgment, probably in the sense of administration in the millennial Kingdom. As well, the apostles had the honor of helping to provide a singular foundation for the church (Ephesians 2:20), and have a special tribute in the New Jerusalem (Revelation 20:14).

b. **Assuredly, I say to you, there is no one who has left**: The twelve may have their unique reward, but there will be universal honor for all who sacrifice for Jesus' sake. Whatever has been given up for Him will be returned to us many times over, both **in this present age, and in the age to come eternal life**.

i. **Many times over** is obviously not meant in a material sense. Jesus did not promise a hundred mothers and a hundred wives. **Many times over** is literal, but spiritual in its fulfillment.

ii. Matthew Poole described some of the ways we get our **many times over**:

- Joy in the Holy Ghost, peace of conscience, the sense of God's love
- Contentment. They shall have a contented frame of mind
- God will stir up the hearts of others to supply their wants, and that supply shall be sweeter to them than their abundance was
- God sometimes repays them in this life, as he restored Job after his trial to greater riches

iii. The principle stands: God will be a debtor to no man. It is impossible for us to give more to God than He gives back to us. Having and keeping the heart of a giver will keep you from being corrupted by riches. We all must do what Psalm 62:10 says: *If riches increase, do not set your heart on them*, and giving is key.

6. (31-34) Jesus again announces His coming fate in Jerusalem.

Then He took the twelve aside and said to them, "Behold, we are going up to Jerusalem, and all things that are written by the prophets concerning the Son of Man will be accomplished. For He will be delivered to the Gentiles and will be mocked and insulted and spit upon. They will scourge *Him* and kill Him. And the third day He will rise again." But they understood none of these things; this saying was hidden from them, and they did not know the things which were spoken.

a. **Behold, we are going up to Jerusalem**: This was not a surprise to the disciples. Even if Jesus had not specifically told them, their movement south from Galilee at about the time of the Passover feast made it easy to understand that Jesus and the disciples would be in **Jerusalem** for Passover.

b. **All things that are written by the prophets concerning the Son of Man will be accomplished**: In saying "**all things,**" Jesus emphasized the aspects **concerning the Son of Man** that were commonly neglected and overlooked by the Jewish people of His day—that the Messiah would suffer and die as a sin-bearing servant.

c. **For He will be delivered to the Gentiles and will be mocked and insulted and spit upon**: Jesus reminded His disciples of His coming suffering and death, emphasizing the shame and humiliation He would bear.

i. **Will be delivered**: This speaks of the *betrayal* of Jesus; one of His own disciples would deliver Him over to the religious leaders for money. Certainly, Jesus did not arrange His own betrayal, yet He confidently said it would happen.

ii. **Will be mocked and insulted and spit upon**: Jesus predicted the humiliation and mocking associated with His coming agony—which on a human level He could not arrange. "They plucked his hair, they smote his cheeks, they spat in his face. Mockery could go no farther. It was cruel, cutting, cursed scorn." (Spurgeon)

iii. **They will scourge Him**: This sharp and brutal whipping was a particular agony and humiliation to endure.

iv. **And kill Him**: The suffering would not end with humiliation and a severe beating. It would continue to the death of Jesus.

v. Taken together, the entire picture is one of great suffering.

• Suffering from the disloyalty of friends

- Suffering from injustice
- Suffering from deliberate insult and humiliation
- Suffering from physical pain
- Suffering from great humiliation and degradation

d. **And the third day He will rise again**: Jesus triumphantly told His disciples that the story would not end with His suffering, humiliation, and death. He would **rise again** in resurrected glory.

i. This was something that Jesus had *no apparent control over*. Yet He confidently announced to His disciples that this would happen.

e. **They understood none of these things**: They heard the words right from the mouth of Jesus, and saw the expression on His face, and still did not understand—because **this saying was hidden from them**. They could not see or understand the truth until God opened their eyes.

i. Perhaps God did not open their eyes to this truth because they couldn't handle it yet. If they really knew what would happen to Jesus, and how different it would be than their own conceptions of riding the coattails of the Messiah to glory, they might have given up right then and there.

ii. "Only at a somewhat later time . . . do the Jewish rabbis appear to have taught that there would be a suffering Messiah ('Messiah ben Joseph') as well as a triumphant Messiah ('Messiah ben Judah')." (Geldenhuys)

7. (35-39) In Jericho, a blind man begs for the attention of Jesus.

Then it happened, as He was coming near Jericho, that a certain blind man sat by the road begging. And hearing a multitude passing by, he asked what it meant. So they told him that Jesus of Nazareth was passing by. And he cried out, saying, "Jesus, Son of David, have mercy on me!" Then those who went before warned him that he should be quiet; but he cried out all the more, "Son of David, have mercy on me!"

a. **As He was coming near Jericho**: One of the most traveled roads from Galilee to Jerusalem went through **Jericho**. When Jesus came to this ancient city, He was not far from Jerusalem and the fate waiting for Him there. Mark 10:46 says the blind man's name was *Bartimaeus*, the son of Timaeus.

i. The blind man couldn't see Jesus, but he could hear Him—so, **hearing a multitude passing by, he asked what it meant**. Instead of giving up because he could not seek Jesus by sight, he sought Jesus the way that he could—by hearing.

ii. In the Gospels of Matthew (20:29) and Mark (10:46), this miracle is said to happen as Jesus and the crowd *were leaving Jericho*. The seeming contradiction in Luke is understood in the light of archaeology, which has discovered that by Jesus' time there were *two* cities of Jericho—the ancient city, and the newer Roman city. The miracle happened in-between these two cities of Jericho, leaving one and entering the other.

b. **He cried out all the more**: The man heard Jesus **was passing by**, and was desperate to get Jesus' attention. He would not be embarrassed, and he would not be shut up. He knew that Jesus was the **Son of David**, meaning the Messiah, and kept shouting for His **mercy**.

i. William Barclay points out there is a difference in the ancient Greek words used to describe the action of the blind man in Luke 18:38 and 18:39, and that they show the blind man's great desperation.

- **Cried out** (Luke 18:38): "An ordinary loud shout to attract attention"

- **Cried out all the more** (Luke 18:39): "The instinctive cry of ungovernable emotion, a scream, an almost animal cry"

c. **Have mercy on me**: The blind man knew he needed **mercy** from Jesus. He didn't think that God *owed* him; he wanted **mercy**.

8. (40-43) Jesus heals the blind man.

So Jesus stood still and commanded him to be brought to Him. And when he had come near, He asked him, saying, "What do you want Me to do for you?" He said, "Lord, that I may receive my sight." Then Jesus said to him, "Receive your sight; your faith has made you well." And immediately he received his sight, and followed Him, glorifying God. And all the people, when they saw *it*, gave praise to God.

a. **Jesus stood still**: Nothing could stop Him on His journey to Jerusalem, yet He **stood still** to answer a persistent plea for mercy.

b. **What do you want Me to do for you?** This is a wonderful, simple question God has not stopped asking. Sometimes we go without when God would want to give us something simply because we will not answer this question, and we *do not have because we do not ask* (James 4:2).

i. Jesus asked this question with full knowledge that this man was blind. He knew what he needed and what he wanted, but God still wants us to tell Him our needs as a constant expression of our trust and reliance on Him.

c. **Lord, that I may receive my sight**: The blind man knew how to submit to Jesus—he called Jesus "**Lord**" and asked to **receive** his **sight**.

e. **Receive your sight; your faith has made you well**: Jesus granted the man's request and healed him of blindness. Jesus connected the man's healing with the man's **faith**. There were many notable aspects of this man's faith that made him ready to receive from Jesus.

- It was faith that wanted Jesus
- It was faith that knew who He was
- It was faith that knew what he deserved from Jesus
- It was faith that could tell Jesus what it wanted
- It was faith that could call Jesus **Lord**

f. **He received his sight, and followed Him, glorifying God**: The blind man, now healed and saved, began to follow Jesus. The way of Jesus became his way. This was especially significant considering that Jesus was on His way towards Jerusalem to die.

Luke 19—The Triumphal Entry

A. Jesus and Zacchaeus

1. (1-4) Zacchaeus climbs a tree and risks ridicule to see Jesus.

Then *Jesus* entered and passed through Jericho. Now behold, *there was* a man named Zacchaeus who was a chief tax collector, and he was rich. And he sought to see who Jesus was, but could not because of the crowd, for he was of short stature. So he ran ahead and climbed up into a sycamore tree to see Him, for He was going to pass that *way*.

a. **Jesus entered and passed through Jericho**: Jericho was an ancient and important city, and as Jesus passed through the city on His way to Jerusalem, it seems that the reason was to meet with this **man named Zacchaeus**.

i. Jericho was a prosperous city. "It had a great palm forest and world-famous balsam groves which perfumed the air for miles around. Its gardens of roses were known far and wide. Men called it 'The City of Palms.' Josephus called it 'a divine region,' 'the fattest in Palestine.' The Romans carried its dates and balsam to world-wide trade and fame." (Barclay)

b. **Zacchaeus, who was a chief tax collector**: Zacchaeus was not only a tax collector, but a **chief tax collector**—and the Jews hated men like him. This was not only due to their natural dislike of taxes, but more so because of the practice known as tax farming; the collector made his profit on whatever *extra* he could get away with charging his victims. A tax collector was highly motivated to make the taxes as high as possible.

i. When the tax collectors came to John the Baptist, asking how they could get right with God, he told them *collect no more than what is appointed for you* (Luke 3:13). If you were a tax collector and you were rich, you were a rogue.

ii. Morris on **chief tax collector**: "The title is not found anywhere else, so its precise significance is not known, but it seems to point to the head of the local taxation department."

iii. The name **Zacchaeus** means "pure one." This man was anything but pure—until he received Jesus. "He should by his name have been a puritan (in the best sense), but he was an arch-publican, a public sinner, not simple, but subtle, a griping extortioner, a rich but wretched sycophant." (Trapp)

c. **He sought to see who Jesus was**: Zacchaeus wanted to set his eyes on Jesus; he *sought after Him*. Perhaps Zacchaeus had heard that Jesus accepted people like him; he longed to see this remarkable Man Jesus for himself.

d. **He was of short stature**: His natural state gave him a disadvantage in seeking after Jesus. It also probably affected his personality; small in size, we can imagine how Zacchaeus was mocked and hated by others—and how he returned the favor by increasing the taxes on his victims.

i. If Zacchaeus had a small heart, he would have given up and not worked to see Jesus. "But Zacchaeus had had a great will to grow rich, and he had found there a way to *that*. And now he had a great will to see Jesus, and he was not the sort of person to be stopped." (Morrison)

e. **He ran ahead and climbed up into a sycamore tree to see Him**: Because Zacchaeus sought Jesus so intensely, he didn't mind doing something that many thought was beneath the dignity of a grown, wealthy man—he climbed up **a sycamore tree**.

i. He climbed the tree like a little boy, and without knowing fulfilled Jesus' word that unless we become like children, we will not see the kingdom of God (Matthew 18:3).

ii. "A traveller describes the tree as being like 'the English oak, and its shade is most pleasing... It is very easy to climb." (Barclay)

iii. "I wish there were more of us who did not mind being laughed at if only what we did helped us to see Jesus." (Maclaren)

2. (5-6) Jesus invites Himself to Zacchaeus' house.

And when Jesus came to the place, He looked up and saw him, and said to him, "Zacchaeus, make haste and come down, for today I must stay at your house." So he made haste and came down, and received Him joyfully.

a. **He looked up and saw him**: Because Zacchaeus worked hard and risked embarrassment to see Jesus, *Jesus saw him* and did not pass him by.

In the best sense, Zacchaeus stood out to Jesus, and Jesus connected with Him.

b. **Zacchaeus, make haste**: Jesus started by calling **Zacchaeus** by name. Jesus knew the importance of a person's name. This may have been the first time Zacchaeus heard someone besides his mother say his name in a kind way.

> i. Saying his name made all the difference; Jesus told **Zacchaeus**, "I know you, and I lay some claim upon you."

> ii. Jesus knew the importance of a name. He said that He calls His sheep by name: *To him the doorkeeper opens, and the sheep hear his voice; and he calls his own sheep by name and leads them out* (John 10:3). In Revelation, we are promised a new name that only God and we know. When we get to heaven, there will be someone there who knows our name.

c. **Make haste and come down**: Jesus told Zacchaeus to *hurry* and to **come down**. If He did not hurry, the opportunity might be lost. If he did not lower himself, he would never meet Jesus.

> i. This says to each, "Come down from your high place." Jesus would never have eaten with Zacchaeus if he stayed in the sycamore tree.

d. **Today I must stay at your house**: Jesus didn't merely want to preach to Zacchaeus and convert him in a spiritual or religious sense. Jesus wanted to have *real relationship* with Zacchaeus, beginning with a meal and time spent together.

> i. Jesus invited Himself to spend time with Zacchaeus, the hated outcast. The early church was despised for its acceptance of outcasts (1 Corinthians 1:26-31), but the early Christians regarded this as something glorious, not shameful.

e. **And received Him**: Jesus would only come into the house of Zacchaeus and into his life *if invited*, if *received*. He received Jesus first, and then started a relationship with Him.

> i. "Christ will not force himself into any man's house, and sit there against the man's will. That would not be the action of a guest, but of an unwelcome intruder." (Spurgeon)

> ii. Perhaps Zacchaeus had a lot of questions, but he didn't ask them from the sycamore tree. He came down from the tree, met Jesus, and then asked Him whatever he wanted to.

f. **And received Him joyfully**: Zacchaeus was *happy* to receive Jesus. Jesus called Zacchaeus to Himself, and it was to *Jesus* that he came, and happily so. Zacchaeus received **Him**, that is, Jesus Himself. Not primarily to a creed or a doctrine, not to a theory, and not to a ceremony, but to Jesus.

i. Jesus was on His way to Jerusalem, and would be received into the city with joy, with what is called *the triumphal entry*. Here, before that, He had a different entry into the heart of just *one man*. This entrance, this reception, seemed to have more lasting results.

ii. Jesus is joyful to receive sinners, and they are joyful to be saved. We know that the joy of Jesus is greater, because it is more blessed to give than to receive.

iii. Zacchaeus is a model to everyone of how to receive Jesus:

- Receive Jesus by seeking after Him with real effort
- Receive Jesus by humbling yourself
- Receive Jesus no matter how sinful or hated you are
- Receive Jesus as He invites you by name
- Receive Jesus without delay
- Receive Jesus by coming down to Him
- Receive Jesus Himself
- Receive Jesus into your *life*, your *home*
- Receive Jesus joyfully
- Receive Jesus despite what others say
- Receive Jesus with repentance and restitution

3. (7-10) Zacchaeus renounces his sin and Jesus proclaims his salvation.

But when they saw *it*, they all complained, saying, "He has gone to be a guest with a man who is a sinner." Then Zacchaeus stood and said to the Lord, "Look, Lord, I give half of my goods to the poor; and if I have taken anything from anyone by false accusation, I restore four-fold." And Jesus said to him, "Today salvation has come to this house, because he also is a son of Abraham; for the Son of Man has come to seek and to save that which was lost."

a. **He has gone to be a guest with a man who is a sinner**: The people (**they all**, not only the religious leaders) thought Jesus had gone too far by associating with a man as bad as Zacchaeus, so they protested.

i. "Jesus Christ did not teach Zacchaeus by going to his house that character was of no consequence; on the contrary, Zacchaeus perceived at once that character was of the greatest consequence, and so he stood forth, and said 'Behold, Lord, the half of my goods I give to the poor; and if I have taken anything from any man by false accusation, I restore him fourfold.'" (Spurgeon)

b. **Look, Lord…I restore fourfold**: In receiving Jesus and spending just a little time with Him, Zacchaeus knew he had to repent and make restitution. First he just sought after Jesus. But in seeking Jesus, he also came to seek repentance.

i. Zacchaeus cheerfully offered to do as much or even more than the law demanded. The promise to make restitution to **anyone** he had wronged was remarkable; "Considering the way he had made his money it was unlikely that this would be a short list." (Morris)

ii. *Can a life change this quickly?* Yes. Not every habit in the life of Zacchaeus changed immediately, but the heart changed, and there was some evidence of life-change immediately.

c. **Today salvation has come to this house**: Jesus knew that the repentant Zacchaeus was saved, rescued from the bondage, power, guilt, and penalty of his sin. The word was no longer **sinner** but **salvation**, and Jesus told everyone.

i. Jesus commanded the rich young ruler to give away everything (Luke 18:18-23); but for Zacchaeus it was enough to make restitution to those he had wronged. Jesus knew Zacchaeus by name and knew exactly what *he* must do to repent and be right with God and man.

ii. In Luke 18:24-27, Jesus said that it was impossible with man for the rich to enter into heaven, but it is possible with God. This is a fulfillment of that promise. Zacchaeus became a joyful giver, thus showing God's *impossible* work in him, but the young ruler went away sorry, holding on to his riches.

d. **Because he also is a son of Abraham**: Since Zacchaeus was so hated by his fellow Jews, they probably often said that he wasn't a "real" Jew. Jesus wanted everyone to know that Zacchaeus really was a **son of Abraham**, both by genetics and by faith, because he really, joyfully received Jesus.

i. The priests of Jericho (it was a Levitical city) had probably often condemned Zacchaeus and called on him to give to the poor. But after meeting Jesus, such a sacrifice was done joyfully. Love for Jesus can motivate us for greater things than legalism, guilt, or manipulation can ever do.

e. **The Son of Man has come to seek and to save that which was lost**: Jesus explained why He sought and extended friendship to a notorious sinner like Zacchaeus. Jesus came precisely to save people like Zacchaeus.

i. Zacchaeus *really* believed on Jesus. A true **son of Abraham** was not only descended from Abraham genetically, but also had the *faith* in God Abraham had.

ii. Even though Zacchaeus sought Jesus, it turns out that *he* was the one who **was lost**, and *Jesus sought him* (**has come to seek**). Zacchaeus was lost to his parents, lost to the religious, lost to his community, lost to whatever friends he might have had—yet in a sense, not lost to God. "As the story of his conversion unfolds, his seeking Jesus (Luke 19:3) turned out to be the result of Jesus' first seeking him (Luke 19:10)." (Pate)

iii. The entire account with Zacchaeus gives us a remarkable who, what, where, when, why, and how of receiving Jesus.

- *Who* Jesus wants to receive Him: those lost

- *What* Jesus wants with those who receive Him: relationship

- *Where* Jesus wants to go: down to him

- *When* Jesus wants you to receive Him: immediately, quickly

- *Why* Jesus wants you to receive Him: to be with Him, to connect with Him in life

- *How* Jesus wants you to receive Him: joyfully

B. The parable of the stewards.

1. (11) The purpose of the parable.

Now as they heard these things, He spoke another parable, because He was near Jerusalem and because they thought the kingdom of God would appear immediately.

a. **He was near Jerusalem**: Jericho is not a great distance from Jerusalem, and as Jesus neared the city, the disciples and others expected Jesus to show Himself as Messiah and the political savior of Israel (**they thought the kingdom of God would appear immediately**).

i. Passover was coming soon. According to Josephus, more than two million pilgrims poured into Jerusalem in this season. There was also great messianic expectation, strengthening the idea that **the kingdom of God would appear immediately**.

ii. George MacDonald wrote a pretty rhyme about their confused expectations:

They were all looking for a King,
To slay their foes and lift them high.
He came a little baby thing,
That made a woman cry.

b. **Because they thought the kingdom of God would appear immediately**: Jesus spoke this parable to warn His disciples that He would depart and return again before the kingdom came in full glory, and to tell them how to conduct themselves in His absence.

i. "It was an emblem of His own departure to a far country to receive a kingdom. It taught in figure that *first* there must be departure, and the long absence of the King, before the Kingdom could come in its full glory." (Morrison)

ii. The following parable is rich in historical allusions. "The Saviour probably derived the details of this parable from the actual history of Archelaus, the son of Herod, who after his father's death went to Rome to receive the sovereignty over part of his father's kingdom in accordance with the intentions of his father's testament. Its confirmation by the Roman emperor was necessary, because Herod's empire in reality formed part of the Roman Empire. A Jewish deputation at that time also went to Rome to dispute Archelaus's claim to kingship, bit the emperor nonetheless appointed him as ruler (though not as a full sovereign king) over half of his father's kingdom." (Geldenhuys)

2. (12-13) The master distributes **minas**—units of money.

Therefore He said: "A certain nobleman went into a far country to receive for himself a kingdom and to return. So he called ten of his servants, delivered to them ten minas, and said to them, 'Do business till I come.'"

a. **A certain nobleman went into a far country to receive for himself a kingdom and to return**: This parable is different from the parable of the talents in Matthew 25. Here, ten servants were each given an equal amount of money, worth about three months of wages for a working man.

i. God distributes some gifts differently, according to His own pleasure; others are universally given to every believer—such as the gospel, which is given to each Christian in equal measure.

ii. **Delivered to them ten minas**: It isn't that each servant received **ten minas**, but that **ten** were distributed to the group as a whole, one to each of the ten servants.

b. **Do business till I come**: While the master was away, receiving his kingdom, the servants were expected to **do business**—to use the resources that the master gave them, and to use them to the utmost.

3. (14) The rebellion of the citizens.

"But his citizens hated him, and sent a delegation after him, saying, 'We will not have this *man* to reign over us.'"

a. **But his citizens hated him**: These were the **citizens** of the nobleman, who lived in the area he ruled. These were not the servants who received the minas.

b. **We will not have this man to reign over us**: These citizens **hated him**, and they made it clear to the nobleman. In Jesus' parable, the nobleman did nothing to deserve this rejection; it was only because the citizens had hearts full of hate.

4. (15-19) The first two servants give account to their master.

"And so it was that when he returned, having received the kingdom, he then commanded these servants, to whom he had given the money, to be called to him, that he might know how much every man had gained by trading. Then came the first, saying, 'Master, your mina has earned ten minas.' And he said to him, 'Well *done*, good servant; because you were faithful in a very little, have authority over ten cities.' And the second came, saying, 'Master, your mina has earned five minas.' Likewise he said to him, 'You also be over five cities.' "

a. **Having received the kingdom, he then commanded these servants, to whom he had given the money, to be called to him**: When the master returned, he dealt first with his servants. He later dealt with the rebellious citizens, but they were not his first concern. He first wanted to know how faithful his servants had been in his absence.

b. **Then came the first, saying, "Master, your mina has earned ten minas."** The first servant brought a good report. He did business with his master's mina, and had ten more to show for it. This was an impressive 1000% increase.

i. The first servant heard beautiful praise from his master: **Well done, good servant; because you were faithful in a very little, have authority over ten cities**: Because he demonstrated faithful handling of the master's resources, he was given authority over ten cities in the kingdom his master just received.

ii. **Have authority**: The reward for faithful service is not rest, but *more* service. This is entirely pleasing to the servant of God. "The reward of work well done was more work to do....The great reward of God to the man who has satisfied the test is more trust." (Barclay)

c. **Master, your mina has earned five minas**: The second servant brought another good report. He did business with his master's mina and had five more to show for it, a 500% increase.

i. Each of the servants credited the gift of the master (**your mina**) for the work instead of their own effort or intelligence. "Not my pains, but thy pound hath done it." (Trapp)

ii. He was also rewarded, though not with the words "**Well done, good servant**." The number of cities he was given authority over was in proportion to his faithfulness in managing the master's resources.

5. (20-26) The third servant gives account to his master.

"Then another came, saying, 'Master, here is your mina, which I have kept put away in a handkerchief. For I feared you, because you are an austere man. You collect what you did not deposit, and reap what you did not sow.' And he said to him, 'Out of your own mouth I will judge you, *you* wicked servant. You knew that I was an austere man, collecting what I did not deposit and reaping what I did not sow. Why then did you not put my money in the bank, that at my coming I might have collected it with interest?' And he said to those who stood by, 'Take the mina from him, and give *it* to him who has ten minas.' (But they said to him, 'Master, he has ten minas.') For I say to you, that to everyone who has will be given; and from him who does not have, even what he has will be taken away from him."

a. **Master, here is your mina, which I have kept put away in a handkerchief**: The third servant did not have a good report. He did not obey the master's command to *do business till I come*. Burying the master's resources underground was not wise or good.

i. The third servant excused his disobedience by claiming that his master was so powerful that he didn't need the servant's help (**you collect what you did not deposit, and reap what you did not sow**).

b. **Out of your own mouth I will judge you, you wicked servant. You knew that I was an austere man**: The master did not reward the third servant. Instead, he rebuked him because the great power of the master should have inspired the servant to greater diligence, not to disobedience and laziness.

i. It would have been easy for this servant to do *something* with his master's resources (**Why then did you not put my money in the bank?**). Yet out of disobedience, he did *nothing*.

ii. This helps us to understand the plan of the master. It was not to make money by his servants, but to make *character* in them. He didn't need them to make money, but they needed to work with him to build their character.

c. **Take the mina from him, and give it to him who has ten minas**: The third servant had everything taken from him. He remained his master's servant, and in his house, but was left with nothing. He proved himself unable to manage his master's things, and was given nothing to manage.

i. Jesus emphasized this by saying, **"For I say to you, that to everyone who has will be given; and from him who does not have, even what he has will be taken away from him"**. "The paradoxical, almost oxymoronic, statement reflects the spiritual axiom earlier recorded in Luke 8:18: Whoever is faithful to the Lord will be rewarded and whoever is not will suffer loss. Light received brings more light; light refused brings the night." (Pate)

ii. "In the Christian life we do not stand still. We use our gifts and make progress or we lose what we have." (Morris)

iii. The main point of this parable is clear; the kingdom will be delayed, so we must concentrate on being faithful servants in the meantime. Our Master has gone away to a far country, and will one day return with His kingdom. In the meantime, we are commanded to do business with what He has given us until He returns.

iv. "By the *ten minas* given to *each*, we may understand the Gospel of the kingdom given to each person who professes to believe in Christ, and which he is to improve to the salvation of his soul. The *same* word is given to all, that all may believe and be saved." (Clarke)

v. When our Master returns, He will come to reward us according to our faithfulness, and we will be rewarded with different levels of authority in His kingdom.

vi. The unfaithful servants were those who thought that because their Master was so mighty, He did not need their help. But the issue is not His need of my help; the issue is my need to help Him and my need to be part of His work.

6. (27) Judgment day comes for the master's enemies.

"But bring here those enemies of mine, who did not want me to reign over them, and slay *them* before me."

a. **But bring here those enemies of mine**: The servants all had to answer for their work in the master's absence, but at least none of them were guilty of treason. Now the master dealt with his **enemies**, the rebellious citizens mentioned in Luke 19:14, who *hated him* and said, "*We will not have this man to reign over us.*"

i. **Who did not want me to reign over them**: They could try and deny the reign of the master as much as they pleased, but it would get them nowhere. He would rule over them one way or another.

b. **And slay them before me**: The servants of the master each had to answer to him, but so did his enemies. They met with certain, final judgment. This dramatic and strong ending shows that responding to the reign of Jesus is a life-or-death decision.

C. Jesus enters Jerusalem.

1. (28) On to Jerusalem.

When He had said this, He went on ahead, going up to Jerusalem.

a. **When He had said this**: After carefully correcting His followers as to the true nature of His kingdom and His mission, Jesus went steadfastly towards Jerusalem.

i. "At last Jerusalem, the temple city in which the greatest and holiest drama on earth will be staged the following week, is in immediate vicinity." (Geldenhuys)

b. **He went ahead, going up to Jerusalem**: Knowing full well what awaited Him, knowing that He must endure the cross before receiving the kingdom, Jesus went. In His suffering, we should *admire*, not *pity* Jesus. He knew exactly what was before Him.

i. John 11:57 makes it clear that there was a price on Jesus' head, and He was a wanted man. Despite all that, Jesus came into Jerusalem in the most public way possible.

2. (29-34) Careful preparations are made for the entrance ceremony.

And it came to pass, when He came near to Bethphage and Bethany, at the mountain called Olivet, *that* He sent two of His disciples, saying, "Go into the village opposite *you,* where as you enter you will find a colt tied, on which no one has ever sat. Loose it and bring *it* here. And if anyone asks you, 'Why are you loosing *it?'* thus you shall say to him, 'Because the Lord has need of it.'" So those who were sent went their way and found *it* just as He had said to them. But as they were loosing the colt, the owners of it said to them, "Why are you loosing the colt?" And they said, "The Lord has need of him."

a. **Go into the village opposite you, where as you enter you will find a colt tied**: As Jesus came to this last, critical week before the crucifixion, He carefully and deliberately sent His disciples to make arrangements for His arrival into Jerusalem. Jesus had been to Jerusalem many times before, but there was something very special about *this* journey to Jerusalem.

b. **You will find a colt tied, on which no one has ever sat**: Jesus rode this relatively humble animal into Jerusalem. Instead of coming on a horse as a conquering general, He came on a **colt**, as was customary for royalty. He came to Jerusalem as the Prince of Peace.

i. "The ass was the mount of a man of peace, a merchant or a priest. A king might ride an ass on occasion, but he would be more likely to appear on a mighty war-horse. Zechariah's prophecy saw Messiah as the Prince of peace." (Morris)

ii. "This entry into Jerusalem has been termed the *triumph* of Christ. It was indeed the triumph of *humility* over *pride* and worldly grandeur; of *poverty* over *affluence*; and of *meekness* and *gentleness* over *rage* and *malice*." (Clarke)

iii. **On which no one has ever sat**: F.B. Meyer observed that this is an illustration of how God requires of us *undivided loyalty*; that the seat of authority is for Jesus and Jesus alone. He also noted that Jesus may require of us only one brief service of renown or notice; and if this is His plan, we will find satisfaction in it.

c. **The Lord has need of him**: Seemingly, this was a pre-arranged borrowing or rental of this animal for the use of Jesus. The disciples needed to tell the owners that it was for the use of Jesus.

i. "Normally, animals such as donkeys (for the poor) and horses (for the wealthy) were made available by their owners for travelers for a price or, at times, to be borrowed." (Pate)

ii. "What a singular conjunction of words is here, 'the Lord' and 'hath need!' Jesus, without laying aside his sovereignty, had taken a nature full of needs; yet, being in need, he was still the Lord and could command his subjects and requisition their property." (Spurgeon)

iii. "*Hath need of them*: not for any weariness: he who had travelled on foot from Galilee to Bethany, could have gone the other two miles; but that he might enter into Jerusalem as was prophesied of him, Zechariah 9:9." (Poole)

3. (35-40) Jesus enters the city to a humble display of praise and honor.

Then they brought him to Jesus. And they threw their own clothes on the colt, and they set Jesus on him. And as He went, *many* spread their clothes on the road. Then, as He was now drawing near the descent of the Mount of Olives, the whole multitude of the disciples began to rejoice and praise God with a loud voice for all the mighty works they had seen, saying: " 'Blessed *is* the King who comes in the name of the LORD!' Peace in heaven and glory in the highest!" And some of the Pharisees called to Him from the crowd, "Teacher, rebuke Your disciples." But He answered and said to them, "I tell you that if these should keep silent, the stones would immediately cry out."

a. **Threw their own clothes on the colt...spread their clothes on the road...began to rejoice and praise God with a loud voice**: The crowd extravagantly honored Jesus and praised God for sending this King unto Jerusalem, saying **Blessed is the King who comes in the name of LORD!**

i. The idea of a victorious, conquering king entering a city was well known in that time. Typically, a victorious king came into a city escorted by the citizens of his kingdom and his army. As he entered, songs were sung in praise and acclamation of the conqueror and he came with symbols of his victory and authority. Finally, he came into the city's prominent temple and made a sacrificial offering to honor the gods and associate himself with them.

ii. The Gospels take these well-known forms and turn them on their head. Jesus entered Jerusalem with a relatively humble and motley escort and singing. The only symbols of His power were a humble donkey and palm branches. Upon entering the city, He did not offer sacrifices, but He challenged the religious status quo and cleansed the temple.

b. **Teacher, rebuke Your disciples**: The crowd's praise made Jesus' enemies uncomfortable; it made them object to the praise being offered. It made them know they were being defeated. John 12:19 says that on this day, *The Pharisees therefore said among themselves, "You see that you are accomplishing nothing. Look, the world has gone after Him!"*

i. Nothing tells Satan and his followers that they have lost like the praises of God ringing in their ears. Satan loses, because when God's people are really worshipping, their hearts and minds are on Him—and not on sin, self, or Satan's distractions.

c. **I tell you that if these should keep silent, the stones would immediately cry out**: Jesus said this when the Pharisees told Him to quiet those who praised Him and received Him as King. On *this* day, Jesus was going to be praised. For most of His ministry, Jesus did everything He could to discourage people from publicly celebrating Him as Messiah. Here Jesus invited public praise and adoration as Messiah.

i. **The stones would immediately cry out**: The idea of creation itself praising God may seem strange, but the Bible speaks about it in a few places—trees, hills, oceans, rivers, mountains, valleys, cattle and creeping things, birds and fields all give praise to God (Psalm 148:7-13, Psalm 96:11-12).

ii. Yet the stones stayed silent on that day, because all the multitude praised Jesus: **the whole multitude of the disciples began to rejoice.** "And yet, I suppose, those disciples had their trials as we have ours. There might have been a sick wife at home, or a child withering with disease." (Spurgeon) Yet they *all* praised Him!

d. **With a loud voice for all the mighty works they had seen**: Their praise was filled with remembrance. They remembered all the mighty works they saw Jesus do, such as the raising of Lazarus from the dead (John 12:17-18). They told of the great things God had done in their lives.

i. A great indictment against much of our praise is that it is mindless. We do not have anything specific in our minds that we praise God for, things that we have seen Him do in our lives. Anyone who says, "Praise the Lord!" should be able to answer this question: "Praise Him for *what*?"

4. (41-44) Jesus weeps over Jerusalem.

Now as He drew near, He saw the city and wept over it, saying, "If you had known, even you, especially in this your day, the things *that make* for your peace! But now they are hidden from your eyes. For days will come upon you when your enemies will build an embankment around you, surround you and close you in on every side, and level you, and your children within you, to the ground; and they will not leave in you one stone upon another, because you did not know the time of your visitation."

a. **As He drew near, He saw the city and wept over it**: This was a deeply moving moment for Jesus. His tears were not for His own fate in Jerusalem, but for the fate of the city itself.

i. "*Wept* might be rendered 'wailed'; Jesus burst into sobbing as he lamented lost opportunity." (Morris)

ii. "The cry was that of a frustrated desire. He had visited the city, with the desire to deliver it from the things of destruction; and with the offers of the things of peace. The spiritual blindness of the rulers and people was such that they did not discern the meaning of the visitation. The result was inevitable. There could be no escape from the destruction." (Morgan)

b. **If you had known, even you, especially in this your day, the things that make for your peace!** This was a turning point for the Jewish people. Their leaders had rejected Jesus, and most of the people followed their leaders. Yet if they **had known** Jesus and His work as Messiah, they might have been spared the destruction to come.

i. In some old copies of the Bible, they removed the passage about Jesus weeping here, because they thought that if Jesus were perfect, He would not weep. But the perfection of Jesus demands that He weep at this occasion, when Israel rejected their only opportunity to escape the destruction to come.

ii. Jesus here showed the heart of God, how even when judgment must be pronounced, it is never done with joy. Even when God's judgment is perfectly just and righteous, His heart weeps at the bringing of the judgment.

c. **If you had known, even you, especially in this your day, the things that make for your peace!** Jesus mourned over the fact they did not know the time of the Messiah's coming, the **day** prophesied by Daniel: **this your day**.

> i. **This your day** was so important because it was likely *the day* prophesied by Daniel that *Messiah the Prince* would come unto Jerusalem. Daniel said that it would be 483 years on the Jewish calendar from the day of the decree to restore and rebuild Jerusalem to the day the Messiah would come to Jerusalem. By the reckoning of Sir Robert Anderson, this was fulfilled 483 years later to the day (by the Jewish reckoning of 360 day years, as in Daniel 9:25).

> ii. This is the day mentioned in Psalm 118:24: *This is the day the LORD has made; we will rejoice and be glad in it.*

d. **The things that make for your peace**: The name *Jerusalem* means "city of peace"; but the city of peace did not know the **things that make for your peace**. Jesus knew that their desire for a political Messiah would bring total destruction in less than a generation.

e. **Days will come upon you when your enemies will build an embankment around you**: Jesus predicted five specific aspects of the Roman attack upon Jerusalem:

- The building of an embankment
- The surrounding of the city, laying siege
- The destruction of the city
- The killing of the city's inhabitants
- The complete leveling of the city

> i. The historian Josephus described in detail the **embankment around** Jerusalem; how it utterly shut up the city before the Romans totally destroyed them (*Wars of the Jews*, 5.12.1-3).

> ii. From Josephus: "All hope of escaping was now cut off from the Jews, together with their liberty of going out of the city. Then did the famine widen its progress, and devour the people by whole houses and families; the upper rooms of women and infants that were dying by famine, and the lanes of the city were full of the dead bodies of the aged; the children also, and the young men wandered about the market places like shadows, all swelled with the famine, and fell down dead wheresoever their misery seized them. For a time the dead were buried; but afterwards, when they could not do that, they had them cast down from the wall into the valleys beneath. When Titus, on going his rounds along these valleys, saw them full of dead bod-

ies, and the thick putrefication running about them, he gave a groan, and spreading out his hands to heave, called God to witness this was not his doing." (Cited in Spurgeon. He added: "There is nothing in history to exceed this horror. But even this is nothing compared with the destruction of a soul.")

5. (45-48) The cleansing of the temple.

Then He went into the temple and began to drive out those who bought and sold in it, saying to them, "It is written, 'My house is a house of prayer,' but you have made it a 'den of thieves.'" And He was teaching daily in the temple. But the chief priests, the scribes, and the leaders of the people sought to destroy Him, and were unable to do anything; for all the people were very attentive to hear Him.

a. **He went into the temple and began to drive out those who bought and sold in it**: This seems distinct from the cleansing of the temple courts mentioned in John 2:13-22, which happened towards the beginning of Jesus' earthly ministry. Yet the purpose was the same; to drive out the merchants, who in cooperation with the priests cheated visitors to Jerusalem by forcing them to purchase approved sacrificial animals and currencies at high prices.

i. Barclay notes, "A pair of doves could cost as little as 4p outside the Temple and as much as 75p inside the Temple." This is almost *20 times* more expensive.

ii. Yet Jesus' anger was against **those who bought** as well as those who **sold in it**. "Sellers and buyers viewed as one company—kindred in spirit, to be cleared out wholesale…The traffic was necessary, and might have been innocent; but the trading spirit soon develops abuses which were doubtless rampant at that period." (Bruce)

iii. What Jesus did was important more as an acted-out parable than for what it accomplished in itself. "There is no indication, nor is it likely, that any lasting reform was achieved; no doubt the tables were back for the rest of the week, and Jesus took no further action." (France)

b. **My house is a house of prayer**: The merchants operated in the outer courts of the temple, the only area where Gentiles could come and pray. Therefore, this place of prayer was made into a marketplace, and a dishonest one (**a 'den of thieves'**).

i. Mark's record contains the more complete quotation of Jesus' reference to Isaiah 56:7: *Is it not written, "My house shall be called a house of prayer for all nations?"* (Mark 11:17). The point was that Isaiah prophesied, and Jesus demanded that the temple be a place for *all nations* to pray. The activity of **all those who bought and sold in the** outer courts made it impossible for any seeking Gentile to come and pray.

ii. "In that uproar of buying and selling and bargaining and auctioneering prayer was impossible. Those who sought God's presence were being debarred from it from the very people of God's House." (Barclay)

c. **And He was teaching daily in the temple**: After running the merchants out of the temple courts, Jesus boldly continued His work of public teaching and healing (Matthew 21:14). He was able to continue because the people wanted to hear Him (**for all the people were very attentive to hear Him**).

Luke 20—Question and Answer with Jesus

"These answers of His were not the sharp retorts of smartness, but the final utterances of a wisdom which revealed the ignorance of the questions." (Morgan)

A. The religious leaders question the authority of Jesus.

1. (1-2) The religious and political leaders question Jesus.

Now it happened on one of those days, as He taught the people in the temple and preached the gospel, *that* the chief priests and the scribes, together with the elders, confronted *Him* and spoke to Him, saying, "Tell us, by what authority are You doing these things? Or who is he who gave You this authority?"

a. **The chief priests and the scribes, together with the elders, confronted Him**: Jesus didn't look for these great debates with the religious leaders. He wanted to teach the people and tell them about God's good news. Yet the questioners came to Him, and He answered them with great wisdom and power.

b. **Tell us, by what authority are You doing these things?** Jesus showed great courage by boldly entering Jerusalem and driving out the corrupt merchants from the temple courts. Now, the religious leaders wanted to know by what right Jesus did such things—especially because He did not have traditional rabbinical training.

i. This was not the beginning of the official suspicion of Jesus by the religious authorities. Yet His cleansing of the temple and public teaching made Jesus of even greater concern to them. "Jesus' teaching, preaching, and surely His cleansing of the temple (Luke 19:45-46), were viewed by the officials as highly controversial if not adversarial." (Pate)

2. (3-8) Jesus answers their question with another question.

But He answered and said to them, "I also will ask you one thing, and answer Me: The baptism of John; was it from heaven or from men?"

And they reasoned among themselves, saying, "If we say, 'From heaven,' He will say, 'Why then did you not believe him?' But if we say, 'From men,' all the people will stone us, for they are persuaded that John was a prophet." So they answered that they did not know where *it was* from. And Jesus said to them, "Neither will I tell you by what authority I do these things."

a. **The baptism of John; was it from heaven or from men?** By replying with this question, Jesus did not *evade* their question. Instead, He used the question to explain who He was and to expose the hypocrisy of the leaders. If John was from God, then he was right in proclaiming Jesus as the Messiah—and if this was true, then Jesus had all authority.

i. "Since John, like Jesus, was not a rabbi, the authorities' response to the one would affect their response to the other." (Pate)

b. **They answered that they did not know where it was from**: This response showed they were not sincere seekers of truth. They cared more about winning the argument against Jesus than in knowing the truth.

i. "If you do not recognize authority when you see it, He said in effect, no amount of arguing will convince you of it." (Geldenhuys)

c. **Neither will I tell you by what authority I do these things**: When they showed themselves to be insincere seekers, Jesus refused to answer their question. Jesus had great care and compassion for the sincere seeker, but not for cynical critics and manipulators.

i. If we want answers from Jesus, we must deal rightly with the truth that has already been revealed. These men knew that John said Jesus was the Messiah, and were not willing to accept it.

B. The parable of the tenant farmers.

1. (9-16a) A parable about a landowner and his tenants.

Then He began to tell the people this parable: "A certain man planted a vineyard, leased it to vinedressers, and went into a far country for a long time. Now at vintage-time he sent a servant to the vinedressers, that they might give him some of the fruit of the vineyard. But the vinedressers beat him and sent *him* away empty-handed. Again he sent another servant; and they beat him also, treated *him* shamefully, and sent *him* away empty-handed. And again he sent a third; and they wounded him also and cast *him* out. Then the owner of the vineyard said, 'What shall I do? I will send my beloved son. Probably they will respect *him* when they see him.' But when the vinedressers saw him, they reasoned among themselves, saying, 'This is the heir. Come, let us kill him, that the inheritance may be ours.' So they cast him out of the vineyard and killed *him*. Therefore what will the owner of the vineyard

do to them? He will come and destroy those vinedressers and give the vineyard to others."

a. **A certain man planted a vineyard, leased it to vinedressers**: This sort of tenant farming arrangement was a common practice in Jesus' day, especially in Galilee. Archaeologists have discovered records of this same sort of dispute between landowners and tenant farmers.

b. **Planted a vineyard**: This parable had more than a cultural connection; it was also rooted in the Old Testament. Jesus' first listeners would remember that the **vineyard** was used in the Old Testament as a picture of Israel (Isaiah 5:1-7). In this parable, the tenants (the **vinedressers**) represented the religious leaders among the Jewish people.

c. **Leased it to vinedressers**: The **vinedressers** didn't buy the vineyard, and they did not make it. They were allowed to work it by a generous owner, yet they turned against the owner, and would one day would answer for their rebellion.

i. This parable tells us that God, the owner of all, is more patient with rebels than we would ever be, and that there will be a final day of reckoning.

d. **What shall I do? I will send my beloved son**: The owner of the vineyard repeatedly tried to receive what was rightfully His from the vineyard and those who worked it. They rejected each of the three servants he sent to receive what was due to him, so finally he sent his **beloved son**, thinking, "**Probably they will respect** *him*."

e. **This is the heir. Come, let us kill him, that the inheritance may be ours**: The renters of the vineyard foolishly thought they could benefit from killing the son who had or would inherit the vineyard. They were seriously wrong in this foolish assumption.

i. "Jeremias surmises that the farmers may have assumed from the arrival of the son that the owner had died. So if they killed the sole heir, the vineyard would pass into their hands as first claimants." (Pate)

ii. "In a day when title was sometimes uncertain, anyone who had had the use of land for three years was presumed to own it in the absence of an alternative claim." (Morris)

iii. This parable tells us that Jesus knew He was the Son—the Son of God—and that He knew that He would be killed soon.

2. (16b-19) Jesus applies the parable.

And when they heard *it* **they said, "Certainly not!" Then He looked at them and said, "What then is this that is written: 'The stone which the builders rejected Has become the chief cornerstone'? Whoever falls on**

that stone will be broken; but on whomever it falls, it will grind him to powder." And the chief priests and the scribes that very hour sought to lay hands on Him, but they feared the people; for they knew He had spoken this parable against them.

a. **Certainly not!** The religious leaders understood the parable immediately and objected that Jesus compared *them* to the rebellious and foolish tenants (**they knew He had spoken this parable against them**). In their blindness they thought, "This could never be *us*."

b. **The stone which the builders rejected Has become the chief cornerstone**: Jesus taught them from Psalm 118, because this Psalm described the coming of the Messiah to Jerusalem, and Jesus had been officially presented to Israel at the Triumphal Entry. The hostility of the Jewish leaders showed that this Messianic **stone** was being **rejected**, even if He was initially greeted with hosannas.

i. "Jesus' connection of the rejected son and the rejected stone seems to suggest that He is explaining the people's query about the treatment of the son." (Pate)

c. **Stone . . . chief cornerstone**: Jesus is often likened unto a stone or a rock in the Bible. He is the rock of provision that followed Israel in the desert (1 Corinthians 10:4). He is the stone of stumbling (1 Peter 2:8). He is the stone cut without hands that crushes the kingdoms of this world (Daniel 2:45).

i. The **cornerstone**, "designated in antiquity the stone used at the building's corner to bear the weight or the stress of the two walls. It would have functioned somewhat like a 'keystone' or 'capstone' in an arch or other architectural form. It was the stone which was essential or crucial to the whole structure." (Fitzmyer, cited in Pate)

d. **Whoever falls on that stone will be broken; but on whomever it falls, it will grind him to powder**: Anyone who comes to Jesus will be **broken** of their pride and self-will, but those who refuse to come will be crushed by Christ in judgment.

C. God and Caesar.

1. (20-22) The Pharisees try to entrap Jesus.

So they watched *Him,* and sent spies who pretended to be righteous, that they might seize on His words, in order to deliver Him to the power and the authority of the governor. Then they asked Him, saying, "Teacher, we know that You say and teach rightly, and You do not show personal favoritism, but teach the way of God in truth: "Is it lawful for us to pay taxes to Caesar or not?"

a. **That they might seize on His words, in order to deliver Him to the power and the authority of the governor**: Public opinion had kept them from stopping Jesus. Now, the enemies of Christ tried to turn the tide of public opinion against Him by making Jesus appear to side with the Roman government.

i. **Spies**: The original has the idea, "*I let down, to set in ambush. One who crouches in* in some secret place to *spy, listen, catch,* or *hurt*... No doubt the persons mentioned in the text were men of the basest principles, and were *hired* by the malicious Pharisees to do what they attempted in vain to perform." (Clarke)

b. **Teacher, we know that You say and teach rightly, and You do not show personal favoritism, but teach the way of God in truth**: This was an obvious and clumsy attempt to influence Jesus with flattery. They hoped Jesus was insecure or foolish enough to be impressed by their hollow praise.

i. "Here is a fair glove, drawn upon a foul hand." (Trapp)

c. **Is it lawful for us to pay taxes to Caesar or not?** Jesus' dilemma with this question was simple. If He said that taxes *should* be paid, He could be accused of denying the sovereignty of God over Israel (making Himself unpopular with the Jewish people). If He said that taxes *should not* be paid, He made Himself an enemy of Rome.

i. Rome had long required the Jews of Palestine to pay taxes, and at least since A.D. 6 they were forced to pay taxes directly into the emperor's treasury. Some Jewish patriots (such as the Zealots) refused, not wanting to recognize Roman rule as legitimate. Most others reluctantly paid it.

2. (23-26) Jesus answers their question.

But He perceived their craftiness, and said to them, "Why do you test Me? Show Me a denarius. Whose image and inscription does it have?" They answered and said, "Caesar's." And He said to them, "Render therefore to Caesar the things that are Caesar's, and to God the things that are God's." But they could not catch Him in His words in the presence of the people. And they marveled at His answer and kept silent.

a. **Why do you test Me?** If there was some exasperation in the voice of Jesus as He said this, it was not only on His own behalf. It is easy to imagine that Jesus thought, "Why do you keep testing Me when you always lose? How long will you try to get the best of Me?"

b. **Whose image and inscription does it have?** Essentially, Jesus said "You recognize Caesar's civil authority when you use his coins, therefore you are obliged to pay him the taxes he asks for."

i. "The denarii bore the head of Tiberius and the inscription *TI. CAE-SAR DIVI AVG. F. AVGVSTVS* (Tiberius Caesar, son of the divine Augustus, Augustus). The image and inscriptions of ancient coins would have been understood as a property seal; the coins *belonged* to Caesar." (Pate)

ii. A spiritual lesson can be learned from what is inscribed on coins issued in the United States, because each phrase has an important association in the Christian life.

- In God we Trust
- Liberty
- E. Pluribus Unum (Out of Many, One)

c. **Render therefore to Caesar the things that are Caesar's**: Jesus affirmed that the government makes legitimate requests of us. We are responsible to God in all things, but we must be obedient to government in matters civil and national.

i. Peter said it like this: *Fear God. Honor the king.* (1 Peter 2:17) "Jesus is saying that we are citizens of heaven and earth at the same time." (Morris)

ii. "Every Christian has a double citizenship. He is a citizen of the country in which he happens to live. To it he owes many things. He owes the safety against lawless men which only a settled government can give; he owes all public services." (Barclay)

iii. "*Render* generally means 'give back' (whereas the verb they had used in verse 17 was simple 'give'). It is the verb for paying a bill or settling a debt; they owe it to him." (France)

d. **And to God the things that are God's**: Everyone has the image of God impressed upon them. This means that we belong to God, not to Caesar, or not even to ourselves.

i. "It establishes the *limits*, regulates the *rights*, and distinguishes the *jurisdiction* of the two *empires* of *heaven* and *earth*. The *image* of *princes* stamped on their *coin* denotes that temporal things belong all to their government. The *image* of God stamped on the *soul* denotes that all its faculties and powers belong to the Most High, and should be employed in his service." (Clarke)

ii. If the Jews had rendered unto God His due, they would have never had to render *anything* to Caesar. In New Testament times, they would never have endured the occupying oppression of the Roman Empire if they had been obedient to their covenant with God.

e. **They could not catch Him in His words**: Jesus gave a wise and appropriate answer to their question. Nevertheless, they took this perfect answer and twisted it into an accusation in Luke 23:2, when they accused Jesus of *forbidding to pay taxes to Caesar*—when He actually said just the opposite

D. A question about the resurrection.

1. (27-33) The Sadducees ask Jesus a ridiculous question.

Then some of the Sadducees, who deny that there is a resurrection, came to *Him* and asked Him, saying: "Teacher, Moses wrote to us *that* if a man's brother dies, having a wife, and he dies without children, his brother should take his wife and raise up offspring for his brother. Now there were seven brothers. And the first took a wife, and died without children. And the second took her as wife, and he died childless. Then the third took her, and in like manner the seven also; and they left no children, and died. Last of all the woman died also. Therefore, in the resurrection, whose wife does she become? For all seven had her as wife."

a. **The Sadducees, who deny there is a resurrection**: The Sadducees were the ancient version of the modern liberal theologians. They were anti-supernaturalistic, only accepting the first five books of Moses as authentic—and disregarding what was written in those books when it pleased them to do so. They did not believe in immortality, spirits or angels.

i. The name *Sadducees* came from the name of the priestly family *Zadok* (as in Ezekiel 44:15); it was something like saying, "Zadokites." It was the priestly faction or party. (Pate)

ii. "They were the conservative, aristocratic, high-priestly party, worldly minded and very ready to cooperate with the Romans, which, of course, enabled them to maintain their privileged position." (Morris)

b. **Now there were seven brothers**: The Sadducees asked Jesus a hypothetical (and ridiculous) question, hoping to show that the idea of the resurrection was nonsense. Based on Deuteronomy 25:5-10, if a married man died childless, it was his brother's responsibility to impregnate his brother's widow and then count the child as the deceased husband's descendant. The Pharisees imagined elaborate circumstances along these lines and raised the question, "**Therefore, in the resurrection, whose wife does she become?**"

i. This practice of a brother-in-law marrying the widow of his brother is known as *levirate marriage*. The term comes from the Latin "lavir," meaning "brother-in-law." This is the specific idea in the question.

ii. "Probably, this was one of the stock stories they were in the habit of telling in order to cast ridicule upon the resurrection." (Spurgeon)

2. (34-36) Jesus corrects their misunderstanding of resurrection life by showing it is life of an entirely different order.

And Jesus answered and said to them, "The sons of this age marry and are given in marriage. But those who are counted worthy to attain that age, and the resurrection from the dead, neither marry nor are given in marriage; nor can they die anymore, for they are equal to the angels and are sons of God, being sons of the resurrection."

a. **Neither marry nor are given in marriage**: First, Jesus reminded them that life in the resurrection is quite different from this life. It does not merely continue this world and its arrangements, but it is life of a completely different order.

i. This passage has made many wonder if marriage relationships will exist in heaven, or if those who are husband and wife on earth will have no special relationship in heaven. We are not told enough about life in the world beyond to answer in great detail, but we can understand a few principles.

- Family relationships will still be known in life in the world beyond. The rich man Jesus described in the afterlife was aware of his family relationships (Luke 16:27-28)

- The glory of heaven will be a relationship and connection with God that surpasses anything else, including present family relationships (Revelation 21:22-23)

ii. If it seems that life in **the resurrection** that Jesus spoke of here does not include some of the pleasures of life we know on earth, it is only because the enjoyments and satisfactions of heaven far surpass what we know on earth. We can't be completely certain what life in glory beyond will be like, but we can know with certainty that no one will be disappointed with the arrangements (Revelation 22:1-5).

iii. This question is not merely theoretical. There will be many in heaven who have had more than one spouse, for any number of reasons. Jesus here told us that jealousy and exclusion will have no place in heaven.

iv. This Biblical understanding of heaven is dramatically different from the more sensual dreams of heaven, such as those found in Islamic and Mormon theology. "Mahomet, as he professed that himself had a special license given him by God to know what woman he would, and to put them away when he would; so he promised to all his votaries and adherents the like carnal pleasures at the resurrection." (Trapp)

b. **Nor can they die anymore, for they are equal to the angels and are sons of God, being sons of the resurrection**: Second, Jesus reminded us that life in heaven is eternal and shares some characteristics of the existence that angels now experience—though they will be even greater, being called **sons of God** and **sons of the resurrection**, titles not given to angelic beings in the New Testament.

i. If there is no death in the life to come, there is no need for procreation.

ii. The most obvious point must not be neglected: Jesus told the Sadducees that angels were real. "In fact, Jesus' use of angels contains a double thrust since the Sadducees denied their existence." (Carson)

3. (37-40) Jesus proves the resurrection from the Scriptures.

"But even Moses showed in the *burning* bush *passage* that the dead are raised, when he called the Lord 'the God of Abraham, the God of Isaac, and the God of Jacob.' For He is not the God of the dead but of the living, for all live to Him." Then some of the scribes answered and said, "Teacher, You have spoken well." But after that they dared not question Him anymore.

a. **The God of Abraham, the God of Isaac, and the God of Jacob**: Jesus demonstrated the reality of the resurrection using only the Torah, the five books of Moses, which were the only books the Sadducees accepted as authoritative. If Abraham, Isaac and Jacob did not live on in resurrection, then God could not say that He is **the God of Abraham**, and would instead say, "I *was* the God of Abraham."

i. This emphatically tells us that those departed from this life in the Lord *live*.

- They live *personally*—they are still individuals in the life to come
- They are *mentioned by their names*—they are known and not anonymous
- They are *free from all sorrow*, never to die and to live as sons of God
- They are *not lost*—we know where they are, and they also know

ii. "Children of God, it is in the highest degree proper that you should think of things as your Father thinks of them; and he saith that 'all live unto God.' Let us correct our phraseology by that of Scripture, and speak of departed saints as inspiration speaks of them…in our family we shall number brothers, and sisters, and friends, whose bodies lie in the churchyard and shall speak of those who have crossed the border, and passed within the veil, as still our own." (Spurgeon)

b. **He is not the God of the dead but of the living, for all live to Him**: This demonstrates that there is a resurrection, and life beyond, despite what the unbelieving and doubting Sadducees thought and taught. Jesus answered well, and both His friends and enemies recognized it.

> i. "A living God is the God of living men; and Abraham, Isaac, and Jacob are still alive." (Spurgeon)

E. Using a question, Jesus warns the religious leaders.

1. (41-44) Jesus asks a question: How can the Messiah be both the **Son of David** and the **Lord** of David?

And He said to them, "How can they say that the Christ is the Son of David? Now David himself said in the Book of Psalms: 'The LORD said to my Lord, "Sit at My right hand, till I make Your enemies Your footstool."' Therefore David calls Him 'Lord'; how is He then his Son?"

a. **How can they say that the Christ is the Son of David?** When the scribes and Pharisees and Sadducees questioned Jesus, they tried to make Him look bad or trap Him. Jesus didn't do the same with His questions to them. Instead, He got to the heart of the matter—"Do you really know who I am?"

> i. Jesus tested their notion that they already knew all about the Messiah. He asked them to consider that they may not know everything about the Messiah, and may have something to learn.

b. **Therefore David calls Him 'Lord'; how is He then his Son?** Quoting Psalm 110:1, Jesus noted that King David called the Messiah his **Lord**. This means that the Messiah is not only the **Son of David** (a popular Messianic title), He is also the **Lord** of David. As Revelation 22:16 says, He is *both the root and offspring of David.*

2. (45-47) Jesus warns about the hypocrisy of the scribes.

Then, in the hearing of all the people, He said to His disciples, "Beware of the scribes, who desire to go around in long robes, love greetings in the marketplaces, the best seats in the synagogues, and the best places at feasts, who devour widows' houses, and for a pretense make long prayers. These will receive greater condemnation."

a. **Who desire to go around in long robes**: The scribes were men of leisure, who watched while others worked. **Love greetings**: They demanded recognition from others for their standing with God. **The best seats**: They demanded the special benefits of status and privilege.

b. **Devour widows' houses**: Perhaps the scribes pretended to help the widows, and instead used their position of trust to take from them. Perhaps they received gifts from well-meaning widows and mismanaged them. Perhaps they solicited gifts from widows with false promises.

i. In that day a Jewish teacher could not be paid for teaching, but he could receive gifts. Apparently, many scribes used flattery and manipulation to get big gifts from those who could least afford to give them, such as widows.

ii. Many of the Jews of Jesus' day taught that teachers were to be respected almost as God; they said that they deserved more honor and respect than any other people in life did. They taught that the greatest act someone could do is give money to a teacher. Of course, it was the teachers themselves who taught this!

c. **For a pretense make long prayers**: The scribes thought they were more spiritual because of their **long prayers**. But Morgan rightly said that when a man is away from his wife, and the journey is short, the letters are short—but the farther he is from his wife, the longer the letters become. Morgan said that some people must be a long way from God because their prayers are so long!

d. **These will receive greater condemnation**: The scribes represent a complete contrast to the picture of how a disciple should live—as a servant, as a child, as one carrying a cross. Jesus said we should notice what they do, as well as what they say, and especially that we should notice their *destiny*.

i. The scribes were experts at projecting a religious image, but a religious image before men isn't what God looks for in us. God is concerned about our religious *reality*, not the image.

Luke 21—Jesus Warns of Jerusalem's Fall and His Return

A. A widow's sacrificial gift.

1. (1-2) Jesus observes the widow's giving.

And He looked up and saw the rich putting their gifts into the treasury, and He saw also a certain poor widow putting in two mites.

a. **He looked up and saw the rich putting their gifts into the treasury**: At the temple, Jesus noticed a long line of rich people who put in a lot of money, perhaps making some kind of display to call attention to their gifts.

i. The line at the offering box and the pride shown by the rich men in their giving shows us that it isn't necessarily more spiritual to have an offering box instead of passing offering bags. It isn't a matter of right and wrong, but a matter of which is an easier way for people to give in a way that doesn't call attention to their gifts.

b. **He saw also a certain poor widow putting in two mites**: This poor widow must have been a welcome sight to a weary Jesus, who endured a storm of questions from His enemies.

i. **He saw also**: Jesus sees us when we give. He notices how much we give, but is far more interested in the faith and motive and heart in giving than simply the amount.

c. **Two mites**: According to Poole's calculations, the value of a mite can be determined like this: a denarii is one day's wage, and equals six meahs; one meah equals two pondions; one pondion equals two issarines; one issarine equals eight mites. When you figure it all out, two mites is 1% of a denarii—1% of a day's wage.

i. The ancient Greek word *lepton* literally means "a tiny thing," and so in the Old English was translated *mite*, which comes from the word for a "crumb" or "very small morsel."

ii. She gave **two mites**, not just one. The widow might have kept one coin for herself, and no one would blame her if she did. Giving one meant giving half of all her money. Instead, she gave with staggering generosity.

2. (3-4) Jesus assesses the widow's gift.

So He said, "Truly I say to you that this poor widow has put in more than all; for all these out of their abundance have put in offerings for God, but she out of her poverty put in all the livelihood that she had."

a. **This poor widow has put in more than all**: Jesus did not say that she put in more than *any one* of them. He said that she put in **more than all** of them—all of them put together. The others gave out of **their abundance**; she gave sacrificially, **out of her poverty**.

i. Jesus' principle here shows us that before God, the *spirit* of giving determines the value of the gift more than the amount. God doesn't want grudgingly given money or guilt money. God loves the cheerful giver.

ii. The widow's gift and Jesus' comment on it also shows us that the value of a gift is determined by what it *costs* the giver. This is what made the widow's gift so valuable. David refused to give God *that which cost me nothing* (2 Samuel 24:24).

iii. Jesus' principle here shows us that God does not *need* our money. If God needed our money, then *how much* we give would be more important than our *heart* in giving. Instead, it is *our* privilege to give to Him, and we need to give because it is good for us, not because it is good for God.

b. **Out of her poverty**: The woman was poor because she was a widow and had no husband to help support her. It also may be significant that Jesus had just criticized the scribes as those *who devour widow's houses* (Luke 20:47). Then a lone widow made a spectacular contribution. Perhaps a scribe devoured her house.

i. The widow challenged the mindset that says, "I'll give when I have more." The widow had virtually nothing, yet was a giver. This means that we can all please God with our giving just as much as the richest man can please God with his giving. Whatever we give sacrificially to God, He sees it and is pleased

B. Jesus speaks of future events.

1. (5-6) Jesus makes an amazing prediction concerning the temple.

Then, as some spoke of the temple, how it was adorned with beautiful stones and donations, He said, "These things which you see; the days will come in which not *one* stone shall be left upon another that shall not be thrown down."

a. **As some spoke of the temple**: This temple was originally rebuilt by Zerubbabel and Ezra (Ezra 6:15), but greatly expanded and improved by Herod. It was the center of Jewish life for almost a thousand years. The temple was so revered that it was customary to swear by the temple (Matthew 23:16), and speaking against the temple could be considered blasphemy (Acts 6:13).

i. After Herod, the temple was huge—nearly 500 yards/meters long and 400 yards/meters wide. Herod's rebuilding work started in 19 B.C., and was only completed in A.D. 63, taking more than eighty years. It was finished only seven years before it was destroyed.

b. **How it was adorned with beautiful stones and donations**: The temple wasn't just big, it was also beautiful. The Jewish historian Josephus said that the temple was covered on the outside with gold plates, that were so brilliant that when the sun shone on them, it was blinding to look at. Where there was no gold, there were blocks of marble of such a pure white that from a distance travelers thought there was snow on the temple mount.

i. As great as the temple was, Jesus never hesitated to claim that He was greater than the temple (Matthew 12:5). For many Jews of that day, the temple had become an idol—it began to mean more to the people than God Himself did.

ii. Good things can become the worst idols, and sometimes God sours or takes away even good things that we make our idols

c. **Not one stone shall be left upon another that shall not be thrown down**: Some 40 years after Jesus said this, there was a widespread Jewish revolution against the Romans in Palestine. The rebels enjoyed many early successes, but ultimately Rome crushed the rebellion. Jerusalem was leveled, including the temple—just as Jesus said.

i. It is said that at the fall of Jerusalem, the last surviving Jews of the city fled to the temple, because it was the strongest, most secure building in the city. Roman soldiers surrounded it, and one drunken soldier started a fire that soon engulfed the whole building. Ornate gold detail work in the roof melted down in the cracks between the stone walls of the temple; and to retrieve the gold, the Roman commander ordered that the temple be dismantled stone by stone. The destruction was so complete, that today there is true difficulty learning exactly where the temple was.

2. (7) His listeners ask about the events connected with the temple's destruction.

So they asked Him, saying, "Teacher, but when will these things be? And what sign *will there be* when these things are about to take place?"

a. **Teacher, but when will these things be?** Astounded by the prediction of Jesus, the disciples asked a logical question. This question begins one of Jesus' most famous teachings, often called the *Olivet Discourse* because Matthew 24:3 tells us Jesus said these things seated on the Mount of Olives.

i. Matthew 24 seems to have a more complete account of this teaching, and it is helpful to answer questions about the Luke account from the more complete recording in Matthew.

ii. Both Matthew and Luke make it clear that Jesus spoke *both* of the coming destruction of Jerusalem, *and* of the ultimate end of the age and His glorious return. Prophetically, the two are connected, though separated by many centuries.

iii. "We must regard the siege of Jerusalem and the destruction of the temple as being a kind of rehearsal of what is yet to be." (Spurgeon)

iv. "Most divines think that God in the destruction of Jerusalem intended to give a specimen of the general conflagration, and ruin of the world at the last day; so as the signs of the same kind with those seen before Jerusalem was destroyed, shall be seen before the great and terrible day of our Lord's coming to judge the world." (Poole)

b. **What sign will there be when these things are about to take place**: The reply of Jesus to these questions, recorded in both Matthew 24 and here in Luke 21, has in mind both the coming destruction upon Jerusalem in the near term *and* the ultimate return of Jesus at the end of the age. Luke's record focuses more on the first aspect.

i. Matthew recorded the much more specific answer to this question, pointing to what Jesus called *the abomination of desolation* (Matthew 24:15 and following).

3. (8) To walk in these dangerous times, do not follow false leaders.

And He said: "Take heed that you not be deceived. For many will come in My name, saying, 'I am *He,*' and, 'The time has drawn near.' Therefore do not go after them."

a. **Take heed that you not be deceived**: From the outset, Jesus warned the disciples that many would be deceived as they anticipated His return. There have been times in the history of the church when rash predictions were made and then relied upon resulting in great disappointment, disillusionment, and falling way.

> i. One notable example of this was the prophetic expectation in 1846 with William Miller in the United States. Because of his prophetic interpretations, calculations, and publications, there were hundreds of thousands in the United States who were convinced that Jesus would return in 1846. When He did not, there was great disappointment, with some falling away, and some cultic groups spawned from the prophetic fervor.

b. **For many will come in My name**: Jesus knew that many would come after Him, claiming to be the political and military messiah for Israel. One striking example of this was a man named Bar Kokhba, who 100 years after Jesus many Jews considered to be the messiah. He started a widespread revolution against the Romans and enjoyed early success, but was soon crushed.

c. **Therefore do not go after them**: Tragically, those who rejected Jesus when He came to them as Messiah ended up following after false messiahs who led them into nothing but death and destruction. In rejecting the truth, they were vulnerable to greater deception.

> i. When the Romans came against Jerusalem, "Josephus tells, too, of six thousand refugees who perished in the flames of the temple porticos deluded by a 'false prophet, who had on that day proclaimed to the people in the city that God commanded them to go up to the temple court, to receive there the tokens of their deliverance" (*J. W.* 6.285). They were deluded by charlatans and would-be messengers of God." (Pate)

4. (9-11) To walk in these dangerous times, do not be frightened by catastrophes commonly associated with the end times.

"But when you hear of wars and commotions, do not be terrified; for these things must come to pass first, but the end *will not come* immediately." Then He said to them, "Nation will rise against nation, and kingdom against kingdom. And there will be great earthquakes in various places, and famines and pestilences; and there will be fearful sights and great signs from heaven."

a. **When you hear of wars and commotions, do not be terrified**: What Jesus said here applied both to the coming destruction of Jerusalem and the yet-to-be fulfilled return of Jesus at the end of the age.

i. In some sense, there were **wars** preceding the destruction of Jerusalem, because the Romans were frequently at war with the Jews, the Samaritans, the Syrians, and others during this period. In the broader Roman Empire, there were notable **earthquakes** before Jerusalem was destroyed. There were **famines**, such as the one mentioned in Acts 11:28. In the greater Roman Empire, there were **fearful sights** such as the destruction of Pompeii, only seven years before Jerusalem was destroyed. There were **signs in the heavens**, such as a comet that looked like a sword in the sky over Jerusalem before its destruction.

b. **For these things must come to pass first, but the end will not come immediately**: Yet Jesus specifically said that *none* of these things are the specific signs of His immediate coming. Matthew 24:8 described these things as *the beginning of sorrows*, more literally *the beginning of labor pains*. Just as is true with labor pains, we should expect that the things mentioned—**wars**, **famines**, **earthquakes**, and so on—would become *more frequent* and *more intense* before the return of Jesus, without any one of them being the specific sign of the end.

i. **These things must come to pass first**: "These things must happen because they are part of the prophetic programme of the End-time in general, and so are divinely decreed; but they do not usher in the *immediate* end. The fall of Jerusalem and the events leading up to it were morally, though not chronologically, of an eschatological character." (Geldenhuys)

5. (12-15) Jesus describes what His disciples must expect to endure.

"But before all these things, they will lay their hands on you and persecute *you*, delivering *you* up to the synagogues and prisons. You will be brought before kings and rulers for My name's sake. But it will turn out for you as an occasion for testimony. Therefore settle *it* in your hearts not to meditate beforehand on what you will answer; for I will give you a mouth and wisdom which all your adversaries will not be able to contradict or resist."

a. **But before all these things, they will lay their hands on you and persecute you**: This was and is true both of the time preceding the destruction of Jerusalem and the time preceding the ultimate return of Jesus in glory. Disciples will be persecuted, but they must not regard any season of such suffering, no matter how severe, as the specific sign of the end.

b. **Delivering you up to the synagogues and prisons**: This indicates persecution from both religious and secular sources. Disciples of Jesus must expect both.

c. **But it will turn out for you an occasion for testimony**: From the Book of Acts on, there have been countless times when persecution has given Christians the opportunity to preach and give **testimony** to those they could otherwise never reach with the message, such as **kings and rulers**.

d. **I will give you a mouth and wisdom which all your adversaries will not be able to contradict or resist**: Jesus *personally* promised special grace, special help to His people in such circumstances.

i. **Not to meditate beforehand on what you will answer**: "The Greek word for 'to prepare beforehand,' *promeletan*, was a technical expression for practicing a speech in advance." (Pate)

6. (16-19) To walk in these dangerous times, when all others turn against you, persevere and take a firm stand.

"You will be betrayed even by parents and brothers, relatives and friends; and they will put *some* of you to death. And you will be hated by all for My name's sake. But not a hair of your head shall be lost. By your patience possess your souls."

a. **You will be betrayed**: Christians must expect to suffer, not only from enemies outside the church, but also from traitors among believers (**parents and brothers, relatives and friends**). Because of this, some would even die (**put some of you to death**).

b. **You will be hated by all for My name's sake**: It is strange to think that men and women would be **hated** for the sake of Jesus, who was and is only love and goodness. Yet, of course, it is true.

c. **By your patience possess your souls**: The word for **patience** here is the great Greek word *hupomone*. It speaks of a strong endurance, not a passive waiting. We endure, trusting the promise of Jesus that ultimately, in *eternal* perspective, **not a hair of your head shall be lost**.

7. (20-24a) To walk in these dangerous times, flee Jerusalem when armies begin to surround it.

"But when you see Jerusalem surrounded by armies, then know that its desolation is near. Then let those who are in Judea flee to the mountains, let those who are in the midst of her depart, and let not those who are in the country enter her. For these are the days of vengeance, that all things which are written may be fulfilled. But woe to those who are pregnant and to those who are nursing babies in those days! For there will be great distress in the land and wrath upon this people. And they will fall by the edge of the sword, and be led away captive into all nations."

a. **But when you see Jerusalem surrounded by armies**: This warning focused on the nearer aspects of the greater prophecy, was virtually ignored by the Jews in A.D. 70 when Roman **armies** circled Jerusalem.

b. **Let those who are in Judea flee to the mountains**: Many Jews expected the Messiah to return in glory when hostile Gentile armies surrounded Jerusalem. However, Christians in Jerusalem knew what Jesus had said, and they obeyed Him, fleeing across the Jordan River mostly to Pella. Few, if any, Christians perished in the fall of Jerusalem.

i. The ancient Christian historian Eusebius wrote that Christians fled to Pella in response to "an oracle given by revelation." (*History of the Church*, 3.5.3, cited in Morris)

c. **For these are the days of vengeance**: The Roman conquest of Jerusalem A.D. 70 was complete. History records that 1.1 million Jews were killed and another 97,000 were taken captive in one of the worst calamities ever to strike the Jewish people. Jesus warned them to avoid it.

i. When the Romans were done with Jerusalem in A.D. 70, not a single Jew was left alive in the city. The Romans eventually renamed the city *Aelia Capitolina*; and for many years would not allow a Jew to even enter what was formerly known as Jerusalem, except on one day a year, the anniversary of the fall of the city and the destruction of the temple, when Jews were invited to come and mourn bitterly.

ii. "From the commencement of the history of the Jewish nation, God through His servants warned them clearly that if they behaved unfaithfully and wickedly they would reap disastrous retribution. Cf. especially the striking words of Deuteronomy 28:15-68. There is almost no form of calamity that visited the Jews during the Roman-Jewish war, not mentioned here in Deuteronomy." (Geldenhuys)

iii. Truly Jesus meant it when He said **these are the days of vengeance**. This is why He wept over Jerusalem (Luke 19:41-44), because He could see the massive devastation to come upon this city He loved, and why He warned all who would listen how they could flee from the coming destruction.

8. (24b) Jerusalem will be trampled by the Gentiles until the times of the Gentiles are over.

"And Jerusalem will be trampled by Gentiles until the times of the Gentiles are fulfilled."

a. **Jerusalem will be trampled by Gentiles**: After the destruction of Jerusalem and the dispersion of the Jews predicted by Jesus in the previous verses, there would come a long period when Jerusalem would be dominated **by Gentiles**.

i. After thousands of years of exile, a Jewish state was miraculously established in Israel again in 1948. It was not until 1968 that Israel controlled Jerusalem, but still today they yield the rule and the administration of the most central piece of Jerusalem—the Temple Mount—to Gentile rule (the Palestinian Authority). It can be argued that prophetically speaking, Jerusalem is still **trampled by Gentiles**.

b. **Until the times of the Gentiles are fulfilled**: When these **times of the Gentiles** *are* completed, the author believes that the remaining seven-year period appointed to the Jewish people in Daniel 9 begins. The calamities described in following verses will come in this period.

i. "The Gentiles shall not always tread down Jerusalem." (Trapp)

ii. "It is highly likely that Jesus intended by this phrase to suggest that the moment will come when Gentiles will no longer possess Jerusalem and that when such a time is fulfilled, the nation of Israel will repossess her land." (Pate)

9. (25-28) When the final period of calamity hits the world, look up—your redemption is on the way.

"And there will be signs in the sun, in the moon, and in the stars; and on the earth distress of nations, with perplexity, the sea and the waves roaring; men's hearts failing them from fear and the expectation of those things which are coming on the earth, for the powers of heaven will be shaken. Then they will see the Son of Man coming in a cloud with power and great glory. Now when these things begin to happen, look up and lift up your heads, because your redemption draws near."

a. **Signs in the sun, in the moon, and in the stars; and on the earth distress of nations, with perplexity**: History records no adequate fulfillment of these words in A.D. 70 or immediately following. Jesus here looked to the later aspects of the ultimate fulfillment of His return and the end of the age.

i. This kind of total chaos and calamity is described in horrific detail in Revelation 6, 8-9, and 15-18. All this will culminate in the dramatic, spectacular return of Jesus, coming with His church to this earth.

b. **Then they will see the Son of Man coming in a cloud with power and great glory**: Again, history records no adequate fulfillment of these words in A.D. 70 or immediately following. Jesus has turned from describing what is (from our perspective) the past to describing events to come.

c. **Now when these things begin to happen, look up and lift up your heads, because your redemption draws near**: The things that will **begin to happen** are described in Luke 21:25-27. Jesus assured believers on the earth at that time to be ready, because the time of great tribulation they experience will not last forever, but Jesus will return in glory soon.

10. (29-33) When you see these signs (spoken of in Luke 21:25-26), you know that the end is very near.

Then He spoke to them a parable: "Look at the fig tree, and all the trees. When they are already budding, you see and know for yourselves that summer is now near. So you also, when you see these things happening, know that the kingdom of God is near. Assuredly, I say to you, this generation will by no means pass away till all things take place. Heaven and earth will pass away, but My words will by no means pass away."

a. **Look at the fig tree**: The fig tree is just one example of a tree that buds before summer; no special reference to Israel seems to be intended (as indicated by the words, **and all the trees**). The idea is that when a fig tree buds, there is an inevitable result—summer is near, and fruit is coming. In the same way, when these signs are seen, the coming of Jesus in glory with His church to this world will inevitably follow.

b. **This generation will by no means pass away till all things take place**: Jesus did not refer to His *own* generation and that of the disciples, but of the **generation** that sees those signs; *they* will also see the very end. This is God's promise that He will not prolong what Jesus called the Great Tribulation (Matthew 24:21) forever.

i. There is also a strong case to be made that Jesus meant *the Jewish people* by the term **this generation**, meaning that they would not perish (despite terrible persecution and attempted genocide) until these things were fulfilled.

ii. "*Genea* can mean three things: (1) the descendants of a common ancestor; (2) a set of people born at the same time; (3) the period of time occupied by such a set of people, often in the sense of successive sets of people. It cannot be said without further ado, therefore, that *genea* necessarily means generation." (Pate)

c. **Heaven and earth will pass away, but My words will by no means pass away**: No mere man could truthfully say this. Jesus claimed that His words were the very words of God—and they are.

11. (34-36) How to live in the last days.

"But take heed to yourselves, lest your hearts be weighed down with carousing, drunkenness, and cares of this life, and that Day come on you unexpectedly. For it will come as a snare on all those who dwell on the face of the whole earth. Watch therefore, and pray always that you

may be counted worthy to escape all these things that will come to pass, and to stand before the Son of Man."

a. **But take heed to yourselves**: We must **take heed** because there are certain things that will make one unprepared—**carousing, drunkenness, and cares of this life**. Each of these things can make us unprepared for the day of Jesus' return. They make the heart **weighed down**.

i. According to Morris, **carousing** literally refers to the hangover that comes after a time of intoxication.

b. **It will come as a snare on all those who dwell on the face of the whole earth**: Jesus here spoke of His coming from a different angle. In Luke 21:25-26, He spoke of unmistakable calamity to shake the earth before the coming of Jesus. In Luke 21:34-36, Jesus said that He would come as a surprise, a **snare**, and emphasized the importance of readiness.

i. This is because the second coming of Jesus has two distinct aspects, separated by an appreciable time. The first aspect comes suddenly, unexpectedly, **as a snare**, in a time of peace and safety. The second comes with great anticipation to a world almost destroyed by the judgment of God, with Jesus coming to the earth with His people from heaven.

ii. Those who are ready for the *first* aspect of His coming would **be counted worthy to escape all these things**, the things of great calamity to come to the earth. They would instead **stand before the Son of Man**. These are those who are caught up together with Jesus, to meet the Lord in the air (1 Thessalonians 4:17), to escape the tribulation to come upon the earth.

iii. What Jesus spoke of at this part of Luke's record of the Olivet Discourse applied to those **of the whole earth**, not only those who lived in Jerusalem or Judea. This speaks of much more than what happened to Jerusalem in A.D. 70.

c. **Watch therefore**: Because this is relevant to **the whole earth**, we must **watch**. Anyone who watches will never be caught in a **snare**; a failure to watch prevents us from being ready.

d. **Pray always that you may be counted worthy to escape those things that will come to pass**: Jesus told His followers to **pray always**, that they may be found worthy to **escape all these things that will come to pass**. The good news in Jesus is that we don't have to go through this calamity that is coming. He will take as many as are ready before this calamity begins.

i. In a lesser and more immediate sense regarding the destruction of Jerusalem, those who listened to and obeyed Jesus escaped the horrible destruction that came upon the city.

ii. Regarding the far greater destruction that is coming upon the whole earth, those who listen to and obey Jesus can escape the horrible destruction that will come.

12. (37-38) The public nature of Jesus' ministry.

And in the daytime He was teaching in the temple, but at night He went out and stayed on the mountain called Olivet. Then early in the morning all the people came to Him in the temple to hear Him.

a. **In the daytime He was teaching in the temple**: Luke emphasizes the public, open character of Jesus' teaching work, even teaching **early in the morning** at the most public place in Jerusalem. Jesus did not hide in these few days before His betrayal, arrest, and crucifixion.

b. **At night He went out and stayed on the mountain called Olivet**: Like many Galileans who came to Jerusalem for Passover, Jesus essentially camped out on Mount Olivet in the days leading up to Passover.

Luke 22—*The Last Supper; Jesus Is Betrayed*

A. The Last Supper.

1. (1-6) Judas seeks to betray Jesus.

Now the Feast of Unleavened Bread drew near, which is called Passover. And the chief priests and the scribes sought how they might kill Him, for they feared the people. Then Satan entered Judas, surnamed Iscariot, who was numbered among the twelve. So he went his way and conferred with the chief priests and captains, how he might betray Him to them. And they were glad, and agreed to give him money. So he promised and sought opportunity to betray Him to them in the absence of the multitude.

a. **Now the Feast of Unleavened Bread drew near, which is called Passover**: The *time* is significant, because at **Passover** Jerusalem was also crowded with Messiah-expecting multitudes.

i. Because it was a major feast, many of the people who had heard and seen Jesus in the region of Galilee were in Jerusalem. They generally had respect and great expectation for Jesus and His ministry.

b. **For they feared the people**: The **chief priests and the scribes** did not fear God, but they did fear **the people**. They were not afraid to kill the Son of God; they just had to find a politically smart way to do it.

c. **Satan entered Judas**: Satan prompted and perhaps even guided Judas in his crime. This does not diminish Judas' personal responsibility, because none of this was done *against* the will of Judas, but with it. This shows that the real enemy of Jesus was Satan, even more than Judas was an enemy.

i. Many have wondered about the motives of Judas; some have even said that he might have had a *noble* motive, such as wanting to put Jesus in circumstances where He *had* to show Himself as Messiah. The Bible indicates no such praiseworthy intention.

ii. **Judas, surnamed Iscariot**: The name **Iscariot** may mean that he was from Kerioth, a city in southern Judea. This would make Judas the only *Judean* among the other disciples, who were all Galileans. Some wonder if Judas resented the leadership of the Galilean fishermen among the disciples, and finally had enough of it. Others think the name **Iscariot** is linked to the word *sicarius*, meaning "assassin"— a connection to the Jewish zealots who carried out underground warfare against the Roman occupiers.

iii. It may well be that Judas followed Jesus from selfish motives, expecting to receive a position of great status and prestige when Jesus came triumphantly to Jerusalem as Messiah. When Jesus came and it was evident that He was not going to be the kind of Messiah Judas had hoped for, he may have lashed out against Jesus and opened this door to Satan out of spite. Jesus didn't give Judas what his selfish heart wanted, so Judas felt his ties to Jesus were broken. In essence, Judas may have said, "You betrayed me by not being the kind of Messiah I wanted. So I will betray You."

d. **They were glad, and agreed to give him money**: Matthew 26:14-16 says that Judas asked them, *What are you willing to give me if I deliver Him to you?* This shows that *Judas* approached them and asked for a price. This points to the motivation of simple *greed*.

i. One may also think about Satan's motive. The death of Jesus on the cross was the great defeat of Satan. Why did the devil steer things towards that course? Yet Satan is not all-knowing; perhaps he did not *know* how these events would turn against him. Nevertheless, Satan knows the Bible, so he *should* have known.

ii. A better explanation is the fact that Satan is not all-wise; even if he did know that the death of Jesus would *crush his head*, his hatred got the best of him. Since Satan is the great deceiver, he has no doubt deceived himself, and may actually believe that he could or can win over Jesus.

e. **So he promised and sought opportunity to betray Him**: God would use the wicked works of Judas to further His eternal plan. This was the appointed time for Jesus to go to the cross, but before Judas' treachery, the religious leaders did not intend to do it at the time out of a fear of the people.

2. (7-13) Preparations for the Passover.

Then came the Day of Unleavened Bread, when the Passover must be killed. And He sent Peter and John, saying, "Go and prepare the Passover for us, that we may eat." So they said to Him, "Where do You

want us to prepare?" And He said to them, "Behold, when you have entered the city, a man will meet you carrying a pitcher of water; follow him into the house which he enters. Then you shall say to the master of the house, 'The Teacher says to you, "Where is the guest room where I may eat the Passover with My disciples?"' Then he will show you a large, furnished upper room; there make ready." So they went and found it just as He had said to them, and they prepared the Passover.

a. **Then came the Day of Unleavened Bread**: This must have been a very moving commemoration for Jesus. Passover remembers the deliverance of Israel from Egypt, which was the central act of redemption in the Old Testament. Jesus now provided a new center of redemption to be remembered by a new ceremonial meal.

i. "The phrase 'the day of unleavened bread' is a generic description of the week-long feast...It originally celebrated the beginning of harvest, but later was combined with Passover." (Pate)

b. **A man . . . carrying a pitcher**: This was an unusual sight, because **carrying a pitcher** was typically a woman's work, and men generally carried liquids in animal skin containers. This would be a distinctive sign to the disciples.

c. **The Teacher says to you**: The scene here implies secrecy, and Jesus had good reason to quietly make arrangements for Passover. He didn't want Judas to betray Him before He could give a final talk to the disciples.

d. **Eat the Passover with My disciples**: The mention of **Passover** brings up complicated issues of the precise calendar chronology of these events. The main complicating issue is that Matthew, Mark, and Luke present this meal Jesus will have with His disciples as the Passover meal—normally eaten with lamb which was sacrificed on the day of Passover with a great ceremony at the temple. Yet John seems to indicate that the meal took place before the Passover (John 13:1), and that Jesus was actually crucified on the Passover (John 18:28).

i. "Possibly the best explanation is that there were different calendars in use. Jesus died as the Passover victims were being slain according to the official calendar; but he had held the Passover with his followers the previous evening, according to an unofficial calendar." (Morris)

ii. A similar solution is suggested by Adam Clarke: "It is a common opinion that our Lord ate the Passover some hours before the Jews ate it; for the Jews, according to custom, ate theirs at the *end* of the *fourteenth* day, but Christ ate his the preceding even, which was the beginning of the same sixth day, or Friday; the Jews begin their day at *sunsetting*, we at midnight. Thus Christ ate the Passover on the *same day* with the Jews, but not on the *same hour*."

iii. None of the synoptic Gospels mention a lamb at the Passover meal. This may be because they could not obtain one before the official day of Passover. In addition, Jesus may have wanted it this way, to emphasize the idea that *He* was the Passover sacrifice.

3. (14-18) Jesus eats the Passover with His disciples.

When the hour had come, He sat down, and the twelve apostles with Him. Then He said to them, "With *fervent* desire I have desired to eat this Passover with you before I suffer; for I say to you, I will no longer eat of it until it is fulfilled in the kingdom of God." Then He took the cup, and gave thanks, and said, "Take this and divide *it* among yourselves; for I say to you, I will not drink of the fruit of the vine until the kingdom of God comes."

a. **With fervent desire I have desired**: This was a passionate moment for Jesus. It wasn't so much that He was saying goodbye to His disciples, as much as now He arrived at the central reason why He came to man: to institute a new covenant with men, based on His own sacrifice. This was not the beginning of the end; it was the beginning of the beginning.

b. **He took the cup**: In the following verses, Luke tells us Jesus also *took the cup after supper* (Luke 22:20). It seems that Jesus took the cup both before and after the bread. According to the customs of a Passover dinner, this was nothing unusual—there were normally four different cups of wine ceremonially sipped during the meal.

c. **I will not drink of the fruit of the vine until the kingdom of God comes**: Jesus has not yet celebrated a Passover in heaven. He is waiting for all His people to be gathered to Him; then there will be a great supper, known as the marriage supper of the Lamb (Revelation 19:9). This is the fulfillment in the kingdom of God Jesus longs for.

4. (19-20) Jesus reinterprets Passover, instituting the New Covenant.

And He took bread, gave thanks and broke *it*, and gave *it* to them, saying, "This is My body which is given for you; do this in remembrance of Me." Likewise He also *took* the cup after supper, saying, "This cup *is* the new covenant in My blood, which is shed for you."

a. **He took bread, gave thanks and broke it, and gave it to them**: When the bread was lifted up at Passover, the head of the meal said: "This is the bread of affliction which our fathers ate in the land of Egypt. Let everyone who hungers come and eat; let everyone who is needy come and eat the Passover meal." Everything eaten at the Passover meal had symbolic meaning. The bitter herbs recalled the bitterness of slavery; the salt water remembered the tears shed under Egypt's oppression. The main course of the meal, a lamb freshly sacrificed for that particular household, did not symbolize anything connected to the agonies of Egypt. It was the sin-bearing sacrifice that allowed the judgment of God to pass over the household that believed.

i. The Passover created a nation; a slave mob was freed from Egypt and became a nation. This new Passover also creates a people; those united in Jesus Christ, remembering and trusting His sacrifice.

b. **This is My body which is given for you…This cup is the new covenant in My blood**: Jesus didn't give the normal explanation of the meaning of each of the foods. He reinterpreted them in Himself, and the focus was no longer on the suffering of Israel in Egypt, but on the sin-bearing suffering of Jesus on their behalf.

i. "The words 'this is my body' had no place in the Passover ritual; and as an innovation, they must have had a stunning effect, an effect that would grow with the increased understanding gained after Easter." (Carson)

ii. This is how we *remember* what Jesus did for us. As we eat the **bread**, we should remember how Jesus was broken, pierced, and beaten with stripes for our redemption. As we drink the **cup**, we should remember that His blood, His life was poured out on Calvary for us.

iii. This is how we *fellowship* with Jesus. Because His redemption has reconciled us to God, we can now sit down to a meal with Jesus, and enjoy each other's company.

c. **This is My body which is given for you…This cup is the new covenant in My blood**: The precise understanding of these words from Jesus have been the source of great theological controversy among Christians.

i. The Roman Catholic Church holds the idea of *transubstantiation*, which teaches that the bread and the wine *actually* become the body and blood of Jesus.

ii. Martin Luther held the idea of *consubstantiation*, which teaches the bread remains bread and the wine remains wine, but by faith they are the same as Jesus' actual body. Luther did not believe in the Roman Catholic doctrine of transubstantiation, but he did not go far from it.

iii. John Calvin taught that Jesus' presence in the bread and wine is real, but only spiritual, not physical. Zwingli taught that the bread and wine are significant symbols that represent the body and blood of Jesus. When the Swiss Reformers debated the issue with Martin Luther at Marburg, there was a huge contention. Luther insisted on some kind of physical presence because Jesus said, "**this is My body**."

He insisted over and over again, writing it on the velvet of the table, *Hoc est corpus meum*—"**this is My body**" in Latin. Zwingli replied, "Jesus also said I am the vine," and "I am the door," but we understand what He was saying. Luther replied, "I don't know, but if Christ told me to eat dung I would do it knowing that it was good for me." Luther was so strong on this because he saw it as an issue of believing Christ's words; and because he thought Zwingli was compromising, he said he was of *another spirit* (*andere geist*). Ironically, Luther later read Calvin's writings on the Lord's Supper (which were essentially the same as Zwingli's) and seemed to agree with, or at least accept Calvin's views.

iv. Scripturally, we can understand that the **bread** and the **cup** are not *mere* symbols, but they are powerful pictures to partake of, to enter into, as we see the Lord's Table as the new Passover.

v. "Let the papists and Lutherans say what they can, here must be two figures acknowledged in these words. The *cup* here is put for the wine in the cup; and the meaning of these words, *this is my blood of the new testament*, must be, this wine is the sign of the new covenant. Why they should not as readily acknowledge a figure in these words, *This is my body*, I cannot understand." (Poole)

vi. "What is certain is that Jesus bids us commemorate, not his birth, nor his life, nor his miracles, but his death." (Carson)

d. **This cup is the new covenant in my blood**: Remarkably, Jesus announced the institution of a **new covenant**. No mere man could ever institute a **new covenant** between God and man, but Jesus is the God-man. He has the authority to establish a **new covenant**, sealed with blood, even as the old covenant was sealed with blood (Exodus 24:8).

i. The **new covenant** concerns an inner transformation that cleanses us from all sin: *For I will forgive their iniquity, and their sin I will remember no more* (Jeremiah 31:34). This transformation puts God's Word and will in us: *I will put My law in their minds, and write it on their hearts* (Jeremiah 31:33). This covenant is all about a new, close relationship with God: *I will be their God, and they shall be My people* (Jeremiah 31:33).

ii. We can say that the **blood** of Jesus made the **new covenant** possible, and it also made it sure and reliable. It is confirmed with the life of God Himself.

5. (21-23) Woe to the betrayer.

"But behold, the hand of My betrayer *is* with Me on the table. And truly the Son of Man goes as it has been determined, but woe to that

man by whom He is betrayed!" Then they began to question among themselves, which of them it was who would do this thing.

a. **Behold, the hand of My betrayer is with Me on the table**: This would seem to indicate that Judas was *present* when Jesus passed the bread and the cup to His disciples. This is a matter of debate among students of the Bible.

b. **The Son of Man goes as it has been determined**: It was **determined** by prophecy that the Messiah should be betrayed (Psalm 41:9). Nevertheless, **woe to that man** who actually betrayed the Messiah. Judas could never claim that he helped Jesus by fulfilling prophecy. He was and is fully accountable for his sin before God.

i. "The fact that God overrules the evil that bad people do as he brings his purposes to pass does not make them any the less evil." (Morris)

c. **They began to question among themselves, which of them it was**: Judas kept his secret well, because none of the other disciples seemed to suspect him.

B. Final teachings to the disciples.

The fullness of this marvelous discourse must be gathered from all four gospels—especially from John chapters 13-16.

1. (24-27) Jesus teaches about true greatness.

Now there was also a dispute among them, as to which of them should be considered the greatest. And He said to them, "The kings of the Gentiles exercise lordship over them, and those who exercise authority over them are called 'benefactors.' But not so *among* you; on the contrary, he who is greatest among you, let him be as the younger, and he who governs as he who serves. For who *is* greater, he who sits at the table, or he who serves? *Is* it not he who sits at the table? Yet I am among you as the One who serves."

a. **A dispute among them, as to which of them should be considered the greatest**: It's almost frightening to think that after Jesus poured three years of His life into these men, after they saw the character of Jesus on display in almost every conceivable circumstance; that now, at the final hours before His betrayal, arrest, and crucifixion, they argued about which of them was the greatest.

i. This seems to have been a common topic of conversation among the disciples (Matthew 18:1, Matthew 20:20-26, Mark 9:33-34, Luke 9:46).

b. **Which of them should be considered the greatest**: We might think that Jesus would settle the issue by saying *He* was the greatest. Instead, Jesus answered their question by what He *did*. John 13:3-5 tells us that Jesus washed their feet after supper, and He may have spoken these words about true greatness as He washed their feet, or after He was finished.

i. In fact, the supreme patience of Jesus was displayed in His gentle correction of His squabbling disciples. He obviously had great things weighing down His mind, yet He gently taught and corrected them.

c. **The kings of the Gentiles exercise lordship over them**: The world exercises authority and power with a certain style, all ultimately self-exalting. Jesus wasn't like that, and neither should His followers be. In fact, the **greatest** should be like the **younger** (not favored by society, the outcast), and the one who **governs** should be like one who **serves**.

i. The idea of being called **benefactors** is really the idea of getting credit. Many people will only serve if they can be assured of getting proper credit.

ii. "In the ancient world it was accepted that age gave privileges; the youngest was, by definition, the lowliest." (Morris)

d. **For who is greater, he who sits at the table, or he who serves? Is it not he who sits at the table?** The world regards the one who is served as **greater**, but Jesus showed us that true greatness is in serving, more than in being served.

i. Cultures have always envied the person whom others serve. In ancient China, rich people sometimes grew long, long fingernails, so long they could do nothing for themselves—and this was seen as a sign of status.

ii. But the people who are really great in our lives are the servants. If the President took a month off, no one would really miss it; but if all the trash collectors in the country took the month off, we would notice. Jesus is trying to re-arrange our thinking, our priorities.

d. **Yet I am among you as the One who serves**: Living as a servant really is the *best* way to live. We are no longer concerned for our own honor and credit; we don't walk around with hurt feelings and disappointed expectations, because all we want to do is to serve. We can always do what we want to do, because we can always serve somehow.

i. Jesus did not mean that if you serve in a lowly place, you will always be given a great place. He meant that in God's eyes, the lowly place *is* the great place. "Service given, not gained, is the true greatness, for it is the sign of real fellowship with the Lord Himself." (Morgan)

ii. "The very greatness of God is finally demonstrated, not in the height and the glory of His eternal throne, but in the depth and grace

of His amazing stoop to our humanity and to the death of the Cross."
(Morgan)

iii. " 'King of kings' is a title full of majesty, but 'servant of servants' is
the name which our Lord preferred when he was here below." (Spurgeon)

2. (28-30) The reward for the disciples.

**"But you are those who have continued with Me in My trials. And I
bestow upon you a kingdom, just as My Father bestowed *one* upon
Me, that you may eat and drink at My table in My kingdom, and sit on
thrones judging the twelve tribes of Israel."**

a. **I bestow upon you a kingdom**: The disciples would receive a unique
reward, because they are the ones who have **continued with** Jesus in His
trials. Jesus appreciated and valued the support He received from His
disciples.

b. **I bestow upon you a kingdom**: The apostles will have special status in
the Kingdom of God. They will **sit on thrones judging the twelve tribes
of Israel**, and their names will be on the twelve foundations of the wall of
the New Jerusalem (Revelation 21:14).

i. Being a servant does not mean that we are unrewarded. Quite the
opposite; God's greatest servants receive the greatest rewards. But a
great servant does not serve for the sake of reward, but for the sake of
God's glory.

3. (31-34) Jesus warns Peter of his coming fall.

**And the Lord said, "Simon, Simon! Indeed, Satan has asked for you,
that he may sift *you* as wheat. But I have prayed for you, that your
faith should not fail; and when you have returned to *Me,* strengthen
your brethren." But he said to Him, "Lord, I am ready to go with You,
both to prison and to death." Then He said, "I tell you, Peter, the rooster shall not crow this day before you will deny three times that you
know Me."**

a. **Indeed, Satan has asked for you**: Jesus was aware of a spiritual battle
behind the scenes. Peter was no doubt ignorant of the fact that **Satan has
asked for you, that he may sift you as wheat**—Satan wanted to completely crush and defeat Peter.

i. Apparently, Satan *wanted* to do much more against Peter than the
Lord would allow. Satan could not do whatever he wanted against
Peter, but he had to *ask* God for permission.

ii. "Satan desires that in the sifting process 'no wheat shall remain',
but that all (like Judas) will be blown away like chaff." (Geldenhuys)

b. **But I have prayed for you**: Satan did not completely crush Peter, but that had nothing to do with Peter himself. It was because Jesus prayed for Peter.

i. It is both wonderful and moving to remember that Jesus prays for His people, protecting us from Satan (Hebrews 7:25, Revelation 12:10). Surely there are many times that we would have perished, but Jesus prayed for us and protected us.

c. **That your faith should not fail**: Peter's faith would falter but **not fail**. Jesus did not see the temporary lapse that was to come as a failure of faith, because He knew that Peter would return to Him.

i. In the Christian life, we may falter, but we must never fail. If we have denied Jesus in some way, then we must return to Him immediately.

ii. And, having returned, we must turn our focus towards helping others—**when you have returned to Me, strengthen your brethren**. The one who returns after faltering isn't necessarily to be excluded or encouraged to become self-focused, but they should reach out and strengthen the brethren.

d. **Lord, I am ready to go with You, both to prison and to death**: Peter did not consciously lie here; rather he was unaware of both the spiritual reality and the spiritual battle that Jesus could see. Peter merely looked to how he *felt* at the moment, and at the moment he felt pretty brave.

i. Relying on how you *feel* at the moment is not a stable foundation. Peter felt brave at the moment, but would soon be intimidated before a humble servant girl, and deny to her that he even knew Jesus.

ii. "It is sometimes easier to bear a great load for Christ than a small one. Some of us could be martyrs at the stake more easily that confessors among sneering neighbors." (Maclaren)

e. **I tell you, Peter, the rooster shall not crow this day before you will deny three times that you know Me**: Jesus told Peter the truth about himself and the situation, not to discourage him, but to let him know there was a spiritual reality and a spiritual battle that he unaware of, but that Jesus knew well.

i. "Was it not well that Peter should know how weak he was; that he might become truly penitent and converted?" (Meyer)

ii. "Fitzmyer catches the sense of the prophecy—Peter's 'triple denial will come so quickly that a cock will not even be able to crow twice.'" (Pate)

4. (35-38) Jesus calls the disciples to readiness.

And He said to them, **"When I sent you without money bag, knapsack, and sandals, did you lack anything?" So they said, "Nothing." Then He said to them, "But now, he who has a money bag, let him take** *it,* **and likewise a knapsack; and he who has no sword, let him sell his garment and buy one. For I say to you that this which is written must still be accomplished in Me: 'And He was numbered with the transgressors.' For the things concerning Me have an end." So they said, "Lord, look, here** *are* **two swords." And He said to them, "It is enough."**

a. **But now, he who has a money bag, let him take it, and likewise a knapsack**: The intent of Jesus seems to be, "I am on the point of leaving you, and when I am gone, you must use common-sense means for provision and protection." Such practical considerations were not needed before, but were needed now.

i. The disciples had been sent out to do ministry without Jesus before (Luke 10:1-17), but then they were received with goodwill and hospitality. Now they faced a hostile world without Jesus and must be prepared.

b. **This which is written must still be accomplished in Me: "And He was numbered with the transgressors"**: Jesus had previously told His disciples that He would be rejected and crucified (Luke 17:25, 18:31-33). Here, Jesus told them that this would happen soon.

c. **For the things concerning Me have an end**: This seems to have the sense of, "This will all be accomplished soon."

d. **It is enough**: When offered the swords, Jesus said this, meaning "Enough of this kind of talk" and was a firm way of ending the conversation. Jesus did not mean, *two swords will be enough to battle the crowd that comes to arrest Me.*

i. "Jesus' answer, 'Enough of this', is to be preferred to that of, 'it is enough.' The latter might imply that Jesus affirmed the disciples' suggestion, acknowledging that two swords would be sufficient for the conflict. But the context clearly rules out that rendering." (Pate)

ii. It seems that the disciples didn't understand what would happen in the next several hours. Later, Christians also did not understand what Jesus meant here. "In his notorious papal bull *Unam Sanctum*, Boniface VIII (A.D. 1302) built on this text his doctrine that the Pope has the right to exercise secular as well as spiritual autocratic rule over mankind—the two swords, he said, are the spiritual sword and the secular sword." (Geldenhuys)

C. Jesus' agonized prayer in the Garden of Gethsemane.

1. (39-46) Jesus' agony in the garden.

Coming out, He went to the Mount of Olives, as He was accustomed, and His disciples also followed Him. When He came to the place, He said to them, "Pray that you may not enter into temptation." And He was withdrawn from them about a stone's throw, and He knelt down and prayed, saying, "Father, if it is Your will, take this cup away from Me; nevertheless not My will, but Yours, be done."

a. **He went to the Mount of Olives, as He was accustomed**. Jesus had spent nights there during that week (Luke 21:37), and He refused to change the routine, even though it meant that Judas could easily find Him.

b. **Pray that you may not enter into temptation**: As Jesus began to pray in the Garden of Gethsemane (Matthew 26:36 and Mark 14:32 name it so), He began by warning the disciples of *their* need to pray. Jesus Himself needed to pray for strength to pass the difficult ordeal to come. The disciples had their own ordeal to face, and needed all the more to **pray that you may not enter into temptation**—that is, to *give into* temptation.

i. "The words 'enter into temptation' (*perasmon*) mean to succumb to its evil power (cf. Luke 22:46; 11:4)." (Pate)

c. **He knelt down and prayed**: Here is the passionate account of an eye-witness (one of the disciples), who reported this to Luke. Only an eyewitness would remember a detail such as Jesus praying **about a stone's throw** away from the disciples.

i. "The usual manner of prayer at that time was to pray in a standing position. That Jesus knelt down proves the violence of His struggle in Gethsemane." (Geldenhuys)

d. **Father, if it is Your will, take this cup away from Me**: Jesus knew what the Father's will was, yet was in great agony of soul. The agony did not come from any lack of desire to do the will of God, but because Jesus would go to the cross as a sacrifice for sins. He was no victim of circumstances beyond His control, and unlike any animal sacrifice, He went with full knowledge. He willingly resolved to lay down His life.

i. Repeatedly in the Old Testament, a cup is a powerful picture of the wrath and judgment of God.

- *For in the hand of the LORD there is a cup, and the wine is red; it is fully mixed, and He pours it out; surely its dregs shall all the wicked of the earth drain and drink down* (Psalm 75:8)

- *Awake, awake! Stand up, O Jerusalem, you who have drunk at the hand of the LORD The cup of His fury; you have drunk the dregs of the cup of trembling, and drained it out* (Isaiah 51:17)

- *For thus says the LORD God of Israel to me: "Take this wine cup of fury from My hand, and cause all the nations, to whom I send you, to drink it"* (Jeremiah 25:15)

ii. The **cup** didn't represent death, but judgment. Jesus was unafraid of death, and when He had finished His work on the cross—the work of receiving and bearing and satisfying the righteous judgment of God the Father upon our sin—when He finished that work, He simply yielded Himself to death as His choice.

iii. Jesus became, as it were, an enemy of God, who was judged and forced to drink the **cup** of the Father's fury, so we would not have to drink from that cup. Taking this figurative cup was the source of Jesus' greatest agony on the cross.

iv. "I am never afraid of exaggeration, when I speak of what my Lord endured. All hell was distilled into that cup, of which our God and Savior Jesus Christ was made to drink." (Spurgeon)

e. **Nevertheless not My will, but Yours, be done**: Jesus came to a point of decision in Gethsemane. It wasn't that He had not decided nor consented before, but now He had come upon a unique point of decision. He drank the cup at Calvary, but the decision once for all to drink that cup came at Gethsemane.

i. A sinless man battled Satan, sin, self, and temptation in a garden and lost—saying, "My will not Yours, be done" and the loss impacted all mankind. The second Sinless Man battled Satan, sin, self, and temptation in another garden and won—saying, "**Not My will, but Yours, be done**"—and its impact touches people from every tribe and tongue.

2. (43-44) In His agony, Jesus is strengthened by angels.

Then an angel appeared to Him from heaven, strengthening Him. And being in agony, He prayed more earnestly. Then His sweat became like great drops of blood falling down to the ground.

a. **Then an angel appeared to Him from heaven, strengthening Him**: In response to Jesus' prayers, the Father did not take the cup from Jesus; but He strengthened Jesus by angelic messengers to be able to take, and drink, the cup.

i. These two verses—Luke 22:43-44—are the subject of some debate regarding the manuscript evidence for their inclusion. Some modern translations exclude them as not belonging to the original. Yet, "The text critical difficulty of vv. 43-44 does not admit to a conclusive answer. The oldest manuscript evidence is divided." (Pate)

ii. Perhaps these angels—sadly—did the work that the sleeping disciples did not do. John Trapp said that Jesus received this, "To show that he had been made himself lower than the angels, Hebrews 2:7, he received comfort from an angel that was his servant."

b. **Being in agony, He prayed more earnestly**: In His agony, Jesus **prayed more earnestly**, to the point where **His sweat became like great drops of blood falling down to the ground**. Luke did not say that Jesus' sweat *was* blood, but that it was *like* blood; either in the way that it poured off His brow, or because it was tinged with blood from the burst capillaries and dilated pores on His brow.

i. "His perspiration was so profuse that it was like blood spilling on the ground." (Pate)

ii. However, "There have been cases in which persons in a debilitated state of body, or through horror of soul, have had their sweat tinged with blood. . . . Cases sometimes happen in which, through *mental pressure*, the pores may be so dilated that the blood may issue from them; so that there may be a bloody sweat." (Clarke)

iii. "The old physician Galen gives an instance in which, through extremity of horror, an individual poured forth a discoloured sweat, so nearly crimson as at any rate to appear to have been blood. Other cases are given by medical authorities." (Spurgeon)

iv. **He prayed more earnestly**: "He bent, as it were, all his nerves, he intended the utmost activity of his spirit and of his speech; to make atonement for our dull and drowsy devotions." (Trapp)

3. (45-46) Jesus warns His disciples.

When He rose up from prayer, and had come to His disciples, He found them sleeping from sorrow. Then He said to them, "Why do you sleep? Rise and pray, lest you enter into temptation."

a. **He found them sleeping from sorrow**: The disciples were also filled with **sorrow**; but instead of praying, they slept. Jesus woke them and encouraged them to pray.

b. **Rise and pray, lest you enter into temptation**: They were followers of Jesus, and following Him would now bring a testing and a trial they could not have imagined. Jesus encouraged them to do this for *their sake*, thinking of them and their good instead of how they failed to support Him.

D. Jesus' arrest and arraignment.

1. (47-53) Jesus is betrayed and arrested.

And while He was still speaking, behold, a multitude; and he who was called Judas, one of the twelve, went before them and drew near to

Jesus to kiss Him. But Jesus said to him, "Judas, are you betraying the Son of Man with a kiss?" When those around Him saw what was going to happen, they said to Him, "Lord, shall we strike with the sword?" And one of them struck the servant of the high priest and cut off his right ear. But Jesus answered and said, "Permit even this." And He touched his ear and healed him. Then Jesus said to the chief priests, captains of the temple, and the elders who had come to Him, "Have you come out, as against a robber, with swords and clubs? When I was with you daily in the temple, you did not try to seize Me. But this is your hour, and the power of darkness."

a. **Behold, a multitude**: The number of those sent to arrest Jesus shows that the religious leaders clearly regarded this as a dangerous operation to be done without risk of riot or failure.

i. "According to John 18:3, 12, Roman soldiers also formed part of the crowd." (Pate)

ii. The **multitude** also included the **captains of the temple** (Luke 22:52). "The captain of the Temple, or the Sagan, as he was called, was the official who was responsible for the good order of the Temple; the captains of the Temple here referred to were his lieutenants who were responsible for carrying out the actual arrest of Jesus." (Barclay)

b. **Drew near to Jesus to kiss Him**: Judas warmly greeted Jesus, even giving Him the customary **kiss**. But the **kiss** only precisely identified Jesus to the authorities who came to arrest Him. Apparently, Jesus was normal enough in appearance so that it was necessary that Judas specifically identify Him for the sake of those arresting Him. Judas chose to identify Jesus by greeting Him with a **kiss**.

i. "When a disciple met a beloved Rabbi, he laid his right hand on the Rabbi's left shoulder and his left hand on the right shoulder and kissed him. It was the kiss of a disciple to a beloved master that Judas used as a sign of betrayal." (Barclay)

c. **Judas, are you betraying the Son of Man with a kiss?** Of course, Jesus knew the irony of being betrayed with a warm greeting; so He essentially asked Judas, "Are you so dead to all feeling that you can kiss and betray?" Judas is a good example of a seared conscience.

i. The betrayal of Jesus was terrible sin, and Judas bears full responsibility for it. Yet God, in His providence, used it as the best way to deliver Jesus into the hands of His adversaries.

• If they captured Jesus in a fight or if Jesus ran and hid until they found and caught Him, it would show that He was an unwilling victim

- If Jesus surrendered Himself, it might excuse His murderers or be seen as suicide

- If it happened accidentally, it would lessen the full effect of the bitter cup Jesus was about to drink

- "No; he must be betrayed by his friend, that he may bear the utmost depths of suffering, and that in every separate circumstance there may be a well of grief" (Spurgeon)

d. **And one of them struck the servant of the high priest and cut off his right ear**: John 18:10 identified this unnamed swordsman as Peter. When Peter used sword-power, he could only cut off ears; but using the power of the Word of God, he could pierce hearts for God's glory (Acts 2:37).

i. "When the Church takes sword in hand, it usually shows that it does not know how to wield it, and as often as not has struck the wrong man." (Maclaren)

ii. Luke, with his medical precision, identified the ear as the **right ear**. Assuming Peter was right-handed, the only way to cut off someone's right ear in this manner is if you attack from *behind*. It's likely—though not certain—that Peter attacked from behind.

iii. Jesus stopped this foolish and ineffective bloodshed by saying, "**Permit even this**." "He told His disciples who had resorted to violence, 'Let it be as far as this.' Colloquially we might render these words, 'Stop it! No more of this!'" (Pate)

e. **And He touched his ear and healed him**: Even here, Jesus was present to clean up the mess His disciples left behind. He healed the damage done by Peter.

f. **Your hour, and the power of darkness**: Jesus explained why He went with the **chief priests, captains of the temple, and the elders** and the many soldiers that came to arrest Him. He did not put up a fight because now was the time for the religious leaders to do to Jesus what they wanted to do all along—to arrest and kill Him. By all outward appearance it would seem to be their **hour**, not Jesus'.

2. (54-60) Peter denies that he knows or is associated with Jesus.

Having arrested Him, they led *Him* and brought Him into the high priest's house. But Peter followed at a distance. Now when they had kindled a fire in the midst of the courtyard and sat down together, Peter sat among them. And a certain servant girl, seeing him as he sat by the fire, looked intently at him and said, "This man was also with Him." But he denied Him, saying, "Woman, I do not know Him." And after a little while another saw him and said, "You also are of them."

But Peter said, "Man, I am not!" Then after about an hour had passed, another confidently affirmed, saying, "Surely this *fellow* also was with Him, for he is a Galilean." But Peter said, "Man, I do not know what you are saying!" Immediately, while he was still speaking, the rooster crowed.

a. **They led Him and brought Him into the high priest's house**: Luke did not record the details of this appearance before Caiaphas, the high priest, and a hastily gathered greeting of the Sanhedrin council (Matthew 26:57-68). Luke will begin his focus at the official, daylight meeting of the council (Luke 22:66).

i. Before Jesus came to the home of **Caiaphas** (the official high priest), He was led to the home of Annas, who was the ex-high priest and the "power behind the throne" of the high priest (according to John 18:12-14 and John 18:19-23).

b. **But Peter followed at a distance**: Peter was concerned for Jesus and wanted to know what would become of Him. Yet he did not have the courage for a clear association with Jesus, and therefore he **followed at a distance**. This **distance** would make it much more difficult for Peter to admit his association with Jesus when he was questioned.

i. The rest of the disciples fled. Peter **followed at a distance**, hoping to prove wrong Jesus' prediction that He would deny and forsake Him at His death.

c. **Peter sat among them**: Finding warmth around their fire and hoping to blend in, Peter put himself among the servants of those who arrested and persecuted Jesus. Having forsaken the fellowship of the fleeing disciples, Peter did not, at this time, want to be identified as a follower of Jesus.

d. **But he denied him**: Peter denied Jesus in at least three specific ways. First, Peter denied even knowing Jesus (**Woman, I do not know Him**); then he denied being a follower of Jesus (**Man, I am not**); finally he denied that he was even from Galilee (**Man, I do not know what you are saying!**).

i. Matthew 26:74 says that at the last denial Peter even began *to curse and swear*, hoping that it would help distance himself from association with Jesus.

3. (61-62) Jesus looked at Peter, and Peter remembered the word of Jesus.

And the Lord turned and looked at Peter. And Peter remembered the word of the Lord, how He had said to him, "Before the rooster crows, you will deny Me three times." So Peter went out and wept bitterly.

a. **And the Lord turned and looked at Peter**: At the crowing of the rooster, Jesus looked through the crowd around Him, and made eye contact with Peter. Peter was immediately convicted of his sin; not only of his denial of Jesus, but also of the pride that led him to think he could never deny Him.

i. The ancient Greek word for **looked** "usually signifies a look of interest, love, or concern." (Liefeld)

b. **Peter remembered the word of the Lord**: Sadly, he remembered it too late, *after* he had sinned. At the moment, Peter's only reaction was that he **wept bitterly**—yet he would be restored.

i. It was appropriate for him to weep bitterly at that moment, but Peter was not without hope. As much as Jesus' promise that Peter would deny Him was true, so was the promise that *your faith should not fail* (Luke 22:32). Peter fell, but had not fallen away.

4. (63-65) Jesus is beaten and mocked.

Now the men who held Jesus mocked Him and beat Him. And having blindfolded Him, they struck Him on the face and asked Him, saying, "Prophesy! Who is the one who struck You?" And many other things they blasphemously spoke against Him.

a. **Now the men who held Jesus mocked Him and beat Him**: Luke did not record the proceedings of this first, nighttime trial of Jesus before the high priest and the hastily gathered council (Matthew 26:57-68). He did record what happened immediately after that trial—that Jesus was mocked and beaten by the religious authorities.

b. **Having blindfolded Him, they struck Him on the face**: Blinded, Jesus endured these slaps and punches in pain and perhaps with a concussion. Matthew 26:67 and Mark 14:65 add that they also spat in His face.

i. It is easy to think that they did this because they didn't know who He was. That is true in one sense, because they would not admit to themselves that He was indeed the Messiah and the Son of God. Yet in another sense it is not true at all, because by nature man is an enemy of God (Romans 5:10, Colossians 1:21). For a long time man waited to *literally* hit, slap, and spit in God's face.

- Omnipotence must be held captive and its glory mocked
- Goodness must be smitten, stricken, bruised, assaulted
- Omniscience must seem to be blinded
- The face of God's perfect love must be struck and punched
- Divine justice must be defied

ii. Therefore God had His glorious work to do; yet all the while the sinfulness of man was on full display.

- They found sin to be a *game*
- They found the cruelty of sin to be *delicious*
- They found sin to be *multiplied*

c. **Prophesy! Who is the one who struck You?** If Jesus were to draw on His rightful resources of divine power and authority, He could say *exactly* who struck Him. Jesus could also say everything there was to know about that man. Yet in all this, Jesus refused to draw on the resources of His divine power and authority, and instead faced this as a Spirit-strengthened *man*.

i. "However, the very thing they mocked, Jesus' prophetic ability, had just been ironically vindicated in the previous scene: Peter denied his Lord three times, just as Jesus predicted." (Pate)

ii. It was important for Jesus to face this abuse, though it was painful for Jesus to endure and painful for His followers to consider.

- It was important to demonstrate that the proper reply to hate is not more hate, but love

- It was important to demonstrate His trust in God the Father, that God would vindicate Him and He did not need to defend Himself

- It was important so that those who are abused and humiliated can find refuge in a God who knows what they experience

iii. "I must also call him *victorious*. His persecutors could not make him give way to anger. They could not destroy his mercy; they could not slay his love; they could not cause him to think of himself; they could not make him declare that he would go no further with his work of saving sinners now that men began to scoff at him, and smite him, and despitefully use him." (Spurgeon)

5. (66) Jesus' second trial before the Sanhedrin.

As soon as it was day, the elders of the people, both chief priests and scribes, came together and led Him into their council, saying,

a. **As soon as it was day**: On the night of His betrayal and the day of His crucifixion, Jesus actually stood on trial several times, before different judges. The order of events can be summarized.

i. Jesus was first brought to the home of Annas, the ex-high priest and the "power behind the throne" of the high priest (John 18:12-14, John 19-23).

ii. Then Jesus was brought to the home of Caiaphas, the sitting high priest. There He was placed on trial before an ad-hoc gathering of the Sanhedrin still during the night (Matthew 26:57-68), when false witnesses were brought before the council and the high priest demanded to know of Jesus if He was the Son of God. To this question, Jesus replied: *"It is as you said. Nevertheless, I say to you, hereafter you will see the Son of Man sitting at the right hand of the Power, and coming on the clouds of heaven." Then the high priest tore his clothes, saying, "He has spoken blasphemy! What further need do we have of witnesses? Look, now you have heard His blasphemy! "What do you think?" They answered and said, "He is deserving of death."* (Matthew 26:64-66)

iii. After that, the beating described in Luke 22:63-65 began.

iv. Then **as soon as it was day** the Sanhedrin gathered again, this time in official session, and they conducted the trial described in Luke 22:66-71 (and mentioned in Matthew 27:1-2).

b. **The elders of the people, both chief priests and scribes, came together and led Him into their council**: This daytime meeting of the Sanhedrin council was necessary, because by the Sanhedrin's own laws and regulations, the night trial described in Matthew 26:57-68 was illegal.

i. According to Jewish law, all criminal trials must begin and end in the daylight. This second trial was necessary, because they knew the first one—the *real* trial—had no legal standing.

ii. According to Jewish law, only decisions made in the official meeting place were valid. The first trial was held at the home of Caiaphas, the high priest, so they called together this trial, held at **their council**.

iii. According to Jewish law, criminal cases could not be tried during the Passover season.

iv. According to Jewish law, only an acquittal could be issued on the day of the trial; guilty verdicts had to wait one night to allow for feelings of mercy to rise.

v. According to Jewish law, all evidence had to be guaranteed by two witnesses, who were separately examined and could not have contact with each other.

vi. According to Jewish law, false witness was punishable by death; nothing is done to the many false witnesses in Jesus' trial.

vii. According to Jewish law, a trial always began by bringing forth evidence for the innocence of the accused before the evidence of guilt was offered; this was not the practice here.

viii. "The whole procedure was designed for mercy; and even from Luke's summary account, it is clear that the Sanhedrin, when it tried Jesus, was far from keeping its own rules and regulations." (Barclay)

6. (67-71) The interrogation of Jesus at His second trial before the council.

"If You are the Christ, tell us." But He said to them, "If I tell you, you will by no means believe. And if I also ask *you*, you will by no means answer Me or let *Me* go. Hereafter the Son of Man will sit on the right hand of the power of God." Then they all said, "Are You then the Son of God?" So He said to them, "You *rightly* say that I am." And they said, "What further testimony do we need? For we have heard it ourselves from His own mouth."

a. **If You are the Christ, tell us**: They wanted to hear from Jesus Himself if He claimed to be the Messiah. Again, this was all a formality because they had already passed judgment on Jesus with the illegal trial held the night before (Matthew 26:57-68), where essentially the same question was asked (Matthew 26:63).

b. **If I tell you, you will by no means believe**: Given the circumstances—that Jesus had already been found guilty and that the present trial was only a show—this was the perfect response. They pretended to have an open mind and ask sincere questions, but it wasn't true—only pretense.

c. **Hereafter the Son of Man will sit on the right hand of the power of God**: This was essentially the same reply Jesus gave to the high priest at the earlier trial (Matthew 26:64). Jesus warned them that though they sat in judgment of Him now, He would one day sit in judgment of them—and with a far more binding judgment.

i. **Hereafter**: "'Hereafter!' 'Hereafter!' Oh, when that hereafter comes, how overwhelming it will be to Jesus' foes! Now where is Caiaphas? Will he now adjure the Lord to speak? Now, ye priests, lift up your haughty heads! Utter a sentence against him now! There sits, your victim upon the clouds of heaven. Say now that he blasphemes, and hold up your rent rags, and condemn him again. But where is Caiaphas? He hides his guilty head he is utterly confounded, and begs the mountains to fall upon him." (Spurgeon)

ii. **Of the Power**: "*Power* is a typically Jewish reverential expression to avoid pronouncing the sacred name of God (which might have laid Jesus open to the charge of blasphemy, though ironically it was precisely that charge on which he was condemned, Matthew 26:65!)." (France)

d. **What further testimony do we need?** At this daytime trial, they made no effort to find testimony against Jesus, because the witnesses at the nighttime trial had hopelessly contradicted themselves (Matthew 26:59-60). Therefore they avoided witnesses at this daytime trial.

Luke 23—Jesus' Trial, Death and Burial

A. Jesus on trial before Pilate and Herod.

1. (1-7) The first trial before Pilate.

Then the whole multitude of them arose and led Him to Pilate. And they began to accuse Him, saying, "We found this *fellow* perverting the nation, and forbidding to pay taxes to Caesar, saying that He Himself is Christ, a King." Then Pilate asked Him, saying, "Are You the King of the Jews?" He answered him and said, *"It is as* you say." So Pilate said to the chief priests and the crowd, "I find no fault in this Man." But they were the more fierce, saying, "He stirs up the people, teaching throughout all Judea, beginning from Galilee to this place." When Pilate heard of Galilee, he asked if the Man were a Galilean. And as soon as he knew that He belonged to Herod's jurisdiction, he sent Him to Herod, who was also in Jerusalem at that time.

a. **Led Him to Pilate**: The Roman government did not allow the Jewish leaders the authority to execute a criminal. The religious leaders sent Jesus to Pontius Pilate, the Roman governor over the region of Judea.

i. The Jewish leaders had reason to expect a favorable result when they went to Pilate. Secular history shows that he was a cruel, ruthless man, completely insensitive to the moral feelings of others. Surely, they thought, **Pilate** will put this Jesus to death.

ii. Philo, the ancient Jewish scholar from Alexandria, described Pilate: "His corruption, his acts of insolence, his rapine, his habit of insulting people, his cruelty, his continual murders of people untried and uncondemned, and his never-ending gratuitous and most grievous inhumanity." (Barclay)

b. **We found this fellow perverting the nation, and forbidding to pay taxes to Caesar, saying that He Himself is Christ, a King**: At the same time, the religious leaders knew Pilate would be unconcerned with the accusation of blasphemy before the religious council. Therefore they brought Pilate three false accusations:

- That Jesus was a revolutionary (**perverting the nation**)
- That Jesus incited the people not to pay their taxes (**forbidding to pay taxes to Caesar**)
- That Jesus claimed to be a king in opposition to Caesar (**saying that He Himself is Christ, a King**)

c. **Then Pilate asked Him, saying, "Are You the King of the Jews?"** We can only wonder what Pilate thought when he first saw Jesus, when he saw this beaten and bloodied Man before him. Jesus didn't look especially regal or majestic as He stood before Pilate, so the Roman governor was probably sarcastic or ironic when he asked, **"Are You the King of the Jews?"**

i. "Pilate was evidently not alarmed by the charge brought against Jesus. Why? Apparently at first glance he saw that the man before him was not likely to be a pretender to royalty in any sense that he need trouble himself about…The [you] in an emphatic position in verse [Matthew 27:]11 suggests this = *You* the King of the Jews!" (Bruce)

d. **It is as you say**: Jesus gave no majestic defense and performed no instant miracle to save His own life. Instead, Jesus gave Pilate the same simple reply He gave to the high priest (Matthew 26:64).

e. **I find no fault in this Man**: *This was Pilate's verdict.* Though Pilate was a cruel, ruthless man, he wasn't stupid. He could see through the motives of the religious leaders and had no problem in estimating Jesus and the whole situation by the declaration, "**I find no fault in this Man.**"

f. **But they were the more fierce**: In response, the religious leaders became **more fierce**, and emphasized their accusation that Jesus was a leader of insurrection (**He stirs up the people**). This was a crime that any Roman governor would be concerned with.

g. **And as soon as he knew that He belonged to Herod's jurisdiction, he sent Him to Herod**: Pilate remained perplexed and unwilling to stand behind his verdict that Jesus was not guilty. So he sent Jesus to Herod, because Jesus was from Galilee, the area where Herod ruled.

i. "The city of *Nazareth*, in which Christ had continued till he was thirty years of age, and that of *Capernaum*, in which he principally resided the last years of his life, were both in *Lower Galilee*, of which *Herod Antipas* was tetrarch. Pilate was probably glad of this opportunity to pay a little respect to Herod, whom it is likely he had irritated, and with whom he now wished to be friends." (Clarke)

ii. "The word 'sent off' [**sent Him to**] (*anepempsen*) was a technical word for sending a prisoner from one authority to another (see Acts 25:21)." (Pate)

2. (8-12) The trial before Herod Antipas, son of Herod the Great.

Now when Herod saw Jesus, he was exceedingly glad; for he had desired for a long *time* to see Him, because he had heard many things about Him, and he hoped to see some miracle done by Him. Then he questioned Him with many words, but He answered him nothing. And the chief priests and scribes stood and vehemently accused Him. Then Herod, with his men of war, treated Him with contempt and mocked *Him*, arrayed Him in a gorgeous robe, and sent Him back to Pilate. That very day Pilate and Herod became friends with each other, for previously they had been at enmity with each other.

a. **When Herod saw Jesus, he was exceedingly glad; for he had desired for a long time to see Him**: Herod had surely heard much about Jesus, but his only interest was a desire to be amused and entertained. This son of Herod the Great never took Jesus seriously.

i. "Certain of the old writers delight to remark that as there were four evangelists to do honor to our Lord, so were there four judges to do him shame. Annas and Caiaphas, Pilate and Herod." (Spurgeon)

b. **He hoped to see some miracle done by Him**: Herod gave his attention to Jesus and was even **exceedingly glad** to see Him. He wanted to hear from Jesus (on Herod's own terms) and wanted to see Jesus do a **miracle**. Yet for all this, Herod's interest in Jesus was not sincere and was to his condemnation, not his praise.

i. At one time, Herod Antipas had expressed some religious interest. He heard the Word of God from John the Baptist (Mark 6:20), yet intending to continue in his sin and hardened against God and His Word, Herod became dead to conscience.

ii. At this point, Herod only wanted to hear from Jesus what *he* wanted to hear (**he questioned Him with many words**). He wanted Jesus to prove Himself, demanding a miracle. Many today also demand a miracle from Jesus as evidence, and it may be true that Jesus thinks of them as He thought of Herod.

iii. "There was left to Herod no feeling towards Jesus but the craving after something new, the desire to be astonished, the wish to be amused.... There sits the cunning prince, divining what the wonder will be; regarding even displays of divine power as mere showman's tricks, or magician's illusions." (Spurgeon)

c. **Then he questioned Him with many words, but He answered him nothing**: Herod governed over Galilee, where Jesus spent most of His ministry. He had countless opportunities to hear Jesus again and again—Jesus did not speak in secret meetings in hidden places. All this led Jesus to understand the truth about Herod: he was not a sincere seeker.

i. Herod thought, "Let's hear an answer from the Great Teacher! Let's see a miracle from the Miracle Man!" Jesus may have thought in response, "I have nothing for you, the murderer of My cousin John the Baptist." "He who answered blind beggars when they cried for mercy is silent to a prince who only seeks to gratify his own irreverent curiosity." (Spurgeon)

ii. Jesus understood that Herod was a wretched, shallow man and had therefore **nothing** to say to Him. The same man who murdered John the Baptist now regarded Jesus as a miracle performer for his own entertainment. Even when others **vehemently accused Him**, Jesus had nothing to say to Herod.

d. **Then Herod, with his men of war, treated Him with contempt and mocked Him**: The **contempt** and mockery showed what Herod really thought of Jesus. When Jesus refused to entertain him, Herod entertained himself by mistreating Jesus.

i. "The mockery made it plain that Herod did not take the charge seriously. That is the really frightening thing about the incident. With the Son of God before him Herod could only jest." (Morris)

e. **That very day Pilate and Herod became friends**: Significantly, Herod and Pilate **became friends** that day. They found no common ground except their opposition to Jesus.

i. "I do hope if there are any here that are true-hearted Christians if they have had any ill-will towards one another they will think it a great shame that Herod and Pilate should be friends, and that any two followers of Jesus should not be friends at the sight of the suffering Master." (Spurgeon)

ii. To this point, Luke 23 shows three different groups who hated and rejected Jesus.

- Because of fear and envy, the religious leaders hated Jesus
- Pilate knew something of who Jesus was, but was unwilling to make an unpopular stand for Him
- Herod didn't even take Jesus seriously; he was only interested in amusement and entertainment

3. (13-17) The second trial before Pilate.

Then Pilate, when he had called together the chief priests, the rulers, and the people, said to them, "You have brought this Man to me, as one who misleads the people. And indeed, having examined *Him* in your presence, I have found no fault in this Man concerning those things of which you accuse Him; no, neither did Herod, for I sent you back to him; and indeed nothing deserving of death has been done by Him. I will therefore chastise Him and release *Him*" (for it was necessary for him to release one to them at the feast).

a. **Having examined Him in your presence, I have found no fault in this Man . . . indeed nothing worthy of death has been done by Him**: Pilate clearly and eloquently declared Jesus innocent of any crime. This was the result of his careful examination of both Jesus and the evidence brought against Him.

b. **I will therefore chastise Him and release Him**: Pilate did not suggest a light punishment for Jesus. The Roman custom of scourging was a brutal whipping. The blows came from a whip with many leather strands, each having sharp pieces of bone or metal at the ends. It reduced the back to raw flesh, and it was not unusual for a criminal to die from a scourging, even before crucifixion.

i. *This was not just.* An innocent man does not deserve even a light punishment, much less the severe one suggested by the words, "**I will therefore chastise Him.**"

c. **For it was necessary for him to release one to them at the feast**: Pilate believed he had a way for Jesus to escape death. He planned to release Him according to the custom of releasing a prisoner every Passover season.

i. Pilate perhaps thought, "If this Man claimed to be king and is even the slightest bit hostile to Rome, then the crowd will love him. These Jewish leaders don't want Jesus to go free, but the crowd will sympathize with Him."

4. (18-25) The crowd makes its choice.

And they all cried out at once, saying, "Away with this *Man,* and release to us Barabbas"; who had been thrown into prison for a certain rebellion made in the city, and for murder. Pilate, therefore, wishing to release Jesus, again called out to them. But they shouted, saying, "Crucify *Him,* crucify Him!" Then he said to them the third time, "Why, what evil has He done? I have found no reason for death in Him. I will therefore chastise Him and let *Him* go." But they were insistent, demanding with loud voices that He be crucified. And the voices of these men and of the chief priests prevailed. So Pilate gave sentence that it

should be as they requested. And he released to them the one they requested, who for rebellion and murder had been thrown into prison; but he delivered Jesus to their will.

a. **Away with this Man, and release to us Barabbas**: The crowd, whom Pilate was convinced would release Jesus, instead condemned Him. Because of this, Pilate did not find the courage to oppose both the religious leaders and the crowd.

b. **But they shouted, saying, "Crucify Him, crucify Him!"** This was a strange, almost insane scene: a cruel, ruthless Roman governor trying to win the life of a miracle-working Jewish teacher against the strenuous efforts of both the Jewish leaders and the crowd.

i. "Their *loud cries* give the impression that a riot was beginning to build up. It must have been obvious to Pilate that the situation was becoming increasingly ugly." (Morris)

ii. We may imagine that many in this crowd had, just a few days before, cried out "Hosanna" to Jesus. Yet it is probable that most of these who cried, "**Crucify Him!**" were local residents of Jerusalem, not the pilgrims from Galilee and other places who welcomed Jesus on the day He entered Jerusalem.

c. **And he released to them the one they requested, who for rebellion and murder had been thrown into prison; but he delivered Jesus to their will**: The crowd rejected Jesus and embraced Barabbas, whose name means *son of the father*, and who was a terrorist and a murderer.

i. If anyone should be able to say, "Jesus died for me," it was Barabbas. He knew what it was to have Jesus die on his behalf, the innocent for the guilty.

d. **He delivered Jesus to their will**: This was how Pilate perceived his actions, and was *partly* true. In a larger sense, Jesus was delivered to His Father's will and the eternal purpose of God—predestined before the world was ever created—would certainly be accomplished.

B. Jesus dies and is buried.

1. (26) Simon carries Jesus' cross.

Now as they led Him away, they laid hold of a certain man, Simon a Cyrenian, who was coming from the country, and on him they laid the cross that he might bear *it* after Jesus.

a. **As they led Him away**: Even before Jesus was to be scourged, His physical condition was weak. It is reasonable to assume that Jesus was in good physical condition up until the night of His arrest.

i. "The rigors of Jesus' ministry (that is, travelling by foot throughout Palestine) would have precluded any major physical illness or a weak general constitution." (Dr. William Edwards in the article "On the Physical Death of Jesus Christ" from the *Journal of the American Medical Association*, 3/21/86)

ii. Yet during the 12 hours between 9 p.m. Thursday and 9 a.m. Friday, Jesus suffered many things, both physically and in the high-stress challenges that took a toll on Him physically.

- Jesus suffered great emotional stress in the Garden of Gethsemane, as indicated when *His sweat became like great drops of blood* (Luke22:44). "Although this is a very rare phenomenon, bloody sweat (hematidrosis or hemohidrosis) may occur in highly emotional states or in persons with bleeding disorders. As a result of hemorrhage into the sweat glands, the skin becomes fragile and tender" (Edwards)

- Jesus suffered the emotional stress of abandonment by His disciples

- Jesus suffered a severe physical beating at the home of the high priest

- Jesus suffered a sleepless night

- Jesus suffered, being forced to walk more than two and a half miles

- All of these factors made Jesus especially vulnerable to the effects of scourging

iii. Before Jesus took the cross, He was whipped—scourged—as Pilate had earlier promised (*I will therefore chastise Him*, Luke 23:16). "Scourging was a legal preliminary to every Roman execution, and only women and Roman senators or soldiers (except in cases of desertion) were exempt." (Edwards)

iv. The goal of the scourging was to weaken the victim to a state just short of collapse and death. "As the Roman soldiers repeatedly struck the victim's back with full force, the iron balls would cause deep contusions, and the leather thongs and sheep bones would cut into the skin and subcutaneous tissues. Then, as the flogging continued, the lacerations would tear into the underlying skeletal muscles and produce quivering ribbons of bleeding flesh. Pain and blood loss generally set the stage for circulatory shock. The extent of blood loss may well have determined how long the victim would survive the cross." (Edwards)

v. "The severe scourging, with its intense pain and appreciable blood loss, most probably left Jesus in a pre-shock state. Moreover, hematidrosis had rendered his skin particularly tender. The physical and mental abuse meted out by the Jews and the Romans, as well as the lack of food, water, and sleep, also contributed to his generally weakened state. Therefore, even before the actual crucifixion, Jesus' physical condition was at least serious and possibly critical." (Edwards)

b. **As they led Him away**: Before Jesus was led away, His clothes were stripped off. This was painful and opened wounds that had just begun to heal.

i. "When the soldiers tore the robe from Jesus' back, they probably reopened the scourging wounds." (Edwards)

c. **As they led Him away**: As Jesus was led to crucifixion, He was—like all victims of crucifixion—forced to carry the wood He would hang upon.

i. The weight of the entire cross was typically 300 pounds (136 kilograms). The victim only carried the crossbar, which weighed anywhere from 75 to 125 pounds (34 to 57 kilograms). When the victim carried the crossbar, he was usually stripped naked, and his hands were often tied to the wood.

ii. The upright beams of a cross were usually permanently fixed in a visible place outside of the city walls, beside a major road. It is likely that on many occasions, Jesus passed by the very upright He would later be crucified upon

d. **They laid hold of a certain man**: The weakened condition of Jesus required this. The man's name was **Simon**, and he was from Cyrene in North Africa (modern-day Libya).

i. No doubt, **Simon** was visiting Jerusalem as a Passover pilgrim from his native land (some 800 miles or 1300 kilometers away). He knew little if anything about this Jesus and had no desire to be associated with this Man who was condemned to die as a criminal.

ii. Yet the Romans were the law, and Simon was not given a choice—**they laid hold of** him, and **on him they laid the cross that he might bear it**. Perhaps he was chosen because he was an obvious foreigner and more conspicuous in the crowd.

iii. Wonderfully, we have reason to believe that Simon came to know what it *really means* to take up one's cross and follow Jesus. There is some evidence to suggest that his sons became leaders among the early Christians (Mark 15:21 and Romans 16:13).

2. (27-31) Jesus speaks to the **Daughters of Jerusalem**.

And a great multitude of the people followed Him, and women who also mourned and lamented Him. But Jesus, turning to them, said, "Daughters of Jerusalem, do not weep for Me, but weep for yourselves and for your children. For indeed the days are coming in which they will say, 'Blessed *are* the barren, wombs that never bore, and breasts which never nursed!' Then they will begin 'to say to the mountains, "Fall on us!" and to the hills, "Cover us!"' For if they do these things in the green wood, what will be done in the dry?"

    a. **A great multitude of the people followed Him**: It was customary for a **great multitude** to follow a condemned criminal on his way to crucifixion. It was intended to be a public event.

        i. According to the customs of crucifixion, a Roman guard led with a sign that carried the man's name and crime, calling out the name and the crime along the way to the place of crucifixion. They usually didn't take the shortest way so as many people as possible could see how the Roman Empire treated its enemies.

    b. **Daughters of Jerusalem, do not weep for Me, but weep for yourselves and for your children**: With good reason, certain women **mourned and lamented** when they saw Jesus being treated in this fashion. Jesus essentially told them, "Don't weep for Me, weep for those who reject Me."

        i. "As for the words themselves, they are especially noteworthy, because they constitute the last connected discourse of the Savior before he died. All that he said afterwards was fragmentary and mainly of the nature of prayer." (Spurgeon)

        ii. **Blessed are the barren**: "Normally, Jewish custom did just the opposite, praised motherhood and stigmatized the barren. But the days of the fall of Jerusalem would be so severe that women would far prefer not to have children, rather than have them go through the ordeal that awaited the city." (Pate)

    c. **For if they do these things in the green wood, what will be done in the dry?** The idea is, "If this is the fate of the innocent (Jesus referring to Himself), what will happen to the guilty?"

        i. Jesus spoke this in a more immediate sense, knowing the fate to come upon Jerusalem. "With his calm, prophetic eye he looks beyond the intervening years and sees Jerusalem besieged and captured. He speaks as though he heard the awful shrieks which betokened the entrance of the Romans into the city, and the smiting down of young and old, and women and children." (Spurgeon)

ii. Jesus spoke this in a greater sense, knowing the fate of all who reject Him. "Ye need not weep because Christ died one-tenth so much as because your sins rendered it necessary that he should die. You need not weep over the crucifixion, but weep over your transgression, for your sins nailed the Redeemer to the accursed tree. To weep over a dying Savior is to lament the remedy; it were wiser to bewail the disease." (Spurgeon)

3. (32-33) Jesus is crucified.

There were also two others, criminals, led with Him to be put to death. And when they had come to the place called Calvary, there they crucified Him, and the criminals, one on the right hand and the other on the left.

a. **When they had come to the place called Calvary**: There was a specific place outside the city walls of Jerusalem, yet still close, where people were crucified. At this **place called Calvary** Jesus died for our sins, and our salvation was accomplished. **Calvary** means, "place of a skull," and it was the place where criminals were crucified.

i. "It is a telling criticism that Fitzmeyer, a Jesuit theologian, observes in an aside comment on v. 32 that the account of Jesus' road to the cross says nothing about the fourteen stations of the cross, such as the falls of Jesus, the meeting with His mother or with Veronica ('true image'). Such later traditions, though certainly sentimental in appeal, seem to have no historical basis." (Pate)

b. **There they crucified Him**: In the days when the New Testament was first written, the practice of crucifixion needed no explanation. In the many generations since then, most people do not appreciate what a person experienced in the ordeal of execution by crucifixion.

i. "Although the Romans did not invent crucifixion, they perfected it as a form of torture and capital punishment that was designed to produce a slow death with maximum pain and suffering." (Edwards)

ii. The combination of scourging and crucifixion made death on the cross especially brutal. The victim's back was first torn open by the scourging, then the clotting blood was ripped open again when the clothes were torn off before crucifixion. The victim was thrown on the ground to fix his hands to the crossbeam, and the wounds on the back were again torn open and contaminated with dirt. Then, as the victim hung on the cross each breath caused the painful wounds on the back to scrape against the rough wood of the upright beam.

iii. When the nail was driven through the wrists, it severed the large median nerve. This stimulated nerve produced excruciating bolts of fiery pain in both arms, and often gave the victim a claw-like grip in the hands.

iv. Beyond the extreme pain, the major effect of crucifixion was to restrict normal breathing. The weight of the body, pulling down on the arms and shoulders, tended to fix the respiratory muscles in an inhalation state and hinder exhalation. The lack of adequate respiration resulted in severe muscle cramps, which further hindered breathing. To get a good breath, the victim had to push against the feet, and flex the elbows, pulling from the shoulders. Putting the weight of the body on the feet produced searing pain, and flexing of the elbows twisted the hands hanging on the nails. Lifting the body for a breath also painfully scraped the back against the rough wooden post. Each effort to get a proper breath was agonizing, exhausting, and led to a sooner death.

v. "Not uncommonly, insects would light upon or burrow into the open wounds or the eyes, ears, and nose of the dying and helpless victim, and birds of prey would tear at these sites. Moreover, it was customary to leave the corpse on the cross to be devoured by predatory animals." (Edwards)

vi. Death from crucifixion could come from many sources: acute shock from blood loss; being too exhausted to breathe any longer; dehydration; stress-induced heart attack, or congestive heart failure leading to a cardiac rupture. If the victim did not die quickly enough, the legs were broken, and the victim was soon unable to breathe because of the posture of the crucified person.

vii. How bad was crucifixion? We get our English word *excruciating* from the Roman word "out of the cross." "Consider how heinous sin must be in the sight of God, when it requires such a sacrifice!" (Clarke)

c. **There they crucified Him**: The most significant thing about Jesus' suffering was that He was not, in any sense, the victim of circumstances. He was in control. Jesus said of His life in John 10:18, *no one takes it from Me, but I lay it down of Myself.* It is terrible to be forced to endure such torture, but to freely choose it out of love is remarkable.

i. This was the most important act of this most important life, and this is reflected even in ancient secular histories. The existing mentions of Jesus in ancient extra-biblical literature each highlight His death on the cross.

- A letter written by Mara bar Serapion to his son (ca. A.D. 73)
- Josephus, the Jewish historian (ca. A.D. 90)

- Tacitus, the Roman historian (ca. A.D. 110-120)
- The Babylonian Talmud (ca. A.D. 200)

d. **The criminals, one on the right hand and the other on the left**: In His death, Jesus was identified with sinners—He was crucified between two criminals.

4. (34-38) Jesus on the cross.

Then Jesus said, "Father, forgive them, for they do not know what they do." And they divided His garments and cast lots. And the people stood looking on. But even the rulers with them sneered, saying, "He saved others; let Him save Himself if He is the Christ, the chosen of God." The soldiers also mocked Him, coming and offering Him sour wine, and saying, "If You are the King of the Jews, save Yourself." And an inscription also was written over Him in letters of Greek, Latin, and Hebrew: THIS IS THE KING OF THE JEWS.

a. **Father, forgive them, for they do not know what they do**: The love of Jesus never fails. On the cross, He prayed even for His executioners, asking God the Father to not hold this sin against them.

i. Jesus probably prayed in this manner for His enemies all through His ministry. This prayer was heard and noted, because He had no quiet place to pray.

ii. In this, Jesus fulfilled His own command to *love your enemies, bless those who curse you, do good for those who hate you, and pray for those who spitefully use you and persecute you* (Matthew 5:44).

b. **For they do not know what they do**: In this, Jesus recognized the blindness of His enemies in His prayer. This did not excuse the guilt of those who put Jesus on the cross, but Jesus set His enemies in the best possible light in His prayer to the Father. We must pray with the same heart, after the same pattern.

i. "If ignorance does not excuse a crime, it at least diminishes the atrocity of it. However, these persons well knew that they were crucifying an *innocent* man; but they did not know that, by this act of theirs, they were bringing down on themselves and on their country the heaviest judgments of God. In the prayer, *Father, forgive them!* that word of prophecy was fulfilled, *He made intercession for the transgressors*, Isaiah 53:12." (Clarke)

c. **And they divided His garments and cast lots**: On the cross, Jesus retained no material possessions. Even the clothes on his back were taken and **divided** by the roll of the dice. This shows that Jesus came all the way down the ladder to accomplish our salvation. He let go of absolutely everything—even His clothes—becoming completely poor for us, so we could become completely rich in Him.

> i. 2 Corinthians 8:9 says it like this: *For you know the grace of our Lord Jesus Christ, that though He was rich, yet for your sakes He became poor, that you through His poverty might become rich.*

d. **Even the rulers with them sneered… The soldiers also mocked Him**: Jesus was not honored or encouraged as He hung on the cross. Instead He was scorned and mocked. His religious enemies said, **"He saved others; let Him save Himself if He is the Christ, the chosen of God."** Yet it was precisely because He did *not* save Himself that He can save others. It could be rightly said that *love* kept Jesus on the cross, not nails.

e. **An inscription also was written over Him in letters of Greek, Latin, and Hebrew:** THIS IS THE KING OF THE JEWS: In John 19:21, we read that the religious leaders among the Jews objected to this title. They felt it was *false*, because they did not believe that Jesus was **the King of the Jews**. They also believed it was *demeaning*, because it showed Rome's power to humiliate and torture even the "**King of the Jews**." Yet Pilate would not alter this, and when asked to take down the inscription, he answered, *What I have written, I have written* (John 19:22).

> i. "The written *charge* (or *titulus*) was normally carried before a criminal on the way to execution, or hung around his neck, and would then be fixed to the cross, thus reinforcing the deterrent effect of the punishment." (France)

> ii. "This venerable eulogy and epitaph, set upon our Saviour's cross, proclaimed him King of all religion, having reference to the Hebrews; of all wisdom, to the Greeks; of all power, to the Latins." (Trapp)

5. (39-43) A criminal on a cross finds salvation.

Then one of the criminals who were hanged blasphemed Him, saying, "If You are the Christ, save Yourself and us." But the other, answering, rebuked him, saying, "Do you not even fear God, seeing you are under the same condemnation? And we indeed justly, for we receive the due reward of our deeds; but this Man has done nothing wrong." Then he said to Jesus, "Lord, remember me when You come into Your kingdom." And Jesus said to him, "Assuredly, I say to you, today you will be with Me in Paradise."

a. **One of the criminals who were hanged blasphemed Him**: One of the criminals crucified with Jesus joined in the mockery and scorn. He reasoned that if Jesus *were* the Messiah, He should save those who are being crucified with Him (**save Yourself and us**).

b. **But the other, answering, rebuked him**: Both Matthew (Matthew 27:44) and Mark (Mark 15:32) indicate that *both* criminals mocked Jesus. Though at first they both mocked Jesus, in the hours spent on the cross, one of the criminals came to see things differently, and to actually put his trust in Jesus.

- This second criminal respected God (**Do you not even fear God**)
- He knew his own sin (**under the same condemnation . . . we indeed justly, for we receive the due reward of our deeds**)
- He knew Jesus (**this Man has done nothing wrong**)
- He called out to Jesus (**he said to Jesus**)
- He called out to Jesus as Lord (**he said to Jesus, "Lord . . ."**)
- He believed Jesus was who He said He was (**remember me when You come into Your kingdom**)
- He believed the promise of everlasting life from Jesus

i. "It is worthy of remark, that this man appears to have been the first who believed in the *intercession* of Christ." (Clarke)

c. **Assuredly, I say to you, today you will be with Me in Paradise**: Jesus answered the trust of the second criminal, assuring him that his life after death would be **with** Jesus, and be in **Paradise**, not torment.

i. Here is something truly remarkable: a deathbed conversion, and may fairly be said to be the only Biblical example of a last-minute salvation. There *is* one deathbed conversion in the Bible, so that no one would despair; but *only one*, so that no one would presume.

ii. Significantly, this thief who trusted in Jesus at the last moment goes to the same heaven everyone else does. This may not seem fair, but in the larger picture it gives glory to the grace of God, not to human merit in salvation. In heaven, we will all be filled to the full with joy and reward; but the degree of our faithfulness now determines how big our container for joy and reward will be in heaven, though all will be filled to the fullest they can hold.

iii. **In Paradise**: "Paradise (*paradeisos*), a Persian word meaning 'garden, park,' was used in the Septuagint for the Garden of Eden (Genesis 2:8). It then became a type of the future bliss for God's people in Isaiah 51:3…In the present passage it represents the state of bliss which Jesus promised to the criminal directly after death." (Pate)

iv. This assurance was so important to Jesus that it cost Him something. It *hurt* Jesus to even say these words. "Since speech occurs during exhalation, these short, terse utterances must have been particularly difficult and painful." (Edwards)

v. Jesus answered the second criminal far beyond his expectation.

- The thief on the cross had some distant time in mind; Jesus told him **today**
- The thief on the cross asked only to be remembered; Jesus said **"you will be with Me"**
- The thief on the cross looked only for a kingdom; Jesus promised him **Paradise**

6. (44-46) Jesus dies on the cross.

Now it was about the sixth hour, and there was darkness over all the earth until the ninth hour. Then the sun was darkened, and the veil of the temple was torn in two. And when Jesus had cried out with a loud voice, He said, "Father, 'into Your hands I commit My spirit.' " Having said this, He breathed His last.

a. **There was darkness over all the earth until the ninth hour**: The remarkable darkness over all the earth showed the agony of creation itself in the Creator's suffering. "Origen (*Contra Celsus*, ii,33) and Eusebius (*Chron.*) quote words from Phlegon (a Roman historian) in which he makes mention of an extraordinary solar eclipse as well as of an earthquake about the time of the crucifixion." (Geldenhuys)

i. A Roman historian named Phlegon wrote: "In the fourth year of the 202nd Olympiad, there was an extraordinary eclipse of the sun: at the sixth hour, the day turned into dark night, so that the stars in heaven were seen; and there was an earthquake." (Cited in Clarke)

ii. The crucifixion took place during Passover season, and Passover is always held at a full moon. A *natural* eclipse of the sun is impossible during a full moon.

b. **The veil of the temple was torn in two**: The tearing of the temple veil signified at least two things. First, now man has free access to the throne of grace by the cross. Second, no one should ever think again that God dwells in temples made with hands.

i. Matthew 27:51 notes that the temple was torn *from top to bottom*. God tore it from heaven instead of man tearing it from earth.

c. **When Jesus had cried out with a loud voice**: Jesus cried out something with **a loud voice**, *then* He spoke to God the Father in the lines that follow. John 19:30 tells us what He said: *it is finished*, which is one word in the Greek (*tetelestai*—"paid in full"). This was the cry of a winner, because

Jesus had paid in full the debt of sin we owed, and had finished the eternal purpose of the cross.

i. At some point before He died, before the veil was torn in two, before He cried out *it is finished*, an awesome spiritual transaction took place. The Father set upon Jesus all the guilt and wrath our sin deserved, and He bore it in Himself perfectly, totally satisfying the wrath of God for us.

ii. As horrible as the physical suffering of Jesus was, this spiritual suffering—the act of being judged for sin in our place—was what Jesus really dreaded about the cross. This was the *cup*—the cup of God's righteous wrath—that He trembled at drinking (Luke 22:39-46, Psalm 75:8, Isaiah 51:17, Jeremiah 25:15). On the cross, Jesus became, as it were, an enemy of God who was judged and forced to drink the cup of the Father's fury. He did it so we would not have to drink that cup.

iii. Isaiah 53:3-5 puts it powerfully: *He is despised and rejected by men, a Man of sorrows and acquainted with grief. And we hid, as it were, our faces from Him; He was despised, and we did not esteem Him. Surely He has borne our griefs and carried our sorrows; yet we esteemed Him stricken, smitten by God, and afflicted. But He was wounded for our transgressions, He was bruised for our iniquities; the chastisement for our peace was upon Him, and by His stripes we are healed.*

iv. "Reader! *one drop* of this cup would bear down thy soul to endless ruin; and these agonies would annihilate the universe. He suffered *alone*: for the people there was none with him; because his sufferings were to make an atonement for the sins of the world: and in the work of redemption he had no helper." (Clarke)

v. "The fact that He could raise His voice, when normally a crucified person could barely gasp for breath, indicates that Jesus was still in control of His destiny." (Pate)

d. **Father, into Your hands I commit My spirit**: His work on the cross accomplished, with prayer Jesus yielded His living **spirit** to God the Father as He yielded His body to death on the cross. This shows that Jesus gave up His life when He wanted to and how He wanted to. No one took His life from Him; He gave it up when His work was finished. Jesus is not a victim we should pity, but a conqueror we should admire.

i. Save your pity for those who reject the complete work of Jesus on the cross at Calvary; for those preachers who do not have the heart of Paul in 1 Corinthians 1:23, when he proclaimed the center of the Christian message: *we preach Christ crucified.*

ii. **I commit My spirit**: "Or, *I will commit my spirit-I deposit my soul in thy hands*. Another proof of the *immateriality* of the soul, and of its *separate* existence when the body is dead." (Clarke)

e. **Having said this, He breathed His last**: Once the work of the cross was accomplished, Jesus felt no further need to endure the suffering. He yielded His living **spirit** to God the Father and He yielded His body to death on the cross and **breathed His last**.

i. "The words of v. 46, 'Jesus expired' ('breathed out His life'), can be seen to echo Genesis 2:7. There it is said that God breathed into Adam the breath of life, and he became a living soul. The one God breathed into the breath of life—Adam; the other breathed out the breath of life—Jesus. The latter paid the consequences for the sin of the former in order to inaugurate a new creation." (Pate)

7. (47-49) The reaction of bystanders at Jesus' death.

So when the centurion saw what had happened, he glorified God, saying, "Certainly this was a righteous Man!" And the whole crowd who came together to that sight, seeing what had been done, beat their breasts and returned. But all His acquaintances, and the women who followed Him from Galilee, stood at a distance, watching these things.

a. **When the centurion saw what had happened, he glorified God**: At the expiration of Jesus on the cross, the Gentile centurion immediately gave glory to God and understood Jesus for who He was (**Certainly this was a righteous man**).

i. Surely, this centurion had seen many people crucified before. Yet there was something so remarkable about Jesus that he said something about Him that he could say about no one else.

ii. This is a picture of all who come to Jesus through the cross, fulfilling Jesus' promise *if I am lifted up from the earth, will draw all peoples to Myself* (John 12:32).

b. **The whole crowd who came together to that sight, seeing what had been done, beat their breasts and returned**: Others went home sadly; they were too close to Jesus to see how remarkable His death was, and they forgot His promise to rise again.

8. (50-56) Jesus is buried in the tomb of Joseph of Arimathea.

Now behold, *there was* a man named Joseph, a council member, a good and just man. He had not consented to their decision and deed. *He was* from Arimathea, a city of the Jews, who himself was also waiting for the kingdom of God. This man went to Pilate and asked for the body of Jesus. Then he took it down, wrapped it in linen, and laid it in a tomb

that was **hewn out of the rock, where no one had ever lain before. That day was the Preparation, and the Sabbath drew near. And the women who had come with Him from Galilee followed after, and they observed the tomb and how His body was laid. Then they returned and prepared spices and fragrant oils. And they rested on the Sabbath according to the commandment.**

a. **This man went to Pilate and asked for the body of Jesus**: Customarily, the bodies of crucified criminals were left on their crosses to rot or be eaten by wild animals. But the Jews wanted no such horror displayed during the Passover season, and Romans were known to grant the corpses to friends or relatives for proper burial.

i. Joseph did *not* serve Jesus in many ways, but he did serve Him in ways no one else did or could. It was not possible for Peter, James, John, or even the many women who served Jesus to provide a tomb, but Joseph could and did. We must serve God in whatever way we can.

b. **That day was the Preparation, and the Sabbath drew near**: They were unable to properly prepare the body of Jesus for burial because of the coming Sabbath. So in hurried preparation, Jesus' body was placed in a borrowed tomb.

i. "In the hours of crisis it is often the Peters who have sworn loyalty to Jesus with big gestures and fullness of self-confidence, that disappoint, and it is the secret and quiet followers of the Master (like Joseph, Nicodemus and the women) that do not hesitate to serve Him in love—at whatever the cost." (Geldenhuys)

c. **Laid it in a tomb that was hewn out of the rock, where no one had ever lain before**: Tombs like this were very expensive. It was quite a sacrifice for Joseph of Arimathea to give his tomb to Jesus, but Jesus would only use it for a few days.

Luke 24—The Resurrected Jesus

A. The resurrection of Jesus is discovered.

1. (1-3) Women followers of Jesus discover the empty tomb of Jesus.

Now on the first *day* of the week, very early in the morning, they, and certain *other women* with them, came to the tomb bringing the spices which they had prepared. But they found the stone rolled away from the tomb. Then they went in and did not find the body of the Lord Jesus.

a. **Now on the first day of the week, very early in the morning**: Jesus was crucified on Friday (or on Thursday by some accounts). After His entombment, the tomb was sealed and guarded by Roman soldiers (Matthew 27:62-66). The tomb stayed sealed and guarded until discovered by these women **on the first day of the week, very early in the morning**.

i. A rich man like Joseph of Arimethea would likely have a tomb carved into solid rock; this tomb was in a garden near the place of crucifixion (John 19:41). The tomb would have a small entrance and perhaps one or more compartments where bodies were laid out after being wrapped with linen strips smeared with spices, aloes, and ointments. Customarily, the Jews left these bodies alone for a few years until they decayed down to the bones, then the bones were placed in a small stone box known as an ossuary. The ossuary remained in the tomb with the remains of other family members.

ii. The entrance to the tomb was blocked by a heavy circular-shaped stone, securely rolled in a channel, so only several strong men could move it. This was done to ensure that no one would disturb the remains.

iii. John 19:42 specifically tells us that the tomb of Joseph of Arimethea that Jesus was laid in was close to the place of Jesus' crucifixion (and each of the two suggested places for Jesus' death and resurrection bear this out). Joseph probably didn't like it that the value of his family tomb decreased because the Romans decided to crucify people nearby; yet it reminds us that in God's plan, the cross and the power of the resurrection are always permanently and closely connected.

iv. "This became the day of Christian worship (cf. Acts 20:7). The change from the traditional and biblical Sabbath is in itself a strong evidence of the Resurrection because it shows the strength of the disciples' conviction about what happened on that day." (Liefeld)

b. **They, and certain other women with them**: These women are of special note. **They** refers to the women from Galilee who saw Jesus put in the tomb (Luke 23:55-56). Luke agrees with Mark 15:47 and Matthew 27:61 that **they** included *Mary Magdalene* and *Mary the mother of James* (Luke 24:10). The **certain other women with them** included *Joanna,* (Luke 24:10) and others, unnamed (*and the other women with them*, Luke 24:10).

i. "These women came first, by a wonderful providence, before the apostles, to confute that impudent lie made by the priests, that the disciples had stolen the body away." (Trapp)

c. **Came to the tomb bringing the spices which they had prepared**: The body of Jesus was hastily prepared for burial by Joseph of Arimathea and Nicodemus (John 19:38-41). The women came to properly complete the hurried job performed immediately after Jesus' death.

i. Mark 16:3 tells us that the women discussed the problem of what to do with the heavy stone blocking the entrance to the tomb.

d. **But they found the stone rolled away from the tomb. Then they went in and did not find the body of the Lord Jesus**: The actual *event* of Jesus' resurrection is nowhere described, but the discovery of it is recorded in some detail. Here, the women who intended to give Jesus' body a more proper burial discover that the stone was rolled away from the tomb, and that the body of Jesus was not inside the tomb.

i. "This lack of spectacular detail itself speaks for the historicity of the New Testament documents. There is no attempt on the part of the writers to embellish the event of the Resurrection." (Pate)

ii. Matthew 27:65-66 reminds us that there was a guard set round the tomb. The stone could not have been rolled away by the women (they were not strong enough) or by the disciples (even if they were brave enough, they could not overcome the armed guards). No one else would have wanted to roll away the stone, and Matthew 28:2 tells us that it was an angel who rolled it away.

iii. The stone was not rolled away to let Jesus out. John 20:19 tells us that Jesus, in His resurrection body, could pass through material barriers. The stone was **rolled away** so that others could see in and be persuaded that Jesus Christ was and is risen from the dead.

2. (4-8) The angelic announcement of the resurrection.

And it happened, as they were greatly perplexed about this, that behold, two men stood by them in shining garments. Then, as they were afraid and bowed *their* faces to the earth, they said to them, "Why do you seek the living among the dead? He is not here, but is risen! Remember how He spoke to you when He was still in Galilee, saying, 'The Son of Man must be delivered into the hands of sinful men, and be crucified, and the third day rise again.'" And they remembered His words.

a. **As they were greatly perplexed about this**: Once the women saw the stone rolled away and the tomb empty, their immediate reaction was that they were **greatly perplexed**. They did not expect to find an empty tomb. This shows that the resurrection accounts cannot be the product of wishful thinking; they were not even *expecting* that it could happen.

b. **Two men stood by them in shining garments**: Even as angels announced the birth of Jesus (Luke 2:8-15), so they also announced the resurrection of Jesus. The announcement of His birth was made to a few humble people, considered unimportant by the culture; His resurrection was announced by angels to a few women.

c. **Why do you seek the living among the dead?** This was a wonderfully logical question. The angels seemed almost surprised that the women were surprised; after all, the angels had heard what Jesus said regarding His resurrection, and they knew the women had heard it also. They naturally wondered why the women were surprised.

i. "Jesus is not to be thought of as dead: therefore he is not be sought among the dead." (Morris)

ii. "As places of burial were unclean, it was not reasonable to suppose that the *living* should frequent them; or that if any was missing he was likely to be found in such places." (Clarke)

iii. The angels' question made a point: the **living** are not to be found among the **dead**. We should not expect spiritual life among those who do not have it. Many look for Jesus in dead things—religious traditionalism, formalism, man's rules, human effort and ingenuity. We find Jesus only where there is resurrection life, where He is worshipped in Spirit and in truth.

d. **He is not here**: These were some of the most beautiful and important words ever spoken by an angel to men. One may look all over Jerusalem and see countless thousands of tombs, but one will never find the tomb of Jesus—because **He is not here**.

i. Every so often someone claims to have found evidence of the tomb of Jesus or the bones of Jesus. Each claim is found to be untrue, while the testimony of the angels is proved true over and over again: **He is not here**.

ii. Even the beginning of the resurrection account refutes many of the false alternative theories suggested by some.

- The wrong-tomb theory is answered by Luke 23:55; the women knew exactly which tomb Jesus was buried in

- The wishful-thinking theory is answered by Luke 24:4 and 24:11, which note the surprise of the women and the disciples of the news of Jesus' resurrection

- The animals-ate-the-body theory is answered by the presence of the stone (Luke 24:2)

- The swoon theory is answered by the presence of the stone (Luke 24:2)

- The grave-robber theory is answered by the presence of the Roman guard and seal (Matthew 27:62-66)

e. **The Son of Man must be delivered into the hands of sinful men, and be crucified, and on the third day rise again**: To the women, it must have seemed like a long time ago that Jesus said these words (Luke 18:31-33). Nevertheless, they needed to remember His words and the angels remind them of what He said.

i. **Must** is the critical word here; just as much as the crucifixion of Jesus was necessary and ordained, so was His resurrection. Jesus would have never come to the place of Calvary unless there was also an empty tomb of resurrection there, also.

f. **And they remembered His words**: The first notes of hope were sounded in the hearts of the women when they **remembered** Jesus' words. The empty tomb, the presence of angels, the words of the angels in and of themselves could not change their hearts—but **His words** could change and cheer their hearts.

3. (9-11) The women tell the apostles and are not believed.

Then they returned from the tomb and told all these things to the eleven and to all the rest. It was Mary Magdalene, Joanna, Mary *the mother* of James, and the other *women* with them, who told these things to the apostles. And their words seemed to them like idle tales, and they did not believe them.

a. **Then they returned from the tomb and told all these things to the eleven and to all the rest**: The women who saw the evidence of the resurrected Jesus and remembered His words were excited about what seemed to be the most wonderful news possible—that Jesus *was* alive and had triumphed over death.

> i. They would not be excited if Jesus had only somehow miraculously survived the ordeal of the cross. The news that He was alive meant so much more to them than knowing Jesus was a *survivor*; it meant He was the conqueror over death and that He was everything they had hoped for and more.

b. **It was Mary Magdalene, Joanna, Mary the mother of James, and the other women with them**: These were the women mentioned in Luke 24:1 as those who discovered the empty tomb. Three are mentioned specifically, and then an unnamed group of **other women**. These were given the privilege of being the first to tell others of the risen Jesus.

> i. The only references to **Mary Magdalene** in the Gospels concern her as a witness of the crucifixion (Mark 15:40 and John 19:25) and of the resurrection (all four gospels) and as one from whom Jesus had cast out seven demons (Luke 8:2, Mark 16:9).

> ii. **Joanna** is mentioned in Luke 8:2 as one of the women who accompanied Jesus and provided for His needs. She is also noted in Luke 8:2 as the wife of Chuza, who helped manage Herod's affairs (a steward). She was likely a woman of privilege and resources.

> iii. **Mary the mother of James** is only mentioned in connection with the resurrection appearances of Jesus. She was apparently the mother of one of the apostles, James the Less (not James the brother of John).

c. **Their words seemed to them like idle tales, and they did not believe them**: Despite their excitement, the testimony of the women was not believed. In fact, to the apostles, it seemed as if the women told **idle tales**, a medical word used to describe the babbling of a fevered and insane man (according to Barclay).

> i. "In the first century the testimony of women was not deemed authoritative. Luke's inclusion of the incident serves to emphasize his high regard for women." (Pate)

> ii. "The disciples were not men poised on the brink of belief and needing only the shadow of an excuse before launching forth into a proclamation of resurrection. They were utterly skeptical." (Morris)

4. (12) The apostles come to believe.

But Peter arose and ran to the tomb; and stooping down, he saw the linen cloths lying by themselves; and he departed, marveling to himself at what had happened.

a. **But Peter arose and ran to the tomb**: We know from John 20:3-8 that both Peter and John ran to the tomb together. They saw grave clothes, but not as if they had been ripped off after a struggle. They saw the grave clothes of Jesus lying in perfect order, as if a body had just passed out of them (John 20:6-7). When John saw that, he believed, and Peter marveled. They had not seen the risen Jesus, but they knew that something *powerful* had happened to cause a body to leave behind the grave clothes in such a manner.

b. **Marveling to himself at what had happened**: Peter and John both observed what was in the tomb and John believed (John 20:8). This tells us that Peter analyzed the situation; he knew something spectacular had happened because of the condition of the grave clothes, but because he had forgotten the words of Jesus (John 20:9), he did not yet understand and *believe* the way John had.

i. You can know that Jesus rose from the dead, but unless you know His words, it won't make sense. Without knowing the life and teachings of Jesus:

- You don't know that the resurrection means that the payment that Jesus offered on the cross was perfect and complete

- You don't know that the cross was the payment and the empty tomb is the receipt

- You don't know that death has no hold on redeemed man

- You don't know that when God's love and man's hate battled at the cross, God's love won

- You don't know that because Jesus was raised from the dead, we can be resurrected in Him

B. On the road to Emmaus.

1. (13-16) Jesus joins two disciples on a road.

Now behold, two of them were traveling that same day to a village called Emmaus, which was seven miles from Jerusalem. And they talked together of all these things which had happened. So it was, while they conversed and reasoned, that Jesus Himself drew near and went with them. But their eyes were restrained, so that they did not know Him.

a. **Two of them were traveling that same day to a village called Emmaus**: On this Sunday, these two disciples traveled to Emmaus from Jerusalem. As they walked together (probably returning from the Passover celebration in Jerusalem), it gave them opportunity to talk.

i. These weren't famous apostles; they were simple and half-anonymous followers of Jesus. "I take it as characteristic of the Lord that in the glory of His resurrection life He gave Himself with such fullness of disclosure to these unknown and undistinguished men…. He still reveals Himself to lowly hearts. Here is the Saviour for the common man. Here is the Lord who does not spurn the humble." (Morrison)

ii. "There is considerable uncertainty about the original location of the village of Emmaus. Luke mentions that it was about seven miles (literally, 'sixty stadia') from Jerusalem. If he meant round-trip, the reference would fit rather nicely with a town Josephus identified as Emmaus, which he located thirty stadia from Jerusalem." (Pate)

iii. "Luke almost certainly obtained his information from one of the two disciples, and probably in writing. The account has all the effect of personal experience." (Plummer, cited in Geldenhuys)

b. **They conversed and reasoned**: As they talked, they spoke of the things that were biggest on their hearts—**all of these things which had happened**—the things regarding the arrest and crucifixion of Jesus.

c. **Jesus Himself drew near and went with them**: Jesus came alongside these disciples, and **went with them** for a while. Yet for a time, they were miraculously prevented from seeing who Jesus was.

i. "When two saints are talking together, Jesus is very likely to come and make the third one in the company. Talk of him, and you will soon talk with him." (Spurgeon)

2. (17-24) The disciples explain what they talked about.

And He said to them, "What kind of conversation *is* this that you have with one another as you walk and are sad?" Then the one whose name was Cleopas answered and said to Him, "Are You the only stranger in Jerusalem, and have You not known the things which happened there in these days?" And He said to them, "What things?" So they said to Him, "The things concerning Jesus of Nazareth, who was a Prophet mighty in deed and word before God and all the people, and how the chief priests and our rulers delivered Him to be condemned to death, and crucified Him. But we were hoping that it was He who was going to redeem Israel. Indeed, besides all this, today is the third day since these things happened. Yes, and certain women of our company, who arrived at the tomb early, astonished us. When they did not find His body, they came saying that they had also seen a vision of angels who said He was alive. And certain of those *who were* with us went to the tomb and found *it* just as the women had said; but Him they did not see."

a. **What kind of conversation is this that you have with one another as you walk and are sad?** Jesus opened the conversation by asking them what they had talked about. From this, we can know that Jesus had walked silently with them for a while, just listening as they carried on the conversation.

i. It was evident in their countenance (and perhaps even in their manner of walking) that they were **sad**. Jesus knew both what they already knew (that they were sad), and what they did not yet know (that they had no reason to be sad).

b. **Are You the only stranger in Jerusalem, and have You not known the things which happened here in these days?** Jesus probably smiled when they said this. He knew pretty well what had **happened here in these days**.

c. **What things?** In saying this, Jesus skillfully played along with the conversation, encouraging the men to reveal their hearts. Even though He knew their hearts, there was value in them saying it to Jesus.

d. **The things concerning Jesus of Nazareth**: The men explained what they did know about Jesus.

- They knew His name and where He was from
- They knew He was a **Prophet**
- They knew He was **mighty in deed and word**
- They knew He was **crucified**
- They knew He promised to **redeem Israel**
- They knew others had said He rose from the dead

e. **We were hoping**: These disciples had a hope disappointed. Their hope was not truly disappointed, but in some ways their hope was misguided (**that it was He who was going to redeem Israel**). Jesus would show them that their true hope was fulfilled in Him and His resurrection.

f. **Just as the women had said**: The only thing these disciples had to go on was the testimony of others, but they were slow to believe. The report of the women meant little to them, and the report of Peter and John who had seen the grave clothes meant little—because **Him they did not see**.

i. Jesus wanted to know from them what He wants to know from us today: can we believe without seeing with our own eyes? We can believe and must believe based on the reliable eyewitness testimony of other people.

3. (25-27) Jesus teaches them why the Messiah *had* to suffer.

Then He said to them, "O foolish ones, and slow of heart to believe in all that the prophets have spoken! Ought not the Christ to have suffered these things and to enter into His glory?" And beginning at Moses and all the Prophets, He expounded to them in all the Scriptures the things concerning Himself.

a. **Slow of heart to believe**: Jesus told them that the problem with their belief was more in their **heart** than their *head*. We often think the main obstacles to belief are in the head, but they are actually in the **heart**.

b. **Ought not the Christ to have suffered these things and to enter into His glory?** They should have believed what **all the prophets have spoken**, that the Messiah would suffer first and then be received in glory.

- They were common, simple men
- They had lost hope
- They had lost joy—a sense of spiritual desertion
- They had not lost desire—they still loved to talk about Jesus
- They had not yet seen the *necessity* of the cross

    i. The prophets spoke in Isaiah 53:3-5: *He is despised and rejected by men, a Man of sorrows and acquainted with grief. And we hid, as it were, our faces from Him; He was despised, and we did not esteem Him. Surely He has borne our griefs and carried our sorrows; yet we esteemed Him stricken, smitten by God, and afflicted. But He was wounded for our transgressions, He was bruised for our iniquities; the chastisement for our peace was upon Him, and by His stripes we are healed.*

    ii. Isaiah 50:5-7 is another example of what the prophets taught concerning this. *The Lord GOD has opened My ear; and I was not rebellious, nor did I turn away. I gave My back to those who struck Me, and My cheeks to those who plucked out the beard; I did not hide My face from shame and spitting. For the Lord GOD will help Me; therefore I will not be disgraced; therefore I have set My face like a flint, and I know that I will not be ashamed.*

    iii. Daniel 9:26 shows another prophecy regarding these things: *The Messiah shall be cut off, but not for Himself.*

    iv. Zechariah 12:10 is yet another example: *They will look on Me whom they pierced. Yes, they will mourn for Him as one mourns for his only son, and grieve for Him as one grieves for a firstborn.*

c. **And beginning at Moses and all the Prophets, He expounded to them in all the Scriptures the things concerning Himself**: Jesus began to teach them what was surely one of the most spectacular Bible studies ever taught. **Beginning in Moses and all the Prophets**, He told them all about the Messiah.

> i. "It is a sign to us that He is still the same, though He has passed into the resurrection glory, that He still goes back to the old familiar Scripture which He had learned beside His mother's knee." (Morrison)

> ii. He told them that the Messiah was:

> - The Seed of the Woman, whose heel was bruised
> - The blessing of Abraham to all nations
> - The High Priest after the order of Melchizedek
> - The Man who wrestled with Jacob
> - The Lion of the Tribe of Judah
> - The voice from the burning bush
> - The Passover Lamb
> - The Prophet greater than Moses
> - The captain of the Lord's army to Joshua
> - The ultimate Kinsman-Redeemer mentioned in Ruth
> - The son of David who was a King greater than David
> - The suffering Savior of Psalm 22
> - The Good Shepherd of Psalm 23
> - The wisdom of Proverbs and the Lover of the Song of Solomon
> - The Savior described in the prophets and the suffering Servant of Isaiah 53
> - The Princely Messiah of Daniel who would establish a kingdom that would never end

> ii. "The Savior, who knows the Word of God perfectly, because of His intimate union with the Spirit who is its Primary Author, expounded to them in broad outline all the Scriptures that referred to Him, from the first books of the Old Testament and right through to the end." (Geldenhuys)

> iii. "We should not understand this as the selection of a number of proof-texts, but rather as showing that throughout the Old Testament a consistent divine purpose is worked out, a purpose that in the end meant and must mean the cross." (Morris)

d. **Expounded to them in all the Scriptures**: This describes *how* Jesus taught them. The idea of expounding is to simply let the text speak for itself; exactly what a Bible teacher should do his or her best to do.

i. The ancient Greek word for **expounded** (*diermeneuo*) has the idea of sticking close to the text. In another passage when Luke used this word, it is expressed with the word *translated* (Acts 9:36). When Jesus explained things **concerning Himself** in the Old Testament, He didn't use fanciful allegories or speculative ideas. He **expounded**, which means He stuck close to the text.

ii. "The Scripture was a familiar book to them. And what did our Lord do when He met with them? He took the book they had studied all their lives. He turned to the pages that they knew so well. He led them down by the old familiar texts." (Morrison)

4. (28-32) Jesus is revealed to the disciples on the road to Emmaus.

Then they drew near to the village where they were going, and He indicated that He would have gone farther. But they constrained Him, saying, "Abide with us, for it is toward evening, and the day is far spent." And He went in to stay with them. Now it came to pass, as He sat at the table with them, that He took bread, blessed and broke *it,* and gave it to them. Then their eyes were opened and they knew Him; and He vanished from their sight. And they said to one another, "Did not our heart burn within us while He talked with us on the road, and while He opened the Scriptures to us?"

a. **He indicated that He would have gone farther**: Jesus acted as if He might continue on farther, but did not want to force His company on these disciples. **But they constrained Him** shows that even though they didn't know this was Jesus in their midst, they knew they wanted to spend as much time as they could with this man.

i. "It is a very strong word that, 'they constrained him'; it is akin to the one which Jesus used when he said, 'The kingdom of heaven suffereth violence.' They not only invited him, but they held him, they grasped his hand, they tugged at his skirts, they said he should not go." (Spurgeon)

b. **He took bread, blessed and broke it**: These men were not present at the last supper Jesus had with his twelve disciples; they knew nothing of the sacramental nature of breaking bread in theological terms.

i. "It was in no sense a sacramental meal, as we use that word sacrament in our theology. It was a frugal supper in a village home of two tired travellers, and another. Yet it was then—in the breaking of bread, and not in any vision of resurrection splendor—that they knew that their companion was the Lord." (Morrison)

c. **Then their eyes were opened and they knew Him**: Though it was not what might be called a sacramental meal, there was something in it that showed them who the mysterious and wise guest was. Before their eyes were restrained (Luke 24:16); now **their eyes were opened**, and *He was known to them in the breaking of bread* (Luke 24:35).

> i. Morrison suggested several ways that they might have recognized Jesus in the breaking of bread:

> - The way He took the place of host with "the quiet air of majesty"
> - The way He gave the blessing over the meal they would eat
> - The pierced hands that gave them the bread

> ii. "However it was, whether by word or hand, they felt irresistibly that this was He. Some little action, some dear familiar trait, told them in a flash this was the Christ." (Morrison)

> iii. Jesus may be right in front of you, walking with you and sitting down with you at every meal—and your eyes could be restrained from seeing Him. We therefore should pray that God would open our eyes to see Jesus as He is, as being with us all the time.

d. **He vanished from their sight**: As soon as their eyes were opened to who Jesus was, He left miraculously, and they both said what was on their hearts. Their hearts burned as they heard Him speak and teach.

e. **Did not our heart burn within us while He talked**: Even when they didn't know it was Jesus, even when they didn't believe He was risen from the dead, their heart still burned because of the ministry of God's Word and of Jesus, the Living Word of God.

> i. God's word can have this same effect on our heart, even when we don't know that it is Jesus doing that work.

> ii. Neither of them knew the other's heart burned until Jesus left. After that, they could have a fellowship of flaming hearts together. One reason Jesus left was so that they would love one another, and minister to one another.

5. (33-35) They tell the good news.

So they rose up that very hour and returned to Jerusalem, and found the eleven and those *who were* with them gathered together, saying, "The Lord is risen indeed, and has appeared to Simon!" And they told about the things *that had happened* on the road, and how He was known to them in the breaking of bread.

a. **So they rose up that very hour and returned to Jerusalem**: After a seven-mile walk one way, they were so excited that they went seven miles back—and probably much faster on the return. They had the passion to tell the great news of Jesus' resurrection.

b. **The Lord is risen indeed, and has appeared to Simon**: They had mutual confirmation of the resurrection of Jesus. Though the risen Jesus was not physically in their midst, His resurrection had been confirmed by more than two witnesses.

C. Jesus teaches His disciples and ascends into heaven.

1. (36-43) Jesus appears to the eleven.

Now as they said these things, Jesus Himself stood in the midst of them, and said to them, "Peace to you." But they were terrified and frightened, and supposed they had seen a spirit. And He said to them, "Why are you troubled? And why do doubts arise in your hearts? Behold My hands and My feet, that it is I Myself. Handle Me and see, for a spirit does not have flesh and bones as you see I have." When He had said this, He showed them His hands and His feet. But while they still did not believe for joy, and marveled, He said to them, "Have you any food here?" So they gave Him a piece of a broiled fish and some honeycomb. And He took *it* and ate in their presence.

a. **As they said these things, Jesus Himself stood in the midst of them**: This seems to be the same late Sunday meeting Jesus had with the eleven described in John 20:19-25. In his Gospel, John specifically wrote that Jesus appeared to them *when the doors were shut* (John 20:19). It seems that Jesus suddenly, and perhaps miraculously, appeared to the disciples in the midst of a closed room without making an obvious entrance.

b. **Peace to you**: These were words with new meaning, now that Jesus had risen from the dead. Now, true peace could come between God and man and among men.

i. "About the Lord there were the air and style of one who had peace himself, and loved to communicate it to others. The tone in which he spake peace tended to create it. He was a peace-maker, and a peace-giver, and by this sign they were driven to discern their Leader." (Spurgeon)

c. **Behold My hands and My feet, that it is I Myself**: Jesus first displayed His wounded **hands** and **feet** to the disciples. In this Jesus wanted to establish both His identity and His bodily existence, and that it was in a transformed state *the same body* He had before the cross, upon the cross, and set in the tomb.

i. It is remarkable to consider that the resurrection body of Jesus retains the wounds He received in His sufferings and crucifixion. There are many possible reasons for this.

- To exhibit the wounds to the disciples, that they would know that it was the very same Jesus

- To be the object of eternal amazement to the angels
- To be His ornaments, trophies of His great work for us
- To memorialize the weapons with which He defeated death
- To serve as advocates in His perpetual intercession for us
- To preserve the evidence of humanity's crime against Him

ii. "In the apostles' case the facts were tested to the utmost, and the truth was not admitted till it was forced upon them. I am not excusing, the unbelief of the disciples, but I claim that their witness has all the more weight in it, because it was the result of such cool investigation." (Spurgeon)

d. **Handle Me and see**: Jesus wanted to assure them that He was a real, physical body, though of a different order than our own bodies. The resurrected Jesus was not a ghost or phantom.

i. "He distinctly denied that His resurrection was of His Spirit only, for He invited them to touch His hands and His feet. The evidences of a material body are abundant." (Morgan)

ii. "The account is precisely concerned to refute the notion that Jesus only arose in spirit, or as a ghost. Rather, He arose in spirit and in body; that is, in a spiritual body." (Pate)

e. **A spirit does not have flesh and bones as you see I have**: Some make much of the fact that Jesus said His body had **flesh and bones** and not the more normal phrasing of *flesh and blood*. The idea is that perhaps the resurrection body of Jesus did not have blood, and perhaps neither will ours. It is also possible that Jesus said **flesh and bones** because blood could not be felt, but bones can be discerned by touch.

f. **They still did not believe for joy, and marveled**: Curiously, for that moment **joy** kept them from faith. This may have been true in the sense that we may believe something to be too good to be true. Yet it is also true that God wants from us a *reasoned, thought-out* faith, not a giddy easy-believism. Jesus wanted them to *think* and believe.

i. "Then a great joy, like a tide, swept over them. And they could not believe, they were so glad. Not long ago Christ found them sleeping for sorrow (Luke 22:45), and now He found them disbelieving for joy. Do not forget, then, that joy can hinder faith. It may be as great a foe to faith as sorrow sometimes is." (Morrison)

ii. There were several times previous to this when joy hindered faith, in the sense of something being too good to be true.

- In Genesis 45:25-26, Jacob could not believe that Joseph was alive, because the news seemed to be too good

- In Job 9:16, Job said that if God would have answered him, he would not have believed it
- In Psalm 126:1, it seemed too good to be true that God would rescue Israel from captivity
- When Peter was set free from prison in Acts 12, the church didn't believe it (Acts 12:13-14)

iii. "Their joy was so great that for a moment it was even an impediment to their faith." (Geldenhuys)

g. **Have you any food here?** To demonstrate both His identity and the reality of His spiritual body, Jesus ate in their presence. In most of Jesus' resurrection appearances, He eats with the disciples.

i. This would be another powerful evidence that *this was the same Jesus*, doing something with them that He did many times before.

2. (44-48) Jesus teaches His disciples.

Then He said to them, "These *are* the words which I spoke to you while I was still with you, that all things must be fulfilled which were written in the Law of Moses and *the* Prophets and *the* Psalms concerning Me." And He opened their understanding, that they might comprehend the Scriptures. Then He said to them, "Thus it is written, and thus it was necessary for the Christ to suffer and to rise from the dead the third day, and that repentance and remission of sins should be preached in His name to all nations, beginning at Jerusalem. And you are witnesses of these things."

a. **These are the words which I spoke to you while I was still with you**: Jesus *almost* said, "I told you so" by reminding them that all had happened just as He said it would. To help His disciples take it all in, **He opened their understanding, that they might comprehend the Scriptures**.

i. It must have been before this that the disciples were actually born again by God's Spirit, when Jesus breathed on them and they received the Holy Spirit (John 20:22).

ii. "In that one hour, in the upper chamber with Christ, Scripture became a new book to the disciples. Never forget how earnestly and constantly our Lord appealed to the testimony of the Word." (Morrison)

b. **It was necessary for the Christ to suffer and to rise from the dead the third day**: Jesus wanted them to understand that the cross was not some unfortunate obstacle that had to be hurdled. It was a **necessary** part of God's redemptive plan for man, and that it would be in the name of a crucified and risen Savior that **repentance and remission of sins** would be brought to the world.

i. "They were told by their great Master what to preach, and where to preach it, and how to preach it, and even where to begin to preach it." (Spurgeon)

ii. **Should be preached in His name**: To preach the gospel in Jesus' name means to:

- Preach it under His orders
- Preach it on His authority
- Preach it knowing repentance and remission of sin come by the virtue of His name
- Refusing to preach it in our own name

c. **You are witnesses of these things**: Jesus solemnly told them that they were **witnesses of these things**. Not only **witnesses** of the events surrounding the work of Jesus, but also of the commission itself to spread the gospel. This was a work they were all mutually responsible for.

d. **Beginning at Jerusalem**: Their work was to begin at Jerusalem; there are many reasons why it was fitting for the preaching of the gospel to begin there.

- Because the Scriptures say it should be so (Isaiah 2:3, Joel 2:32)
- Because that is where the facts of the gospel took place, and the truth of those facts should be tested straightaway
- To honor the Jewish people and to bring them the gospel first
- Because it is good to begin where we are tempted not to begin
- Because the time is short and it is good to begin near to where we are
- Because it is good to begin where we may expect opposition

3. (49-53) The Ascension of Jesus.

"Behold, I send the Promise of My Father upon you; but tarry in the city of Jerusalem until you are endued with power from on high." And He led them out as far as Bethany, and He lifted up His hands and blessed them. Now it came to pass, while He blessed them, that He was parted from them and carried up into heaven. And they worshiped Him, and returned to Jerusalem with great joy, and were continually in the temple praising and blessing God. Amen.

a. **I send the Promise of My Father upon you**: They could not do the work Jesus had called them to do unless they were **endued with power**

from on high, and that power would come as the Holy Spirit was poured out upon them.

b. **He lifted up His hands and blessed them . . . while He blessed them**: Jesus continued to appear to His people for 40 days following His resurrection. Eventually came the day when He would ascend to heaven. When He did, Jesus left the earth blessing His Church, and He continues to bless them, as much as His people will receive.

> i. Nothing but blessing had ever come from those hands; but now, Jesus stands as the High Priest over His people to bless them. "Thus He remains until He comes again, His hands uplifted, and His lips pronouncing the blessedness of His own." (Morgan)

> ii. When Jesus blesses His people, it isn't just a pious wish like "I hope things work out for you" or "I hope you will be feeling better." Instead, the blessing of Jesus has inherent *power* within it.

> iii. "If he has blessed you, you *shall* be blessed, for there is no power in heaven, or earth, or hell, that can reverse the blessing which He gives." (Spurgeon)

> iv. "While we see those uplifted hands, there can be no room for doubt or fear, when other menacing hands are stretched out to harm us or vex us. Whether in life or death, in adversity or prosperity, in sorrow or in joy, we know by that token that we are safe." (Morgan)

d. **He was parted from them and carried up into heaven**: Jesus had to ascend so that confidence would be put in the power and ministry of the Holy Spirit, not in the geographical presence of Jesus.

> i. Acts 1:3 tells us that this ascension into heaven happened 40 days after Jesus' resurrection. He spent those 40 days proving the truth of His resurrection and preparing His disciples for His departure.

> ii. "He rises by his own power and majesty; he needs no help....He proved the innate power of his Deity, by which he could depart out of the world just when he willed, breaking the law of gravitation, and suspending the laws usually governing matter." (Spurgeon)

> iii. "It was unthinkable that the appearances of Jesus should grow fewer and fewer until finally they petered out. That would have effectively wrecked the faith of men." (Barclay)

> iv. "The ascension differs radically from Jesus' vanishing from the sight of the disciples at Emmaus and similar happenings. There is an air of finality about it. It is the decisive close of one chapter and the beginning of another." (Morris)

e. **And they worshiped Him, and returned to Jerusalem with great joy, and were continually in the temple praising and blessing God**: This shows the wonderful result of the ministry of Jesus in the disciples' lives.

- **They worshiped Him**: This means they knew that Jesus was God, and they gave Him the honor He deserves

- They **returned to Jerusalem**: This means they did just what Jesus told them to do. They were obedient

- **With great joy**: This means they *really believed* Jesus rose from the dead, and let the joy of that fact touch everything in their life

- **Continually in the temple praising and blessing God**: This means that they lived as *public* followers of Jesus, and could not hide their love and worship towards Him

  i. "A little before, they could not believe for joy. Now they were joyful just because they believed." (Morrison)

  ii. When God does this kind of work in His people, we say "**Amen.**"

Bibliography

Barclay, William *The Gospel of Matthew, Volume 1* and *Volume 2* (Philadelphia: The Westminster Press, 1975)

Bruce. A.B. "The Synoptic Gospels" *The Expositor's Greek Testament, Volume 1* (London: Hodder and Stoughton, ?)

Calvin, John *A Harmony of the Gospels: Matthew, Mark, and Luke Volumes 1, 2, and 3* Translator: A.W. Morrison (Grand Rapids, Michigan: Eerdmans Publishing, 1972)

Carson, D.A. "Matthew" *The Expositor's Bible Commentary, Volume 8* (Grand Rapids. Michigan: Zondervan, 1984)

Clarke, Adam *The New Testament of Our Lord and Saviour Jesus Christ, Volume II* (New York: Eaton & Mains, 1832)

France, R.T. *The Gospel According to Matthew* (Leicester, England: Inter-Varsity Press, 1985)

Geldenhuys, Norval *Commentary on the Gospel of Luke* (Eerdmans Publishing, 1988)

Hill, David *The Gospel of Matthew* (Grand Rapids, Michigan: Eerdmans Publishing, 1981)

Lane, William L. *The Gospel of Mark* (Grand Rapids, Michigan: Eerdmans, 1974)

Maclaren, Alexander *Expositions of Holy Scripture, Volume 6* and *Volume 7* (Grand Rapids, Michigan: Baker Book House, 1984)

Meyer, F.B. *Our Daily Homily* (Westwood, New Jersey: Revell, 1966)

Morgan, G. Campbell *An Exposition of the Whole Bible* (Old Tappan, New Jersey: Revell, 1959)

Morgan, G. Campbell *Searchlights from the Word* (New York: Revell, 1926)

Morgan, G. Campbell *Commentary on the Gospel of Matthew* (Old Tappan, New Jersey: Revell, 1979)

Morris, Luke *Luke, an Introduction and Commentary* (Inter-Varsity Press, Leicester, England, 1988)

Poole, Matthew *A Commentary on the Holy Bible, Volume III: Matthew-Revelation* (London: Banner of Truth Trust, 1969, first published in 1685)

Robertson, A.T. *Word Pictures in the New Testament, Volume 1* (Nashville, Tennessee: Broadman Press, 1930)

Spurgeon, Charles Haddon *The Gospel of Matthew* (Old Tappan, New Jersey: Revell, 1987)

Spurgeon, Charles Haddon *The New Park Street Pulpit, Volumes 1-6* and *The Metropolitan Tabernacle Pulpit, Volumes 7-63* (Pasadena, Texas: Pilgrim Publications, 1990)

Stott, John *Christian Counter-Culture: The Message of the Sermon on the Mount* (Downers Grove, Illinois: Inter-Varsity Press, 1978)

Trapp, John *A Commentary on the Old and New Testaments, Volume Five* (Eureka, California: Tanski Publications, 1997)

Wessel, Walter W. "Mark" *The Expositor's Bible Commentary, Volume 8* (Grand Rapids, Michigan: Zondervan, 1984)

Wiersbe, Warren W. *The Bible Exposition Commentary, Volume 1*, Mark (Wheaton, Illinois: Victor Books, 1989)

As the years pass I love the work of studying, learning, and teaching the Bible more than ever. I'm so grateful that God is faithful to meet me in His Word. This commentary on the Gospel of Luke is dedicated to our grandson Jay in his very first year.

Thanks once again to Debbie Pollacia for her proofreading help. She's remarkably patient with my work, even when I make the same mistakes through a manuscript. Even more, I thank Debbie for her prayer support through the years.

I am often amazed at the remarkable kindness of others, and thanks to all who give the gift of encouragement. With each year that passes, faithful friends and supporters become all the more precious. Through you all, God has been better to me than I have ever deserved.

After more than 20 years of pastoral ministry in California and 7 years of work with Calvary Chapel Bible College Germany, David Guzik accepted the call to serve the congregation of Calvary Chapel Santa Barbara in July 2010. David and Inga-Lill live in Santa Barbara.

You can e-mail David at
ewm@enduringword.com

For more resources by David Guzik, go to
www.enduringword.com

For more Bible resources by David Guzik, go to:

www.enduringword.com